DISSEMINAL

CHAUCER

Disseminal
CHAUCER

Rereading *The Nun's Priest's Tale*

PETER W. TRAVIS

University of Notre Dame Press

Notre Dame, Indiana

Library of Congress Cataloging-in-Publication Data

Travis, Peter W.
Disseminal Chaucer : rereading The nun's priest's tale / Peter W. Travis.
   p. cm.
  Includes bibliographical references and index.
  ISBN-13: 978-0-268-04235-6 (pbk. : alk. paper)
  ISBN-10: 0-268-04235-7 (pbk. : alk. paper)
  1. Chaucer, Geoffrey, d. 1400. Nun's priest's tale. 2. English poetry—
Middle English, 1100–1500—History and criticism. I. Title.
  PR1868.N63T73   2010
  821.1—dc22

                            2009038253

For my sons — Sean, Jared, Matthew

Contents

Acknowledgments   ix

Introduction   1

ONE
The Nun's Priest's Body, or Chaucer's Sexual Genius   29

TWO
The Nun's Priest's Tale as Grammar School Primer, Menippean
Parody, and *Ars Poetica*   51

THREE
Close Reading: Beginnings and Endings   119

FOUR
Chaucer's Heliotropes and the Poetics of Metaphor   169

FIVE
The Noise of History   201

SIX
Chaucerian Horologics and the Confounded Reader 267

SEVEN
The Parodistic Episteme: Learning to Behold the Fox 303

EIGHT
Moralitas 335

Notes 351

Works Cited 392

Index 416

Acknowledgments

Many of us who love Chaucer can trace the trajectory of our careers back to a few powerful mentors. My own fascination began in a year-long Chaucer course taught at Bowdoin College by William S. Williams. At the University of Chicago, I reread all of Chaucer's works in graduate courses taught by Jerome Taylor. And in my first few years at Dartmouth College, I had the good fortune to team-teach *The Canterbury Tales* with Alan Gaylord, from whom I learned most of what I know about the craft of teaching. I am deeply indebted to these extremely inspiring role models. I am also very indebted to two younger medievalists in my home department: George Edmondson, whose love of all thing theoretical has rejuvenated my readiness to pursue some of my riskier scholarly adventures, and Monika Otter, who has read the entirety of this book with caring critical attention and who has been a most generous and inspiring colleague. Searching for my critical voice over the past thirty-some years has led me into invigorating exchanges with many others. At MLA conventions, meetings of the Medieval Academy, the Medieval Institute at Western Michigan University, New Chaucer Society conferences, as well as more specialized conferences, I have had the privilege of joining a community of thinkers whose various ways of reading Chaucer have brought the field to a extraordinarily high level of sophistication. For sharing their ideas and listening to my own, I want especially to thank Kathleen Ashley, Theresa Coletti, Sarah Stanbury,

Lee Patterson, Jim Rhodes, James Goldstein, Ross Arthur, Sylvia Tomasch, Robert Hanning, Sealy Gilles, Robert Stein, Dan Rubey, Joel Kaye, Richard Neuse, Thomas Hahn, Paul Strohm, Lisa Kiser, Steven Kruger, Carolyn Collette, Chris Baswell, Warren Ginsberg, Frank Grady, Robert Myles, and Bill Askins. Other individuals whose scholarly work has been profoundly significant remain so numerous that I'll try to recognize them at appropriate points in the book itself. Yet here I want to acknowledge Derek Pearsall, whose magisterial Variorum edition of *The Nun's Priest's Tale* remains the most important resource and appraisal of its kind.

I am grateful to the National Endowment for the Humanities for their extremely generous support, and above all to Dartmouth College, whose sabbatical schedule and senior faculty fellowship program have provided me with more than ample time to finally bring this project to completion. I have been privileged at Dartmouth to teach courses on *The Canterbury Tales* and on Chaucer's other works to students of the highest caliber; were it not for their intelligence and critical energy, I am certain I would have pursued my scholarly interests with diminished enthusiasm. I have conducted most of my research in Dartmouth's Baker/Berry Library, whose first-rate staff, especially Laura Braunstein, have provided expert professional assistance. I want to thank Darsie Riccio for her collegiality, and my conscientious undergraduate research assistants— Cordelia Ross, Emma Palley, Fruzsina Molnar, and Lauren Indvik. Finally, Carol Westberg has been a most generous companion, whose love of poetry and of all things wise and beautiful has encouraged me to try to capture in analytic prose some of the pleasures of Chaucer's verse.

I am grateful for permission to reprint in revised form previously published works: to the University of Eichstätt for "Learning to Behold the Fox: Poetics and Epistemology in Chaucer's *Nun's Priest's Tale*," in *Poetry and Epistemology: Turning Points in the History of Poetic Knowledge*, ed. Roland Hagenbuchle and Laura Skandera (1986); to the New Chaucer Society for "*The Nun's Priest's Tale* as Grammar-School Primer," *Studies in the Age of Chaucer: Proceedings* 1 (1986); to the *Journal of Medieval and Renaissance Studies* for "Chaucer's Trivial Fox Chase and the Peasants' Revolt of 1381," *Journal of Medieval and Renaissance Studies* 18 (1988); to the Medieval Academy for "Chaucer's Heliotropes and the Poetics of Metaphor," *Speculum* 72 (1997); to the University of Northern Illinois for "Chaucer's *Chronographiae,* the Confounded Reader, and Fourteenth-Century Measurements of Time," *Disputatio* 2: *Constructions of Time in the Late Middle Ages* (1997); to Boydell and Brewer, Ltd., for "Reading Chaucer *Ab Ovo:* Mock-*Exemplum* in *The Nun's Priest's Tale,*" in *The Performance of Middle English Culture: Essays on Chaucer and the Drama,* ed. James J. Paxson, Lawrence M. Clopper, and Sylvia Tomasch (1998); to the University of Florida for "Thirteen Ways of Listening to a Fart: Noise in Chaucer's *Summoner's Tale,*" *Exemplaria* 16 (2004); and to the University of Notre Dame Press for "The Body of the Nun's Priest, or, Chaucer's Disseminal Genius," in *Reading Medieval Culture: Essays in Honor of Robert W. Hanning,* ed. Robert M. Stein and Sandra Pierson Prior (2005).

Finally, I want to commemorate Chauntecleer and his twelve wives, each named Alice. For a brief time they roamed freely in my barnyard. One spring day—it was May 3—I looked up from my rototiller and beheld Reynard loping in from the woods, followed by his attractive vixen. Chickens elevated in various directions, my family implored me to do something heroic, I vainly arced one arrow from a bow I had fashioned in summer camp years ago: "It semed as that hevene sholde falle." Heaven did not then fall. But a few nights later the fox returned, and for a long time we grieved the loss of those beautiful, self-involved, and so-human critters. It was then I decided I might write a book about chickens.

Introduction

Most readers agree that *The Nun's Priest's Tale* is one of Chaucer's finest poetic achievements. Critics have judged it to be a "virtuoso performance,"[1] "the most consciously aesthetic of Chaucer's productions,"[2] "a summa of Chaucerian artistry,"[3] illustrating "*in parvo* the achievement of *The Canterbury Tales* as a whole."[4] Donald Howard finds it one of the "few places in *The Canterbury Tales* . . . where we hear a neutral voice which might as well be Chaucer's own."[5] And Morton Bloomfield would appear to speak for two generations of readers when he agrees with his own undergraduate professor who once imperiously asserted that "an inability to enjoy [*The Nun's Priest's Tale*] should disqualify anyone from the study of literature."[6] Urbane, playful, humanistic, learned, and quintessentially Chaucerian, *The Nun's Priest's Tale* has rarely suffered from underappreciation.

In addition to inspiring a host of appreciative essays, the *Tale* has prompted numerous scholarly studies concerning the *Tale*'s literary, intellectual, historical, and cultural *mise en scene*. These include studies of its sources and its analogues; its reflections of medieval dream psychology, medical theories, theological debates; its astronomical allusions, musical allusions, scientific allusions, scriptural allusions, and political allusions. These informative pieces have caused little controversy, by and large, because each has contributed to a knowledge that is helpful in preparation for our interpretation of the tale. It is only when scholars actually begin to articulate the *Tale*'s meaning that the fireworks start. Although critics of literature are scarcely known for their collegial harmony of opinion ("What," asks the jejune critic Persse McGarrigle in the academic novel *Small World,* "do you *do* if everybody agrees with you?"),[7] the diversity of readings of *The Nun's Priest's Tale* is nevertheless astonishing. It is also deeply ironic, since beast fables—brief narratives with attached morals— are not considered to be a very difficult genre to decode.[8] And even though *The Nun's Priest's Tale* is obviously a uniquely complex instance of the genre, it too closes with a *moralitas* that graciously empowers readers to discover for themselves the essence of the *Tale*'s meaning:

> But ye that holden this tale a folye,
> As of a fox, or of a cok and hen,
> Taketh the moralite, goode men.
> For Seint Paul seith that al that writen is,
> To oure doctrine it is ywrite, ywis;
> Taketh the fruyt, and lat the chaf be stille.
> Now, goode God, if that it be thy wille,
> As seith my lord, so make us alle goode men,
> And brynge us to his heighe blisse! Amen.
>   (VII.3438–46)[9]

Over the past century one might expect that careful readings of these concluding nine lines would have generated consensus somewhere along the spectrum of Chaucerian scholarship. However, after reviewing all pertinent critiques of this *moralitas,* Derek Pearsall in his invaluable *The Nun's Priest's Tale* in *The Variorum Edition of the Works of Geoffrey Chaucer* reports: "The narrator here bids us find a simple moral, but no two critics agree on what it is, except that it is not what the Nun's Priest says it is."[10] One of the several difficulties in successfully determining the *Tale*'s "moral" obviously lies in the overabundance of "fruit" scattered about its narrative field, for in a poem of only 646 lines, there are numerous embedded apothegms all striving to extrapolate the import of ongoing events. Indeed, every major character—rooster, hen, fox, and narrator— seems to be a frustrated glossator, whose instinctive response to a half-line of narrative is to lift aloft hand, wing, or paw, exclaim "Lo!" and utter a timely axiom or two.

Because the tale's plethora of self-interpreting philosophemes seems to function as an oblique critique of literary criticism generally, a number of readers have felt warned off from any kind of serious interpretative endeavors. Under the puckish rubric "Desiderata," *The Chaucer Review* once requested a magic "Alley-oop machine" that could take five scholars, plus tape-recorder, back in time to ask those questions only Chaucer could answer, such as "What *is* the 'fruyt' of *The Nun's Priest's Tale?*"[11] Talbot Donaldson, in an oft-cited one-liner, has pronounced conclusively that the fruit of *The Nun's Priest's Tale* is its chaff.[12] In his survey of all the tale's criticism up until 1982, Pearsall appears to agree with Donaldson's anti-interpretative interpretation. After dividing "Interpretative Studies" of the tale into "Moral Interpretation" (surveyed in seven pages), "Exegetical Interpretation" (five pages), "Skepticism Concerning Moral and Exegetical Interpretation" (two pages), and "Political Interpretation" (one page), Pearsall arranges the bulk of the tale's criticism (surveyed in sixteen pages) under the rubric "Noninterpretative Evaluation."[13] These studies, which focus generally upon the *Tale's* satiric and mock-heroic rhetorical voices, constitute in Pearsall's opinion "the traditional and central critical approach to *The Nun's Priest's Tale.*"[14] For Pearsall, it is quite acceptable for critics to evaluate the tale (that is, appreciate its range of literary styles), but it is folly to attempt to *interpret* the tale (that is, explicate its meaning). In fact, Pearsall rather pointedly concludes that it is really quite useless to search for the ultimate import of *The Nun's Priest's Tale* because "the fact that the tale has no point is the point of the tale."[15] To put it another way, since Chaucer's poem seems to have so brilliantly anticipated, parodied, and deconstructed the extrapolative importunities of our critical profession, sheer admiration might be our wisest option: dwarfling scholar had best retire and leave the field free and clear to Chaucer's gigantic genius.

Indeed, there is much in the *Tale* that mocks all our scholarly endeavors. The hubris of erudition, as Peter Elbow observes, is embodied in Chauntecleer himself, whose most distinctive characteristic as avian humanist is "to stretch away from earth"—in his crowing, his astronomizing, his glozings, and his cocky style of loving.[16] Because modern and postmodern critics, especially those of a theoretical bent like me, are forever prepared to stretch into the stratosphere, if we were ever to gloss this tale in an unusually clever way we would surely be setting up our own critical *jouissance* as a special target of its ironies. "Unlike fable," Charles Muscatine famously asserted years ago, the "*Nun's Priest's Tale* does not so much make true and solemn assertions about life as it tests truths and tries out solemnities. If you are not careful, it will try out your solemnity too; it is here, doubtless, trying out mine."[17] An especially poignant moment underscoring the experience of critical self-deflation regularly effected by this tale occurred at an MLA session when a paper entitled "Chauntecleer and Partlet Identified" attracted a flock of curious scholars. What the paper eventually proved was that the tale's hero and heroine were actually Golden Spangled Hamburg chickens.[18] No one, except the most erudite experts in the history of chicken breeding, could have disagreed.[19] But to find oneself suddenly brought so low on the great chain of academic being, mucking about in the taxonomies of poultry identification, must have been a sobering experience. And a salutary experience it may have been as well, because a fundamental reason that *The Nun's Priest's Tale* remains remarkably unresponsive to our golden-spangled critical ambitions, I believe, is that one of its major commitments is to demonstrate, not only its own resistance, but the adamantine resistance of *all* literature to traditional critical practices.

But precisely because the literary world of *The Nun's Priest's Tale* is so imaginatively creative and quintessentially Chaucerian, certain stalwart critics in past generations have insisted that if we cannot decrypt Chaucer's intent in this, his signature piece of poetry, we can scarcely feel confident about our interpretations of any of his other major works. Contending that *The Nun's Priest's Tale* is a bibliocosm of *The Canterbury Tales* and arguing that *The Canterbury Tales,* in turn, with its Genesis-like opening and Last Judgment–like closure, constitutes a literary variant of the history of Christian salvation, at least one school of thought has argued that Chaucer's beast fable is best interpreted in the same ways the Bible, its most sacred textual referent, was traditionally understood. This means that Chauntecleer, strutting around his terrestrial paradise, is rather like Adam before the fall; Pertelote, gracious Everywoman and harridan Archwife, is equivalent to Eve; the clever and insouciant fox is, well, quite similar to the Devil, or perhaps the snake.[20] The tale unquestionably invites this kind of associative thinking, even from readers far removed from the prevenient grace of neo-Robertsonian exegesis. Undoubtedly, if one squints in the right spirit, one can readily descry—in a roosting-peg, a dry ditch, a convenient tree, and various struttings, frettings, and awkward flights—the major types of salvation history. And if one is somewhat uncertain about the prefabricated certitude of these typological equations, one can choose to dilute biblical allegory with ethical tropology occasionally modified by contemporary history: Chauntecleer might become a priest (or any holy man), the fox might become a heretic (or a Franciscan), and Chauntecleer's peasant mistress, the widow, might become the church (or at least an exemplary Christian).[21]

There is of course no question that Chaucer employed various forms of biblical citation and scriptural allusion throughout his poetic career, braiding into his texts familiar images and phrases that alert the reader to the sacred referents that are being parodied, transcontextualized, and redeployed. Whereas in most forms of literary parody the target text is itself the object of critical scrutiny, in biblical parody the dynamics are typically reversed, the Bible serving as the textual authority against which characters and events reflected in the parodic text are themselves to be judged. But the narrator of *The Nun's Priest's Tale* appears to be intent upon an even more complex form of parody, biblifying his animal creatures so that he may just as expertly unbiblify them. Chauntecleer at tale's end remains an oversexed and underrepentant pagan. Pertelote, despite the narrator's archly misogynistic asides, remains the testy wife, attractive *lemman,* and loving sister she has always been. The fox slithers six ways to Sunday under every exegetical hedge, his only consistent meaning being what he most consistently is: a fox. What appears to be the primary parodic target in this fable is neither the Bible itself nor the animal characters inside their barnyard paradise, but rather our own hermeneutical desires to unite the two. Thus it would appear that one major subject of interrogation in this literary *hortus inconclusus* is ultimately the reader as overextended exegete, whose proclivities toward knee-jerk biblicism and hyper-*allegoresis* are in need of the finest cathartics parody can provide.

But this does not mean that critical attempts to descry in *The Nun's Priest's Tale* patterns of epic proportion and cosmic significance are entirely out of order. In an ambitious study entitled "Food, Laxatives, and

Catharsis in Chaucer's *Nun's Priest's Tale*," Patrick Gallacher focuses upon the prevalence of food in the tale, both its consumption and expulsion, most notably the widow's diet, the chickens foraging for grain, the narrator's inability to "bulte it to the bren" (VII.3240), the closing exhortation to take the fruit and leave the chaff, and Pertelote's prescription of "lawriol, centaure, and fumetere, / . . . ellebor, / . . . katapuce . . . [and] gaitrys beryis" (VII.2963–65) as purges for her husband's imbalanced humors. Citing a large body of medieval theological tracts but concentrating especially on Plato's *Timaeus*, Gallacher argues for an implicit contrast in the tale between the body of the divinely constructed universe, which is in such perfect balance that "it is fed, ecologically enough and immanently, by its own waste,"[22] and the human body, which "is in a state of constant flux and mutability—of ingestion, respiration, and purgation, of being filled and emptied."[23] Relying upon numerous medieval examples of the well-balanced consumption of food as a holistic sign— an analogue to taking advice sensibly, to digesting the meaning of texts properly, and to communing the Eucharistic mysteries—Gallacher argues that Chaucer's fable points toward a model of the perfect human life as well as toward a "model of total continuous intelligibility in the universe."[24] Accordingly, the ideal mode of interpretative understanding entertained in the *Tale* is nothing less than utopian: it "must explicitly reconcile the literal and the metaphorical, the physical and the spiritual, the empirical and the transcendent, the universal and the particular; it is, in fact, the sum total of all answers to all questions."[25]

In *Chaucer and Menippean Satire*, F. Anne Payne agrees that physical eating is an important behavior in the fable. But in a chapter entitled "The Eaters and the Eaten in *The Nun's Priest's Tale*," her assessment of the heuristic significance of consumption is diametrically opposed to Gallacher's.[26] Rather than a trope directing us toward an understanding of the well-balanced moral and spiritual life in a divinely ordered universe, she sees eating as a powerful reminder of the meaningless violence of human life and the inevitable horrors of death:

> The fate of all but God is to be eaten eventually. Power, which ultimately only God has, is the ability to eat, by destroying or consuming or manipulating offending bodies which are obstructive

or uncooperative and which, in some way, provide food for the eater's desires.[27]

Payne's dystopian vision of the alimentary disorders of the natural world, a violent site of devourers consuming devourees, embraces an anxious conviction that the narrator of the tale is himself intent on taking us in— devouring our good will with his "lies," "inconsistencies," and "covert, sly, and gleeful attacks on serious thinkers,"[28] laughing at "men's rooster-like concerns," and belittling "their futile attempts at explanation."[29] Speaking in "the voice of the devil," the Nun's Priest is a verbal trickster whose only "fruit is the morality of the arch-destroyer," a "knowledge that destroys all sense of beauty, all joy, all impulse toward freedom."[30] So when the Priest opens his mouth to speak, Payne concludes, "like Chauntecleer, we ought to fly into the most convenient tree, not stay in the fox's mouth the while, for we have been in the process of being beguiled by a master with intents every bit as wicked as the fox's."[31]

Payne's fearful vision of the bestial world of *The Nun's Priest's Tale* is radically different from Gallacher's trust in the existence of a salvific *telos* to that world's literary design. Gallacher's and Payne's studies are similar in significant ways, however, especially in their shared sense that the tale is a monad of Chaucer's poetic, intellectual, and theological imagination, and in their deep conviction that the fabulous world it creates is a simulacrum of the real world Chaucer would wish we all might adequately understand. Indeed, their belief that a single beast fable could be such a capacious literary microcosm is similar to the attitude in Malcolm Lowry's *Under the Volcano* of the consul who respectfully kept a volume of *Peter Rabbit* in his vast and eclectic library: "'Everything is to be found in *Peter Rabbit*,' the consul liked to say."[32] Furthermore, and quite importantly, both Gallacher and Payne see *The Nun's Priest's Tale* as a metafable concerned with the problematics of literary interpretation and its effects upon the reader, Gallacher trusting in Chaucer's investment in some kind of readerly progress towards an elevated unity of Being, Payne fearing that the reader may end up abused, ground down, and consumed. And what these two studies most symptomatically demonstrate is the contentious pattern of almost all extended interpretations of the tale. In ways that are both fascinating and frustrating, for several generations *The Nun's*

Priest's Tale has inspired intracritical disputes between hermeneutical extremes—secular versus spiritual, theoretical versus pragmatic, serious versus ironic, didactic versus antididactic, trusting versus wary, interpretative versus anti-interpretative, and so on. These kinds of debates are of course scarcely new to Chaucer criticism, but in a way that is quite distinctive *The Nun's Priest's Tale* has generated a peculiarly riven and walleyed critical canon. And inside this critical canon there is an unusual amount of nervous tension generated by a felt need to create some kind of synaptic arc across a large conceptual space positioned within dyadic sets of interdependent but mutually exclusive discourses.

This book attempts to conceptualize that synaptic arc by first asking a very basic question: What in fact *is* the genre of *The Nun's Priest's Tale*? In addition to beast fable, it has been defined as a sermon, an *exemplum,* a comedy, a tragedy, a tragicomedy, a satire, an epyllion, a mock epic, a romance, a fabliau, even a fictional *poème à clef.* It includes bits of many other kinds of literature as well: fortunate fall motifs are intercalated with fascicles of the *Fürstenspiegel* ("mirror of princes"), the *consolatio,* and the *disputatio,* which in turn are set off against discursive snippets relating to theology, psychology, astronomy, gastronomy, philosophy, and the proper measurements of time. In fact, *The Nun's Priest's Tale* is such a polygeneric kaleidoscope of literary kinds that from a distance it resembles what W. K. Wimsatt once saw when he took in the panoptic world of Northrop Frye's *Anatomy of Criticism* in one acerbic glance: "Superimposed fourth-of-July pinwheels, with a reversing sequence of rocket engines."[33]

In order to give some critical order and generic stability to our reading of *The Nun's Priest's Tale,* I will employ a principal concept throughout this book: a fully theorized understanding of parody. Over the past generation, the inner workings of parody have belatedly been accorded the nuanced attention they deserve. A verbal construct whose primary object of imitation is typically another verbal construct, literary parody is both an intertextual and a self-referential genre. Normally based on at least one other work of literature, parody is a prime example of a meta-fictional artifact whose ultimate concern is the nature and value of art— its construction, contamination, transcontextualization, and interpretation. One must be especially foolhardy or self-assured to write parody: as a literary form of literary criticism, parody is the art of art glossing art, and thus it must stand up to being judged according to the aesthetic norms it itself employs in judging its target text. The target text functions first as an empowering model in that its literary achievements must be intimately understood in order that they may be imitated, critiqued, and then superseded as the parodic text aspires to an even more demanding aesthetic ideal. Accordingly, the literary parodist must needs be an accomplished poet as well as an achieved critic whose parodic *ars poetica* is itself a work of art.

Although various critics have expressed their appreciation for *The Nun's Priest's Tale*'s intertextual playfulness—calling its style "ironic," "satiric," or "parodic"—rarely has it been argued that the entire tale is a sustained parody, in part because there is obviously no one textual referent, in part because there is no apparent ideational target other than such grand notions as "the follies of human nature" or "the sin of pride." Accordingly, at this early point in my analysis of *The Nun's Priest's Tale* I find it worth introducing two instances of literary nomenclature that will provide assistance in forthcoming chapters: encyclopedic parody, as defined by Mikhail Bakhtin,[34] and Menippean anatomy, as defined by Northrop Frye.[35] Both Bakhtin and Frye group under these closely related rubrics a variety of literary works that take pleasure in resisting traditional generic classifications. Cornucopian and labyrinthine, these works tend to favor colliding literary styles, disorderly narrative forms, multiple authorial perspectives, and conflicting points of view. Often placed in unusual settings, their world of intellectual reference entertains the entirety of Western thought, and while their principal comic butt is consistently the archetypal *philosophus gloriosus,* they raise, even though they refuse to answer, a series of important questions about the limits of human knowledge and the ultimate purpose of man. Like Cervantes' *Don Quixote,* Sterne's *Tristram Shandy,* and Joyce's *Ulysses, The Nun's Priest's Tale* (as small as they are large) is a fair example of Menippean anatomy—a concatenated mixture of textual appropriations, scholarly allusions, and protean voices all channeled through an authorial persona so chameleonesque that he burlesques the reliable and the unreliable narrator at the very same moment.

To illustrate just a few of the *Tale*'s Menippean features, I turn to Maurice Hussey's *The Nun's Priest's Prologue and Tale,* an edition that for years

served as a preparatory text for the British A-level exams. Hussey provides a memorable outline of the tale's narrative and nonnarrative parts:

[1–54   Prologue]
55–115   Introduction of human and bird characters
116–141   The Tale (I): The Dream
142–175   Pertelote's interpretation (based upon Cato)
176–203   Her medical advice
204–217   Chauntecleer's rejection of her interpretation
218–283   The first example: the murder of the pilgrim
284–296   Brief moralization upon murder and punishment
297–343   The second example: deaths by drowning
344–355   The third example: the death of St Kenelm
356–360   The reference to Scipio's dream
361–371   The reference to Joseph's dreams
372–384   Citation of classical examples:
              (i) Croesus (372–374)
              (ii) Andromache (375–384)
385–390   Chauntecleer's conclusion
391–420   The Tale (II)
421–433   Astronomical interlude
434–440   Chauntecleer's fears
441–448   Digression upon rhetoric
449–459   Introduction of the Fox
460–463   Digression upon treachery
464–485   Digression upon Predestination
486–558   The Tale (III) with moralization (486–500)
559–564   Sermon upon Flattery
565–571   The Tale (IV): The attack upon Chauntecleer
572–575   Digression upon Destiny
576–580   Digression upon Venus
581–588   Digression upon Richard I
589–608   Classical lamentations:
              (i) Troy (589–595)
              (ii) Carthage (596–602)
              (iii) Rome (603–608)

609–636   The Tale (V): The Chase
637–638   Couplet upon Fortune
639–669   The Tale (VI): The Escape
670–680   The Moral
[691–696   Epilogue]³⁶

This is an editorial tour-de-force. Contending that the tale itself is a mere 175 lines long while the rest of whatever the poem is takes up the remaining 521 lines, Hussey's seemingly straight-faced plot outline is meant to illustrate the amount of rhetorical ornamentation that has been superimposed upon the basic *materia,* or field, of the story. Chopped up into six unequal parts, "The Tale" is repeatedly arrested in its narrative forward progress as digressions, interludes, moralizings and amplifications take over center stage, the most egregious being a 250-line one-sided debate between Pertelote and Chauntecleer on the meaning of dreams. Nevertheless, despite its many divagations, Hussey hopes the reader might eventually discover some principle that would accord narrative or ideational unity to the *Tale*'s disparate elements:

> This list may make the Tale look absurdly fragmented. This is not the case. It is left to the individual reader to decide whether there is not a relevance among so many irrelevances, a consistency within so many seeming inconsistencies. In so far as they refer to human problems and predicaments they may be allowed to enhance the Tale rather than to distract from it.³⁷

In response to Hussey's formalist reservations, it is useful to recall how the craft of poetry in the Middle Ages was understood to be similar to constructing an edifice out of standard elements, each of which could be appreciated in isolation before being fitted into a larger design. As Robert Jordan remarks in *Chaucer and the Shape of Creation,* "[t]he typical Chaucerian narrative is literally 'built' of inert, self-contained parts, collocated in accordance with the additive, reduplicative principles which characterize the Gothic edifice."³⁸ Further, as John Dagenais notes in his study of medieval reading practices, the "particular texture of [medieval] reading," with "its starts and stops and bumps and skips," may have been much more tolerant of a particled and inorganic artistic design than our modern reading practices are today.[39] But none of this means that Hussey's negative criticism of the *Tale*'s "absurdly fragmented" structure is altogether wide of the mark, for one of the fable's parodic strategies is precisely to place on the critical fault line the whole complex matter of artistic unity by testing the reader's tolerance for "so many seeming inconsistencies" in the *Tale*'s unique narrative structure.

Although Chaucer's contemporaries would surely have appreciated the *Tale*'s experimentations with narrative form, what for them made *The Nun's Priest's Tale* first and foremost a powerfully unified reading experience is something rarely touched on in its critical history. As we shall see at considerable length in chapter 2, from start to finish Chaucer has constructed the *Tale* so as to evoke his readers' memories of their early grammar school studies in literature and literary criticism—reading assignments, translations from Latin into English and back again, exercises requiring the identification and imitation of a wide variety of tropes and figures of thought, amplifications and abbreviations of rhetorical passages from the preceptive handbooks, as well as critical glosses and prudential themes defending truths discovered in the texts of the classical *auctores*. The backbone to this curricular program was Priscian's *preexercitamina*, a sequence of fourteen or so linguistic, literary, and rhetorical exercises. Significantly, the first exercise, Fabula, begins with students' composing a careful paraphrase of the main features of an Aesopian beast fable— precisely the medieval assignment that Hussey unwittingly completes in his exacting outline of *The Nun's Priest's Tale*. Thus, in response to the question, What *is* the genre of *The Nun's Priest's Tale*, my first answer constitutes the first major assertion I wish to make in this book. Chaucer's *The Nun's Priest's Tale* is a Menippean anatomy invoking his readers' vivid memories of specific grammar school literary assignments, parodically redeploying those exercises inside an instructively innovative and metapoetic environment, and thus revitalizing their educative power to effect a reinterrogation of what the essence of literature may be.

The second major assertion I wish to make proceeds directly from the first. Despite its modest size, the tale into which Chaucer reinscribes his readers' early educational exercises is nothing less than a simulacrum of the entire world of Western thought and letters. Many readers have remarked how this fable feels like a mock-*summa,* a miniaturized synopticon of Western learning, as it knowingly appropriates to its own purposes all kinds of biblical, classical, and medieval tropes, topics, and texts beginning historically with the first book of Genesis and the fall of Troy. One topos organizing the *Tale* is familiar from the *paideia* tradition, wherein the humanist subject ascends into the intellectual stratosphere with the assistance of all seven of the liberal arts. *The Nun's Priest's Tale* accords special attention to each of the seven liberal arts (especially, as we shall see, the trivial arts), but the *Tale*'s flight plan—namely, lift off, wobble, swerve, and crash—is a seriocomic parody of our high-minded readerly aspirations. But this does not mean that the *Tale* is anti-intellectual or anti-academic. In fact, the narrator expects his readers to be *au courant* with state-of-the-art issues dear to the late fourteenth-century intelligentsia, such as recent philosophical interrogations of the nature of motion, change, and time coming out of the universities of Paris and Oxford. Nor does it mean that the *Tale* is designed to be read as a satire, Menippean or otherwise. In this regard it is radically different from *The Merchant's Tale.* An equally learned and jumbled ingathering of Biblical, classical, and medieval discourses, *The Merchant's Tale* is so personally embittered that it finally is not even a satire *manqué* (it has no socially redeeming intent) but rather a misanthropic screed whose ultimate purpose is the complete desecration of all that we value in Western art and culture. By contrast, *The Nun's Priest's Tale* is poetry that glories in the wondrousness of poetry, a celebration of all that we hold sacred in Western art and culture, and a personal tribute to the very tradition of humane letters that inspired Chaucer's career and informs his genius.

My final definition of the genre of *The Nun's Priest's Tale* is the most important of the three because it will control all the arguments I advance in this book. In addition to redeploying his and his readers' early grammar school literary exercises and in addition to refunctioning powerfully significant texts from the great tradition of Western letters, *The Nun's Priest's Tale* is also Chaucer's premier work of self-parody. Written near the end of his career, serving as the gratifying climax to Fragment VII (the "literature fragment"), *The Nun's Priest's Tale* is rich with allusions to his other Canterbury tales as well as to earlier poems, such as his dream visions, written well before *The Canterbury Tales* had got under way. One reason Chaucer has chosen to quote and mimic his past works is consistent with other examples of authorial self-parody: preempting the dull critic, the artist selects, exaggerates, and spotlights the essential features of her craft in order to invite a more fully nuanced rereading of her artistic achievements.[40] *The Nun's Priest's Tale* in this regard is Chaucer's *apologia pro sua arte.* But the most profound matters foregrounded in *The Nun's Priest's Tale* are not in fact Chaucer's advertisements of his past or present achievements; rather, they are poetological *problems* that Chaucer has wrestled with from the beginning of his career and now wants to address in a concentrated, experimental, and parapoetical environment. So while asserting that *The Nun's Priest's Tale* is Chaucer's premier instance of self-parody, in the same breath I am asserting that it is his signature *ars poetica*: a fable wherein he contextualizes, critiques, deepens, and refunctions the most pressing concerns of a humanist poet writing in the late fourteenth century in England.

Of all Chaucer's pressing areas of concern in this his *ars poetica,* the most significant is his own readers. Who are my ideal readers? Who are my real readers? How do my readers read? Do they detect the differences between irony, parody, and satire? Do they read poetry for a message? Do they ever change because of the poetry they read? Do my readers invent my authorial intent? Are my readers my own best fictions? What in fact *is* the act of reading? Of all the literary genres, parody is unusually dependent on its reader, because in order for parody to succeed *as parody* not only must its reader already know the target text and appreciate its distinctive artistic features, but the reader must be able to appreciate the subtleties of the latter-day text as it both emulates and critiques its predecessor. This means the more accomplished and pluriform the choreographies of the target texts, the more complex and pluriform the parody, especially if the parodic text is intent on paying homage to the genius of its precursors. It is perhaps not surprising in this regard that the experimentations of contemporary dance, honoring the past while striving to supercede its precursors through slantwise mimickings of earlier styles, is a fertile analogy to the intertextual poetics of parody. In *A Map of Mis-*

reading, Harold Bloom invented six oedipal "ratios" designating six major stratagems available to the young poet as he deliberately "misreads" the voice of the all-powerful forebear: *clinamen, tessera, kenosis, demonization, askesis,* and *apophrades.* In her excellent book *Intertextuality,* Mary Orr transposes (and feminizes) the clunkiness of Bloom's occult terms into the graceful movements of dance, six ways of the young artist's answering back to the dominant *auctoritates:*

> The first is a sidestep away from the precursor's footwork. The second is a leap invented by the precursor but used as a different dance step by the newcomer. The third is a flat-footed jump to claim independence as dancer from the precursor's dance tradition. The fourth describes a dance movement so quintessentially anchored in dance that the precursor's use of it seems amateur. The fifth is a dance movement of withdrawal of movement as dance, leaving the sixth a dance movement that so retranslates the precursor's most original dance step that this appears derivative.[41]

It is Chaucer's hope, I believe, that in the process of rereading *The Nun's Priest's Tale* his readers will learn to recognize the play, nuance, and originality of the steps he takes even when he is "literally" repeating pieces from his past repertoire, or the movements of his precursors, line by line. Prizing apart parodic imitation from poetic innovation is of course a challenging assignment for any reader, and at times there's really little point in trying to tell the dancer from the dance. Even so, as readers retrace the poet's steps with care, learning to engage in the labile conversation between tradition and the individual talent, readers at the same time are fashioning a dialogue between their own interpretative past and the enfranchising opportunities offered by the parodic text in the present. In her exemplary study *A Theory of Parody,* Linda Hutcheon notes how parody is "both a personal act of supersession and an inscription of literary-historical continuity."[42] And so it may be for the reader, whose experience of responding to sophisticated parody at a deep level may effect a "personal act of supersession" even while the reader's continuities as a reading subject remain intact. Artistic freedom is always a major issue at work in parody, as Margaret Rose has emphasized—freedom not only from the textual determinants of literary traditions but, in the case of self-parody, freedom from the voices, modes, and styles of one's own past creations.[43] In a similar fashion, therefore, a wider degree of artistic freedom is made possible by the inscription in most parodies of a "naïve reader" or "mock reader," whose inadequacies the ideal reader, or the increasingly more sophisticated reader, is expected to acknowledge, correct, and supersede.[44]

Thus, in order adequately to appreciate the parapoetic choreographies of *The Nun's Priest's Tale*, it is essential that we concentrate on the act of reading itself. And this means we will need to read selected passages very closely and very attentively. Chaucerian studies have always appreciated the value of close reading, especially during the 1960s, 1970s, and 1980s when much interpretive work was composed under the formalist influence of New Criticism. Now, in the early twenty-first century, it is possible that Chaucerians are poised to return to close reading with renewed interest and even, perhaps, with a more theorized understanding of what "close reading" might mean and be. In fact, one topic suggested for the 2006 New Chaucer Society Conference was "Chaucer and Close Reading." The proposers' hope was to fill a single session, but reportedly more than forty relevant abstracts were submitted; consequently, close to twenty "close reading" papers were eventually delivered, and the conference is now remembered by many of its participants as the "close reading" conference. Why this sudden explosion of interest in close reading? Some Chaucerians may currently see close reading as occasioning a healthy return to practical criticism after the putative demise of high theory. However, it is my conviction that close reading actually brings theoretical issues even more clearly to the fore, and that theory, which is always already inscribed in the literary text, deconstructs the cognitive certainties that have been associated with close reading in the past. Designed as a sequence of microscopic readings informed by a variety of medieval and postmodern theoretical issues and held together by the generic paradigm of tri-leveled Menippean parody, this study will be taking its fair share of critical risks. Yet in the end I hope this book successfully articulates a significantly new reading of *The Nun's Priest's Tale*. And if, as I claim, *The Nun's Priest's Tale* is Chaucer's signature *ars poetica*, my hope is that *Disseminal Chau-*

cer will provide a new way, perhaps a radically new way, of thinking about everything that Chaucer has written.

In chapter 1, "The Nun's Priest's Body, or Chaucer's Disseminal Genius," I elucidate the meaning of the book's title, *Disseminal Chaucer*. As is well known, under the influence of Jacques Derrida, dissemination in the past few decades has developed into an extremely complex set of interrelated ideas. Playing upon the fortuitous resemblance between "semen" and "seme," Derrida is gesturing toward the dispersal of semantic meaning in every text—a dispersal that is both a wasteful dissipation of semiological meanings and at the same time an excessive surplus of unlimited meanings. Although, according to Derrida, dissemination can never actually be defined, its very resistance to lexical categories serves as a critique of the idea that any text, literary or otherwise, can be owned, controlled, limited, or appropriated in the name of some legitimate reading or authoritative source.[45] Unlike polysemy (favored by humanists in celebration of a text's plurality of meanings), in the disseminal text "no series of semantic valences can any longer be closed or reassembled. . . . The lack and the surplus can never be stabilized in the plenitude of a form."[46] Derrida's "anti-idea" of dissemination provides surprisingly coherent depth to a central topos in the Middle Ages wherein language, especially poetic language, was seen as a form of problematic sexual emission. The medieval anxiety about these linguistic emissions played itself out around the question of *control* (how are these energies contained and directed?), *gender* (is the language of poetry masculine, feminine, or heteroclite?), and *fertility* (do these signifiers bring life to the signified, or do they die in a wasteful expenditure of onanastic desire?).

In the Epilogue to *The Nun's Priest's Tale*, Harry Bailly, the host of the Canterbury pilgrimage, waxes ecstatic because he has finally discovered the supersexual hero of his dreams. The focal point of Harry's imaginative gaze is the Priest's "every stoon" (VII.3448)—testicles so potent, Harry is persuaded, that were the Priest a "trede-foul" he could sexually service "hennes . . . / moo than seven tymes seventene" (VII.3451–54). I argue that the Priest's celibacy, sexual potency, and hypermasculinity all participate in a long-lived aesthetic debate concerning the tradition of the "virile poetic style." From classical treatises by Seneca, Horace, and Tacitus advocating the potency of figurative language to medieval interventions by Matthew of Vendôme and Geoffrey of Vinsauf on the same issue, there is an underlying anxiety that poetic language may in fact be effeminate, infertile, and wild. While embodying in Harry's fantasy a parodic exaggeration of the ideologies of the virile style, Chaucer is responding with equal subtlety to a closely related trope of linguistic sexuality and literary paternity contained in the medieval figure of Genius. Tracing the development of Genius in the works of Bernardus Silvestris, Alanus de Insulis, and Jean de Meun, I argue that the Nun's Priest is in fact Chaucer's clandestine figure of Genius who, as Nature's priest, consort, and envious antagonist, is also a transparent surrogate for the male poet. Thus, like Derrida, Chaucer is interested in the problematics of linguistic dissemination, in language's "always already divided generation of meaning."[47] But Chaucer is equally concerned with style and genre, with the tincture and the texture of the literary text, issues that are given symbolic expression through the natural colors of the Priest's flesh and the "low mimetic" register of his clothing. In sum, the Epilogue to *The Nun's Priest's Tale* serves as a critical gloss to medieval linguistic dissemination, to the "virile style" as celebrated in Western poetological discourse, and to the style and genre of the *Tale* to which it is appended.

Chapter 2, "*The Nun's Priest's Tale* as Grammar School Primer, Menippean Parody, and *Ars Poetica*," details those salient elements in the medieval grammar school curriculum that we need to appreciate in order to understand Chaucer's transmutation of these assignments into literary-critical exercises for his contemporary readers. As I have already noted, Priscian's *preexercitamina,* a sequence of progymnasmatic exercises whose primary purpose was to teach students how to read and write poetry, served as the spine of the early grammar school linguistic and literary curriculum. As we shall see in this chapter, readily recognizable parodies of these assignments are scattered throughout *The Nun's Priest's Tale.* Thus, in any one of his curricular exercises, Chaucer may be seen as parodying a student's imperfect imitation of a textbook's exaggerated imitation of a much-admired set piece of a classical master. In order to succeed as critical instruction, Chaucer must of course rely upon his readers' readiness to make progress toward a more refined understanding of the creative interplay within parody's layerings of texts. Accordingly, at this juncture I venture a fuller outline of the operative components of parody, marking out parody's formal and performative similarities to and differences from satire and irony, as well as providing an overview of the place of *The Nun's Priest's Tale* within the Menippean parodic tradition.

In the latter part of chapter 2 I concentrate on three curricular parodies that foreground three literary skills of paramount importance to Chaucer's poetic vocation. The first poetic skill is the art of textual imitation. In a passage much admired for its rollicking high humor, the Nun's Priest uncharacteristically names his *auctor* (Geoffrey of Vinsauf), even as he transposes one of the *Poetria Nova*'s rhetorical set pieces (how might one honor the tragic death of King Richard I?) into a mock-heroic lament in honor of Chauntecleer's imminent death. While enormously entertaining, Chaucer's seriocomic reapplication of Geoffrey's model apostrophings actually raises several significant concerns about *translatio studii,* such as the increasingly limited agency of the poet's political voice in a constantly diminishing public arena (the tragic death of a *chicken?*). The second poetic skill is the art of translation. When, in the middle of their debate about the meaning of dreams, Chauntecleer suddenly decides to impress his wife by translating *mulier est hominis confusio* into "Womman is mannes joye and al his blisse" (VII.3163–66), we are likely to have several responses. I am persuaded that this compressed "mistranslation" is meant to work as a parody of the problematics of translation itself: the *aporia* between the two counterpointed texts is so absurdly cavernous that it makes room for every possible thesis to carom about in a free-for-all exchange on the supreme fiction of truth-in-translation. Finally, I explore Chaucer's parodic interrogation of irony, focusing on the narrator's casually misogynistic fifteen-line riff, which he concludes with an audacious *volte-face:* "Thise been the cokkes wordes, and nat myne; / I kan noon harm of no womman divyne" (VII.3265–66). So distinctive are Chaucer's ironies that "Chaucerian irony" is often denominated as a class unto itself. But if a poet is able to remove the irony from his own ironies at every whim (as Chaucer appears to be doing here), how can the reader be confident she is ever successful in descrying an author's ironic intent? With the assistance of recent theoretical studies of irony, I argue that this antifeminist passage provides one of Chaucer's most concentrated self-critiques:

not only is the passage a pluriform display of irony and counter-irony in action, it is an interrogation of the limits, or what Stanley Fish has called the "risky business," of irony.

Chapter 3, "Close Reading: Beginnings and Endings," interrogates the problematics of close reading even as it employs the stratagems of a peculiar kind of close reading practice. In the first section, "Mock-*Exemplum,* or Reading *Ab Ovo,*" I place under scrutiny the *Tale's* opening portrait of the peasant widow and her puritan lifestyle, a description that is almost always accepted as a standard-issue *exemplum* whose main purpose is to serve as the "moral ground of the poem."[48] Instead, I believe this to be a parody, a mock-*exemplum* that works as a cautionary corrective to our careless reading habit of narrowing a colorful spectrum of literary kinds (including parody) into the monochromatic patterns of what Susan Suleiman has called "authoritarian fictions."[49] The chapter's second section, "Mock-*Moralitas,* or the *Folye* of Close Reading," provides a theorized close reading of the *Tale's* ending. Because medieval readers understood the trivial arts—especially grammar and rhetoric—as foundational to *enarratio,* the *techne* of interpreting works of literature, they were all well trained in the art of close reading. Yet as Suzanne Reynolds demonstrates in *Medieval Reading,* when closely examining a text's grammatical configurations and rhetorical tropes, medieval readers eventually reached a hermeneutic impasse: how is it possible to determine whether a word is to be taken literally (that is, grammatically) or figuratively (in other words, rhetorically) unless one arbitrarily settles the matter by actually *inventing* the author's "real intent"?[50] In the *moralitas* of *The Nun's Priest's Tale,* Chaucer offers retrospective guidance on how to read his tale. But a close reading of the *language* of these directions reveals that Chaucer deliberately intensifies the "trivial" tension among the grammatical, the rhetorical, and the logical inflections of his words. As terminal case studies firmly framing the central arguments of Chaucer's *ars poetica,* these two parodic exercises in close reading illustrate why it is that both the genres of literature and the language of literature are so resistant to our interpretative overtures at every turn.

In chapter 4, "Chaucer's Heliotropes and the Poetics of Metaphor," I interrogate Chaucer's explorations of the essence of poetry, which, of course, is metaphor. Throughout his career Chaucer meditated on metaphor's figurative possibilities and philosophical dimensions, and, like several other medieval poets, inscribed his private reading of metaphor by troping on the ubiquitous medieval icon for all metaphors, the heliotrope. Chaucer's first great heliotrope is the daisy in the Prologue to *The Legend of Good Women*. In the month of May the poet's ardor is so extreme that he can do nothing under the sun but worship "[t]he 'dayesye,' or elles the 'ye of day'" (Prologue to *LGW*, 184), whom he perceives intermittently to be a flower, a divine being, and his female beloved. Inside his dream the poet and his heliotropic beloved are joined by the God of Love and Queen Alceste, both of whom are dressed in floral, regal, and heliocentric attire. The poet is now accompanied by a confusing embarrassment of heliotropes: even though they are all meta-metaphors, they are all transgressively dissimilar both in their "proper" and their "figural" attributes. Chaucer's most daunting heliotrope is Chauntecleer, whose rooster-knowledge of the "absolute sun" was the envy of every medieval astronomer, poet, and timekeeper. As a human/animal "category mistake" writ large, however, the figure of Chaucer's champion heliotrope argues that metaphor is not only the defining feature of the art of poetry and of the knowable world, but that metaphor's own brilliance is so powerful that poetry appears capable of transforming Chaucer's readers into heliotropes themselves.

Chapter 5, "The Noise of History," focuses on answering one very challenging question: Why did Chaucer insert his only overt reference to the 1381 Uprising (the most earth-shattering political event of his lifetime) into the carnivalized comedy of a fictional fox chase in *The Nun's Priest's Tale*? To arrive at an answer, I begin by tracing the early development of Chaucer's interest in the political and historiographical significance of percussive sound. Within Chaucer's *oeuvre* there are four major percussive explosions of historical/political noise, each parodying from a distance Boethius's famous comparison of sound waves to the motion of concentric rings created by a stone thrown into a body of water. In the dysfunctional historiographical world of *The House of Fame,* Chaucer translates Boethius's dropped stone into a projectile of destructive power. At the center of *The Parlement of Foules,* the dreamer hears a huge political "noyse" whose source proves to be a raucous debate among a nation of birds—a discordance that may embody Chaucer's partisan sympathies concerning the class antagonisms of the 1381 Uprising. Chaucer's third masterstroke of historical/political noise is the great fart at the center of *The Summoner's Tale,* a disseminal noise whose many "meanings" I arrange in a critical design parodying the analytic structure of the *Tale's* twelve-spoked cartwheel. Chaucer's sonic masterpiece is the fox chase in *The Nun's Priest's Tale,* a brouhaha of a free-for-all end-of-the-world hullabaloo. In the very center of this pandaemoniacal comedy, we are stopped short by an unexpected *comparatio* between this barnyard noise and the murderous shouts of "Jakke Strawe and his meynee" (VII.3394) as the rebels slaughtered their Flemish victims in the Peasants' Revolt. How significant is it to integrate "history" and "literature" in such a violently disequilibrating way? Indeed, what is Chaucer saying here about the poetic semiotics and the political semiotics of noise? In the chapter's conclusion I provide answers to these questions; suffice it to say here that the dissonance of this comic yet troubling passage demonstrates once again the noisesome resistance of literature to the auditory "harmonics" of comfortably available interpretative strategies.

In chapter 6, "Chaucerian Horologics and the Confounded Reader," I contextualize five medieval ways of assessing time as an introduction to Chaucer's egregiously convoluted determination of the precise time that the events of *The Nun's Priest's Tale* putatively happened. Twice elsewhere in *The Canterbury Tales* Chaucer constructs an inordinately complex and "scientific" temporal periphrasis. In the Prologue to *The Man of Law's Tale,* Harry manages to ascertain, since the sun had run a bit more than a half hour more than the fourth part of its course through the artificial day, and since the shadow of every tree at that very moment was absolutely equal in length to the tree's height, and since the date of the day could be inferred or known to be the eighteenth day of April, and since the sun had ascended precisely forty-five degrees into the sky, that it is exactly "ten of the clokke" (II.14). In an equally tortured set of scientific maneuvers, in the Prologue to *The Parson's Tale* Chaucer also arrives at a precise determination of the time. Only a few scholars have felt called upon to test the accuracy of these two *chronographiae.* Holding Chaucer's authoritative source, Nicholas of Lynn's *Kalendarium,* in one hand, *The Canterbury Tales* in another, mindful as well of the principal powers of the astrolabe and the different modalities of medieval measurements of time, what these scholarly readers eventually discover is quite astonishing: each of Chaucer's two temporal determinations is, ultimately, quite "wrong."

The *chronographia* at the center of *The Nun's Priest's Tale* takes the prize for the complexities and profundities of its "wrongness." The Nun's Priest's *chronographia* is introduced by an intercalation of verbal beginnings and endings so contradictory and self-canceling that almost all editors have felt some kind of emendation is necessary. In point of fact, Chaucer's well-educated readers would instantly have recognized this word problem as a sophisticated parody of the myriad *incipit/desinit* sophisms they had studied at length in the universities' logical curriculum. A close reading of Chaucer's parodic mensuration of time in *The Nun's Priest's Tale* eventually arrives at a significant interpretative impasse, something called in formal medieval logic *vis confundendi*. With the assistance of Nicole Oresme's magnum opus, *Tractatus de Commensurabilitate vel Incommensurabilitate Motuum Celi*, a contemporary treatise on the role of "error" in our determining the commensurability or incommensurability of time, I conclude this chapter by demonstrating how our interrogation of each of Chaucer's earthbound "errors" in temporal calculations is part of a heuristic exercise designed not only to stymie the reader but ultimately to educate the reader in the direction of scientific skepticism and metaphysical understanding.

In chapter 7, "The Parodistic Episteme: Learning to Behold the Fox," I take as my point of departure the Nun's Priest's mock-defense of the truthfulness of his own fable: "This storie is also trewe, I undertake, / As is the book of Launcelot de Lake, / That wommen holde in full greet reverence" (VII.3211–13). Relying upon a *preexercitamina* exercise as its parodistic base text, the narrator's "double" or "triple" defense of his fable's veridicality is, of course, comically ironic. Whether constructions of the imagination might possibly fashion a truth transcending the binary "law of the excluded middle" is, unsurprisingly, one of the preeminent metafictional questions addressed in Chaucer's *ars poetica*. However, for Chauntecleer, the question of truth-in-fiction is also a matter of life-and-death urgency. Waking from his horrific dream, he recalls an image of a "beest" that was "lyk an hound," whose "colour was bitwixe yelow and reed," and whose intent was to "han had me deed" (VII.2899–2902).

But because Chauntecleer has not yet had the *experience* of any such hound-like animal, he neither *knows* what that animal is nor is he able to give it a *name*.

At one level this is not a problem, for the standard position among medieval philosophers was that an animal upon seeing its enemy reacts instantly, not by using "reason," but "from natural instinct." Well aware of this orthodox reading of animal faculty psychology, as he watches his hero "up . . . sterte" on first sight of the fox, the narrator provides the appropriate epistemic gloss: "For natureelly a beest desireth flee / Fro his contrarie, if he may it see, / Though he never erst hadde seyn it with his ye" (VII.3279–81). Evidently, then, Chaucer's rooster-hero did not have to extrapolate the empirical "truth" of his dream in order to respond knowingly (and appropriately) to the reality that that dream proleptically represents. But an intimately related and much more compelling question relates to Chaucer's reader: graced with the powers of human reason, is this reader able to extrapolate a truth from the image of a fox inside a dream inside a feigned fable without having experienced its applicability to an indeterminate and unnamed future referent? Or, to cast the question more generally, does Chaucer's *ars poetica* embody a representation of reality more verdical, instructive, and liberating, for example, than those realized in the five tales that immediately precede it in Fragment VII? Arguing that each of these preceding tales is designed as a parodic experiment in the aesthetics of partial failure, my answer, unsurprisingly, is in the affirmative: living up to all the advance hype, *The Nun's Priest's Tale* is the fragment's epistemic success story, its parodic *summa*, its supreme literary fiction.

In my final chapter, "*Moralitas*," I rearticulate the theoretical precepts and methodologies that distinguish this study from recent readings of *The Nun's Priest's Tale* as well as from preeminent modes of Chaucer criticism developed over the past two decades. I conclude my analysis of Chaucer's *ars poetica* by suggesting how *The Nun's Priest's Tale* invites readers to respond creatively by inventing a practical agenda in their own art of living.

I wish, finally, to address two more words in my title: "Chaucer" and "Rereading." Whether or not the signifieds of three closely related nominals—namely, "Chaucer," "the Nun's Priest," and "the narrator"—are identical, whether they are nearly impossible to prize apart, or whether they are absolutely discrete subjectivities are all challenging critical questions. In his recent book *Textual Subjectivity,* A. C. Spearing takes issue with the contemporary practice of reading each Canterbury tale as a dramatic monologue emanating from a pilgrim-voice readily distinguishable from the more "reliable" voice of Chaucer the author. Spearing insists that in most tales, as in most medieval fiction, the narrating voice "does not represent a speaking individual, real or fictional, but is merely one element in the rhetoric of storytelling."[51] While allowing that Chaucer "was truly interested in the possibility of connections between stories and their tellers," Spearing contends "he was only at early, exploratory stages" of a literary "development he was only beginning."[52] It should not come as a surprise that the question of to whom the narrative "I" in Chaucer's poem refers is yet another metapoetical issue parodically foregrounded in *The Nun's Priest's Tale.* However, until I address precisely how Chaucer, a.k.a. the Nun's Priest, a.k.a. the narrator copes with this matter, I will simply try to allocate these individual nominals with caution, or with what might best be called an imperfect imprecision.

Although "rereading" often serves as a mere placeholder in the titles of books and articles, because *The Nun's Priest's Tale* concludes with its author's enjoining his readers to set about reading the *Tale* again, I hope in this book to revitalize this rather tired gerund. Chaucer's authorial request is unusual only because the sentiment is included within the literary text itself. As Matei Călinescu demonstrates in *Rereading,* great writers have repeatedly insisted on the absolute necessity of rereading: "One cannot *read* a book," writes Nabokov, "one can only reread it."[53] And of course critics are in full agreement. Călinescu cites Michael Riffaterre, who argued that in order to read a poem adequately one has to read it at least twice: first, by adopting an attitude in which the text functions as if it were "mimetic" (not easily done, of course, with a beast fable) and then "by submitting it to a 'retroactive' or 'hermeneutic' reading in which the previously hidden significance of the poem reveals itself," and thus manages "to get beyond 'mimesis' and reach the higher level of 'semiosis.'"[54] Thus "[t]he question of concealed meaning," Călinescu continues, "haunts the act of rereading, particularly as it comes to focus on tiny textual details, idiosyncratic formulations, letter combinations, patterns of occurences of names and dates, and other such matters."[55] Focusing on many textual details in *The Nun's Priest's Tale, Disseminal Chaucer* is obviously committed to rereading with extreme care. But as we progress through this book I hope that we also manage to keep the totality of Chaucer's literary performance resonant in our minds. The smallest riff, in other words, needs to be heard as part of a developing sequence, a shifting harmonics of sense and sound. To encourage this breadth of appreciation, I drew an analogy earlier in this introduction between the aesthetics of Chaucer's poetics and the choreographies of modern dance. To add another set of metapahors to our rereading of the *Tale,* I'd like to invoke another complementary art form, music, as embodied in the unique achievement of the jazz pianist Art Tatum:

> Tatum's style was notable for its touch, its speed and accuracy, and its harmonic and rhythmic imagination. No pianist has ever hit notes more beautifully. Each one—no matter how fast the tempo—was light and complete and resonant, like the letters on a finely printed page. Vast lower-register chords were unblurred, and his highest notes were polished silver. . . . His speed and precision were almost shocking. Flawless sixteenth-note runs poured up and down the keyboard, each note perfectly accented, and the chords and figures in the left hand sometimes sounded two-handed. Such virtuosity can be an end in itself, and Tatum was delighted to let it be in his up-tempo flag-wavers, when he spectacularly became a high-wire artist, a scaler of Everests. Tatum's bedrock sense of rhythm enabled him to play out-of-tempo interludes or whole choruses that doubled the impact of the implied beat, and his harmonic sense—his strange, multiplied chords, still largely unmatched by his followers, his laying on of two and three and four melodic levels at once—was orchestral and even symphonic.[56]

I suggest that Whitney Balliett's paean to Tatum's jazz genius could just as easily be celebrating Chaucer's poetic virtuosities. The style of each artist is unique; each has synthesized and transcended the traditions of the past; each has a perfect ear. This present study, anatomizing a series of Chaucerian "chords" and "figures," is obviously a longish book on a short-ish tale. But if our goal is to arrive at an appreciation of the fullness of Chaucer's "harmonic imagination," as well as to understand that "synap-tic arc" uniting poetic performance and parodic free play, I believe it is imperative that we first attend to Chaucer's achievements riff by riff— a few notes, and a few chords, at a time.

ONE

The Nun's Priest's Body,
or Chaucer's Sexual Genius

*The poet would be much safer if he did not
commit himself to the Word, but in ironic detachment
exploited the infinite ambiguities of speech. Or he could retreat to the
safety of a socio-religious order, give up his claim to verbal priesthood,
and turn "mouthpiece." Both roads have been taken; but they lead to self-
abnegation. The poet as a fool must be a corrupter of words, a punster,
rhymster, verbal trickster, for there is no other way to break the disgraceful
bonds into which words have fallen. But if he is not also, and ultimately,
priest—if he is not a parson disguised as a fool rather than a fool disguised as
a parson—speech will be "wanton" rather than sacramental: "Why, sir, her
name's a word; and to dally with that word might make my sister wanton."*

—SIGURD BURCKHARDT

Fragment VII of *The Canterbury Tales,* a linked sequence of six quite
radically different narratives, has for a long time been appreciated as a
sustained metapoetic interrogation of the aesthetic ramifications and the
linguistic dimensions of Chaucer's own literary art. In 1967, Alan Gaylord argued that Fragment VII was Chaucer's "literary fragment," whose

premier subject is "the art of story telling" itself.[1] In 1984, Helen Cooper maintained that the "basic question" of "the status of language" is so much its focus that Fragment VII could be known as Chaucer's linguistic fragment.[2] More recently, the fragment has been explored as an experimentation in the genres of partial, or parodic, failure—the ice-cold uncomedy of the Shipman's fabliau; the spiritual ferocities of the Prioress's boy martyrology; the narrative and prosodic pratfalls of Chaucer's *Sir Thopas*; the monitory confusion of a thousand proverbs running amok in the *Melibee*; the anti-cathartic effect of a hundred tragedies promised by the Monk.[3] While each of these five tales can simultaneously be read straight as well as askew, an artistic success as well as a parodic near-miss, as a literary collocation they appear to be seeking some form, voice, and vision that would embody, unify, or transcend their partialities and imperfections.

I am persuaded that Fragment VII's metapoetic quest for a fully realized supreme fiction, that is, *The Nun's Priest's Tale,* is complemented, recoded, and parodied by Harry Bailly's quest throughout this fragment for the supremely masculine male. Most dramatically, nearing the end of the fragment, Harry believes that he has finally discovered in the person of the Monk the sexual superman of his dreams. We "borel men," he confesses unabashedly to the Monk, we ordinary men are nothing but puny "shrympes": we are incapable of satisfying our wives in bed, just as we are unable to generate heirs that are anything but "sklendre" and "feble" (VII.1955–58). By contrast, Harry can see that the Monk is a sexual champion, big of "brawnes and bones," who would be and should be a "tredefowel aright," copulating with such indefatigable vigor that he would beget "ful many a creature" (VII.1941–48). But the Monk fails to live up to Harry's supermanly vision, the only apparent reason being his perceived failure at the art of storytelling. Interrupted by the Knight after his seventeenth straight "tragedie," the Monk has now deflated, in Harry's eye, into less than a shrimp, his superhuman testicular potencies as teensy as those Canterbury bells tinkling and "clynkynge" on his horse's bridle. So it is only at the end of the fragment that Harry finally turns, with little apparent optimism, to the Nun's Priest, hoping for a "swich thing as may oure hertes glade" (VII.2810). But if the Nun's Priest's unimposing horse, a "jade" both "foul" and "lene" (VII.2812–13), is a metonym of its owner's person, then this priest's artistic and sexual powers may prove to be as disappointing as the Monk's.

As I noted in the introduction, a broad consensus in Chaucer studies has maintained for generations that the beast fable told by the Nun's Priest about Chauntecleer, Pertelote, and Russell the fox is a brilliant artistic success. However, in this first chapter I do not want to start off by immediately analyzing the *Tale* itself. Rather, since Harry Bailly in many ways is Chaucer's first internalized reader, I want to follow Harry's critical progress by moving beyond the *Tale* to its end-link. In lines repeating some of the terms of his earlier hyperbolic praise of the Monk, Harry at fragment's end finally provides a physical portrait of the Priest, a portrait, I wish to emphasize, pointedly lacking in the *General Prologue* itself:

> "Sire Nonnes Preest," oure Hooste seide anoon,
> "I-blessed be thy breche, and every stoon!
> This was a murie tale of Chauntecleer.
> But by my trouthe, if thou were seculer,
> Thou woldest ben a trede-foul aright.
> For if thou have corage as thou hast myght,
> Thee were nede of hennes, as I wene,
> Ya, moo than seven tymes seventene.
> See, whiche braunes hath this gentil preest,
> So gret a nekke, and swich a large breest!
> He loketh as a sperhauk with his yen;
> Him nedeth nat his colour for to dyen
> With brasile ne with greyn of Portyngale.
> Now, sire, faire falle yow for youre tale!"
> And after that he, with ful merie chere,
> Seide unto another, as ye shuln heere.
>
> (VII.3447–63)

As seen through Harry Bailly's scopophilic imagination, the Nun's Priest has morphed from an indeterminate former state into a mightily impressive physical personage: even before checking out his great neck, his large breast, and his brawny physique, Harry's netherward gaze remarks upon the quality of the Priest's "breche, and every stoon" (that is, his undershorts and his [many?] testicles). Here, finally, stands Harry's macho man in all his somatic glory: were it not for his spiritual calling, Harry allows, the Priest would prove to be a "trede-foul aright" able to service hens "moo than seven tymes seventene." In addition to his hypermasculinity and his hypersexuality, two more striking physical aspects catch Harry's attention: the Priest's penetrating eyesight ("He loketh as a sperhauk with his yen") and his undyed ruddy complexion: "Him nedeth nat his colour for to dyen / With brasile ne with greyn of Portyngale."

No doubt Harry's quest for a manly alter-ego reveals a great deal about his personal identity anxieties as well as ongoing marital tensions with his wife Goodelief, whom he represents as an emasculating, henpecking spouse threatening to give up her distaff, take up Harry's knife, and do with it as she will.[4] And no doubt this unusual epilogue—unusual in part because several of its lines appear in slightly modified form and with greater textual authority in Harry's earlier praise of the Monk[5]—reveals something about Chaucer's personal interests in the problematics of manliness, whatever manliness may mean and be.[6] In addition, however, I wish to argue that the physical realization of Harry's sexual ideal at the end of Fragment VII contains a quite specific aesthetic and hermeneutic agenda. To be precise, the Epilogue to *The Nun's Priest's Tale* is Chaucer's complex position statement about the power, medium, and appropriate style of his own literary art, serving as a retroactive critical commentary on the *Tale* itself. Each of the Nun's Priest's attributes—his spiritual calling, his manly physique, his X-ray vision, his homely breeches, his ruddy complexion, his refusing any dyes, his seminal potencies, and his "every stoon"—each of these attributes engages themes and tropes found in Western aesthetic debates ranging from classical treatises on style to those found in the Middle Ages and the Renaissance. Thus, understanding the major stylistic norms embodied in the Nun's Priest's masculine person means, first, tracing their articulation in the works of various classical, medieval, and Renaissance authorities. And, second, it means tracing the masculine figure of Genius-as-Priest, developing from the *genii* of Bernardus Silvestris's *De Cosmographia* and provided full human form in the Genius figures of Alanus de Insulis and Jean de Meun. Although Alice Miskimin asserts that "[t]he archetypal image of Natura's priest, Genius, never appears directly in Chaucer's poems,"[7] I believe that, with only the slightest amount of indirection, Genius does in fact appear in the physical person of Chaucer's Nun's Priest; and that, through the Priest's genial mix of hypermasculinity, priesthood, celibacy, and sexual potency, Chaucer is invoking and critiquing the artistic ideologies he embodies.

The ambition of this opening chapter is thus to ascertain Chaucer's assessment of the stylistic precepts, linguistic themes, and artistic principles he invokes through Harry's hypersexual vision of this disseminating literary genius. But because the ultimate task is to define Chaucer's aesthetic position (and not merely Harry's), we need to acknowledge the puzzling absence of the Nun's Priest's body, as well as its presence. We must address, that is, that manuscript issue already briefly alluded to: of all the pilgrims, it is only the Nun's Priest's body that is marked by a pure absence from the reifying ground of the *General Prologue*. Corresponding, I suggest, to Derrida's "affirmation of the nonorigin" of linguistic signifiers, this manuscript aporia helps to configure the Nun's Priest's body as Chaucer's sign of linguistic dissemination. In addition, as a symptomatic projection of Harry's homoerotic desires and his fears of castration, this absent/present body exposes the "disseminal" anxieties at the core of the very traditions that have made its formation possible. Harry's unintentional parody of these aesthetic ideals, in other words, contains Chaucer's own critique of the traditional celebrations of language's potency and of literature's hypermasculine valence. And while within the *Canterbury Tales* manuscripts this unusual portrait works as an unexpected conclusion to Fragment VII, it may also be viewed as a prolegomenon to the metapoetic issues interrogated within *The Nun's Priest's Tale* itself.

VIRILE POETICS

In her essay "Virile Style," Patricia Parker focuses on the anxiety of many classical and neoclassical poets that their literary language is forever on the verge of succumbing to effeminacy.[8] In an epistle written in 1527, for example, Erasmus takes aim at an "effeminate" Ciceronian style to which he feels his fellow humanists were ever in danger of losing their manhood. We need a language "more genuine," he writes, "more concise, more forceful,

less ornate, and *more masculine*"⁹ (italics in Parker's original). In *Timber;
or Discoveries,* Ben Jonson similarly called for styles that *ossa habent, et
nervos* (that would have "bones and sinews") as against a style that is
"fleshy . . . fat and corpulent . . . full of suet and tallow."¹⁰ In these and
other contributions to the Renaissance debates on style, the keyword is
nervus, denoting sinews, but also the sexual male member, and, by extension, force, energy, and manly strength.¹¹ Only its opposite, *enervis,* appears with greater critical frequency, marking the omnipresent danger of
slipping into an effeminate writing style of unmanly excess and weakness,
a literary aesthetic that is again translated into "the metaphorics of the
male body."¹²

We see the same sexual anxieties in these texts' Roman originals.
In one of his *Epistles,* for instance, Seneca treats of "a degenerate style of
speech" that has the "mincing" (*infracta*) and "womanish" (*effeminatus*)
gait of the *cinaedus,* that is, the penetrated partner in sexual relations
between men.¹³ Tacitus, mixing misogyny and anti-Orientalism, records
his hostility to the more copious, "Asiatic" and "effeminate" style of Cicero, consistently using *enervis* (weak, effeminate) as well as *fractum* (broken, impotent) as pejoratives.¹⁴ Not to be outdone, Horace plays on his
own name, Quintus Horatius Flaccus, by characterizing a flaccid style as
akin to a slack and useless member (*ad unum / mollis opus*), as opposed
to a "firm" (*constans*) male virility.¹⁵ These fears of paralyzing impotence
invariably extend into an aggressive denigration of the feminine and even
more fiercely of the passive homosexual. Quintilian, for example, while
praising the good circulation, healthy complexion, firm flesh, and shapely
thews of the writer whose style is properly virile, condemns that man who
would seek to enhance his literary graces by the use of depilatories and
cosmetics and the wearing of dress effeminate and luxurious, rather than
tasteful and dignified. In fact, Quintilian discusses a whole range of such
unmanly behavior: "the plucked body, the broken walk, the female attire,"
all signs of "one who is *mollis* and not a real man" but rather a womanish, passive male.¹⁶

Staunchly opposing this overdressed effeminacy is the Spartan style
and physical frame of the real man. "It is with eloquence as with the
human frame," writes Tacitus. "There can be no beauty of form where
the veins are prominent, or where one can count the bones: sound health-

ful blood must fill out the limbs, and riot over the muscles, concealing the sinews in turn under a ruddy complexion and a graceful exterior."[17] While policing proper male sexual identity is clearly a core concern in all of these aesthetic protestations, what is equally and perhaps even more fundamentally at issue is the nature of language itself and the need to monitor the proper relationship between words and things.[18] In the *Institutes,* to take one example, Quintilian admonishes his readers to hold in the highest regard "the things [or content] that are the sinews of any speech [rather than] devote themselves to the futile and crippling study of words in a vain desire to acquire the gift of eloquence."[19] This privileging of the masculinity of the signified over the effeminacy of the free-floating signifier is, of course, a recurring trope in the history of Western thought and one to which we shall return.

In the Middle Ages, the precepts of literary style, sexual desire, regulated language, and the male body were bound together in ways powerfully indebted to the classical Latin tradition, yet their articulation was positioned within an ethical, religious, and educational context that was distinctive to their time. In the twelfth and thirteenth centuries, for example, the classroom study of the Latin language and the literary arts served as an ongoing object lesson in proper masculine attitudes and behavior. Matthew of Vendôme's *Ars Versificatoria,* to take one mainstream case study, combines sexually transparent *exempla* in order to illustrate to its schoolboy readers the attractions of proper schemes and tropes and the barbarity of improper ones. Apocope, Matthew explains without skipping a beat, is the name for the dropping of a letter in writing, while it is also the name for the act of penile castration;[20] syncopation, which leaves out certain sounds in a line of verse, Matthew analogizes to "the thick penis [that] cuts off the sounds of intercourse."[21] It is not surprising that Matthew's program of grammatical and sexual instruction finds room to lambaste effeminate poetasters, whom he calls, relying upon Quintilian, "the category of vicious and decadent rhetoricians," those "hypocrites who while speaking about virtue wiggle their buttocks."[22] At the same time, as Garret Epp's reading of the *Ars Versificatoria* illustrates, Matthew's instruction in grammatical solecism and prosodic transgression often leads him into a potentially promiscuous queering of his own heteronormative mandates.[23] And this is not surprising, since many standard classroom texts, such as the *Ars amatoria*, the *Achilleid*, and *Pamphilus*, profile the male body as an object of admiration even while instructing "young boys . . . about sexual violence as a method of defining their manhood and controlling their own lives."[24]

Thus, in order to define a new, fourteenth-century style of literary manliness, Chaucer reassembles a large number of conventional signifiers and fashions them into the Nun's Priest's distinctive personal attributes—his ruddy complexion, his heavyweight testicles, his refusal to apply dyes to his person, his classical bearing, and his athletic physique. And he has been able to do so successfully by integrating these signifiers inside a second tradition, the topos of masculine Genius, a concept deriving from Plato's *Timaeus* and explored before Chaucer by Bernardus Silvestris, Alanus de Insulis, and Jean de Meun. This aesthetic tradition, while also male-centered, does not simply reiterate the anti-effeminacy of the virile style. In striking contrast, the ideology of Genius actually celebrates the feminine, especially the gift of natural procreation. At the same time, however, since the figure of Genius is ultimately a stand-in for the male artist, even while the poet may admire and emulate Nature's gifts, more often than not he is intent on appropriating and displacing her powers of natural procreation with his own powers of literary production.

Bernardus Silvestris's mid-twelfth-century *Cosmographia*, a cosmogenic myth about creation itself, paralleling the world's creation with the creation of humankind, is a case in point. The only absolutely masculine forces in Bernard's universe are the four orders of genius. The "highest" and "lowest" *genii* are the most relevant: Pantomorphus, a deity of the highest regions who is "devoted to the art and office of delineating and giving shape to the forms of things";[25] and the *genii* of the male sexual organs, those "twin brothers" who, along with the "crafty penis," are assigned the task of perpetuating mankind.[26] While this deity and these organs are masculine, the remaining powers in Bernardus's vision of creation are all impressively feminine. Coterminous and nearly coequal with God are the three Neoplatonic Forms: Silva, Natura, and Noys. These sisterly goddesses, shaping and informing the act of creation, suggest in their contiguity with each other and with the divine that God may be ambiguously transgendered. If Bernardus's God has a penis, in other words, it remains invisible and immobile. Instead, as Claire Fanger argues, it is God's capacious "womb" that figures as a "generative aspect of the divine—an aspect that often seems to be represented as ontologically prior to the masculinity that it forms or engenders."[27] In this way, and despite its enormous indebtedness to the *Timaeus* and to Plato's well-known womb-envy complex,[28] Bernard's *Cosmographia* is unusually generous in its celebrations of the ontological priorities of the feminine. Yet the tension found in Plato between form and matter, spirit and flesh, the masculine and the feminine, is found here as well. Even in Bernardus's seemingly holistic universe, a major power struggle between the sexes is dramatized; and ultimately the site of this struggle is the mind of the poet himself, a creator who needs to counter the natural gifts of the feminine with his own phallic phantasies of autogenesis and artistic creation.

Alanus de Insulis's *Complaint of Nature* takes this gender struggle a step further by allegorizing the sexual identity and erotic desires of language itself. The most important figure in the *Complaint* is Nature, vicar and vice-regent of God, *genetrix rerum* of the natural world, whose creative function is to stamp on matter the appropriate form, copying the divine ideas so as to insure an uninterrupted continuance of impermanent entities. Venus, the goddess of Love, is in turn Nature's vicegerent; in obedience to Nature and thus to God, she performs the same divinely approved function of assisting all creatures in being fruitful and in multiplying. The male figure of Genius, a priest who appears only at the end of the *Complaint,* is also fashioned in Nature's image, and, at a further remove, in the image of God. Like Nature, he wears magnificent robes that are continually changing their colors, displaying images of natural objects that appear and disappear. Unlike Nature, but very like the male literary artist for whom he stands, Genius brings things into being by means of his phallic pen.[29] With this he writes upon "the pelt of a dead animal," thus "endow[ing] with the life of their species images of things that kept changing from the shadowy outline of a picture to the realism of their actual being."[30] But in addition to serving as Nature's priest, Genius is also her lover, for by means of a Neoplatonic kiss, he and Nature have begotten a daughter named Truth. Unfortunately, Truth is attended by a shadow sibling of unnamed parentage, the dark and ugly Falsitas, who secretly lies "in wait" in order to disgrace "by deformity" whatever Truth has "graced by conformity."[31]

In exercising his priestly powers, Genius's primary assignment is to excommunicate mankind because of its sexual and grammatical perversions. Having rampantly abused Nature's laws of grammatical copulation, having recklessly changed "he's" into "she's," having converted the active sex into the passive sex, having attempted to be both subject and predicate at once, modern man, Nature complains, no longer is charmed by "the little cleft of Venus" and thus deserves to "be excommunicated from the temple of Genius."[32] Even among "those men who subscribe to Venus' procedures in grammar," Nature laments, "some closely embrace those of masculine gender only, others, those of feminine gender, others, those of common, or epicene gender."[33] And then there are those heteroclite autoeroticists, "disdaining to enter Venus' hall, [who] practice a deplorable game in the vestibule of her house."[34] While Nature asserts that she "bring[s] no charge of dishonourable conduct against the basic nature of Desire, if it restrains itself with the bridle of moderation," she does bring a charge against it "if its tiny flame turns into a conflagration, if its little fountain grows into a torrent, if its luxurious growth calls for the pruning-hook to shorten it, if its excessive swelling needs treatment to heal it."[35] In other words, in the *Complaint,* the wildness of erotic desire is so powerful and in need of such aggressive pruning that its husbandry would appear at times to border on sexual/linguistic castration.

It is obvious from just this abbreviated summary that much insecurity surrounds Alanus's fantastic celebrations of heteronormative poetry and literary paternity. Is it possible that Truth is solely Nature's child, and that Genius's only offspring is a fraudulent figure named Falsehood? Is Genius's language in fact capable of spawning any form of being? Is it perhaps the case that erotic promiscuity is an inherent condition of language itself? To some degree, Alanus acknowledges that Nature's standards of proper coition and art's standards of orthodox writing are both subject to inventive experimentation. Venus herself eventually grows bored with the duplicative process of orthodox sex. Forsaking her husband Hymenaeus, she takes up a life of "fornication and concubinage" with Antigenius, with whom she produces a child called Jocus, or Sport, a churlish buffoon whose lifestyle inspires all manner of linguistic and sexual free play. Yet, as many scholars have noted, Alanus, like his master Matthew of Vendôme before him, cannot himself resist indulging in the onanistic arts practiced by those linguistic perverts he calls "falsigraphers."[36] Looking aghast at "sodomites of style" who take "immeasurable pleasure" in embracing grammatical defects, Alanus nevertheless finds himself falling prey to "barbarolexis," sporting, like his enemies, in the "jubilant fount of his own poetics." Indeed, the extreme floribundence of Alanus's rococo style itself indicates that the effete sins of language he seeks to condemn are only slightly distorted images of his own poetic vocation.

Thus a basic issue addressed throughout *The Complaint of Nature* concerns the transgressive nature of poetry itself: could it be that all tropes are a form of "fornication" and linguistic "concubinage," or, even more dangerously, that all poetry, in fact, is "queer"? Alanus heightens the sexual valence of poetic tropes by equating language's proper hue with the desires of robust innocence and by defining all that is rhetorically "foreign" as tainted with illicit concupiscence, arguing that false grammarians are guilty of "discolour[ing] the colour of beauty by the meretricious dye of desire."[37] But he leaves unresolved the difficulty of distinguishing chaste colors from meretricious ones, or of discriminating between poetry's natural pigmentation and its application of artificial dyes. Adding more complexity to the poetics of artificial colors, as Andrew Cowell has shown, the medieval "dye of desire" topos serves in a variety of texts as "a key medieval site for considering the relation between the literal and the figural, and between the 'natural' body of meaning and the rhetoric in which it was expressed."[38] As we shall see, all of these linguistic, sexual, and poetological issues are encoded in the signature attributes of the Nun's Priest's body.

But before returning to Chaucer's Priest, we need to consider one final literary progenitor: Jean de Meun's figure of Genius. Perhaps more than even *The Complaint of Nature, The Romance of the Rose* is a text about "the process of 'becoming male.' "[39] By stripping away the "[s]tylistic equivocation and polite euphemism" of his forebears, Jean lays bare "the insistent demands of male desire and men's preoccupation with their sexual potency."[40] The powers of the phallus, the duties of the testicles, the fears of castration, the abhorrence of the homosexual, the conquest of the female beloved, the insemination of the Rose, and the allure of the human body (be it naked or fully clothed): these preoccupations, as Alistair Minnis argues in *Magister Amoris*, participate in the "phallocentric demythologization" of earlier works that had been much more explicitly about poetry, language, creation, form, and style.[41] Yet each of the sexual preoccupations in the *Rose* remains a literary preoccupation as well, especially the preoccupation with nakedness and dress. The human body in or out of dress, Minnis suggests, is likely to involve an "integumental hermeneutics," where the "rude and nude" embodies a plain or satiric style, and the elaborately dressed body represents the value of one of the "higher" literary registers.[42] Thus Jean's Genius removes his sacerdotal vestments as Nature's priest to put on secular clothing, leaving "his limbs / More free, as if he would attend a dance,"[43] and later dons the robes of Cupid in order to preach his sermon on the virtues of fleshly copulation: "we all should scriveners / Become."[44] Genius's change of habiliment suggests the ever-shifting relationship between the literal and the figural, whereas his refusal to practice sexually what he preaches spiritually bespeaks another complex reading of the role of the poet's art. A servant of a servant of God, Genius as Nature's "Venerian" priest is expected to practice total sexual restraint even though complete genital functionality is requisite to his vocation.[45] A sexual enthusiastic who nevertheless has taken vows of celibacy,[46] Jean's figure of Genius appears self-conflicting and self-conflicted. But these inconsistencies are apparently symbolic elements essential to defining the vocation of the poet and the powers of his literary craft.

TESTERICAL HERMENEUTICS

Given these classical and medieval traditions of linking the ideal male form and the ideal poetic function, what precisely is the "meaning" of the Nun's Priest's masculine body as it suddenly comes into view at the very end of Fragment VII? This body I think we can now decode as constituting a template of recognizable attributes, all of which focus on defining the principles of a new, fourteenth-century virile style. In accordance with the dictates of the classical ideal, the brawny power and handsome girth of Chaucer's Priest represent the sinewy and muscular qualities of a manly literary aesthetic. His "gret . . . nekke," "large breest," and impressive physique articulate a straightforward, reality-based literary language where the signifieds of *res* are firmly embodied in the *verba* as signs. The Priest's undyed flesh argues for a rhetorical style that eschews elaborate tropes, preferring the unadorned and natural. The natural colors of the Priest's healthy complexion mandate that the *significatio* of poetry be seen to reside in the literal rather than in the spiritual. And even the Priest's homely underpants, his "breech," can be understood as supporting a low-mimetic poetics. In contrast to the well-attired Genius figures in *The Complaint of Nature* and in *The Romance of the Rose*, Harry's priest is visualized as fully naked except for one functional, nondescript covering that just barely hides from sight the potent genitals we are assured it contains. Of course it is the prowess of the Priest's "every stoon" that is the cynosure of Harry's intense admiration. Developing from symbolic and literal genitalia inscribed in various cosmogenic treatises, preceptive grammars, and courtly allegories, the Nun's Priest's "every stoon" demonstrates that the artistic instruments of the male poet are superabundantly potent, capable of generating life as well as satisfying the erotic needs of many women, "Ya, moo than seven tymes seventene."[47]

As an aesthetic pronouncement, the Nun's Priest's *effictio* thus seems to stand secure in its masculine semiotics. In this regard it differs markedly from its classical and medieval predecessors, most of which implement stratagems of misogyny and homophobia in order to elevate the heterosexual virtues of the virile style and to celebrate the powers of male procreation. By contrast, Chaucer's portrait notably omits all explicit denigrations of the effeminate, of the feminine, or of the queer. Any latent womb-envy or anxiety about literary paternity is camouflaged, so to speak, by this priest being a nun's priest rather than Nature's priest and by our understanding that his generative potency is held (just barely) in check by his vows of professional celibacy. Thus does Chaucer's compressed integration of the classical mandates of the virile style and of the traditional medieval ideals of masculine genius appear—at least on first reading—to be complete and unproblematic. And unproblematic it might remain were it not for the fact that Fragment VII's concluding vision of the Priest's hypermasculine body is nothing more or less than an ungrounded figment of Harry's testerical imagination.[48]

Radically different in design from the *effictiones* of the *General Prologue* and clearly the personal projection of its creator, this free-floating somatic vision reveals much about Harry himself: his class prejudices, his over-the-top enthusiasms, his homoerotic fantasies, and his sexual uncertainties. But in addition to being "in character," these personal markers, for Chaucer, work more fundamentally as a complex parody of the abiding need for a hypermasculine literary aesthetic. That is, Chaucer uses Harry's abject relationship to the ideal male body as a way of foregrounding, dramatizing, and parodying the obsessions and fantasies that lurk just beneath the surface of the aesthetic tradition that culminates in the Nun's Priest himself. In dramatically counterpointing the figure of the Priest and the figure of Harry, Chaucer has cleanly split apart the ideological economy of his inherited masculinist culture in order to scrutinize its underlying pathology as well as to honor its enduring strengths. What this means is that the Nun's Priest's body provides a satisfying, if *de trop*, celebration of medieval literary masculinity; at the same time, Harry's affective relationship to that exaggerated ideal acts out the fears and fantasies that necessitate its existence. Thus, Harry's intense admiration of the Nun's Priest's genitals can be seen as "outing" the homoerotic fascinations found in almost all the aesthetic treatises we have reviewed. As in these classical and medieval treatises, so with Harry: it is difficult to determine if the viewer's ultimate desire is to possess or to become the poetic ideal of male virility. Harry's castration anxieties work in a similar fashion. The Priest's raptor vision ("He loketh as a sperhauk with his yen"), which is his only aspect not developed from earlier tropes, jibes with Harry's self-doubts as well as with the sexual insecurities that permeate the heritage of virile stylistics. As Freud has famously argued, there is a "substitutive relation between the eye and the male organ," such that "anxiety about one's eyes . . . is often enough a substitute for the dread of being castrated."[49] In a preemptive maneuver, Harry here converts his fears of being unmanned into the penetrating powers of his oedipal authority, the emasculating gaze of the priestly father. Thus Harry's castration complex, foregrounding the male insecurities that underlie so many medieval paeans to poetic virility, serves as an additional element in Chaucer's critique of the traditions embedded in the Nun's Priest's sources.

At the core of these medieval celebrations of artistic genius lurks an urgent need to give credence to the poet's auctorial mastery over language and to language's capacity to inseminate the signifieds of his desire. However, as we have seen in *The Complaint of Nature*, language's polymorphous desire appears to originate somewhere other than in the author's controlling will. Further, as we have noted while discussing the medieval Genius topos, assertions of literary paternity inadvertently reveal their authors' deep fear that language may itself be impotent and barren. Perhaps in some way the poet is always and already castrated; perhaps language is a discourse of *dis*semination rather than *in*semination. Such medieval apprehensions anticipate a modern critique offered in *Dissemination*, where Jacques Derrida argues that language—an unauthored, ungrounded, and ungenerative play of unending lexical substitutions—is equivalent both to "dissemination" and to "castration":

> No more than can castration, dissemination—which entails, entrains, "inscribes," and relaunches castration—can never become an originary, central, or ultimate signified, the place proper to truth. On the contrary, dissemination represents the affirmation of this nonorigin, the remarkable empty locus of a hundred blanks no meaning can be ascribed to. . . . Castration is that nonsecret of seminal division that breaks into substitution.[50]

In light of Derrida's critique of language's impotence, and in light of the recurring medieval alignment of language with castration, it is imperative, I believe, that the Nun's Priest's celibacy be understood as something more than merely a requisite part of his religious vocation. In terms of the linguistic and artistic ideologies that the Priest embodies, I suggest his celibacy is ultimately a sign of the caponized poet's "castrated" and "disseminal" relationship to the realm of the signified, to the "place proper to truth."

Chaucer's most telling parodic maneuver in destabilizing the authority of this masculinist aesthetic program is situated in a place where the Nun's Priest's body is not to be found. In *The Canterbury Tales*, the "origin," the place of the "ultimate signified," is the portrait gallery of the *General Prologue*. Yet within this fictionalized ground of the real, there is already apparently an absence, a gap. That is, of the thirty pilgrims Chaucer tells us are on the pilgrimage (I.24), only twenty-nine are accounted for. More precisely, the Second Nun appears in one-and-a-half lines, after which there follows a puzzling, line-filling phrase, "and preestes thre" (I.164). After an expert review of the possible explanations of this strange state of affairs, Leger Brosnahan concludes that, in all extant *General Prologue* manuscripts, there is in fact a "hole"; this hole, he speculates, was once filled by a completed portrait of the Second Nun and by a full portrait, "if it were ever written," of her one priest.[51] While I find Brosnahan's "admission of a hole" entirely persuasive, rather than attempt to fill that manhole with an imaginary lost presence, I think it is important that it remain a meaningful absence, serving as an "affirmation of the nonorigin" of the Nun's Priest's body. This powerful gesture, Chaucer's "pre-erasure" of the Nun's Priest's material existence, would thus seem to "castrate" the entire tradition he embodies. For what it means is that everything that the Nun's Priest stands for—centuries' worth of argument in defense of the virile style and of the potent art of male genius—has been cut away from its putative foundation in reality and truth. As a consequence, Chaucer represents these masculinist precepts as now being no more valid than any other constructs of our free-floating imaginations.

But does this mean that Chaucer's intent, from the outset, has been ultimately to destroy these medieval masculinist aesthetic ideals? My answer to this question is a qualified "no." In the figure of one fantastic body (the Nun's Priest) and in the figure of one slightly neurotic fan (Harry Bailly), Chaucer has managed to diagnose and decenter the phallocentric presuppositions of a complex European aesthetic tradition. But ultimately he has chosen to do so by employing the double-voiced poetics of parody rather than the cutting-edge aggressivity of satire. In his critical diagnosis, in other words, it has been his preference to counterbalance the celebratory and the dysfunctional, the positive and the problematic, the enabling and disenabling elements of this tradition. While Chaucer may well be unique among his peers in his commitment to pruning back the tradition, there is no evidence that he is committed to killing it off *tout court*. Indeed, were he intent on completely undoing the medieval precepts of the virile style and of masculine literary Genius, even as an unusually evolved poet he would be in grave danger of cutting himself with his own knife.

To this point we have been interrogating the metapoetic thesis the Nun's Priest's body articulates inside a dramatic tradition of linguistic, stylistic, and literary debates in Western aesthetics. In fact, our appreciation of the richness of that debate and the role of the Nun's Priest's body within it could be further amplified. Examining metapoetic constructions of the text-as-body and of the body-as-text in Matthew of Vendôme's *Ars Versificatoria* and Geoffrey of Vinsaulf's *Poetria Nova,* Robin Hass Birky characterizes the various discursive practices associated with different forms of embodiment in these and other twelfth- and thirteenth-century *artes poetriae.*[52] In their imagery, analogies, arguments, and especially their exemplary *effictiones,* these rhetorical handbooks embrace eight or nine discursive paradigms, four of which are distinctively masculine. *Incarnational rhetoric* stands as the universal masculine ideal: since the divinity of Christ the Word is clothed in human flesh, this incarnational archetype sees literary language as "clothing and/or giving body to the matter of the poem," even though the more that poetic language is "embodied" the more it is in danger of participating in the fallen femaleness of language. *Naked rhetoric* configures a second masculine discourse whose literary nakedness, in contradistinction to "painted texts," signifies a kind of prelapsarian "truth value and innocence."[53] In both of these undersomatized formations (Birky calls them "anti-bodies") it is notable that neither descends into detailed physical specificity either in their imagery or in their illustrative *effictiones. Disembodied rhetoric,* as its name suggests, also airbrushes the particulars of the reified male body well nigh out of existence, preferring to concentrate instead on "the spiritual, cerebral, linguistic, and kinesthetic as masculine arenas."[54] It is only in the domain of the fourth masculine discourse, *effeminized rhetoric,* that "a heightened sense of physicality exists."[55] Influenced by the association of the body with flesh, the flesh with the feminine, and the feminine with the desire it evokes, this masculine style in Matthew of Vendôme's treatise is epitomized by the "distorted, deformed male body" of Davus, a figure whose bulging genitals and premature ejaculation "metaphorically demonstrate meter gone awry," and whose "excessive passion effeminizes him and the poetry he embodies, . . . causing him to spill his seed and leaving him unable to inseminate even a poetic text."[56] Strikingly similar to Derrida's theorizations of linguistic and textual dissemination, effeminized rhetoric, according to the authors of these *artes poetriae,* is a poetics run amok. Vibrant in the fleshiness of its own linguistic pleasures, this poetic discourse must be eschewed because it provokes male desire for the erotic physicality of an overly embodied, that is, feminized, masculine language.

The four major feminine discourses complement the aforementioned masculine poetics to a degree. *Marian rhetoric* and *chaste rhetoric* rehabilitate the feminine aspects of the body and of language by adopting equivalents of those undersomatized masculine traits embraced by incarnational rhetoric and naked rhetoric.[57] Thus the two remaining feminine discourses are the two that are most crucial to defining the proper and improper uses of literary language. These are what Birky calls *pedestalized rhetoric,* "ornate language depicting a courtly or noble subject matter in which both language and woman retain use and value through beauty," and *wanton rhetoric,* "decorated discourse illuminating the sexual nature of female figures that is distrusted . . . for its association with carnality and duplicity by which the language and woman are marked."[58] It is the exclusive charge of pedestalized rhetoric somehow to embrace the carnality of language and the allure of the feminine while maintaining a poetics that is elevated and beautiful. Matthew of Vendôme, in his *effictio* of Helen of Troy, and Geoffrey of Vinsauf, in his *effictio* of the "full picture of female beauty," both provide a detailed description of a fully embodied woman whose physical attractiveness nevertheless remains exemplary. Like Geoffrey's idealized woman-as-text, Matthew's Helen serves not only as "a template with which all other female beauty can be judged," writes Birky, but it "acts as a mini art of poetry for feminized discourse— Helen is poetry incarnate."[59] It is striking that both Matthew and Geoffrey agree that the physical beauty of these textual women provokes a powerful sexual desire in the viewer/reader: how else, Matthew asks, is the Trojan war to be explained? In fact, Matthew directs his reader's gaze towards Helen's pudenda, "the delightful / Dwelling of Venus,"[60] and Geoffrey coyly calls attention to his choice *not* to describe "the parts below: more fitting does the imagination speak of these than the tongue."[61] The sexual desirability of each woman-as-text, rather than a sign of wanton linguistic inveiglements, is thus (perhaps surprisingly) a stylistic quality rendering her even more "pleasurable as a textual body."[62]

In the prescriptive context of these metapoetic bodies, the body of the Nun's Priest stands out as a remarkable departure from all preexisting *effictiones*. Fully enfleshed, sexually robust, and scantily clothed, the Nun's Priest's "heightened sense of physicality" should place him in the category of the déclassé, "distorted," and "deformed" manifestations of effeminized masculine rhetoric. But it obviously does not. Unless the Priest's hypermasculine *effictio* is meant to be read entirely ironically, the physical perfection of his body stands as a mark of literary excellence, an ideal that certainly evokes high praise from its first inscribed reader, Harry Bailly. Men, Matthew of Vendôme explicitly cautions, should not be praised in this fashion: "In praising a woman one should stress heavily her physical beauty. This is not the proper way to praise a man."[63] Chaucer's readers are therefore placed in a novel position at the very end of Fragment VII. Gazing upon the embodiment of what could be called a *pedestalized masculine rhetoric*, readers are asked to view the figure of the Nun's Priest, like the figure of Helen, as "poetry incarnate . . . a mini *ars poetria*."[64] This is itself a hermeneutical challenge. In addition, the reader is asked to recognize that the Nun's Priest's body—not unlike Helen's body—is a site of masculine desire. In Harry's intense enthusiasms, in other words, the male reader sees a reflection of his own pleasure as he gazes upon the discrete parts of this body, with special attention directed toward its skimpily clad genitals. To relegate the erotics of this response exclusively to the interior of Harry Bailly's psyche is thus to undervalue our own felt attraction, as readers, toward the macho beauty and self-contained sexual potency of the Nun's Priest's physical person. Harry's admiration thus operates as a double-voiced heuristic: even while parodying the posturings of the hypermasculinist aesthetic tradition, it celebrates the ubiquity of desire evoked by all genders of embodied discourse. In other words, if we are prepared to recognize our erotic selves in Harry, we may then acknowledge the essential role polymorphous desire plays in our readings of any literary text.

The significance of our desire to fill in certain "gaps" in our experience of reading Chaucer's poetry is a subject that has lately prompted considerable theoretical speculation.[65] As I have suggested, the absence in the *General Prologue* of a portrait of the Nun's Priest is one such gap. Although it serves several metapoetic purposes, what is most obvious is that we already know what is materially lacking at this site of absence, namely, a portrait of the fictional author of *The Nun's Priest's Tale*. In every other major instance our desire for the author—to know the narrator's physiognomy, clothing, class, mindset, and possible intent—is a desire generously gratified *before* we read the tale. However, from the skimpy information provided in the prologue to *The Nun's Priest's Tale* all we are able to learn is the Nun's Priest's vocation, the "foul and lene" condition of his horse, his agreement to satisfy Harry's brusk command to tell a heart-gladdening tale (VII.2810), and Chaucer-the-narrator's out-of-the-blue expression of personal tenderness toward this mysterious nonentity, "This sweete preest, this goodly man sir John" (VII.2820). With nothing but these scattered bits to go on, we are constrained to do what all readers of literature normally do, which is to construct from our experience of reading the *Tale* a voice, certain qualities, and perhaps a sketched-out physical form—all of which we attribute to its creator. However, what we are strategically forced to do next is to compare and contrast the author of our imagination with the "authorized" portrait that suddenly appears after the *Tale* is completed. While the experiences of different readers surely differ, in most cases I suspect the Nun's Priest's *effictio* comes as an arresting shock.

Consequently, the disequilibrating impact of the Nun's Priest's portrait is in my judgment yet another of Chaucer's parodic maneuvers whose major thrust is directed toward our own reading practices. Unsurprisingly, an impressive amount of Chaucer criticism involves interpreting each tale in light of the personal, social, and intellectual characteristics (and limitations) of its teller. And in all likelihood Chaucer viewed variants of such "pseudo-biographical" readings among his contemporaries as not undesirable, for it is impossible to read a verbal collocation without constructing a human voice behind it, and it is quite normal to wish to *know* that speaking subject fully. However, even though Chaucer in all cases but one gratifies our desire to "meet the author" in order to understand the tale, in his strategic placement of the Nun's Priest's portrait he alludes, I believe, to the pitfalls of reading *The Canterbury Tales* in this fashion. In a crucial analysis of these behaviors, H. Marshall Leicester Jr. warns that reading through the lens of the *General Prologue* "allows the frame to tyrannize the individual tales."[66] That is, we twist and constrict a tale's potential meanings in order to make them fit the predefined characteristics of its narrator. In order to become more open-minded, Leicester argues, we need to reverse this practice: rather than posited in advance, the personality of each pilgrim-author "has to be worked out by analyzing and defining the voice created by each tale."[67] It is precisely this reverse order that we are uniquely privileged to experience at the end of Fragment VII. We first read the *Tale* and from it we construct what Birky calls "the body of the text"; only then are we granted a view of its embodied author. Although we might soon set about reinterpreting the *Tale* through the lens of the portrait, a most important critical task has been presented to us, which is to meditate on the significance of that gap between tale and portrait without instantly striving to close it up.

In fact, this space may not be easily bridged. I am not at all persuaded that the Nun's Priest's *effictio* serves in any coherent way as an *accessus* to *The Nun's Priest's Tale*. Nor do I find that the *Tale* works as a literary exposé of the Priest's personality and private concerns (even though an immoderate amount of criticism has read the portrait and *Tale* in precisely this way).[68] Both texts are *artes poeticae*, however, and since both explore some of the same literary issues, they are certainly *in metapoetic dialogue* with each other. Both the *Tale* and its Epilogue address a host of overlapping linguistic and literary issues, but neither is a key that directly unlocks the other's secrets. Their most significant commonality remains Harry Bailly, whose ardent attachment to the sexual potency of the Nun's Priest's body provides a surprisingly modern exposé of our own powers of projection as Chaucer's readers. "Does the text have human form, is it a figure, an anagram of the body? Yes, but of our erotic body," writes Roland Barthes in *The Pleasure of the Text*.[69] "The pleasure of the text," Barthes explains, "is not the pleasure of the corporeal striptease of narrative suspense. . . . [T]he entire excitation takes refuge in the *hope* of seeing the sexual organ."[70] Harry's hope of seeing the Priest's "every stoon" expresses our shared desire as readers to catch a glimpse of the sexual genius hidden within the text of *The Nun's Priest's Tale*. We may ultimately wish to identify that figure as Chaucer. But Chaucer-so-named is as much a figment of the imagination as is the Nun's Priest, which means they are both embodied in the same literary discourse, waiting to be unveiled.

TWO

The Nun's Priest's Tale as Grammar School Primer, Menippean Parody, and *Ars Poetica*

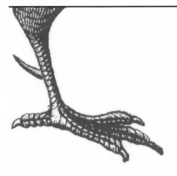

Faciebatque ut qui maiores imitabatur fieret
posteris imitandus.

[*He succeeded in making those who imitated earlier writers
themselves imitable.*]

—JOHN OF SALISBURY

Two of Chaucer's cockiest protagonists, Nicholas and Chauntecleer, are committed to rendering the liberal arts useful in their everyday lives. In *The Miller's Tale,* "hende Nicholas" keeps at "his beddes heed" books and instruments pertaining to three of the quadrivial arts: for astronomy his "Almageste" and his "astrelabie," for arithmetic his "augrym stones," and for music his "gay sautrie" (I.3199–13). Chauntecleer, who had acquired these advanced arts "By nature" (VII.4045), needs the assistance of no man-made instruments. His astronomy he demonstrates daily by crowing precisely at prime; his mathematics is evidenced in his having carefully calculated the degrees, "Twenty degrees and oon, and somwhat moore" (VII.4385), of the sun's progress through Taurus; his native musical genius is displayed by his incomparable singing, "of crowyng nas his peer" (VII.4040). It is only geometry, the most theoretical and abstract of the four mathematical arts, that appears beyond the ken or interest of our two scholar-lovers, perhaps because the earthly forms of Alisoun and Pertelote undulate all but a finger- or wing-tip's touch away.

Although Nicholas "hadde lerned art"—had in the past, that is, studied the trivium—"al his fantasye" (I.3191) is now turned elsewhere. Chauntecleer, by sharp contrast, finds himself returning to those grammar school arts of verbal discourse with a special sense of personal urgency. Like most of us who have gone to school, Chauntecleer is troubled by a horrible dream that tests him in a field of knowledge for which he feels woefully underprepared. Upon waking, Chauntecleer finds solace in books, feathering the pages of one as he debates with his wife about the meaning of dreams. In this debate Pertelote's rhetorical thesis relies upon close analysis of the dream image itself, centering upon its colors and their somapsychotic significance, concluding her arguments with the Catonian apothegm: "Ne do no fors of dremes" (VII.4131). Chauntecleer, proud of having gone to school, on his side of the *disputatio* compares the *effictio* of the dream image to a number of auctorial *narrationes,* which he recounts in a wide variety of literary shapes, ranging from the fulsomely dramatized, plotted, and sententiated story all the way to the wispiest of anecdotes. Like the typical *quodlibetal* debate in the schools, the resolution of this disputation remains open-ended—although these scholastic interlocutors achieve their own closure, as Chauntecleer turns from lore to love, flattering himself and his wife by carefully mistranslating "*In principio, / Mulier est hominis confusio*" (VII.4353–54). Flying down from the beams, he feathers his favorite wife twenty times and treads her twenty times more—a dramatic reminder that we are here very much in the world of the beast fable and that our potent hero is an educated chicken who enjoys more than one natural talent we are left to marvel at, perhaps even to envy.

Even though *The Nun's Priest's Tale* raises the genre of the Aesopic beast fable to the nth power, almost half of its narration is in fact taken up by a scholarly *disputatio* centering on one of Cato's distichs, a debate more than half of which in turn is consumed by a collection of unevenly told literary *exempla,* closing out with an ironic citation and mistranslation of a Latin tag. For Chaucer's literate audience, each of these

characteristics—beast fable, debate, Catonian assertion, Latin translation, and a string of variously told narrative proofs—would have been
poignantly evocative, triggering a collage of bittersweet personal memories from their early years of grammar school linguistic and literary training. Since one of my major contentions in this study is that Chaucer has
designed his unique fable as a palimpsestuous text reworking dozens
of classroom exercises—not only reading assignments, but memoriza-
tions, translations, paraphrasings, glosses, disputations, imitations, and
themes amplifying and defending truths uncovered in the master text—
I open this chapter by sketching out a paradigmatic fourteenth-century
grammar school education in the verbal arts. It is to this kind of instruction that our rooster hero instinctively returns when he attempts to understand the text of his troubling dream.

From the outset I want to emphasize that Chaucer's parodic evocations of the classroom are not designed to satirize the foundations of the
medieval liberal arts curriculum for any perceived imperfections in its
pedagogical principles or literary precepts. Rather, Chaucer takes his readers back to basics in order that they might reexperience, now at a more
sophisticated level, both the profundities and the baffling complexities
of literature. While the primary school curriculum contains the core of
these profundities and complexities, *The Nun's Priest's Tale* also adds layers to its readers' academic recollections by invoking higher disciplines
(such as the quadrivium) as well as more advanced texts studied in the
universities. What holds these striations together, I have been suggesting,
is the coherence of parody, or, more precisely, the coherence of a jumbled
subgenre that is best defined as Menippean parody. To empower my own
uses of this term, in this chapter's midsection I provide a definition of
parody as a genre whose intertextual maneuvers and readerly effects are
quite different from those of its significant siblings, satire and irony, even
though it quite often avails itself of their powers. This theoretical modeling will then enable my transitioning to another plane, wherein I undertake a reading of the *Tale* as an interrogation of some of the most problematic and sophisticated aspects of Chaucer's art. It is these concerns that
transmute a curricular parody into a self-reflexive *ars poetica*. I am not
much interested, in other words, in ferreting out every possible connection

between Chaucer's beast fable and its "sources" in the medieval classroom. Rather, after introducing that curriculum and establishing a set of general academic memories triggered by the *Tale,* my central concern will be the metapoetic issues the beast fable foregrounds. These issues, I believe, constitute the primary focus of Chaucer's *ars poetica.*

THE NUN'S PRIEST'S TALE AS CURRICULAR PARODY

A fundamental literary text for all schoolboys in Greek, Roman, medieval, and Renaissance educational programs was a collection of Aesop's fables. In the Middle Ages, students translated fables from Latin into the vernacular, parsed individual words, and strove to unravel the mysteries of syntactic cruces, all under the tutelage of their *grammaticus.* Each fable was memorized by heart. Students paraphrased and wrote commentaries on their fables; in fact they were required to become fabulators themselves, rewriting fables in different registers in order to master a variety of narrative styles. In the early Middle Ages the standard classroom collection was the forty-two fables of Avianus, versified amplifications of Babrius, whose somewhat ornate literary features were much admired: a fullness of picturesque descriptions; a copious employment of Ovidian and Virgilian phrases; a style of heightened moral seriousness and rhetorical urgency that borders, as Paul Clogan has noted, on the mock-heroic.[1] In the twelfth and thirteenth centuries the classical fables of Avianus were often replaced by Alexander Neckham's *Novus Avianus,* revisions that internalized several of their primary readers' compositional exercises. For instance, Neckham occasionally provides three versions of the same fable—*copiose, compendiose,* and *subcincte*—in order to illustrate the techniques of *amplificatio* and *abbreviato* that students themselves could then emulate. From the mid-thirteenth century forward the Avianus fables were displaced by the popular Romulus collection. More prosaic and less self-consciously rhetorical than those of Avianus, the sixty elegiac verses of the Romulus collection incorporated an array of carefully constructed grammatical challenges revealing their primary employment as texts for basic language instruction.[2] It is striking that in many surviving manuscripts ample interlinear space is in fact provided so that students might insert their commentaries and Latin synonyms.[3] Thus by casting his *ars poetica* as an Aesopian beast fable, Chaucer is reopening that interlinear space— invoking his readers' memories of a time when they were most intimately engaged in the craft of literary analysis, imitation, and production. In the very same gesture, Chaucer zeroes in on the fundamentals of literature itself. The fable's lean characterizations, its no-frills dramatic dialogue, its hyperefficient narrative, and its metaphorical foundations distill the essence of literature to the quick.

While absorbing the essentials of narrative fiction, medieval school-boys were simultaneously introduced to the essentials of *enarratio,* the art of literary criticism. Students began their interpretative endeavors by writing paraphrases, stripping the fables down to what Edward Wheatley calls their " 'true' meaning."[4] But they then made critical advances by composing and defending their interpretative commentaries as well as by responding to the *moralitates* already *in situ.* What is most impressive about these *moralitates* is both their variety and the extraordinary arbitrariness of their applications to individual fables. In his panoptic survey, Wheatley reduces the *moralitates* of medieval fables to six different types: (1) *simple allegory,* where animal characters and their actions are translated into "morally marked human terms";[5] (2) *allegory with social roles,* where the social hierarchies in nature are seen as corresponding to those in human society; (3) *allegory with religious roles,* where certain animals represent certain religious professions; (4) *spiritual allegory,* where the narrative of the fable is "reinterpreted on a metaphysical level";[6] (5) *natural allegory,* where the natural properties of an animal are remarked upon, often by referencing a bestiary; and (6) *exegetical allegory,* where an event in the fable is viewed as mirroring an event in the Bible. While these various forms of *allegoresis* may come as no surprise to medievalists, what is impressive is the lack of any discernible principle in the application of the *moralitates:* "even though a handful of fables had specific readings which followed them across Europe over centuries," writes Wheatley, it is apparent that "any fable could be interpreted according to any allegorical form, at the whim of the reader, or perhaps at the behest of the teacher."[7] Thus by fashioning his *ars poetica* as a beast fable, and especially as a fable

with a complicated *moralitas,* Chaucer is reactivating his readers' early
and quite challenging engagement in the formidable difficulties of literary criticism.

Another basic literary primer, a text which in fact preceded the fables
in the standard course of study, was Cato's distichs, commonly known as
ethica Catonia because they were viewed as teaching the four cardinal virtues.[8] Translated and memorized verbatim, the distichs' more complex linguistic passages served as occasions for grammatical elaboration and even
for debate among students, while the apothegms themselves inspired the
collection of further *sententiae,* both from the classics and from scripture
and scriptural glosses. In the later Middle Ages, as Richard Hazelton has
shown, Cato was accompanied by extensive *glossulae* that contained not
only etymologies, detailed grammatical discussions of the text, and elements of *rhetorica* and *poetria,* but also supplementary material relating
to ethics—such as definitions of the cardinal virtues and their subdivisions, scriptural and patristic quotations and allusions, popular proverbs,
and an abundance of flowers culled from the Roman poets.[9] Essentially
notes for teachers, these *glossulae* constitute "a veritable thesaurus of mediaeval commonplaces,"[10] preserving, along with the distichs, "the ideas,
values, sentiments, and attitudes that flowed out of antiquity into the
Christian mediaeval world."[11] Even though the *liber Catonis* served as
an early reader, like Aesop it is "not by any means to be thought of as
a child's book."[12] Universally admired, ingrained in the memories of all
adults, "quoted literally everywhere,"[13] Cato's authoritative distichs surface throughout medieval literature. However, in his study of Cato's role
in Chaucer, Hazelton argues that Chaucer's treatment is unique; rather
than honoring Cato, Chaucer accords him scant respect, as in *The Nun's
Priest's Tale,* where "the venerable Cato of the moralists appears in a context that reduces all his *auctoritas* to a cackle."[14] Although I agree enthu-
siastically with Hazelton that Chaucer's fable is "a poem that parodies almost all the literary conventions and matters dear to the age,"[15] I would
maintain that by enclosing a Catonian apothegm inside a extended *disputatio* inside a cornucopian curricular environment, *The Nun's Priest's
Tale*'s primary intent is simply to reenergize memories of the many-faceted
foundations of one's education in the liberal arts.

Chaucer's readers were also transported back to the classroom by their recollections of the debates they had engaged in as young scholars. In the universities, disputation was the dominant mode of teaching. Typically, a master set a question that his students would respond to with arguments for and against, and these proffered solutions the master would in turn oppose and challenge, providing qualifications, refinements, and counterarguments. Enigmatic logical propositions were debated in disputations *de sophismatibus*; problems pertaining to the physical sciences were debated in disputations *de questione*; and in perhaps the most inventive debate format, public disputations *de quodlibet* were carried on about any subject whatsoever, and disputants were encouraged to argue for any position no matter how suspect or ludicrous. It is the quodlibetal tradition of "horizontal" debate, where disputation is conducted with no expectation of magisterial resolution, that Thomas Reed has found to have informed the development and reception of English debate poems such as "The Owl and the Nightingale," Chaucer's "The Parliament of Fowls," and Lydgate's "Horse, Goose, and Sheep."[16] Formal disputation was not exclusively a university practice, however, for there is ample evidence that English grammar school teachers (many of them having been trained in dialectics at Oxford) applied the methods of posing questions for debate, but in addition young scholars were expected to initiate formal disputation with each other, both in and out of the classroom.[17] In the judgment of A. F. Leach, in medieval English grammar schools "dialectic was an excellent training for the mind, more especially as it was accompanied by practical work in argument: the boys being set to 'pose' and answer each other, the master 'determining.'"[18] Thus the protracted debate between Chauntecleer and Pertelote concerning the validity of a simple Catonian proposition would have summoned up for Chaucer's readers a wide spectrum of classroom memories even as it poses within its own literary environment a string of disputatious issues concerning the relationship of gloss to narrative, of argument to fable, of authority to experience, of dreams to future contingencies, and of fiction to truth.

Latin was of course the language in which most primary school-texts were written and in which classroom discussions and debates were expected ideally to be conducted. For Chaucer's readers, Latin was the preeminent language of knowledge and learning: it served as the *lingua franca* of the universities as well as the language in which all intellectual texts were written. For the generality of Chaucer's readers Latin was most immediately recognized as the language they had learned in grammar school, where for years they had studied Latin grammar, translated Latin texts, and learned to write Latin verse, Latin prose, and Latin letters. Latin grammar was introduced to beginning students via the rigorous examination of the semantic and syntactic principles at work in illustrative examples—first in individual words (nouns, pronouns, adjectives, verbs, conjunctions, and so forth) and then in phrases and sentences. Latin translation was put into practice by students' taking English sentences called "vulgars," or *vulgaria,* and translating them into "latins," or *latinitates,* and vice versa. *Vulgaria* eventually became the name for teachers' collections of model Latin sentences and their English translations; the earliest printed *vulgaria* reveal that schooolmasters often tried to think up Latin and English sentences that referred to everyday life, contemporary events, and schoolboy humor as a way of sustaining student interest in the linguistic tasks at hand. Therefore, when Chauntecleer closes down his one-sided debate with his wife by suddenly citing a Latin tag, "*In principio, / Mulier est hominis confusio*" (VII.4353–54), he is triggering in Chaucer's readers a recollection of the hundreds of pithy *latinitates* they were once required to translate or construct. And when Chauntecleer decides to provide his own English translation, "Womman is mannes joye and al his blis" (VII.4356), he is at once fulfilling his *vulgaria* assignment and at the same time inspiring a classroom disputation because his brilliant mistranslation effectively dramatizes the wondrous gap that always exists between what translation theorists call the source text and the target text. As I shall demonstrate later in this chapter, Chauntecleer's translation is not simply an "incorrect" translation but also an instructive parody of the entire discourse of translation, exposing translation's curious kinship with the strategies of paraphrase, metaphrasis, gloss, plagiarism, and deconstruction. In addition, it is a speech-act that tellingly instantiates translation's traditional masculinist bias—for as Chaucer's readers and auditors were fully aware, medieval women were marginalized by all things Latin because they were not admitted into the schools or universities.

With this brief introduction to Chaucer's evocation of early class-room practices—through his citation of Aesopian fables, Cato's distichs, the arts of disputation, and the problematics of translation—it is use-ful now to turn to the most famous contemporary description of medi-eval teaching. In his *Metalogicon* (a defense of the study of the classics, of the liberal arts, and especially of the trivium), John of Salisbury describes the duties of the ideal grammarian, or what we would now call the teacher of literature, as they were realized by the master grammar school teacher Bernard of Chartres. Because Bernard's twelfth-century classroom tech-niques are an exemplary representation of teaching methods as they were practiced throughout the later Middle Ages, and because Bernard's meth-ods of literary analysis, imitation, and re-creation are all refashioned in various parodic ways within *The Nun's Priest's Tale,* I quote the passage in full:

On the authority of the same Quintilian, "the teacher of grammar should, in lecturing, take care of such details as to have his students analyze verses into their parts of speech, and point out the nature of the metrical feet which are to be noted in poems." . . . The gram-marian should also point out metaplasms, schematisms, and ora-torical tropes, as well as various other forms of expression that may be present. . . . One will more fully perceive and more lucidly ex-plain the charming elegance of the authors in proportion to the breadth and thoroughness of his knowledge of various disciplines. The authors by *diacrisis,* which we may translate as "vivid represen-tation" or "graphic imagery," when they would take the crude mate-rials of history, plots [*argumenta*], narratives [*fabulae*], and other topics, would so copiously embellish them by the various branches of knowledge, in such charming style, with such pleasing orna-ment, that their finished masterpiece would seem to image all the arts. Grammar and Poetry are poured without stint over the length and breadth of their works. Across this field [*campus*], as it is com-monly called, Logic, which contributes plausibility by its proofs, weaves the golden lightening of its reasons; while Rhetoric, where persuasion is in order, supplies the silvery luster of its resplendent eloquence. Following in the path of the foregoing, Mathematics rides proudly along on the four-wheel chariot of its Quadrivium [Arithmetic, Astronomy, Music, and Geometry], intermingling its fascinating demonstration in manifold variety. . . .

Bernard of Chartres, the greatest font of literary learning in Gaul in recent times, used to teach grammar in the following way. He would point out, in reading the authors, what was simple and according to rule. On the other hand, he would explain grammatical figures, rhetorical embellishment, and sophistical quibbling, as well as the relation of given passages to other studies. . . . He would also explain the poets and orators who were to serve as models for the boys in their introductory exercises [*preexercitamina*] in imitating prose and poetry. Pointing out how the diction of the authors was so skillfully connected, and what they had to say was so elegantly concluded, he would admonish his students to follow their example. And if, to embellish his work, someone had sewed on a patch of cloth filched from an external source, Bernard, on discovering this, would rebuke him for his plagiary, but would generally refrain from punishing him. After he had reproved the student, if an unsuitable theme had invited this, he would, with modest indulgence, bid the boy to rise to real imitation of the classical authors, and would bring about that he who had imitated his predecessors would come to be deserving of imitation by his successors. . . .

A further feature of Bernard's method was to have his disciples compose prose and poetry every day, and exercise their faculties in mutual conferences [comparisons], for nothing is more useful in introductory training than actually to accustom one's students to practice the art they are studying. Nothing serves better to foster the acquisition of eloquence and the attainment of knowledge than such conferences, which also have a salutary influence on practical conduct, provided that charity moderates enthusiasm, and that humility is not lost during progress in learning. A man cannot be the servant of both learning and carnal vice.[19]

There is in fact little in John's description of Bernard's teaching that would have surprised medieval educators. For modern readers, however, at least three of Bernard's major teaching techniques require further commentary. The first involves the diligence, care, and sophistication with which literary texts were studied as phenomena illustrating the rules and problems of grammatical construction. The second educational practice concerns the employment of that popular sequence of compositional exercises known throughout the Middle Ages as the *preexercitamina*. The third unusual mode of instruction concerns John of Salisbury's assumption (relying on Quintilian) that students need to read literature in such a way that all seven of the liberal arts are appreciated as forces operative inside the text. Each of these three educational methods I intend to consider in a preliminary fashion, beginning with the study of grammar.

Like his twelfth-century contemporaries and like educators of the thirteenth and fourteenth centuries, Bernard saw grammar as a powerful and liberating mode of linguistic and literary analysis—one by which texts are broken down into their various linguistic elements, analyzed with extreme care, and then reconstructed. The thoroughness with which medieval students and their masters obsessed about the phonetic, phonemic, morphological, syntactical, and semantic principles of one word in a text—first as a part of speech and then as a word with its own etymological history and philological identity—is quite amazing. This fascination with all matters linguistic began with the earliest classroom assignments in *orthography* (the study of what we would now call graphemes and phonemes). The second part of grammar was a quite sudden leap into *prosody,* the study of verse meter and accentuation, a field that fourteenth-century English school teachers attempted to teach at a high level of sophistication. The third major element of grammar was *etymology,* which actually meant learning everything about the nature of each of the eight parts of speech, memorizing regular conjugations and declensions, and learning irregular features of the language such as deponent verbs and heteroclite nouns. Donatus's *Ars minor,* the *Doctrinale,* and the *Catholicon* were all relied upon to help students systematize these complex issues.

The fourth part of grammar, *syntax,* included two fields of learning: the learning of rules governing sentence structure and the writing of Latin sentences (this is where the *latinitates* and *vulgaria* fit in). After syntax came figures of speech (which were considered examples of irregular syntax): with the Latin Bible as the normative text, students first studied "paradigm" and "parable" and differentiated one from the other; then followed a detailed classification and analysis of a large number of rhetorical tropes. (As we shall see in the first half of chapter 3, this movement from the problematics of parable to the colors of rhetoric is parodied at the beginning of *The Nun's Priest's Tale* where the widow's pseudo-paradigmatic life of "grammatical" restraint is displaced by the "figural" text of Chauntecleer's colorful body.) The next element in the study of grammar was Latin vocabularies, arranged either by topic or by alphabetical order. Then followed a variety of Latin *reading texts* studied over several years (to be discussed later), and in the more advanced grammar school classes students finally learned the art of *dictamen,* the craft of writing letters. Of course, the study of grammar was by no means the sole province of the grammar schools, for it was studied and theorized intensely at the universities, producing in the twelfth and thirteenth centuries the remarkable work of the speculative grammarians, the *Modistae,* as well as grammatical treatises by such specialists as Roger Bacon, Robert Grosseteste, and Robert Kilwardby. Yet despite its status in the universities, grammar had always been understood as first and foremost the nurturing mother to all the other arts, both trivial and quadrivial. In the foundation deed of Winchester College in 1382, William of Wykeham could be speaking for the entirety of the Middle Ages when he writes: "[E]xperience, the mistress of life, already teaches [that] grammar is the foundation, gate, and source of all other liberal arts, without which they cannot be known, nor can anyone arrive at their pursuit. . . . [B]y the knowledge of letters justice is cultivated and the prosperity of human life [is] increased."[20]

As is now apparent in at least a general way, *The Nun's Priest's Tale* is a narrative in which is embedded a number of grammar school exercises that Chaucer parodies, recontextualizes, and reassigns to the adult reader. One heuristic level of these recontextualized exercises can be illustrated briefly by focusing upon two examples that belong to that area of beginning Latin grammatical study designated as *etymology* and *syntax,* the careful analysis of semantic and syntactic cruces. The first test case I have selected occurs in the Nun's Priest's description of the hens' tragic lamentations in response to their husband/lover's imminent death:

Certes, swich cry ne lamentacion
Was nevere of ladyes maad whan Ylion
Was wonne, and Pirrus with his streite swerd,
Whan he hadde hent kyng Priam by the berd,
And slayn hym, as seith us *Eneydos,*
As maden alle the hennes in the clos,
Whan they had seyn of Chauntecleer the sighte.
But sovereynly dame Pertelote shrighte
Ful louder than dide Hasdrubales wyf,
Whan that hir housbonde hadde lost his lyf
And that the Romayns hadde brend Cartage.
She was so ful of torment and of rage
That wilfully into the fyr she sterte
And brende hirselven with a stedefast herte.

(VII.3355–68)

Whether or not any grammatical uncertainty is descried in the pronoun with which the antepenultimate line begins will vary from one reader's response to the next. In an informal polling over the past few years, I have found that there are always a few students in my Chaucer class who remember Pertelote's fiery demise with graphic clarity; there are others who admit to having been momentarily puzzled as to how a classical funeral pyre might have made its way into Pertelote's back yard; and the remainder are either bemused by my off-the-wall question "Who is *she?*" or astonished that anyone could get their literary facts so wrong. In a brief note published in *Explicator,* after remarking that were Pertelote actually to have jumped into the fire "after *her* man," "[s]he would of course become a roast hen, a fried chicken," Richard Zacharias suggests that this confusion may have been intentional: "Chaucer and his priest smile at Dame Pertelote's burned offering in the temple of love and wit."[21] In his Variorum response Pearsall tut-tuts Zacharias for making such a "silly comment."[22] But I think it is appropriate to come to Zacharias's defense not only because of the chutzpah it takes to red-ink "Ambiguous antecedent!" in Chaucer's margins, but because the *pro* and *contra* disputation of a crucial word's grammatical propriety was a daily event in every medieval classroom. Indeed, fourteenth- and fifteenth-century Latin primers and teachers' handbooks demonstrate that pronouns (most notably relative pronouns) were given ample and sustained attention with special emphasis eventually accorded to the matter of ambiguous antecedents.[23] These matters were then more fully theorized in the universities, where pronominal relativity found its way into modistic grammatical speculation, nominalist-realist debates, and fourteenth-century logical and scientific tracts.[24] Yet the exploration of the peculiar semantic and syntactical properties of pronouns (pronouns of course differ radically from common nouns and proper nouns in their laws of scope and reference) was an area of intellectual speculation initiated in the grammar schools at a surprisingly sophisticated level. Indeed, in Chaucer's own poetry, as some readers have noted, the ultimate referential signification of such innocent-looking first person pronouns as "I" is no simple issue.[25] Of course it's not quite fair that our tragic heroine's last appearance should bear such a heavy metagrammatical burden. But the final vision of grieving Pertelote remains slightly problematic: are we meant to remember her as a seriocomic piece of fried chicken or as a lovelorn wife whose cries of woe expire in the heat of their own verbal conflagration?

The second grammatical crux I have selected is a bit more obvious and has inspired a modest degree of critical debate. At the conclusion of a sustained personal profession of his own antifeminist sentiments (or so it had seemed), the narrator suddenly corrects himself and attributes his own thoughts to Chauntecleer, the protagonist of his *Tale*:

> Thise been the cokkes wordes, and nat myne;
> I kan noon harm of no womman divyne.
> (VII.4455–56)

In a free-spirited essay entitled "Chaucerian Wordplay: The Nun's Priest and His *Womman divyne*," Lawrence Besserman calls line 4456 "the most deliciously ambiguous line in all of Chaucer" because it is capable of generating such a wide variety of possible meanings. In fact, because each verbal collocation in this line has at least two possible levels of signification, and because one word, *divyne*, in fact can serve as three different parts of speech capable of bearing eight different meanings, the sentence may support an almost infinite number of interpretations.[26] Besserman illustrates the proposition's polysemy with a semantic and syntactic chart:

I kan	*noon harm*	*of no womman*	*divyne*
I am able	no harm	about any woman	to foretell (v.)
I know	no wrong	about any female (adj.)	to declare
	no sin	of any woman	to guess
	no slander	of any female (adj.)	religious (adj.)
			godly
			theologian (sb.)
			devoted to theology (adj.)
			learned in divinity
			religious poet (sb.)

In his Variorum commentary, Pearsall lets his displeasure with Besserman's lexical and syntactical liberalism be known: line 4456 has one "obvious sense," he proclaims, which is "I cannot conceive of harm in any woman." Yet in light of Besserman's and other critics' insistence that the narrator's assertion is "full of puns and ambiguities," Pearsall concedes that some degree of critical debate is unavoidable: "The confusion here between ambiguity, which is a specific strategic function of a poet's use of language, and the difficulty that a modern reader has in deciding what Chaucer means, especially if he is overreliant on mechanical aids, is inextricable."[27] Now the "mechanical aids" Pearsall disapproves of are the foundations of Besserman's hyperattentive scholarly method, which is "to set down all the meanings for the key words in the line that he can find for the fourteenth century in the *OED* and *MED* (regardless of use and context) and to offer the line as potentially capable of all the permutations of these meanings."[28] Pearsall's assumption is that exfoliating each word's possible meanings is a method of reading antithetical to our proper understanding of the significance of a literary passage. But as we are discovering, Besserman's systematic taxonomizing is absolutely consonant with a dominant methodology of a typical medieval liberal arts classroom.

In the Middle Ages this method of grammatical analysis was often called *distinctiones,* defined by John N. Miner in *The Grammar Schools of Medieval England* as the "preoccupation with the precise meaning of terms" focusing on "the various ways in which a single term can signify."[29] Some of these *distinctio* studies remained at the level of grammatical parsing, teasing apart the closely related but ultimately different meanings, for example, of *inter, intra,* and *infra.* However, in his study of several collections of English grammar school *distinctiones,* Miner remarks on how often these grammatical distinctions are inextricably mixed up with issues that are of a logical, rhetorical, metaphysical, and even theological cast. For example, in one manuscript, British Library MS Harl. 5751, numerous words are seen to enjoy several levels of suppposition, and the one word *panis* is proven to have seven different meanings. Here is Miner's compressed account:

> The word bread (*panis*) can be employed in no less than seven different ways: first, in the sense of material bread (*panis corporalis*), as in the words, "our daily bread"; second, as in spiritual bread, as "man shall eat the bread of angels"; third, as an equivalent to teaching (*doctrina*), "He gave them the bread of life"; fourth, in the sense of repentance (*penitencia*), as "in my bread of tears day and night"; fifth, in reference to the body of Christ, "the bread which I will give you is My flesh"; sixth, referring to Christ himself, "I am the living bread which came down from heaven"; and finally *panis* is the equivalent to a word, as in the Gospel, "Not on bread alone does man live but on every word that proceeds from the mouth of God."
>
> The *distinctio* usually finishes with a verse or two to facilitate the memory; that for *panis,* for example, is as follows:
>
> *Panis corporis est panis spiritualis*
> *Panis doctrina panis penitencia fertur*
> *Est verbum Christus sic eucharistia panis.*[30]

Thus the hermeneutic habit of mind conditioned by the study of *distinctiones* would have prepared a reader for meditating at length upon the semantic as well as syntactic complexities of a proposition like "I kan noon harm of no womman divyne." Of course, grammar masters did not apply equal pressure to every word in a text, else their students would fail to make any progress in their readings. Even the paradigmatic medieval grammatical analysis of a literary masterpiece, Priscian's *Duodecim,* an absolutely enormous word-by-word exegesis of the *Aeneid,* quite sensibly calls it quits after covering the epic's opening twelve lines. What this means for matters at hand, I believe, is that Chaucer embeds only a limited number of truly challenging grammatical, rhetorical, and logical cruces in *The Nun's Priest's Tale*—but these *distinctiones* are, as we shall see in forthcoming chapters, profoundly significant, even as they continue to be wonderfully (and parodically) amusing.

A second cluster of assignments John of Salisbury describes as part of Bernard's teaching practice were the *preexercitamina,* a sequence of "models for the boys in their introductory exercises in imitating prose and poetry."[31] In a critically important article on *The Nun's Priest's Tale,* R. T. Lenaghan suggests in a few compact paragraphs that one way of approaching the *Tale* is precisely via these *progymnasmata* (that is, *preexercitamina*), a program of elementary exercises required of every schoolboy from well before Quintilian and Suetonius to well after Shakespeare and Milton.[32] To my knowledge, no one has followed up on Lenaghan's suggestion.

Although programmatically similar sequences were composed by three different Greek schoolmasters—Theon, Hermogenes, and Aphthonius—it was Priscian's *Preexercitamina,* the Latin adaptation of Hermogenes' *Progymnasmata,* that served throughout the Middle Ages as the progymnasmatic authority.[33] As in their traditional Greek formulations, Priscian's *preexercitamina* progress from simple to more complex and from one category of rhetoric—deliberative, demonstrative, and judicial—to another, "build[ing] each exercise on what the boy has learned from previous exercises, repeating somewhat from the previous exercise and adding something that is new."[34] Priscian arranges the exercises in the following (slightly eccentric) order: fable, narration, *chria, sententia,* commonplace, encomium/vituperation, comparison, impersonation, description, positio, and legislation. All the opening assignments are concerned directly with literature—its creation and interpretation, its ways of marrying manner and subject. *Fable* (as we have already seen) is a series of assignments in which the student rewrites the Aesopic fables in various degrees of amplification and abbreviation. *Narration* requires that several kinds of discourse—namely, the fabulous, the plausible, the historical, and the legal—be rewritten to conform to different narrative models and conventions. *Chria* (or anecdote) and *sententia* (or proverb) explore the ways one can punctuate a story's meaning, the ways a narrative might illustrate a general truth, and the ways of amplifying a truism's significance and applying it to life.

The primary purpose of these exercises in deliberative rhetoric was to teach students how to write poetry by creative imitation and how to interpret poetry both by imitation and by commentary. In narration, for instance, one was asked to rewrite narratives of the *auctores* in five different modes: direct declarative, indirect declarative, interrogative, enumerative, and contrastive. Chauntecleer's assorted narratives illustrating the veracity of dreams are a medley of these five modes. To illustrate *chria*, "the recalling of someone's words or acts or both together, which are suited to a quick explanation and can be offered as a lesson to some person or group,"[35] Priscian offers several anecdotal examples, one being, "'When Diogenes saw a youth behaving shamelessly, he struck the pedagogue with his stick.'"[36] In *The Nun's Priest's Tale* Russell the fox recounts a surprisingly similar *chria:*

> I have wel rad in 'Daun Burnel the Asse,'
> Among his vers, how that ther was a cok,
> For that a preestes sone yaf hym a knok
> Upon his leg whil he was yong and nyce,
> He made hym for to lese his benefice.
> (VII.3312–16)

In the next exercise, *sententia*, Priscian provides more than a dozen examples, such as "Rumor is an evil more swift than any other,"[37] and, as we have already noted, the Nun's Priest includes a large number of *sententiae* in his *Tale*: "For evere the latter ende of joye is wo" (VII.3205), "Wommennes conseils been ful ofte colde" (VII.3256), and so forth.

In the next three exercises (all forms of judicial rhetoric, although Priscian places them much earlier in the sequence than does Hermogenes) the student argues *pro* and then *contra: confirmation* is in favor of a proposition, *refutation* is in opposition, and *commonplace* attempts to balance and resolve both sides of the debate. Priscian suggests that the issue of the truthfulness of a selected literary text (but not "the fables of Aesop or obviously false history")[38] could serve as a proposition to be confirmed or refuted. Chaucer's narrator fails to heed Priscian's warning, however, for the controversial issue he strives to confirm (and thus comes close to refuting) concerns precisely the proscribed matter of his own fable's truthfulness:

> This storie is also trewe, I undertake,
> As is the book of Launcelot de Lake,
> That wommen holde in ful greet reverence.
> (VII.3211–13)

In commonplace, "we magnify the importance of the thing already established or proved," writes Priscian. "It is called a commonplace because it can be applied to every blasphemer, for example, or to every hero, if you prefer."[39] Priscian suggests the student might begin this exercise by stating a general principle, such as "It is only right, oh judges, that you hold in abhorrence all men who are evildoers; but you should especially despise those who dare to attack the gods."[40] In *The Nun's Priest's Tale*, the moment Russell the fox convinces Chauntecleer to close his eyes the better to sing, the narrator launches into a magnificent generalization on the heinousness of flatterers, but rather than judges addressed in courts of law (as with Priscian) his imaginary audience is lords addressed in courts of state:

> Allas, ye lordes, many a fals flatour
> Is in youre courtes, and many a losengeour,
> That plesen yow wel moore, by my feith,
> Than he that soothfastnesse unto yow seith.
> Redeth Ecclesiaste of flaterye;
> Beth war, ye lordes, of hir trecherye.
> (VII.3325–30)

As with commonplace, the more advanced progymnasmatic exercises are forms of extensive public oration, and it is in his parodic allusions to these assignments that the *Tale*'s narrator reveals his skills as an audacious mock-rhetor. In *encomium* one praises a class of human beings, and in *vituperation* one reviles another, each class concretized with specific examples. The narrator's over-the-top praise for Chauntecleer, as in his opening *effictio*, pretty much eclipses any possible encomia for the rest of his gallic kind, including fair Pertelote. As an example of a class that might be reviled, Hermogenes suggests the Despot (Priscian is not explicit on this matter). Of course *The Nun's Priest's Tale* lacks a despot, but it does have a fox, whose murderous nature inspires a sudden outburst from the narrator against "thise homycides alle":

> O false mordrour, lurkynge in thy den!
> O newe Scariot, new Genylon,
> False dissymulour, o Greek Synon,
> That broghtest Troye al outrely to sorwe!
>   (VII.3226–29)

Next, in *comparison,* the student is required to compare two similar subjects according to their various attributes (Priscian gives Ulysses versus Hercules as an example), with the purpose normally of proving that one is greater than the other. As we have already noticed, our narrator chooses to compare not men but women—Chauntecleer's wives and the wives of Troy and Carthage—arguing that the grief of the former was the greater because their screams of tragic suffering were much the louder. In *impersonation* one assumes the voice of a famous literary figure and invents a speech he or she might deliver in a special situation. As we have also just noted, the *Tale*'s narrator takes up this assignment by impersonating *his own voice*, and it is not until speech's end that he belatedly announces he had actually been impersonating his fictional hero all along: "Thise been the cokkes wordes, and nat myne" (VII.4455).

Description is often an exercise in composing realistic detail, like a word-painting, such as the very studied description of the old widow's world at the opening of *The Nun's Priest's Tale*. *Positio* (or abstract situation) is, Priscian explains, "the consideration of some general question

which relates to no particular person or other circumstantial consideration, like a debate over whether sailing or getting married or studying
philosophy is good, without asking for whom; it simply investigates an
issue on its own terms and in light of its own conditions."[41] The very moment Russell slides into Chauntecleer's chickenyard, the Nun's Priest suddenly ascends into an abstract disquisition on foreknowledge ("Goddes
worthy forwityng"), free will ("free choys"), conditional necessity ("necessitee condicioneel") and simple necessity ("symple necessitee")—
even though Priscian warns that philosophical questions should be left
to "the purview of philosophers, for orators are trained in other matters."[42]
Gradually acknowledging his intellectual limits ("I ne kan nat bulte it to
the bren" [VII.3240]) the Nun's Priest abruptly leaves such insolubles to
the philosophers and returns to the art of narration: "I wol nat han to do
of swich mateere; / My tale is of a cok, as ye may heere" (VII.3251–52).
Finally, *legislation* involves rhetorical exercises imitating legal proposals
and judicial cases that might hypothetically be considered in a court of
law. The *Tale*'s celebrated fox chase—where the peasants pursuing the
fox raise the traditional alarums of common law ("'Out! harrow!' and
'Weilaway'")—might possibly qualify as a lowbrow exercise in *legislation*.
And there is no doubt that Chaucer's surprising decision to insert into
this hue and cry the slaughter of the Flemings during the 1381 Uprising
certainly intensifies the juridical implications of this troubling judicial
set-piece.

To this point, then, in our reconstruction of the basic modes of liberal
arts study as practiced in the early years of a typical medieval grammar
school education, we have focused on trivium skills (translation, grammatical analysis, and logical debate especially), on the centrality of a variety of basic texts (Aesopian fables, most notably, and grammatical and
rhetorical primers), as well as on the creative and rhetorical exercises that
constitute Priscian's *preexercitamina*. All of these, I maintain, are touchstones reactivated inside *The Nun's Priest's Tale*; and while some of the
preexercitamina associations I have drawn are surely forced and fanciful,
there is no doubt that the *Tale*'s overall literary *zeitgeist* remains a rich
collocation of early classroom memories. It thus could be argued that the
fable's "best reader" is anyone who is able to recollect the spirit, and perhaps even the letter, of these curricular assignments and is immediately

able to sense the transtextual importance of their evocations. While we have been developing an understanding of the *Tale*'s basic curricular armature, we have also underscored the apparent fragmentariness of its multifascicled form: that is, the fable is a congeries of so many seemingly disparate parts it appears from one critical angle to be a pastiche comparable to a modern painting made up of numerous slivers taken from other, prior works. Thus it is important to emphasize at this moment that the first rule of medieval composition, as Douglas Kelly has explained, is "the tendency of the treatises to favor the small units of discourse,"[43] so that old works are critiqued and modern works are composed with one's primary attention given to the success of the local exercise and with only minor consideration given to its relationship to the overall work. Even so, Chaucer's beast fable so self-consciously pushes that "small unit" practice to the limit that it may belong to a quite unusual literary genre. The parameters of this marginal genre, which I provisionally call "Menippean parody," I will consider in a moment. But before making that move, I wish to recall—as promised—one more pedagogical technique for which Bernard of Chartres was famous, namely, his expectation that students read classical works of literature through the seven liberal arts in order that they might discover the dramatic role played by each of the arts in the text under examination.

That the seven liberal arts constituted the basic structure of medieval academic culture is beyond question: not only did the arts define the structure of the school curriculum, in humanist treatises and in other forms of medieval literature they were typically viewed as sequential steps leading the seeker of knowledge in the direction of the highest form of wisdom. Martianus Capella's fifth-century allegory, *The Marriage of Mercury and Philology*, was the archetypal liberal-arts quest for knowledge: here all seven arts are seen as "the servants of Mercury," who in turn is identified with Hermes Trismegistus, the mythic inventor of languages and letters. Alcuin, in his Christian liberal-arts treatise, the ninth-century *Disputatio de Vera Philosophia*, celebrates the educational importance of the seven liberal arts as "the seven degrees of Philosophy" leading to "the highest truth of Holy Scriptures."[44] Similarly, Honorius of Autun announces in his *De animae exsilio et patria: alias, de artibus* that "[t]he exile of man is ignorance; his native land is wisdom and he reaches it through the liberal arts, each of which is like a city on the road,"[45] the road to "our homeland, true wisdom, which shines forth from the pages of Holy Scripture and reaches perfection in the vision of God."[46] In Alanus de Insulis's twelfth-century *Anticlaudianus,* an allegorical chariot whose parts are constructed out of the seven liberal arts transports Phronesis into the sky in her quest for the Perfect Man, and it is only at the heavens' very summit that Reason proves inadequate, the chariot is left behind, and Theology must show the way. In the *Convivio,* Dante constructs a cosmic scheme for the arts: the seven planetary heavens are the progressive sites of the trivium and quadrivium, while the fixed stars correspond to physics and metaphysics, ethics is lodged in the *Primum Mobile,* and the Empyrean is the ultimate site of theology. Even though Dante relaxes these rigid parallelisms in his *Commedia,* the liberal arts remain such dominant forces in the poem's overall design that an anthology of excellent studies, *The Divine Comedy and the Encyclopedia of Arts and Sciences,* provides a chapter on each of the seven arts.[47]

No collection of critical studies has yet appeared arguing that *The Canterbury Tales* might be read through the lens of the liberal arts. However, one article, Ian Bishop's 1979 study *"The Nun's Priest's Tale* and the Liberal Arts," comes quite close to interpreting Chaucer's beast fable according to the expectations of Bernard of Chartres. The "way in which so much of the syllabus of a fourteenth-century university is enclosed within the narrow and humble compass of the chicken run," writes Bishop, suggests that a "convenient, though not comprehensive, framework for our exploration of the function of the medieval world of learning [reflected in the *Tale*] is afforded by the scheme of the Seven Liberal Arts."[48] Bishop touches briefly on the appearances in the fable of grammar, rhetoric, dialectic, music, and astrology, but he does not inquire very deeply into the instructive work these curricular *artes* perform inside the *Tale* itself, suggesting only, as with the soaring eagle in *The House of Fame,* so with the earth-bound rooster Chauntecleer, that Chaucer is "us[ing] a bird to satirize an academic."[49] As I will demonstrate in considerable detail in succeeding chapters, not only the trivial but the quadrivial arts are called upon to provide techniques of knowledge that assist in interrogating metapoetical and mathematical issues the poem raises. One question we will eventually need to address is whether the seven *artes* in *The Nun's Priest's Tale* are designed to lead the reader toward "true wisdom" and the Empyrean, or in some other direction.

Having completed this fairly extensive review of those specific grammar school materials directly invoked by *The Nun's Priest's Tale*, we are now ready to move toward an interrogation of the genre of the *Tale* itself. As I have already noted, the *Tale* is a potpourri of genres and registers: it could be seen as a comedy, *tragedie manqué*, mock epic, sermon, epyllion, debate, fabliau, exemplum, romance, beast fable, a form of wisdom literature, and much more. The better to understand how these many forms and discourses are contained successfully in one, ultimately unified literary work, we need to define the nature of that capacious genre (or anti-genre) that goes under the name of Menippean satire. After assessing the partial applicability of this literary class to *The Nun's Priest's Tale*, I will then turn to the literary mode I find most instrumental in our interpretation of Chaucer's fable, and that of course is parody.

THE *NUN'S PRIEST'S TALE* AS MENIPPEAN PARODY

"Genre is a necessarily uncertain but certainly necessary construct," writes Howard Weinbrot in *Menippean Satire Reconsidered,* a recent study whose explicit goal is "to reduce the number of works called Menippean satire and to clarify its essential and occasionally overlapping devices and options."[50] Weinbrot's is a formidable task, for literary texts as seemingly unrelated as *Alice in Wonderland, Anatomy of Melancholy, Gulliver's Travels, Hamlet, Moby Dick, Portnoy's Complaint, The Romance of the Rose,* and *The Waste Land* have all been cited as examplars of the form. Even though a clutch of Greek and Latin writers in antiquity (most notably Varro, Seneca, Petronius, Lucian, Martianus Capella, Fulgentius, Ennodius, Apuleius, and Boethius) apparently shared an understanding of a literary form that we now choose to call "Menippean satire," the name itself was not invented until 1581. Another critical problem is that most definitions of Menippean satire acknowledge its unusual resistance to generic definition: here is a literary form that seeks to transgress and deconstruct all traditional literary categories including, perhaps, its own. Attempts to classify the genre are nevertheless abundant. In *Ancient Menippean Satire*, for example, Joel Relihan "urge[s] that the genre is primarily a parody of philosophical thought and forms of writing, a parody of the habits of civilized discourse in general, and that it ultimately turns into the parody of the author who has dared to write in such an unorthodox way."[51] Yet many critics would instantly add that Menippean satire targets not only its own author but also any reader who seeks to impose order on its protean form.

Northrop Frye was the first Western critic to call attention to the importance of the genre. In *Anatomy of Criticism* (1957), Frye suggests that "anatomy" in fact is a more accurately descriptive name than "Menippean satire."[52] Whereas satire normally denotes a form of comically aggressive literature that mocks the world's foibles with the putative purpose of effecting a positive change, the "anatomy" is an encyclopedic potpourri of disparate elements intent on sending up intellectual currents and literary forms but with no apparent commitment to changing the world for the better. Frye implies there are hundreds of examples of the genre in Western literature, including Walton's *Compleat Angler*, Voltaire's *Candide*, Huxley's *Brave New World*, and Burton's *Anatomy of Melancholy* (from which Frye derives the genre's name as well as the title for his book). These works are all "anatomies," writes Frye, because they deal "less with people as such than with mental attitudes"; in this way the anatomy "differs from the novel in its characterization, which is stylized rather than naturalistic, and presents people as mouthpieces of the ideas they represent."[53]

Mikhail Bakhtin's powerfully influential *Problems of Dostoevsky's Poetics*, written in the 1920s but appearing in translation in the West only in 1973, proposed the first full theorization of the form.[54] Preferring his own coinage, "menippea," Bakhtin situates the classical Menippean text inside a larger group of writings in antiquity called "spoudo-geloion" (seriocomical), which share three common traits: "an insistence on examining everything in terms of the present, a deeply critical attitude toward myth, and a love of multifariousness and discordance."[55] Based upon the works of Menippeus (of which only a few fragments remain), the menippea is thus first and foremost a *satura*—that is, a mixture, mish-mash, or "hodge-podge" of styles and forms, a "paradoxical jumble of disparate things."[56] In violation of classical aesthetic norms, prose and poetry are often both included, segments of serious-seeming discourses are juxtaposed to scandalous riffs, and the lowest literary styles are given as much weight as the most dignified. Urbane, ironic, and encyclopedic, eager not only to parody the respected traditions of the intelligentsia but to parody prior parodies of these ideas, the menippea can also be appreciated as a self-reflexive, thoughtful, and "heavily intellectual form."[57]

Bakhtin identifies fourteen major traits to be found in menippeae, even though no single manifestation of the genre embraces all of them. Included in this list are: a spirit of joyful relativity; an unusual freedom of plot and philosophical invention; a readiness to cross-fertilize the fantastic and magical with the crude and banal; a willingness to embrace the world of the gods, the world of the dead, and the world of experience; a delight in abrupt transitions, in the yoking together of disparate things, and in the clash of styles and literary registers; the seemingly haphazard inclusion of many elements from other genres; and a journalistic concern with current and topical issues.[58] Constituting an unbroken tradition from the fragmentary verses of Menippeus to the "polyphonic novels" of Dostoevsky, the bond that ultimately holds the culture of Menippean texts together, be they ancient, medieval or modern, is—according to Bakhtin—their popular, communitarian, and "deeply carnivalized" spirit.

In order to consider the critical relevance of this genre to our immediate understanding of Chaucer's poetry, we need to return briefly to F. Anne Payne's *Chaucer and Menippean Satire*. Payne starts off by listing Bakhtin's fourteen "salient traits" and then adds seven more of her own. These are: a dialogue between a pair of stereotypical characters; one character's being on an "endless quest"; the foregrounding of the theme of freedom; a "courteous intention [on the part of characters] to continue conversing"; a general radiation of "hope" and "titanic energy"; the refusal to represent "God" or any "unquestionable authority"; and the inclusion of "obscenity . . . without pornography."[59] In the remainder of her book Payne analyzes four of Chaucer's texts as Menippean satires—*Boece, Troilus and Criseyde, The Nun's Priest's Tale,* and *The Knight's Tale*—with energetic and sometimes eccentric intensity. However, in her critical analyses Payne quite often sets aside all generic considerations or else selectively remolds her working definition of the genre to accommodate her reading of the text at hand.

Now as we progress from one generic definition to the next—especially from Frye's to Bakhtin's to Payne's—it is possible to sense a menippeanization of Menippean criticism itself, as the proliferation of "salient traits" exerts such a scattering effect that eventually the genre appears to include everything and the kitchen sink. Small wonder, even as far back as 1960, that Alastair Fowler laments that Frye's capacious definition "threatens to prove a baggier monster than the novel."[60] And small wonder in 2005 that Weinbrot, viewing the genre's liberal admissions policy, should characterize the ballooning class we still called Menippean satire as "bulbous."[61] So what then is the essence of Menippean satire? Does it even exist as a distinct literary category? In light of the methodological vagaries at work in every genre classification, answering such questions may ultimately depend on whether, taxonomically, one is a "lumper" or a "splitter." Be that as it may, it appears at the very least, as Weinbrot suggests, that these "salient features" constitute "less a clearly defined genre than a set of variable but compatible devices whose traits support any authorial theme."[62]

Now whether or not one prunes back to an extremely conservative definition or else constructs a liberal Venn diagram of overlapping literary kinds, it still matters to Chaucerians if there were any instances of Menippean satire produced in the Middle Ages. Frye, rather surprisingly, provides no medieval examples. Weinbrot implies that Menippean satire simply disappeared at the end of the classical age until the form was "resurrected in the Renaissance."[63] Relihan, although his study ends with the late Latin revival of the fifth and sixth centuries, is persuaded that there was in fact a twelfth-century "medieval revival" whose major achievements are Bernardus Silvestris's *De Cosmographia* and Alanus de Insulis's *Complaint of Nature*.[64] Payne, unsurprisingly, identifies several medieval Menippean masterpieces—including Alanus de Insulis's *Complaint of Nature* and Jean de Meun's continuation of the *Romance of the Rose*; she also suggests Chaucer might have known certain classical menippeae, specifically, Petronius's *Satyricon*, Seneca's *Apocolocyntosis*, and Apuleius's

Golden Ass.[65] Finally, in *Menippean Satire: An Annotated Catalogue of Texts and Criticism,* Eugene Kirk catalogues only fourteen texts as medieval exemplars among the 738 Menippean satires he contends were written before 1660 in Western Europe, the best known being the two that Relihan also names, Bernardus Silvestris's *De Cosmographia* and Alanus de Insulis's *Complaint of Nature.*[66]

For all the confusion attendant upon the genre's definition and development, assessing the literary features of Menippean satire bears upon our understanding of *The Nun's Priest's Tale* and, in fact, upon our understanding of Chaucer's work more generally. When we read Chaucer's entire oeuvre, Bertrand Bronson once argued in *In Search of Chaucer,* "[w]e are not merely disturbed, we are sometimes disoriented and amazed by the rapid shifts of stylistic level, the apparent sacrifice of achieved effects, the reversals of moods and tone, the abrupt stoppage of narrative momentum, the commingling of colloquial and artificial diction, the breathtaking incorporation of the whole range of language into the working texture of the verse."[67] And especially when we read *The Nun's Priest's Tale* we find these poetic maneuverings so self-consciously intensified that we might be persuaded that here Chaucer takes on the role of the Menippean satirist *par excellence.* There is no doubt that certain features of *The Nun's Priest's Tale* support the possibility of its being seen, minimally, as Menippean satire's well-groomed and diminutive distant cousin. That is, Chaucer's grammar school primer connects easily with that distinctive strain Kirk has identified as "educational" or "didascalic" Menippean satire.[68] The most notable instances in Kirk's list are Macrobius's *Saturnalia* (fifth century), where Macrobius displays shards of ancient learning for his son's edification; Martianus Capella's *Marriage of Mercury and Philology* (fifth century), an allegory of the seven liberal arts written for Martianus's son; Boethius's *Consolation of Philosophy* (fifth century), where Boethius learns about freedom and truth at Lady Philosophy's feet; Bernard's *Cosmographia* (twelfth century), a cosmogenic allegory of the formation of the Perfect Man; and Alanus de Insulis's *Complaint of Nature* (twelfth century), a lamentation of mankind's misuse of the skills acquired from his grammatical and literary textbooks. With one exception, the *Saturnalia,* Chaucer knew these texts and radiated their influence throughout his poetic career.

But despite all this critical preparation, I want now to insist that *The Nun's Priest's Tale* is not in fact a Menippean satire—that is, *if* we choose to accord that problematic term "satire" its modern meaning. While Chaucer takes great pleasure in writing satires authored by fictionalized "others," as in *The Friar's Tale* and *The Summoner's Tale,* and while he enjoys relativizing and reambiguating the myriad tropes of the Satire of the Three Estates tradition in the *General Prologue,* he is essentially an ironist and not a satirist. Chaucer is not a Juvenal, a Rabelais, or a Swift. In fact, parody, as much as irony, is Chaucer's signature trope. But satire is not. So, in one imperious gesture I jettison "satire" as the ruling generic class to which Chaucer's beast fable belongs. And in the same gesture I replace "satire" with "parody." I of course intend to hold on to "Menippean" as a crucial defining term because so many features of the Menippean tradition—be it defined by Frye, Bakhtin, Relihan, Weinbrot, or Payne—remain essential to fine-tuning our appreciation of the form and literary strategies of Chaucer's *ars poetica.* Thus, if a limited set of generic parameters were to provide a structure for better understanding *The Nun's Priest's Tale,* I want to settle the issue by asserting that Chaucer's mock grammar school primer is a *Menippean parody,* or—with even greater precision—a *Menippean didascalic parody.* And while this may mean that the *The Nun's Priest's Tale* ultimately belongs to a generic category of one, its close kinship with the entire Menippean tradition nevertheless sheds light on its unusual, and perhaps unique, literary identity.

Parody, satire, irony: we use these terms easily and on occasion interchangeably because we share a tacit conviction that we all speak the same critical language. But parody, satire, and irony are scarcely equivalents. Since the interrelation among these three modes of poetic address has not been extensively theorized by Chaucerians in recent years, in the next few pages I intend to parse out a fairly contemporary explication of parody and of its relationship to its two kindred tropes. As with my preceding review of curricular materials and educational exercises evoked by the *Tale,* my theorization of the *Tale*'s preeminent generic form will serve as an enabling interpretative superstructure throughout the remainder of this study.

There has been a long-standing tradition, going back at least to Quintilian, that views parody as "pejorative in intent and ridiculing in its

ethos or intended response."[69] Adherents to this popular theory agree
with Gary Saul Morson that parody is always "intended to have a higher
semantic authority than its original and the decoder is always sure of
which voice he or she is expected to agree with."[70] Continuing to insist
that comedy and derision be included in their definitions of parody, even
those who see parody as a form of internalized aesthetic criticism understand those critical norms as being articulated via a one-way mockery of the original, parodistic target. There are however important cor-
rectives to this limiting definition. One liberal voice is W. H. Auden's,
who suggests in his "daydream College for Bards" that the ideal library
should be free of books of literary criticism and instead "the only critical
exercise required of students would be the writing of parodies."[71] Auden's
proposal is in fact close to the medieval classroom practice of writing exaggerated exercises that imitate, emulate, and heighten the tropes of the
original, all as a way of understanding more deeply the achievements of
the master text. Indeed, in classical uses of the term, comedy and ridicule
were in fact *not* considered distinguishing features of parody, as Fred
Householder has shown, and the same holds true for much of the term's
use in the Middle Ages, where parody is often indistinguishable from literary imitation. Another parodic variant well known to both Chaucer and
his readers is what we might call "sacred parody" or "reverential parody":
here features of an authoritative text, such as the Bible or the *Iliad,* are
transliterated into another context in order to underscore the falling-off
between that authority and its latter-day imitations. In such forms of
parody (mock epic being a close analogue), the original is scarcely the target text: rather, it stands as the golden ideal against which the leaden and
plastic behaviors represented within the parodic texts are judged—often
through comic pejoration—and found wanting.

There are other modes of parody where neither the parodistic original nor the parodic successor is the object of corrective criticism. Rather,
a dialogic exchange takes place between two equally achieved discourses,
and the pleasure of the reader's engagement in this exchange derives in
part from the intertextual "bouncing" (to use E. M. Forster's famous term)
between the texts' complicity and distance. Parody is thus a form that
needs to be appreciated as always straddling its own double etymology.
Para, meaning "counter" or "against," may be understood as accentuat-

ing the critical distance (diachronic and otherwise) between the counter-pointed discourses. But *para*, meaning "beside," may be seen as under-scoring the complementary and synchronic parity between two equal texts at play in the same work of art. Thus for these several reasons and for others as well, I insist that Chaucer's comic evocations of certain class-room practices and curricular texts in *The Nun's Priest's Tale* are not satiric critiques of previous modes of literary production and creation. The hy-pothetical schoolboy exercises Chaucer evokes are themselves imitations of earlier works wherein the poet-to-be will eventually discover his own voice and innovative style. In John of Salisbury's words, the master teacher Bernard of Chartres "would bring about that he who had imitated his predecessors would come to be deserving of imitation by his successors."[72] Even though the unsuccessful imitiative exercises were not themselves great works of art, Chaucer's parodic imitations of these imitations fit comfortably inside one of Linda Hutcheon's very important definitions of parody: parody is "an integrated structural modeling process of revising, replaying, inverting, and 'trans-contextualizing' previous works of art."[73]

Parody, as I have been insisting, thus needs to be understood as a genre constitutionally different from satire, even though satire is quite capable of using parody as a vehicle for satiric effect. Parody is essentially an "intramural" genre, to use Hutcheon's term. It involves an internal ex-change between two or more aesthetic norms embedded inside the same literary text: parody thus involves an artful rereading of art itself. But satire is always "extramural." Targeted at the world, it is often driven by an idealistic or moral determination to effect social change in the world—something that parody need not be committed to. Since all forms of art are ultimately—if perhaps problematically—attached to the real, parody inevitably has a pragmatic and even political valence. Nevertheless parody, and here I am thinking of literary parody specifically, is focused preemi-nently on other literatures, as well as on the idea of Literature itself.

Now a major reason that parody and satire are difficult to tease apart is that irony is central to the functionality of both. As we shall see more fully in my case study of irony at the end of this chapter, irony always has an evaluative "edge." Via semantic inversion (*antiphrasis*) and via prag-matic affect (signaling evaluation), irony's "edge" is most typically of a judgmental and pejorative nature: like humor, irony normally succeeds at someone's or something's expense. This makes irony immediately adaptable to the purposes of satire. On the other hand, irony's refusal of semantic univocality is what aligns irony so neatly with parody's similar refusal of structural unitextuality. In literature and in life, we have all experienced the subtle gradations of ironic affect, ranging from the congenial smile to the disdainful smirk to the derisive laugh. At a certain point along this continuum, irony merges with satire. But toward the other end of the spectrum irony merges with parody. This does not mean that parody and satire never overlap, that they never employ each other's services. Rather, there is one type of parody that Hutcheon defines as *satiric parody:* here both the target text and those who share its values are held up to critique. And there is likewise a type of satire she calls *parodic satire:* here the satirizing text aims at certain extratextual follies and uses imitative parodies of those follies as vehicles to achieve its corrective end.[74]

In *A Theory of Parody: The Teaching of Twentieth-Century Art Forms*—an encyclopedic study that I have been relying heavily upon throughout these past few paragraphs—Linda Hutcheon capstones her analysis of parody (P=Parody), satire (S=Satire), and irony (I=Irony) with the "dynamic" Venn diagram of figure 2.1. Hutcheon's diagram provides

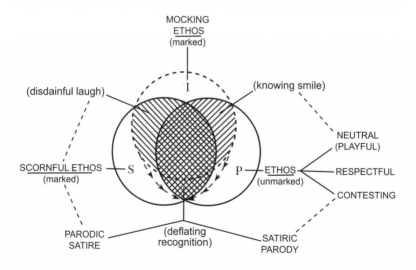

Figure 2.1. The Ethos of Parody, Irony, and Satire[75]

graphic assistance in our understanding the nature of *The Nun's Priest's Tale*'s relationship to parody, satire, and irony. Obviously the *Tale* is positioned on the right side of Hutcheon's diagram, in the shaded area where parody and irony overlap. And while its ethos is predominately "playful," I would submit that in no way does it seek to achieve pure neutrality, or what Hutcheon defines as "a zero degree of aggressivity toward either backgrounded or foregrounded text."[76] It has an edge, and it surely embraces elements of corrective critique. But if its parodic ethos is edgy, the direction of that critical thrust is primarily toward a *faux* reader resistant to or unable to engage fully in the parodic game itself. "There is a long tradition in parodic literature," writes Hutcheon, "of placing readers in tricky positions and forcing them to make their own way." But, she continues, "[t]he rules, if the author is playing fair, are usually in the text itself."[77] These parodic rules, as we shall see, are for the most part subtly evidenced in the *Tale* itself. It is thus important to emphasize that, as parody, *The Nun's Priest's Tale* is not engaged primarily with the early medieval classroom exercises per se as it is with the entire liberal-arts tradition for which these exercises stand. Since that liberal-arts tradition informs all of Chaucer's works, what this means in turn is that Chaucer's beast fable advertises and critiques its author's engagement in the very same arts of literary creation that students studied and imitated from the very earliest stages of their academic careers. As I have already emphatically noted, the *Tale* poses a set of inquiries concerning the nature of poetry, the relative power of Chaucer's vocation, and the "disseminal" difficulties all serious readers experience as they attempt to decode a poet's work.

Having identified the ground of *The Nun's Priest's Tale* as a set of foundational curricular experiences, having situated the tale's genre within the Menippean tradition, and having calibrated its poetic voice by detailing the tonal subtleties of self-reflexive parody, we are now prepared to make a major turn "inward." From this point forward, in other words, our focus will be on how *The Nun's Priest's Tale,* as a Menippean curricular parody, performs its major literary work as Chaucer's *ars poetica.* Relying in part upon their early classroom experiences, Chaucer draws his readers into an interrogation of matters of major importance to the poet's craft. While reevaluating these issues, Chaucer's readers are engaged in a silent dialogue with the poet himself as they become cocreators of the

Tale's localized sites of "meaning." And these sites—each disseminally resistant to critical extrapolation—participate in the *Tale*'s overall self-critical design. Thus, the problematics of narrative beginnings and endings (examined in chapter 3); the illogical powers of metaphor (examined in chapter 4); and the primal substance of poetry, pleasing and unpleasing sounds (examined in chapter 5): to scrutinize these phenomena is to consider the very basic elements of literary creation. Similarly, the limits of human discourse in any attempt to measure the phenomenal world (examined in chapter 6), and the limits of literature in any attempt to represent empirical truth (examined in chapter 7): these "philosophical" sites bear directly upon the poet's ability to guide a reader in the direction of some form of knowledge and understanding. Such are the theoretical touchstones of forthcoming chapters. In the remainder of this chapter, however, I attend to Chaucer's exploration of three basic areas of literary expertise, each practiced in the schools, each an essential element in the craft of the fully achieved poet. These are *imitatio,* as illustrated by Chaucer's transcontextualization of an authoritative text appropriated into a new literary environment; *translatio,* as it is embodied in Chauntecleer's translation of a Latin tag; and finally, the tonal subtlety of *ironia,* as illustrated by the narrator's foregrounding of Chaucer's signature trope. While his readers were instructed extensively in each of these three arts in the schools, via the heuristic powers of parody Chaucer seeks to effect a more sophisticated understanding of the literary and linguistic complexities of his craft.

PARODIC IMITATION: GEOFFREY OVERWRITES GEOFFREY

In *The Light in Troy: Imitation and Discovery in Renaissance Poetry,* Thomas Greene characterizes four ways writers imitate authoritative works from the past.[78] The first mode he designates as *sacramental:* the faithful imitation of a hallowed text, a slavish reproduction suggesting that no form but venerated iteration will successfully keep past and present united. The second mode is *eclectic* or *exploitative* imitation, or what

Renaissance rhetoricians called, unpejoratively, *contaminatio*. Here, allusions, echoes, phrases, and images from a large number of early authors jostle each other indifferently inside the confines of a single modern work. Whereas sacramental imitation is essentially ahistorical, eclectic imitation, according to Greene, has a somewhat developed sense of historicity, but is incapable of dealing at any profound level with the problematics of anachronism. The third imitative mode Greene calls *heuristic:* these works advertise their derivation from their masters' voices, and thus underscore the historicity of their sources while proceeding to distance themselves from their own subtexts. "[T]he informed reader" of the heuristic text, Greene writes, "notes the allusion [to the subtext] but he notes simultaneously the gulf in the language, in sensibility, in cultural context, in world view, and in moral style."[79] Fourth and finally, there is *dialectic* imitation, where, motivated by hostility toward the pressure to imitate, the modern text celebrates the vulnerability of the subtext while also exposing itself to the subtext's potential aggression. Entering into this dialectic of mutual criticism, the contemporary text "assumes its full historicity and works to protect itself against its own pathos."[80]

Although Greene focuses his study on classical and Renaissance texts, with a few passing allusions to "medieval ahistoricism," it is clear not only in Chaucer's writing, but in the entire tradition of medieval humanistic learning and literature, that all four imitative modes were employed by educated writers and understood by educated readers throughout the Middle Ages. As noted earlier in this chapter, detailed literary assignments were given to students wherein they were expected to imitate one rhetorical or narrative technique of the masters while using quite different *materia* as the field upon which the embellishments were to be imposed. These versifying exercises became so popular and sophisticated that in the twelfth century a half-dozen manuals were written by grammar teachers—Matthew of Vendôme, John of Garland, Gervais of Melkely, Eberhard the German, and Geoffrey of Vinsauf—step-by-step preceptive grammars that classified, explicated, and illustrated the arts of invention, exposition, and ornamentation. Throughout, the authors of these manuals included illustrations of their own making, "pure" and often deliberately exaggerated examples of each technique to serve as models for their students to emulate. In Geoffrey of Vinsauf's *Poetria Nova* one such model is the *Apostrophe to Eleustria (England)*, wherein the poet laments the tragic death of Richard the Lion-hearted. By the fourteenth century, this set piece of Latin rhetorical verse had taken on a life of its own, and was disseminated independently in over two hundred manuscripts.

Inside its *Poetria Nova* context, the *Apostrophe to Eleustria* is one of six exercises illustrating the art of apostrophe in a circumscribed literary context: the first exercise rebukes "the man whose mind soars too high in prosperity,"[81] the second cautions the overly proud man, the third is addressed to the overly timid man, and the sixth, a study of ironic apostrophe, mockingly praises the pupil who feels he is the master scholar. The fourth exercise is a sequence of tropes attached to an apostrophe to England, a nation whose position, in this "time of auspicious fortune," is secure "while King Richard lives."[82] And the crucial fifth exercise, also addressed to England, is a capacious illustration of how to express grief in response to the tragedy of King Richard's death. It is a tour-de-force of apostrophes, punctuated by more than a dozen "O!"s, with the dire day itself ("O tearful day of Venus!"), the "soldier of treachery" who murdered Richard, death ("Do you realize, impious death, whom you snatched from us?"), Nature ("you seize precious things, and vile things you leave as if in disdain"), and even God ("why then did you shorten his days?") all serving as addressees of the poet's complaints.[83] What needs to be appreciated here is that this schoolbook exercise is a knowing and serious self-parody: that is, it is self-consciously designed to illustrate as many apostrophic tropes as possible, all within the floribundant style of twelfth-century academic verse.

Now it is precisely this celebrated academic model of apostrophe that the Nun's Priest invokes the moment that his hero is on the brink of death. In order to give voice to the literary emotions appropriate to this gallinaceous calamity, the narrator decides first to apostrophize "destynee"; he then apostrophizes Chauntecleer's erotic goddess, Venus; he then apostrophizes Geoffrey of Vinsauf, the master of rhetoric who taught him how thus to apostrophize; and finally he apostrophizes the very day of the week (Friday) on which this horrible tragedy occurs:

This Chauntecleer stood hye upon his toos,
Strecchynge his nekke, and heeld his eyen cloos,
And gan to crowe loude for the nones.
And daun Russell the fox stirte up atones,
And by the gargat hente Chauntecleer,
And on his bak toward the wode hym beer,
For yet ne was ther no man that hym sewed.
    O destinee, that mayst nat been eschewed!
Allas, that Chauntecleer fleigh fro the bemes!
Allas, his wyf ne roghte nat of dremes!
And on a Friday fil al this meschaunce.
    O Venus, that art goddesse of plesaunce,
Syn that thy servant was this Chauntecleer,
And in thy servyce dide al his poweer,
Moore for delit than world to multiplye,
Why woldestow suffre hym on thy day to dye?
    O Gaufred, deere maister soverayn,
That whan thy worthy kyng Richard was slayn
With shot, compleynedest his deeth so soore,
Why ne hadde I now thy sentence and thy loore,
The Friday for to chide, as diden ye?
For on a Friday, soothly, slayn was he.
Thanne wolde I shewe yow how that I koude pleyne
For Chauntecleres drede and for his peyne.
                                        (VI.3331–54)

Scholars over the past century, as Pearsall's Variorum edition glosses economically illustrate, have generally agreed that Chaucer is intent here on ridiculing something. Manly (1926) reads the beast fable in its entirety as a parody of "the whole apparatus of medieval rhetoric."[84] Baldwin (1927) sees Chaucer pillorying Geoffrey of Vinsauf as "an ass" and lambasting his *Poetria Nova* as "an Ovidian nightmare."[85] Atkins (1943) remarks that here we observe Chaucer "plainly ridiculing the mechanical use of such devices by his usual method of burlesque or parody."[86] Critics in the second half of the past century, appreciative of the profound importance of rhetoric primers in the formation of all medieval poets, tend to direct the satiric thrust away from rhetoric itself and toward something else: Everett (1950), after illustrating Chaucer's extensive use of rhetorical devices in his verse, allows nevertheless that in this passage he is amusing himself at the expense of Geoffrey of Vinsauf.[87] Robert Payne (1963) argues that the allusion to Geoffrey is ridiculous not because the *Poetria Nova* is such, but because the *Tale*'s burlesque displacement from proper to improper context is meant to mock certain "stylistic practices or pretensions."[88] Knight (1973) suggests "Chaucer is not mocking Geoffrey, rather he is self-indulgently flourishing rhetorical language in a holiday mood."[89] Brewer (1973) agrees that Chaucer is not satirizing rhetoric itself. Rather, he "laughs at the rhetorician Geoffroi de Vinsauf in his poem because he is a poor poet—and that is humorous enough in a man who claims to teach the art of poetry. But Geoffroi did not own the art of poetry: he was only one among several who passed on certain rules of composition, which were enshrined in a tradition far greater than he."[90] And Pearsall, at the end of his survey of these and other critics' commentaries, concludes (1982): "Further, the comedy is one of disproportion—using rhetoric, which should adorn a high subject, to deck out a low."[91]

  Now I trust that most twenty-first-century readers would readily concur that Chaucer's imitation of Geoffrey of Vinsauf in this passage is not a satirical swipe at Chaucer's grammar school authority on literary composition, any more than it is a satirical critique of rhetoric *qua* rhetoric. Comic the passage certainly is, and it may well have a "comic" target, but the identity of that target, as Pearsall suggests, is not immediately apparent. One critical challenge is that this passage epitomizes the *Tale*'s habit of deploying the techniques of the mock epic, or what Pearsall calls "high rhetoric adorning a low subject." But the mock epic, as we have already noted, is essentially a satiric genre that sets out not to mock its classical model but rather to use the heroic ethos of a Homer or a Virgil as a norm against which the antiheroic subjects of the modern text are to be judged. In this light, it might be suggested that the *Poetria Nova* passage enjoys the textual authority of a classic, even though it is only a pedagogical set of heightened variations of one classical trope. A second challenge is that the mock-heroic subjects in this text are animals. Animals can certainly serve as satirical vehicles when in beast fables they metaphorize human vanities, pretension, and foibles. But even though Woody Allen suggested years ago that all comedy is tragedy seen from a distance, the *human* fear of violent death does not seem itself to be the target worthy of sustained satirical laughter. So what, then, is the precise "target" of this conspicuously comic piece of literary imitation?

In answer to this question I want to add more precision to the idea that the Nun's Priest's *Poetria Nova* passage is parodic in some general way by asserting that its parodistic object is the very act of literary imitation itself. In other words, while loosely imitating the *Apostrophe to Eleustria,* Chaucer is here invoking, imitating, parodying, and refunctioning certain ways a modern poet might imitate an exemplary model written by a powerful mentor from the past. Thus, if we return to Greene's fourfold taxonomy, we should now be able to appreciate how Chaucer's imitation of the craft of imitation does *not* fit readily into any one of Greene's four modes; rather, it parodies and refunctions each and all at once. The Nun's Priest's *Apostrophe to Eleustria* passage shares some of the characteristics of sacramental imitation: that is, it pretends to be a "faithful reproduction of a hallowed text," but its maladroit attempts to resacralize the present by uniting it with the past are much too literal and much too mechanical to be read entirely "straight." Second, the passage shares the "somewhat developed sense of historicity" of eclectic imitation, but its apparent "inability to deal at any profound level with the problematics of anachronism" is ironically nuanced and thus parodically instructive concerning the problematics of literary anachronism itself. The passage certainly conforms with the third, or heuristic, mode, its imitation of the original striving to move the reader from one aesthetic horizon to the next. But rather than trusting that his "informed" and "sensitized" reader will note "the gulf in the language, in the sensibility, in cultural context, in world view, and in moral style," Chaucer's narrator heavy-handedly highlights each of his numerous rhetorical appropriations, and then—still doubtful of his communicative success—actually provides the very *name* of his authority, Geoffrey of Vinsauf. Fourthly, it could be argued that this passage "assumes its full historicity" by engaging in an agon of mutual criticism with the *Poetria Nova* itself. In other words, while Chaucer's reworking

of the *Apostrophe to Eleustria* obviously foregrounds a radical transformation in aesthetic ideals, there could be as much loss as gain in this evolution in literary styles.

Now the unease some scholars feel when attempting to define the
precise nature of the Nun's Priest's immediate purpose may result from
the fact that this passage is constructed around a series of exaggerated
apostrophes. Of all the tropes in the poet's repertoire, Jonathan Culler has
remarked, apostrophe (at least for Romantic poets) is potentially the most
radical, embarrassing, and mystifying: "It is the pure embodiment of poetic pretention: of the subject's claim that in his verse he is not merely
an empirical poet, a writer of verse, but the embodiment of poetic tradition and of the spirit of poesy."[92] The archetypal apostrophizing poet
pretends to enjoy Orphic powers, a charismatic ability via one vatic vowel
to unite subject and object, living and dead, present and past, literary and
extraliterary. But the very act of apostrophizing calls attention to itself as
an ineffectual speech-act, a willful and pseudo-magical actualization accomplished poetically but not, of course, achieved in fact. Thus, in pre-
tending to bring about the condition to which his apostrophes vocatively
allude—namely, the animation of Destiny, Venus, Friday, and Geoffrey
of Vinsauf himself—the Nun's Priest actually underscores the emptiness
of that rhetorical "O!" all the while foregrounding the difficulties any poetry faces that seeks to make a counterfactual something-or-other happen
in the world.

For all its comedic good spirits, therefore, Chaucer's *Poetria Nova*
passage is doing a good deal of metapoetical work, and much of its industry bears upon its supercharged exchange between tradition and the
individual talent. Pushing back against the pressure to imitate one's forebears, this passage, acknowledging "the rich and intimidating legacy of
the past,"[93] is at once dramatizing the exhaustion of a once-triumphant
apostrophic poetic vocabulary even while contributing, as the Russian
formalists claimed is true of all parodies, to the evolution of literary style.[94]
It may therefore be in its relation to Greene's fourth mode of imitation,
where the contemporary text "assumes its full historicity and works to
protect itself against its own pathos," that Chaucer's parody of literary
appropriation asserts the greatest counter-pressure. In other words, the
"full historicity" of Chaucer's text may be discovered, to a surprising de-

gree, in its own political haplessness and ineffectuality. Chaucer blatantly underscores his text's literary and historical situatedness by naming his twelfth-century authority, Geoffrey, but also by naming that monarch, "worthy kyng Richard," in whose honor Geoffrey's complaint was written. Of course in the past there was but one King Richard of England lamented in an exercise admired by thousands for over two centuries. But there was contemporaneously another King Richard of England. Musing upon these two Richards, looking back, perhaps with envy, to his master Geoffrey, Geoffrey Chaucer might well admire the public mandate that even a classroom bard once assumed was proper to a poet's vocation. "Parody," to quote Hutcheon yet again, "is socially and politically multivalent; its particular uses are never neutral, but they cannot be deduced in advance."[95] Hutcheon's assertion is surely accurate, yet in this instance it is extremely difficult to deduce the social and political valence of the Nun's Priest's rhetorical lament—and this seems to be precisely Chaucer's point. It could be that a late fourteenth-century court poet would be considered a curious anachronism if he were to rear up and apostrophize his nation as does Geoffrey of Vinsauf. It could be that a Richardian poet of the modern age is best advised to conceal his political sentiments inside layers of ironized detachment. It could be that a frazzled rooster is the safest subject upon which to expend one's patriotic and political energies. Two centuries later Queen Elizabeth I will ask, "Know ye not that I am Richard?" after having seen Shakespeare's *Richard II*. Were he of a somewhat similar persuasion, King Richard II might perceive in Chaucer's beleaguered chicken an image of his own political condition. And were he gifted with an unusually anachronistic sensibility—believing in the prophetic powers of poetry—he might even intimate in Chauntecleer's capture his own imminent demise.[96] But Chaucer's interrogations of his own poetry's political ramifications are much too nuanced and noncommittal to allow for such crude historical alignments. Poetry for Chaucer, as he once again demonstrates in this passage, is essentially made out of other pieces of poetry: it is *imitatio* first and *mimesis* second. But this does not render Chaucer's fable absolutely ahistorical or apolitical. Rather, by displacing the pathos of historical grief with the bathos of literary mock-alarums, the Nun's Priest's pseudo-political lament for a royal rooster first invites and then neuters the application of any kind of coercive historical equation. Ultimately, therefore, the politics of the *Apostrophe to Eleustria* passage would appear to reside in its self-conscious erasure of the political. But that erasure need not be absolute, because some historicist residue clearly remains in the reader's processing of the passage—illustrating how even the most free-spirited parody cannot but enjoy a politically corrective edge.

LOST IN THE ORIGINAL, OR
THE ANXIETY OF TRANSLATION

For Chaucer and his contemporaries the art of *translatio studii* meant not only the transportation of an older text into a new literary environment, but also the translation of that text from one language, and language community, into another. On the continent Chaucer was admired in his lifetime as a "grant translateur,"[97] and for good reason: *Boece, A Treatise on the Astrolabe,* and *The Romaunt of the Rose* are all exactingly close translations of important texts, and his lost translation of Innocent III's *De Contemptu Mundi* may have been as well. Other works remain very close to their originals, such as "An ABC," *The Clerk's Tale, The Second Nun's Tale,* and *The Tale of Melibee.* And the majority of Chaucer's remaining works are also dependent upon foreign language sources—in French, Latin, or Italian—which Chaucer normally had at his fingertips as he composed. Nothing is closer to the core of Chaucer's poetic craft than his genius as a translator.

Yet only rarely in his works does one find Chaucer calling attention to the translator's craft—to the translator's intentions, strategies, desired reception, and achieved effects. And when he does so, the effect, rather than clarifying, is quite often difficult to "translate." In the Prologue to *The Legend of Good Women,* for instance, the God of Love reprimands Chaucer for having translated *The Romaunt of the Rose* and the *Troilus,* two works that the deity is persuaded prompted readers to cease paying homage to him. But does Chaucer actually wish us to believe that these two poems, his quite "literal" translation of the French *Romaunt* and his quite "free" adaptation of Boccaccio's Italian *Il Filostrato,* can be categorized in the same breath as "translatiouns"? And what should we then make of

Queen Alceste's defense of Chaucer on the grounds that he "nyste what he seyde" (*LGW,* G.345), that translators like him add nothing to the original and in fact are incapable of understanding the texts they are copying by rote? Are we expected to read her remarks ironically and simply to invert their surface assertions, or are we expected to set them at some strangely askew angle? Elsewhere, Chaucer is not much more helpful. In the headlink to the *Melibee,* Chaucer confesses that in his translation he has added "somwhat moore / Of proverbes" (VI.955–56), but if we were to look at his source, the *Livre de Melibée et de Dame Prudence,* we would find that "somwhat moore" means at least a hundred more proverbs. Nevertheless, Chaucer protests, "Blameth me nat" (VII.961), for the "sentence" of the original and the "sentence" of his translation are exactly the same. In fact, their univocity, he is convinced, is precisely like the univocity of the four gospels: "doutelees hir sentence is al oon" (VII.952). Does Chaucer actually expect us to believe that the addition or subtraction of hundreds of words in any text—such as the *Melibée* or the four gospels—has no effect on that text's meaning?

Chaucer's most sustained discursive consideration of the art of translation would appear to be his Preface to *A Treatise on the Astrolabe,* a Latin instruction manual that he translated into English for his son Lewis. Chaucer explains that in his text, "under full light reules" (that is, phrase-for-phrase rather than word-for-word translation), he will define the "trewe conclusions" (truthful propositions) that would:

> sufficith to these noble clerkes Grekes these same conclusions in Grek; and to Arabiens in Arabik, and to Jewes in Ebrew, and to Latyn folk in Latyn; whiche Latyn folk had hem first out of othere dyverse langages, and writen hem in her owne tunge, that is to seyn, in Latyn. And God woot that in alle these langages and in many moo han these conclusions ben suffisantly lerned and taught, and yit by diverse reules; right as diverse pathes leden diverse folk the righte way to Rome. (*Treatise on the Astrolabe,* 662)

Chaucer then briefly protests that his translation is absolutely not his own creation: "But considre wel that I ne usurpe not to have founden this werk of my labour or of myn engyn. I n'am but a lewd compilator of the labour of olde astrologiens, and have it translatid in myn Englissh oonly for thy doctrine. And with this swerd shal I sleen envie" (*Treatise on the Astrolabe*, 662). Perhaps because the *Treatise* is a scientific rather than a literary text, Chaucer confidently asserts here that the same information is conveyed no matter what language the *Treatise* is written in. This, of course, could be queried. Even so, the surprisingly militant deprecation of others' envy that immediately follows is so intense that it manages to raise once again the question of the translator's creative ownership of the text itself.

The matters foregrounded in this quick review of Chaucer's allusions to the problems of translation are all weighty issues: the truthfulness or untruthfulness of translation; "literal" vs. "free" translation; the relationship of individual words to the text's overall *sentence;* the translator's intent versus his readers' construction of that intent; the translator's craft as noninterventionist compiler; the translator's accountability for the ideas expressed in her translation; the power of any translation to express the same "conclusions" as are in the original. Of course, to arrive at an adequate understanding of Chaucer's philosophy of translation, one would need to analyze all his major works of translation. *The Nun's Priest's Tale* is obviously not one of these works. However, it does contain a passage that is carefully designed to provoke in his readers an articulation of their *own* philosophy of translation.

The Nun's Priest's Tale, as we have repeatedly noted, is a curricular parody intent on reeducating its readers in the art of literary criticism. So, it is clearly appropriate that Chaucer should incorporate a translation exercise into his *ars poetica* and that he should provide—he does this nowhere else—both the Latin original and an English translation for his readers to assess. It is Chauntecleer who provides both texts. Bringing his prolonged lecture on the prophetic power of dreams to a sudden halt, he turns his attention to his wife Pertelote and declaims:

> Now let us speke of myrthe, and stynte al this.
> Madame Pertelote, so have I blis,
> Of o thyng God hath sent me large grace;
> For whan I se the beautee of youre face,
> Ye been so scarlet reed aboute youre yen,
> It maketh al my drede for to dyen;

For al so siker as *In principio,*
Mulier est hominis confusio—
Madame, the sentence of this Latyn is,
'Womman is mannes joye and al his blis.'
For whan I feele a-nyght youre softe syde—
Al be it that I may nat on yow ryde,
For that oure perche is maad so nawre, allas—
I am so ful of joye and of solas,
That I diffye bothe sweven and dreem.

(VII.3157–71)

Most critical commentaries on Chauntecleer's translation have added up to variants of a single observation: this is a very clever joke that any reader with even a smidgen of Latin will fully appreciate and understand. With the exception of Derek Brewer, who doubts that Chauntecleer understood Latin well enough to know what he was doing,[98] critics have assumed that Chauntecleer is his own best audience: he delights in his scholarly cleverness even as he smiles at his beautiful but uncomprehending wife. A few readers have suggested that more is going on here. Peter Elbow, for example, allows that the translation is "exactly wrong and exactly right: wrong, obviously, as a mistranslation; right, however, as the essential explication of *why* woman is man's confusion."[99] Similarly, Charles Owen asserts that "both text and mistranslation are the same."[100] And Ian Bishop suggests that Chauntecleer's translation acts like an allegorical gloss, striving for the *sentence* of the Latin tag: thus Chaucer is here actually satirizing the follies of "glozing."[101]

In my judgment the most productive way of beginning to respond to this translation exercise is to read it as a heuristic parody of the very activity of translation itself, a parody whose reading regimen requires considerable patience as well as creativity to fully explore. Prescriptively, of course, Chauntecleer's translation is inaccurate; in fact, it is in many respects an antitranslation. Yet, just as obviously, there is something about the juxtaposition of these two texts that seems dialogically meaningful: historically, textually, sexually, politically, and theologically, they "speak" to each other. But the most important level of interpretative engagement, I find, is generated by the reader's experience of bouncing back and forth in the semantic and syntactical space between the original Latin and its English translation. In other words, I do not believe Chaucer is expecting his readers to simply supply a proper translation and move quickly on. Rather, by summoning up their "trivial" skills, Chaucer is challenging them to interrogate in a scholarly fashion—as they had been trained in school—the linguistic complexities embedded in the Latin text itself. While his readers may eventually arrive at what they determine to be the best translation, it is also possible that some readers may conclude that this text is curiously resistant to *any* kind of translation.

From among the many superb books on the art of translation, I single out George Steiner's *After Babel: Aspects of Language and Translation* because it economically details the four stages of "hermeneutic motion" any translator must go through:

(1) *Trust:* the investment of belief that there exists in the primary text something that is intended to mean something rather than nothing.

(2) *Aggression:* the incursion of the translator's cognitive faculties into the field of the other text in order to encircle, decipher, and extract what is there and is considered to be of value.

(3) *Incorporation:* the target text proves to be so powerful that it infects the translating text, the inhaled voice in various ways choking or colonizing the interpreting voice.

(4) *Restitution:* a textual dialectic is established, forming a balance of distance and contiguity, with new formats of significance constructed in the space between the two texts.[102]

The high degree of anxiety and aggression expressed in Steiner's hermeneutical model seems appropriate to Chauntecleer's style of translation, one that appropriates from the original whatever is useful and resists all other threats of "contamination." In fact, in contrast to the Nun's Priest's trusting imitations of the *Poetria Nova* passage that we just examined, here the displacing text seeks to obliterate its progenitor almost completely. So it appears that the reader's first step is to undo the hyper-aggressivity of Chauntecleer's English translation in order to reconsider with care the import of the Latin formulation, and then to proceed cautiously toward some form of "restitutition constructed in the space between the two texts."

So what, then, does *In principio* actually mean? The answer to this first step is by no means self-evident. In an article entitled "The Magic of *In Principio*," Morton Bloomfield lists fourteen examples from medieval textual venues illustrating how *in principio* was "a well-known apotropaic formula" used by clergy to exorcize demons at baptism and extreme unction, and more generally "to clear the air of the malignant forces which lay everywhere ready to strike."[103] Thus a primary significance of *in principio* rests not at all in its "literal meaning" but rather in its exorcistic powers. A second understanding of the phrase is generated by its most celebrated context: *in principio* are the first two words both in the book of Genesis and in the Gospel of John. Accordingly, throughout the Middle Ages *in principio* was often understood as signifying the veracity of God's word—"as true as the gospel." It is this level of meaning that Pearsall judges to be the best translation for its localized use in *The Nun's Priest's Tale*.[104] However, to determine the *literal* meaning of the phrase (rather than its apotropaic and synecdochic uses), we might wish to rely upon its literal meaning in its original biblical context. Quite famously, this is precisely what St. Augustine commits himself to discovering in his *Confessions*. But after agonizing for two chapters over the opening sentence of *Genesis*, Augustine confesses to his first auditor, God, that he cannot arrive at the true meaning of *in principio*:

> Let me hear and understand the meaning of the words: In the Beginning you made heaven and earth. Moses wrote these words. He wrote them and passed on into your presence, leaving this world where you spoke to him. He is no longer here and I cannot see him face to face. But if he were here, I would lay hold of him and in your name I would beg and beseech him to explain those words to me. I would be all ears to catch the sounds that fell from his lips. If he spoke in Hebrew, his words would strike my ear in vain and

none of their meaning would reach my mind. If he spoke in Latin, I should know what he said. But how should I know whether what he said was true? If I knew this too, it could not be from him that I got such knowledge. But deep inside me, in my most intimate thought, Truth, which is neither Hebrew nor Greek nor Latin nor any foreign speech, would speak to me, though not in syllables formed by lips and tongue. It would whisper, "He speaks the truth." And at once I should be assured. In all confidence I would say to this man, your servant, "What you tell me is true."

Since, then, I cannot question Moses, whose words were true because you, the Truth, filled him with yourself, I beseech you, my God, to forgive my sins and grant me the grace to understand those words, as you granted him, your servant, the grace to speak them.[105]

Augustine's heart-wrenching difficulties derive in large part from a host of metaphysical complexities concerning the nature of time and eternity, since both modalities meet at the precise point of the world's beginning, its *in principio*. In addition, as Brian Stock explains in *Augustine the Reader*, Augustine's agonies in this passage also instantiate the complexities of the very act of reading itself: "Reading [for Augustine] is a way of linking the past and the future of the self by means of an activity in the present. A text is a plan, a guide, and a map; it is also a puzzle, a labyrinth, 'an immense wood filled with snares and dangers.'"[106] Now it would be much too extreme to imply that Chauntecleer's lighthearted *in principio* is "filled with snares and dangers" equivalent to the gravely serious "snares and dangers" Augustine discovers in the opening words of Genesis. Nevertheless, as we bear down on Chaucer's *in principio*, the phrase begins to take on the appearance of a serious semantic puzzle, and Chauntecleer begins to look like a knowingly cautious translator for having decided to leave the phrase entirely out of his own translation. A few editors of *The Nun's Priest's Tale* have suggested that Chauntecleer's *in principio* means, quite simply, "in the beginning." Therefore, the entire Latin tag needs to be translated as "In the beginning, woman is man's destruction," or "Woman, from the beginning, has been man's ruin."[107] However, in his Variorum-edition gloss, Pearsall asserts that translating *in principio* at this literal level is quite "mistaken"[108] because it is entirely inappropriate to connect the abstract noun *mulier* with the proper noun *Eva*.

Pearsall's "literary-critical" definition of *mulier* in this context is surprisingly similar to the "logical" position concerning the meaning of *mulier* in a similar context taken by medieval philosophers such as Abelard, John of Salisbury, and William of Sherwood. In his *Introduction to Logic,* Sherwood analyzes the semantic difficulties embedded in *Mulier que damnavit salvavit.* This proposition, Sherwood explains, appears to enjoy two distinctly different meanings: "A woman who has damned us has saved us," or, "Woman, who has damned us, has saved us." The first, Sherwood eventually concludes, cannot be valid, for if one replaces *Mulier* with a woman's proper name, one arrives at a logical cul-de-sac, for it is impossible that one and the same woman has both damned us and saved us. Therefore the only valid reading is the second. Sherwood supports his judgment by explaining that the relative pronoun *que* "supposit[s] simply in the third mode."[109] What Sherwood means by this statement had already been clarified by several of his predecessors. John of Salisbury, in his earlier analysis of the same proposition, explains: "these relative expressions should not be conceived as descending to the specific and pointing out some particular person or thing, but rather that they should be understood as remaining general."[110] And Abelard concurs, reasoning that when we say "'woman, who has damned us, has also saved us', [we are speaking] not of one and the same person but of the nature of the female sex . . . for Eve damned us and Mary saved us."[111]

Now even while concentrating on the role of the relative pronoun *que,* what these philosophers are primarily concerned with is an area of logical studies called levels of supposition. Latin, a language without definite articles, indefinite articles, and various demonstrative adjectives, is more frugal than is English in the assistance it provides readers in determining, for example, whether in a certain context the word *homo* is meant to mean "a man," "this man," "mankind," the word "man," "man" as a figure of speech, or something else. To account for these complexities, medieval logicians discriminated among at least six levels of supposition, as Paul Vincent Spade has illustrated in the following "ladder of descent" for the noun "man" (*homo*):

(1) The "improper" (figural) level of supposition: "After six moves the Russian chess player was a man down."

(2) The "material" level of supposition: "Man is a monosyllable."

(3) The "discrete" level of supposition: "That man is my brother."

(4) The "simple" level of supposition: "Man is a species."

(5) The "determinate" level of supposition: "A man is at the door."

(6) The "merely confused" level of supposition: "Every *masseur* is a man."[112]

With the nominative *homo* serving as Spade's key word, and the nominative *mulier* serving as Chaucer's key word, it is clear that the appropriate level of supposition for each term needs to be determined in large part by its syntactical context. But, of course, syntax does not always render the word's level of significance self-evident. And even if the "right answer" for most readers must of necessity accord with "common sense" as well as theological dogma, the difficulties concerning the descent from simple supposition ("woman") to discrete supposition ("that woman") continues to this very day to be a complex issue addressed at length in logical textbooks.

Now as we progress logically in our translation exercise from *mulier* to *hominis* and from *hominis* to *confusio*, it is apparent that Chaunte-cleer's apothegm takes on an even more complicated scholastic cast. Joseph Dane, in a brief essay on the meaning of *Mulier est hominis confusio*, argues that educated medieval readers would recognize the word *confusio* as an important scholarly term alluding to a special logico-linguistic category: *confusio* here is in fact a scholastic pun because "[b]y the late fourteenth century, the words *confusio* and *confuse* were technical terms referring to referential ambiguities of language" (see the "merely confused" level of supposition in Spade's list above).[113] Futhermore, not only are these referential ambiguities made manifest in the several possible semantic meanings of *mulier* and *homo* (that is, their various levels of supposition), but their ambiguities of signification are intensified by the variety of possible syntactic relationships between the two terms. Dane explains:

> In one sense, the relation between the words *mulier* and *homo* are similar to the relation between the words Socrates and *homo*. *Mulier* refers to a woman, but that particular woman confusedly conceived (as in the case of Socrates) is a man (a part of humanity). In this case, *mulier* is the more specific term, *homo* the more general term (in logical terminology, the difference is between "inferior" and "superior" terms). To say *mulier est homo* is simply to predicate the general of the specific (*homo est mulieris confusio*).
>
> But because of the "confused" senses of the word *homo*, which can signify the species humankind as well as masculine individuals, *mulier* can signify the same individuals as *homo* (in the same way that the particular woman, confusedly considered, is a man). What is signified by the word *mulier* is a *confusio* of the word *homo* (*mulier est hominis confusio*).[114]

Although Dane's technical nomenclature is not identical to Spade's suppositional descent, his classification of "superior," "inferior," "general," "specific," and "confused" levels of signification is in general, logical alignment with Spade's semantic categories. Thus as a self-reflexive scholarly pun, the *confusio* effected here by Chaucer's use of *confusio* may be seen as epitomizing the "referential ambiguities" of the entirety of Chauntecleer's Latin formulation. And, as we have noted earlier, the grammatical difficulties created by these several *confusiones* are precisely the kind that schoolboys were expected to uncover by reading texts through the lens of the trivium arts. Thus, it is apparent that the more carefully we read this innocent-looking Latin tag, the more resistant it proves to be to any kind of truly "accurate" translation.

So where, then, are these *confusiones* finally taking us? So far we have been bouncing back and forth between Steiner's two central levels of "hermeneutic motion." That is, as translators we have been acting out our own forms of aggression, "the incursion of the translator's cognitive faculties into the field of the other text in order to encircle, decipher and extract what is there and is considered to be of value." And we have also been sensing the paralyzing counter-effects of incorporation, whereby "the target text proves to be so powerful that it infects the translating text, the inhaled voice in various ways choking or colonizing the interpreting voice." Of course what we need to discover is whether it is possible to arrive at a site of restitution, where "a textual dialectic is established," and where we might finally succeed in constructing "new formats of significance" in "the space between the two texts." But even if we succeed in reaching this site, is it not likely that these "new formats of significance" will in turn catalyze a further dialectics of aggression and counter-aggression?

At this point it might be tempting to protract matters even further by turning to several postmodern translation theorists who argue in various ways that there is no difference between a good translation and a bad translation because no text in one language can be reproduced by another text in another language. Translation, in short, is an impossibility. But I do not intend to take this next theoretical step because Chaucer's preference, I infer, is that his readers engage in these "textual dialectics" after their own fashion. As I have been arguing, the readerly experience of engaging in this kind of intertextual dialectics is a salient effect of Chaucer's overall parodic curriculum. In his parody of literary *imitatio,* as we have just observed, Chaucer invites his readers to "bounce" at many different interpretative angles between the authoritative original and its epigone. Likewise, in his parody of *ironia,* as we shall see next, he prefers that his readers career about inside the theoretical space between the surface utterance and its implied counter-meanings. And here, in his parody of *translatio,* we are similarly encouraged to forestall interpretative closure in order to think constructively about the disseminal nature of language and its resistance to any kind of adequate interpretation/translation.

Yet there is at least one additional problematic in the act of translation that Chaucer brings to the fore, and that involves the cultural values of translation's target audience. Chaucer's audience was surely heterogeneous, including misogynistic and nonmisogynistic members, yet they belonged to a literary culture that tended to view any text awaiting translation as somehow similar to a woman in need of male intervention. As Carolyn Dinshaw has shown extensively in *Chaucer's Sexual Poetics,* medieval readers understood that every act of textual translation "has the potential for revealing the truth and wholeness, the plenitude of the female body, but it also has a potential for turning away from, obliterating, that body; for dissembling and substituting; for estranging truth and fragmenting that wholeness."[115] Thus it is scarcely an accident that Chaucer should have juxtaposed contrary definitions of the nature of woman as grounds for interrogating the problematics of translation itself. That the fox had invited Chauntecleer's mother, as well as his father, to a fateful final dinner is a back story that we readers tend to forget. However, it is impossible to forget that Pertelote is the sole auditor of Chauntecleer's scholarly exercise. Furthermore, as his sister, paramour, and wife, she obviously embodies the semantic field of *mulier* at a most "discrete" level of supposition. Yet Chauntecleer's act of translation ultimately has the effect of "turning from, obliterating" that female embodiment. In fact, not only is Pertelote the victim of what Dinshaw calls translation's potential for dissembling, substituting, estrangement, and fragmentation, from this point onward in the narrative she appears to lose all individual agency, for she utters not a word for the rest of the tale. Whether or not it serves as an objective correlative of translation itself, her muteness is telling. In another literary environment, she might have been able to speak about this obliteration, perhaps by agreeing with those who have suggested every act of translation is ultimately a form of treason.[116] In Chaucer's fable, however, what gets lost in translation is the semantic valence and textual plenitude of the female body—*mulier*, "Womman," and Pertelote. Whether or not Chaucer is knowingly parodying this process of erasure, thereby enjoining his readers to recover that loss and restore that plenitude by revealing (or deconstructing) the Latin text's original "truth" and "wholeness," is one more tricky question concerning the imperfect, indeed impossible, art of translation.

THE RISKY BUSINESS OF IRONY

The central argument I wish to make in this final section is a straightforward one. As careful critics of Chaucer we need to define as precisely as possible the terms we use when attempting to determine the author's intent because that intent is often conveyed through the "silent" intonations of his fictive voice. Accordingly, the major poetic strategy I wish to examine is irony, which is also, by common agreement, Chaucer's signa-ture rhetorical trope.[117] Relying on a few selected studies of irony, most notably Linda Hutcheon's *Irony's Edge* and Claire Colebrook's *Irony,* I hope to demonstrate that calibrating the inner workings of Chaucer's ironies is a necessary, but always risky, business.[118] Setting aside attendant literary phenomena such as Chaucer's dramatic ironies, cosmic ironies, and ironies of fate, I want to focus on Chaucer's verbal and structural iro-nies as pragmatic literary and social performances. That is, rather than a semantic collocation that may be adequately decoded in formal isola-tion, the meaning of an ironic passage in a piece of Chaucer's literature is constructed by a community that, for all its academic credentials, is far from perfectly homogenous. Irony, Mary Louise Pratt tellingly writes, does not so much create "amiable communities" as it comes into being inside "contact zones . . . where cultures meet, clash, grapple with each other, often in contexts of highly asymmetrical relations of power."[119]

The vast industry of irony studies has moved well beyond the trope's most basic definition: irony is a way of saying one thing but meaning something else, so that its literal level of signification is replaced by an unspoken but implicit counter-signified. A more advanced approach rec-ognizes that irony's dynamics are rarely purely oppositional, and that its surface-level assertion is never entirely erased by its ironic intent. Rather, in the space between as well as containing the signifying statement and its signified meaning, there is an oscillating exchange among contradic-tory meanings (some critics have called it a kind of semiotic "bouncing," or dance). There is always a temptation to domesticate, control, and natu-ralize these dancing particles of meaning: "We reduce the strange or in-congruous . . . with which we disagree," Jonathan Culler has written, "by calling them ironic and making them confirm rather than abuse our ex-pectations."[120] On the other hand, Culler continues, irony can be used to "avoid premature closure . . . to give the benefit of the doubt by allowing [a text] to contain whatever doubts come to mind."[121] One way prema-ture closure may be averted is by our acknowledging that irony's ironic intent is determined by the receiver at least as much as it is by its trans-mitter. A fairly homogenous community thus appears to be a necessary prerequisite in order that an ironic message be successfully conveyed, but whether that homogenous community is seen as amiable and inclusive,

or elitist and exclusionary, depends on the local situation and the participants, both of which may vary, sometimes radically, over space and time.

As Linda Hutcheon's V-formation diagram (figure 2.2) of the multiple functions and manifestations of irony illustrates, irony is a complex and pluriform verbal and social behavior. From one set of "liberal"
perspectives, an ironic utterance can be seen as positively ambiguous,
lighthearted, self-deprecating, or corrective. However, from another set
of "conservative" perspectives, it can be seen as negatively ambiguous,
irresponsible, arrogant, or destructive. What does it mean if irony is so
protean and so multivalent that it can invoke such varied responses? Or
is the term "irony" itself entirely inadequate for the phenomena we are
discussing? Without chasing after elusive answers to these questions, I
want to point out that if Chaucerians were asked to stick a pin into one
position on Hutcheon's V-formation figure that most accurately defines
"Chaucerian irony," the range of choices would be extensive. And even if
each of us were provided three choices, the resulting pattern of pins would
range all over the ironic map. In the reception and discussion of papers
delivered in Chaucer conferences over the years, it is quite apparent that
each of us is actually "hearing" Chaucer's tone of ironic intent inside a
unique set of headphones. And yet Chaucerian irony is a critical term that
Chaucerians cannot live without.

As I insist throughout this study, parody is just as important to hearing Chaucer's distinctive literary voice as is irony. Since I wish to argue
shortly that Chaucer in *The Nun's Priest's Tale* parodies his own ironies,
it is important to recall that parody often deploys irony for its own purposes, but normally as a device for rather than as an object of parodic
scrutiny. Like irony, as we have noted, parody operates at two levels: a primary, surface foreground; and a secondary, implied background. Using
ironic inversion and exaggeration, parody is a corrective and instructive
form of artistic imitation, although not necessarily or always at the expense of the parodied text. Differing from quotation and allusion (and
from ambiguity, for that matter) parody almost always has an "edge": it
insists on maintaining an ironic distance from its target text. But while
literary parody's immediate target is typically another work of art, the
more general object of parodic scrutiny may be understood as another
form of coded discourse, another cultural model, another way of seeing

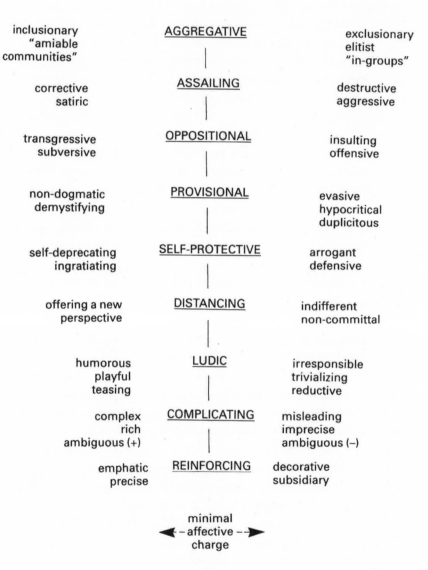

Figure 2.2. The Functions of Irony[122]

the world. Especially in this regard, parody needs to be distinguished from satire. Unlike parody, satire is social in its focus and ameliorative in its intention. Yet the two genres are often fused: satire frequently uses parodic strategies for either expository or aggressive purposes. What keeps the two genres separate is not so much their perspective on human behavior and aesthetic taste, but rather on what is being made into a target. While parody is primarily an intertextual discourse, satire is world-directed, holding up to ridicule the vices and follies of humankind. Both parody and satire are thus at ease with irony's ability to create new but unspoken levels of meaning, but these ironic meanings, we need to emphasize, are forever in danger of misfiring, of not being "properly" received or heard.

There are innumerable moments in Chaucer's texts that dramatize the communicative hazards of irony. *The Merchant's Tale* opens with a protracted encomium to the paradisiacal joys of marriage: "Mariage is a ful greet sacrement. / He which that hath no wif, I holde hym shent" (IV.1319–20). Denominated by most critics a mock-encomium, the Merchant's caustic praise is laced with such bitterness that it would appear nearly impossible to read it straight—yet, very tellingly, some critics have done just that. In *The Franklin's Tale,* after first rejecting Aurelius's adulterous suit in words that could hardly be more explicit, Dorigen, speaking now (as the narrator explains) "in pley" (V.988), sets him the impossible task of removing every stone from the coast of Brittany before she agrees to be his true love; strangely, over time both Aurelius and Dorigen appear to forget the original intent of these playful words, and their de-ironized rereading of their pseudo-contract lands them in a quite problematic situation. A third celebrated instance is the Pardoner's profession to his pilgrim auditors after he has confessed the depths of his own hypocrisy: "I wol yow nat deceyve" (VI.918). Whether this utterance is the effect of a momentary moral paroxysm; whether he means precisely the opposite of what his words say; or whether these words contain a complex confusion of contradictory meanings has been the subject of extensive critical inquiry.[123] The risky business of irony is thus something Chaucer is persistently intent on foregrounding in his poetry as a way of further educating his readers in one of the central elements of his craft. But what if Chaucer were to further ironize his literary ironies by according ironic utterances to a fictional figure whom he might well have supposed would be closely identified with himself? How, in other words, might Chaucer ever expect a reader to discriminate the sliver of ironic space between Chaucer's authorial ironies and the ironies of one of his characters who appears to be a simulacrum of his own person? This of course leads us directly to the Nun's Priest, a fictional figure who, as we have noted, appears nowhere in the *General Prologue* yet who has been commonly (but not universally) accepted as a near stand-in for the arch-poet himself.

It is the morning after Chauntecleer's bad dream, and Russell the fox, having slunk betimes into the chickenyard, is finagling to persuade our hero to close his eyes and sing like his father. At this moment of anxious suspense, the narrator interrupts his narrative with a heated *exclamatio*, warning all "lordes" of the danger of false flatterers:

> Allas, ye lordes, many a fals flatour
> Is in youre courtes, and many a losengeour,
> That plesen yow wel moore, by my feith,
> Than he that soothfastnesse unto yow seith.
> Redeth Ecclesiaste of flaterye;
> Beth war, ye lordes, of hir trecherye.
>   (VII.3325–30)

In a way that relates ultimately to the problematics of irony, a few critics have attempted to identify the target audience of these words. Paull Baum suggests that "ye lordes" indicates the tale was originally written for the entertainment of a clerical audience;[124] Edwin Howard reads it as Chaucer's covert warning to Richard II that "his best friends were a gang of flattering traitors";[125] Baugh, more generally, says "it seems like a rhetorical aside to those to whom it might apply."[126] In other words, these readers would prefer to read the narrator's cautionary words as a fairly "straight" piece of unironic advice. But if we align the passage's obvious rhetorical surpluses alongside the passage's obvious lack of an immediate audience of "lordes" alongside the passage's obvious mock-tragic incommensurabilities between barnyard and court, we surely will find ourselves situating its ethos on the ironic/parodic side of Hutcheon's Venn diagram. That is, we may remain uncertain about how the passage works *parodi-*

cally. We know (with the help of editors) that Chaucer had himself translated a cautionary address concerning courtly hypocrisy in *The Romaunt
of the Rose* (lines 1050–70), but the Nun's Priest's allusion keeps a re-
spectful distance from this far-in-the-background text. It is possible that
the passage may be lightheartedly critiquing other political tracts on the
art of proper governance, but then again it may not. And the passage appears to go nowhere close to sending up Ecclesiastes on "flaterye." Nevertheless, almost all readers in the community of Chaucer scholars would
agree that this piece of concentratedly comic poetry is indubitably *ironic:*
it is an ironic display of high rhetoric running amok, its double-voiced
charge generated by its success in managing to be both "good" and "bad"
poetry at once. Whatever "sentence" it intends to convey is not contained
by the surface utterance (which we cannot read "straight"), but rather
remains implicitly embedded at a "silent" level of communication. Thus
this passage is a fairly uncomplicated example of what Chaucerians mean
by Chaucerian irony—even though the *purpose* of that irony is, in this
instance, yet to be defined.

By contrast, my centerpiece case study is a passage that has prompted
a spectrum of contradictory and confusing readings because, I believe,
this passage is a self-reflexive advertisement of irony's powers, complexities, and risks. It is, in other words, a *parodic* display of irony that also employs irony in its analytic critique. Additionally, whether intentionally or
not, it spotlights both poet and reader as agents unable to control the
slipperiness of irony's "sentential" free-play.

A few moments before the "Allas, ye lordes" passage, and right after
an inconclusive philosophical foray into the theological mysteries of predestination, free will, simple necessity, and conditional necessity, the narrator decides to return to his tale and to matters at hand:

> I wol nat han to do of swich mateere;
> My tale is of a cok, as ye may heere,
> That tok his conseil of his wyf, with sorwe,
> To walken in the yerd upon that morwe
> That he hadde met that dreem that I yow tolde.
> Wommennes conseils been ful ofte colde;

Wommannes conseil broghte us first to wo
And made Adam fro Paradys to go,
Ther as he was ful myrie and wel at ese.
But for I noot to whom it myghte displese,
If I conseil of wommen wolde blame,
Passe over, for I seyde it in my game.
Rede auctours, where they trete of swich mateere,
And what they seyn of wommen ye may heere.
Thise been the cokkes wordes, and nat myne;
I kan noon harm of no womman divyne.

                                (VII.3251–66)

In their citations of this well-known passage, scholars tend to skip the first six lines at the beginning of the quotation provided above, beginning instead with line 4446: "Wommennes conseils been ful ofte colde; / Wommannes conseil broghte us first to wo," and ending with the disclaimer, "I kan noon harm of no womman divyne." Their reason for doing so, it would seem, is to punch up the force of these "opening" words—words that appear to reveal quite directly the speaker's mild, or not-so-mild, misogynistic persuasions. To locate the etiology of these sentiments, some critics inclined toward fictive biography have confected backstory scenarios of the Nun's Priest's personal difficulties with his own troubled masculinity as well as his subaltern relationship to the prioress and her nuns.[127] Critics of another persuasion have heard the author's own voice speaking in these lines, and so have attributed these antifeminist sentiments to Chaucer himself, although usually in a milder and more tolerant vein.[128] But in a tale so charged with rhetorical excess, intellectual parody, and metapoetic free play, how can we be absolutely certain that these solemn lines warning against the counsel of women do not contain some small measure, or some great measure, of irony?

At least one answer to this question is already embedded in the narrator's proclivity towards self-defense. Realizing that his words may prove displeasing to some of his listeners, the narrator explains in line 4452 that he shouldn't be taken seriously: instead, "I seyde it in my game." It is of course very tempting, as well as politically very correct, not to believe him. Or, if we were to give him some benefit of the doubt, we could say that a failed attempt at irony can never be set right. An oft-cited story in irony criticism concerns the mixed reception of Randy Newman's song, "Short People Got No Reason to Live." To those who felt Newman was insensitively mocking the vertically challenged, Newman belatedly explained he was being ironic, choosing a ridiculous object of scorn to highlight the ridiculousness of all kinds of prejudice, be it directed against women, blacks, Jews, or any other minority group.[129] Newman made few new converts by retroactively explicating his ironic intent. Unless here in *The Nun's Priest's Tale* the "Oh-my-God-of-course-I-wasn't-serious" trope is being *parodied,* the taint of sexual chauvinism has not been erased. And even if it is being parodied, its once imagined presence may linger indefinitely.

Two other pieces of the Nun's Priest's declamation can be used to provide more potential evidence of his gender politics. Right after making his two-line assessment of women's cold counsel, the narrator turns to scripture for further justification: a woman's counsel "made Adam fro Paradys to go, / Ther as he was ful myrie and wel at ese." And, later, after providing his "I-was-just-joking" excuse, he gestures again, rather generally, in the direction of the authorities: "Rede auctours . . . And what they seyn of wommen ye may heere." These two maneuvers can be read straight—as they almost always are. Yet there is a possibility that they could be (even should be) read awry. That is, if we were to consider the extraordinary range of patristic and medieval theological, dramatic, and narrative interpretations of the degrees and qualities of culpability shared by Adam and Eve, the narrator's according one hundred percent of the blame to Eve for depriving her poor husband of his merriness and ease is either a sign of an extremely chauvinistic mentality, or else it might be the symptom of some kind of irony at work. Similarly, the narrator's closing advice that we turn to "auctours" to see what they have to say about the matter is surely somewhat troubling in its casual unspecificity. Overgeneralization of scope and vagueness of referent are in fact heuristic maneuvers Chaucer uses throughout his career (as Ida Gordon's careful study of *Troilus and Criseyde* brilliantly illustrates).[130] Thus, it may be more than a possibility that several of the lines in this complex rhetorical piece are ironic, and their seemingly disparate ironies may in fact be part of some larger artistic design that is parodic—and perhaps even satiric—in intent.

At any rate, an irony-free reading of this passage certainly hits very rough going near the end, when the narrator provides his penultimate piece of self-defense: suddenly, and very belatedly, he audaciously asserts, "Thise ben the cokkes wordes and nat myne." In his Variorum edition, Pearsall's note to this line is surprisingly brief: "[T]his is a well-established technique of narration in the novel."[131] But, surely, this one-line zinger is scandalous. At the eleventh hour to pawn your own dubious sentiments off onto a fictional character—a chicken no less—is an outrageous violation of all the principles of reliable narration and of all the expectations of any trusting reader. And then the Nun's Priest concludes his authorial aside with one more doozy: "I kan noon harme of no womman divyne." Perhaps the most ambiguous line in all of Chaucer, this is a minefield of intentional indeterminacy. As we have already noted, Besserman dedicates an entire article to this one line, and Pearsall in his Variorum commentary grudgingly agrees that "the confusion here between ambiguity . . . and the difficulty that a modern reader has in deciding what Chaucer means . . . is inextricable."[132] What Pearsall calls inextricable confusion for the modern reader I prefer to call the risky business of irony. I have left to the end of this close-reading exercise the first piece of evidence that the entire passage needs to be read inside the ethos of irony, and, furthermore, that the entire passage needs to be reread inside the ethos of parody. The most telling signal that the Nun's Priest is a *knowingly* unreliable narrator, and thus a master of irony, is the assertion that gets him going: the reason that Chauntecleer's life is now in peril, he claims, is that he accepted his wife's false counsel: he "tok his conseil of his wyf, with sorwe." But, as any careful reader of the fable knows, in point of literary fact Chauntecleer did precisely the opposite. He did *not* accept his wife's advice, which was: Ignore your dream, dear heart, and take a heap of laxatives. Instead, he insisted on crediting the prophetic power of his dream, warning of future danger to his life: "I shal han of this avisioun / Adversitee . . . / I ne telle of laxatyves no stoor" (VII.3152–54). And *then* he ignores his *own* counsel concerning the prophetic power of dreams.

So, where does all of this leave us? I believe there are several ways that Chaucer's test case in the risky business of irony may be read. Our first option is to read it at a certain characterological level: the Nun's Priest is mildly confused about women but otherwise a first-rate storyteller. Variations of this reading tend to dominate Chaucer criticism. A second option is to read the passage as a knowing display of highly aggressive irony, leaving the reader destitute of any certitude: one extreme variation of this position, as I have noted earlier, is embraced by Anne Payne who, out of frustration, calls the Nun's Priest "the voice of the devil" and "the proverbial father of lies."[133] A third option is to read the passage as a parodic intensification and exploration of the risky business of irony itself. The third reading is the one I endorse. But my articulation of this third way of reading to this point is far from adequate. This is because Chaucer, as he does throughout *The Nun's Priest's Tale,* is here inviting us not only to interpret the exercise presently under scrutiny, but, more importantly, to critique and refine our strategies of interpretation even as we use them. In other words, so far I find my own "hermeneutics of irony" insufficiently attentive to the heuristic opportunities that this parody makes available. In his classic study *A Rhetoric of Irony,* Wayne Booth outlines five kinds of markers that serve readers as "clues" to the "reconstruction" of ironic intention and ironic meaning in written texts:

(1) Straightforward hints or warnings presented in the authorial voice (such as titles, epigraphs, and direct statements)

(2) Violations of shared knowledge (deliberate errors of fact, judgment)

(3) Contradictions within the work ("internal cancellations")

(4) Clashes of style

(5) Conflicts of belief (between our own and that which we might suspect the author is holding)[134]

At least four of these five indicators I have just employed in my demonstration of the ironies at work in the Nun's Priest's "Wommannes conseil" passage. These are: (2) violations of shared knowledge (Eve, for example, is *not* one hundred percent responsible for Adam's fall from grace);

(3) contradictions within the work (Chauntecleer in fact did *not* choose to take his wife's advice); (4) clashes of style (an author *cannot* retroactively blame one of his characters for his own off-color "misspeakings"; and (5) conflicts of belief (Chaucer does *not*—we suspect—share the misogynistic persuasions the narrator professes and then retracts). The first of Booth's ironic "clues" is the only one I have not put to work: (1) direct statements from the author himself. Thus the "hermeneutics of irony" I have been employing appears to be standard critical procedure.

And that's the problem. As Stanley Fish persistently argues in his extensive critique of the central tenets of Booth's book, there are interior contradictions within our habit of pointing to such markers as proof of the presence of irony in a text. "[I]t is obvious," writes Fish, "that [such 'clues'] represent an attempt by Booth to set limits on the operation of irony, so that its undermining of overt or literal meanings will have a fixed and specifiable shape, but unfortunately, they will not do as marks that *signal* the presence of irony (stable or otherwise), because it is precisely *their* presence that is in dispute when there is a debate as to whether or not a particular work is ironic."[135] In other words, irony's presence in a text is a presence of our own making. "Irony," Fish continues, "is neither the property of works, nor the creation of an unfettered imagination, but a way of reading, an interpretive strategy that produces the object of its attention, an object that will be perspicuous to those who share or have been persuaded to share the same strategy. [Accordingly,] *if irony is a way of reading, so is literalness;* neither way is prior to the other, in the sense of being a mode of calculation rather than interpretation; both are interpretive ways, which are set in motion by cues and considerations that are themselves in place as a consequence of an interpretive act."[136]

What I wish to propose, then, is that in his parodic treatment of these and many other ironic "cues" Chaucer is in fact holding up to scrutiny our own agency as encoders and decoders of any literary text. He is, if you will, bouncing Booth's formalist approach off against Fish's deconstructive approach because, in our own reading habits, we actually do the same: we switch back and forth between a literal reading and an ironic reading until we finally make a choice, but even after that willful choice is made, neither the literal meaning nor the ironic meaning cancels the other out. Rather, in the space between as well as in the space containing the surface text and the ironic subtext there is an oscillating exchange of potential signifieds—call it a scene of "exegetical instability," or "semiotic bouncing," or a giddy descent into a *mise-en-abîme.* And while there is always a temptation to domesticate and control these dancing and colliding particles of meaning, I suggest that Chaucer's parodic choreographies invite us to resist premature critical closure because, as a dramatic illustration of linguistic dissemination, verbal irony is beyond our interpretative control. And it is also, ironically, beyond the interpretative control of its own author.

Thus, in addition to providing a rereading of a well-known passage in *The Nun's Priest's Tale,* my goal in this final section has been to call attention to what we are all up to when we read Chaucer. Verbal irony, as several modern studies have revealed, will inevitably complexify, but it can never disambiguate. Because of irony's resistance to interpretative certitude, it is difficult, if not impossible, to treat irony separately from its literary circumstances and its social conditions. If a homogeneous community appears essential for the successful transmission of irony, one would hope that Chaucerians might agree on the nature and quality of what we continue to call Chaucerian irony. It is, after all, considered to be unique to him. But that consensus is not ever likely to be reached. Even so, as one member of that community, I want to conclude this chapter's final case study by asserting that in his "Wommannes conseil" passage Chaucer appears to be sensitively attuned to the many problems of irony, including the meaning-making role performed by that heterogenous and ever-changing community who are his readers. But then I also want to assert that one way Chaucer addresses these matters is simply by flexing his metapoetic muscles: *he* is the parodist in charge.

Like parody, irony has a way of running amok, of undoing the author's intent as well as of exposing the author's artistic and ethical limits. In an excellent article subtitled "Tendentious Jokes in the *Nun's Priest's Tale,*" James Goldstein writes that "Freud's important recognition that jokes can mask hostile and aggressive tendencies suggests that when women and peasants are the butt of Chaucer's jokes, not all the humor must be taken innocently."[137] I agree. As we have seen, in Chaucer's parodic examination of the problematics of translation he constructs a fairly homogeneous community of masculinist readers for whom woman is the already pre-defined other. And the very same abstraction plays a similar role in the Nun's Priest's "Wommannes conseil" passage, a set of pronouncements that scarcely displays "a zero degree of aggressivity" toward one of their parodistic "texts," which is the axiomatic principle of woman's devious nature. Once uttered, the narrator's so-called "ironic" deprecations cannot be decontaminated through irony's playful spirit or by self-parodic retractions of ill intent. In fact, there is no way Chaucer's readers can ever be certain that Chaucer himself did not *mean* these words to be taken straight. As I have already noted, a long-standing assumption in *Canterbury Tales* studies is that discretely different "authorial" voices succeed in expressing themselves through the very same words of a text. However, as we shall see later in this book, prizing apart the voice of a fallible narrator from the voice of an infallible poet is one of those maneuvers (to re-quote Fish) "set in motion by cues and considerations that are themselves in place as a consequence of an interpretive act." Insisting on preserving Chaucer's good name, we may be discovering ironic tropes in places where they were never intended, which is one more demonstration that reading irony is always a risky business.[138]

In a chapter that opened with the early years of a poet's education, that has explored the structure and strategies of Menippean parody, and that concludes with case-study examinations of three skills essential to the poet's craft, we have been tracing certain foundational elements that contributed to Chaucer's evolution into an achieved literary artist. It is appropriate therefore to bring to a close this extensive critical survey by having concentrated on Chaucer's signature trope, which is irony. There is no disagreement that irony is an extremely complex verbal phenomenon, and that Chaucer's mastery of its nuances is superb, and perhaps unique. As a consummate practitioner of irony, Chaucer appears throughout *The Nun's Priest's Tale* to be both self-effacing yet in absolute control, and this is fitting for, as Geoffrey Hartmann notes, irony is "language giving the lie to itself yet still relishing its power."[139] There is no doubt that in parodying his own ironies Chaucer is also reveling in irony's remarkable power. And so when the Nun's Priest audaciously professes, "Thise ben the cokkes wordes and nat myne," Chaucer surely must expect his reader to be flab-bergasted: why is my author not playing by the rules? But he might also be hoping that the reader is able to hear a reassuring response embedded somewhere in the ironic utterance itself. Not to worry, dear reader: cer-tain rules I'll just make up as I go along and you'll have to keep up as best you can, because that's part of the agenda of my didascalic fable—my grammar school primer, my Menippean parody, my personal *ars poetica.*

THREE

Close Reading: Beginnings and Endings

We clearly know what it means to begin; then
why question our certainty by reminding ourselves
that in the realm of thought, beginning is not really a beginner's game.

—EDWARD SAID

Every limit is a beginning as well as an ending.

—GEORGE ELIOT

How to begin? Indeed, how does one know what a proper beginning is? The nearly universal anxiety given voice in these and related questions carries a special set of burdens for the creators of fiction in a traditional Christian culture. Living inside the grand narrative of salvation history at a point far removed from the Alpha and Omega, how can one settle upon any moment that pretends to be an ultimate terminus, an original beginning? And how in turn can this beginning pretend to be the initiator of an event that develops into a pattern so complete that its *finale* is as definitive an end-all as the beginning from which it sprang? Because Christ the Word's act of creation *in principio* hovers over every human artifice, medieval writers were particularly aware of the hubristic resonance of their opening words. What is immediately problematic is that such creators have no direct experience of the termini of which their own artistic boundaries are but attenuated variants. Rather, each author is positioned in a middle whose fictional representations would seem to make sense only if his or her beginnings and endings are grounded in some extrafictional reality. As Frank Kermode has famously remarked, "Men, like poets, rush 'into the middest,' *in medias res,* when they are born; they also die *in mediis rebus,* and to make sense of their span they need fictive concords with origins and ends, such as give meaning to lives and to poems."[1]

One classic way of addressing the urgency of beginnings is to forestall the entire issue. Horace's advice in the *Ars Poetica* was never to begin *abo ovo* (referring to the double-yoked egg of Leda, which, producing Helen and Clytemnestra, initiated the history of Troy); a poet should rather begin, as did Homer in the *Iliad,* "in the middle of the thing," *in medias res.* With a few notable exceptions such as Milton's *Paradise Lost,* Horace's preference for the Homeric and Virgilian model has exerted only a minor influence in the composition of Western fiction. Medieval English writers, for example, never saw fit to open their narratives *in medias res.*[2] Yet the model of epic beginnings remained well known throughout the later Middle Ages because a variety of ways of arranging the parts of a narrative were studied and imitated in the standard school curricula. One of the most influential preceptive grammars in the late Middle Ages, Geoffrey of Vinsauf's *Poetria Nova,* a self-conscious modernization of Horace's *Poetria Antiqua,* both amplifies and "medievalizes" Horace's classical definitions of the artfully constructed narrative. Geoffrey argues that there are two excellent ways of rearranging the sequence of narrative events. The poet can begin either at the end or at the middle of his material:

> Let that part of the material which is first in the order of nature wait outside the gates of the work. Let the end, as a worthy precursor, be first to enter and take up its place in advance, as a guest of more honourable rank, or even as master. Nature has placed the end last in order, but art respectfully defers to it, leads it from its humble position and accords it the place of honour.

The place of honour at the beginning of a work does not reserve its lustre for the end of the material only; rather, two parts share the glory: the end of the material and the middle. Art draws from either of these a graceful beginning.[3]

In the architectonics of literary construction there are thus two narrative beginnings that "share the glory": the end of the original "material" and the middle. But Geoffrey goes on to explain that there are two additional, and "still more brilliant," ways of beginning a narrative. One may begin either with a proverb or an *exemplum:*

If a still more brilliant beginning is desired (while leaving the sequence of the material unchanged) make use of a proverb, ensuring that it may not sink to a purely specific relevance, but raise its head high to some general truth. . . .

No less appropriately do exempla occupy a position at the beginning of a work. The same quality, indeed, shines forth from exempla and proverbs, and the distinction conferred by the two is of equal value.[4]

While honoring the classical ideal of beginning a poetic narrative elsewhere than at its "original" beginning, Geoffrey reveals himself a thoroughly medieval aesthetician when declaring his own preference for beginning with a moral exhortation, either in the form of proverb or *exemplum*. In thus privileging *sententia* over *mythos*, Geoffrey is suggesting that all narratives, no matter how ornate their use of rhetorical figures, are essentially a form of didactic art illustrating useful general principles. The beginning proverb or *exemplum* clearly signalizes the narrative principle that follows and thus initiates a way of reading appropriate to the work as a whole. Indeed, the introductory proverb or *exemplum* may be seen as the middle or the end of a work's *argumentum* in that it provides a distillation of the central point and final purpose to the narrative of which it is an integral part.[5]

In the first half of this chapter I intend to study in considerable detail the exemplary beginning of *The Nun's Priest's Tale*. I undertake this analysis in part because the *exemplum,* as Larry Scanlon has argued in his study of the genre, is the "narrative form [that] dominated later medieval culture, particularly in England."[6] *Exemplum,* Scanlon contends, is the "dominant narrative genre of the Chaucerian tradition": "Of its four most important works, the *Canterbury Tales,* the *Confessio Amantis,* the *Regement of Princes,* and the *Fall of Princes,* only the first is not [in its entirety] an exemplum collection," and yet "at least eight" of Chaucer's twenty-four tales "can be described as exempla or exemplum collections," and these eight include *The Nun's Priest's Tale.*[7] To scrutinize in detail one particular *exemplum* by Chaucer is thus to study the fundamental genre in what Scanlon calls the "Chaucerian tradition." But the more compelling reason I undertake an examination of the opening scene of *The Nun's Priest's Tale* is that Chaucer, while brilliantly in command of the *exemplum* form, is aware of the dangers of our reading every work of literature as if it were already processed into the *exemplum* format. In the way that it plays with the classical-medieval ideal of an exemplary, non–*ab ovo* beginning, the Nun's Priest's opening *exemplum* honors the aesthetic persuasions of Geoffrey of Vinsauf and of Horace before him. Yet at the same time, via the nuanced subtleties of parody, Chaucer's *exemplum* is playing with our expectations that the narrative we are reading is already and always designed in accord with some overarching argument or *sentence.*

In the second half of this chapter I turn to the ending of *The Nun's Priest's Tale,* which I contend is also an instructive parody: that is, it is a brilliantly successful mock-*moralitas.* As with his *exemplum,* this does not mean that Chaucer is criticizing the *moralitas* tradition per se. Rather, he is foregrounding the manner in which medieval readers had been trained to analyze a text as a literary artifact. Revitalizing his readers' memories of their education in the three liberal arts—grammar, rhetoric, and logic— Chaucer explores the "trivial" problematics of language itself. As his most explicit guide on how to interpret a piece of literature, Chaucer's *moralitas* also provides a deconstructive interrogation of the activity of literary criticism. Because the mock-*exemplum* and mock-*moralitas* of *The Nun's Priest's Tale* are both parodic interrogations of the time-honored discipline of close reading, I conclude the chapter by suggesting that close reading appears to be a mode of interpretation resistant to any interpretation that might be provided by close reading itself.

MOCK-*EXEMPLUM,* OR READING *AB OVO*

A povre wydwe, somdeel stape in age,
Was whilom dwellyng in a narwe cotage,
Biside a grove, stondynge in a dale.
This wydwe, of which I telle yow my tale,
Syn thilke day that she was last a wyf
In pacience ladde a ful symple lyf,
For litel was hir catel and hir rente.
By housbondrie of swich as God hire sente
She foond hirself and eek hir doghtren two.
Thre large sowes hadde she, and namo,
Three keen, and eek a sheep that highte Malle.
Ful sooty was hire bour and eek hir halle,
In which she eet ful many a sklendre meel.
Of poynaunt sauce hir neded never a deel.
No deyntee morsel passed thurgh hir throte;
Hir diete was accordant to hir cote.
Repleccioun ne made hire nevere sik;
Attempree diete was al hir phisik,
And exercise, and hertes suffisaunce.
The goute lette hire nothyng for to daunce,
N'apoplexie shente nat hir heed.
No wyn ne drank she, neither whit ne reed;
Hir bord was served moost with whit and blak—
Milk and broun breed, in which she foond no lak,
Seynd bacoun, and somtyme an ey or tweye,
For she was, as it were, a maner deye.

(VII.2821–46)

The standard critical approach in Chaucer studies has been to treat this opening portrait of the widow as a literary exercise containing a fairly readily extrapolated meaning. For several scholars the portrait is an impressively accurate depiction of the socioeconomic realities of fourteenth-century English subsistence farming, a specific form of marginal existence slightly below that of "half-virgater," where insufficient arable land required the cultivation of livestock to flesh out a modest living.[8] A second approach has focused upon the graphic artistry of the portrait, whose naturalism is to be appreciated in the tradition either of classical epic or of early Renaissance genre paintings.[9] A third and quite minor approach has chosen to allegorize the entire scene: for Donovan, Dahlberg, and Englehardt, the widow is a representative of the Church; for D. W. Robertson, the possibility the widow engaged in winnowing underscores the church's responsibility to separate the fruit from the chaff.[10] But the most popular critical take by far has been to emphasize the way this opening scene works as an *exemplum*. Claus Uhlig, for example, sees the widow as an emblem of "*moderatio* and temperance";[11] Charles Watkins feels the portrait underscores the virtues of good health, frugality, and fortitude;[12] John Block Friedman finds the image of the widow "a homiletic commonplace for expressing the eschewing of the life of vanity and the passions";[13] for William Strange she is the "model of man living in humility, free from Fortune";[14] D. W. Robertson sees her as a "model of chastity and sobriety";[15] and Trevor Whittock articulates the most widely shared sense of Chaucer's authorial intent when he asserts that the widow's portrait is "the moral ground of the poem."[16]

These four basic positions need not, of course, be mutually exclusive. One might argue that the portrait is sociologically realistic, that it is artistically part of a tradition of literary genre scenes, that tropologically the widow provides a positive moral example, and that allegorically her life may figure forth the ideals of the Christian church. But clearly these four approaches comprise two distinctly different forms of critical activity: the first two read the widow's portrait as a visual sign or icon, while the second two see the portrait as a form of moral injunction. What is interesting is that these two modes of critical response, the first emphasizing the scene's iconic power and the second emphasizing the portrait's strategies of moral exhortation, are in keeping with the two preeminent ways *exemplum* was originally understood by Aristotle and his Greek contemporaries. Aristotle viewed the *exemplum* as a powerful rhetorical device for producing belief in the general public about matters that do not avail themselves to absolute logical certainty: only enthymeme vied with *exemplum* in its effective conversion of the audience to the acceptance of a general truth. An equally important understanding of *exemplum* was its close association with the *eikon,* a pictorial form of representation, where certain details in an artistic medium (such as inlaid images in a tiled floor) foreground the argument of the scenic design.[17] Thus, the fact that Chaucer scholars have responded to the Nun's Priest's opening scene as either an iconic representation or a tropological injunction is one indication that the widow's portrait is positioned squarely within the European *exemplum* tradition.

A second indication that we are dealing with an *exemplum* in the opening scene of *The Nun's Priest's Tale* is through negative evidence: this passage has not been the site of very much critical controversy. In the Middle Ages and in the Renaissance, *exemplum* was regularly associated with and sometimes even equated with narration itself (one medieval gloss unifies the two activities as *exemplare narrare*).[18] And this association has of course continued into the twenty-first century, so that we often find it difficult to distinguish between an all-purpose narrative (such as the novel) and a narrative with the particular function of serving as a concrete instance of a general truth (a literary form which some critics choose to call the apologue).[19] John Lyons explains that one reason *exemplum* has rarely been an object of extended literary criticism is that, despite its seeming innocence, it is in fact a subtle threat to literary criticism itself: as a narrative with a self-inscribed explicating function, *exemplum* appears to have already used the tools and done the work of literary analysis itself. In *exempla,* the narrative's meaning is theoretically self-evident: all is apparently already made known. Standing halfway between metaphor (which purports to hide its meaning) and fable (which is "sufficiently obscure to awaken the decrypting of literary analysis"), *exempla* advertise themselves as "common property about which we can have few suspicions."[20] And so a second indication that we are here dealing with a carefully modeled *exemplum* is, paradoxically, the fact that the widow's portrait has inspired little in the way of critical controversy.

A third indication that the Nun's Priest's *exemplum* is centrally located within the *exemplum* tradition is also the first of many clear signs that Chaucer is actually providing a critique of the dangerous effects of that tradition upon its unwary readers. This generic self-consciousness is realized in the landscape itself. A depiction of a habitation in a dale beside a grove of trees, Chaucer's type-scene is a remarkably graphic literalization of the word *exemplum*, which in medieval Latin means "a clearing in the woods." According to John Lyons, the term's radical etymology helps illustrate *exemplum*'s relationship to the other forms of discourse that surround it:

> Only the clearing gives form or boundary to the woods. Only the woods permit the existence of a clearing. Likewise, example depends on the larger mass of history and experience, yet without the "clearings" provided by example that mass would be formless and difficult to integrate into any controlling systematic discourse.[21]

Lyons quite naturally assumes, in contrast to the woods, that a clearing is an orderly scene controlled by an enlightened principle of literary husbandry. However, as we are about to see, despite its attempts at domesticating decorum, the Nun's Priest's exemplary clearing is at least as unkempt as the forests that surround it.

Having just proposed a threefold defense of the widow's portrait as a quintessential *exemplum* (it is a rhetorical, iconic, and critically uncontroversial "clearing in the woods"), for the remainder of this section I wish to argue that an exemplary *exemplum* is precisely what it is not. Rather, it is a subtle parody—a mock-*exemplum*—designed to test our own reading of the *exemplum* genre while also testing our ways of reading other kinds of narrative literature. It is absolutely not a parody of the *exemplum* itself; rather, it is primarily a parody of the generic expectations of a readerly sensibility too intent on finding unitary truth in any piece of literature it reads. To see how Chaucer's parodic strategies work, we need first to consider a contrasting Chaucerian passage that is impressively faithful to the requisites of the *exemplum* genre. This passage is the beginning of the *secunda pars* of *The Clerk's Tale*:

> Noght fer fro thilke paleys honurable,
> Wher as this markys shoop his mariage,
> There stood a throop, of site delitable,
> In which that povre folk of that village
> Hadden hir beestes and hir herbergage,
> And of hire labour tooke hir sustenance,
> After that the erthe yaf hem habundance.

Amonges thise povre folk ther dwelte a man
Which that was holden povrest of hem alle;
But hye God somtyme senden kan
His grace into a litel oxes stalle;
Janicula men of that throop hym calle.
A doghter hadde he, fair ynogh to sighte,
And Griseldis this yonge mayden highte.

But for to speke of vertuous beautee,
Thanne was she oon the faireste under sonne;
For povreliche yfostered up was she,
No likerous lust was thurgh hire herte yronne.
Wel ofter of the welle than of the tonne
She drank, and for she wolde vertu plese,
She knew wel labour but noon ydel ese.

But though this mayde tendre were of age,
Yet in the brest of hire virginitee
Ther was enclosed rype and sad corage;
And in greet reverence and charitee
Hir olde povre fader fostred shee.
A fewe sheep, spynnynge, on feeld she kepte;
She wolde noght been ydel til she slepte.
　　　　　　　　　　　　　　　(IV.197–224)

This portrait is a masterpiece in the literary tradition of the medieval Christian *exemplum*. Here, the poverty of the humble town is nonjudgmentally counterpointed against the "honurable" but nearby palace of the marquis. Although Griselde's father Janicula is the poorest man in the village, his poverty is spiritually honorable, for, as the narrator reminds us, Christ's Incarnation occurred in a humble ox's stall. Griselde, although only moderately fair to physical sight, embraces all the beautiful inner virtues of a secular saint: virginity, love of her father, charity towards others, constant busyness, and a mature and steadfast heart. We are given just enough details to see that her virtues are consonant with the world she lives in: her "throop" is humble, yet of "site delitable";

the townspeople gain sustenance from their domestic animals (Griselde's "fewe sheep" are the only kind specified) and from their honest labor in the fields, but only to the degree that the earth is provident. Griselda's moral behavior is exemplary ("no likerous lust"); that she drinks more often of the well than of the tun (an instance of carefully controlled Christian *litotes*) offers another image of the pellucidity of her soul. Written in the plain style of low mimetic Christian pastoral, this carefully designed *sermo humilis* succeeds in no small part because the camera of narrative description is held consistently at a middle distance between the universal and the particular. As in the portrait of the idealized Plowman in the *General Prologue,* we are given just enough specificity to concretize the portrait's reigning spiritual and moral virtues.

What makes this passage a successful *exemplum* is not only its integration of carefully selected particulars inside a controlling sentential discourse, but the certainty embodied in the passage itself concerning the absolute rightness of this integration. In his study of the strategies of the *exemplum* genre, Bruno Gélas calls this integration an agreed-upon *theory of manifestation*:

> [W]hat the *exemplum* implies (that which it introduces) is not only or not primarily a rule, but the belief that the *exemplum*'s relationship to the rule is exactly the relationship which joins anecdotal manifestation to a transcendental truth. In this sense, no exemplarisation is possible except on the grounds of an agreement on a *theory of manifestation* which is also the theory of a reading practice.[22]

As we turn to the Nun's Priest's *exemplum*, what we find is that its theory of manifestation almost immediately calls itself into question. While controlling the relationship of anecdote to transcendent truth, this theory of manifestation, as Gélas argues, is also a theory of reading practice. Thus the *exemplum*'s rules of proper reading are also almost immediately challenged. It is necessary to recognize from the beginning that the only way of successfully tracing out both the parodied and the parodistic theory of manifestation is to read the passage with unusual care. This means we must give slow-motion attention to the smallest details in the text itself and to the roundabouts and cul-de-sacs these details generate in the reader's decoding process. A few critics have allowed that one or two phrases in the portrait of the widow's life are there for the purpose of "humorous exaggeration."[23] But I find the entire *exemplum*, including is opening lines of dutiful sobriety, a witty send-up of the art of right reading and right writing. As the widow's portrait unfolds, its edges begin to fray, its generic outlines start shifting, dissolving, and regrouping. Wrong ideas are allowed to come into the reader's head, various rules of interpretation sashay forth and disappear, so that the whole *exemplum* eventually plays sly havoc with the way a literary narrative is expected to settle into some form of stable significance. Whether or not all these instabilities are themselves controlled by an alternative "theory of manifestation" we will consider in due time.

Here, then, for a second time, is the way *The Nun's Priest's Tale* begins:

> A povre wydwe, somdeel stape in age,
> Was whilom dwellyng in a narwe cotage,
> Biside a grove, stondynge in a dale.
> This wydwe, of which I telle yow my tale,
> Syn thilke day that she was last a wyf
> In pacience ladde a ful symple lyf,
> For litel was hir catel and hir rente.

The descriptive format with which the Nun's Priest opens his beast fable corresponds in a number of ways to the chaste, biblical, and plain style of *The Clerk's Tale*. Various virtues of the common Christian life not only appear actualized in the tale's protagonist, but some are specifically named—poverty ("povre"), "pacience," and (a bit later) "housbondrie." "[W]hilom," that most reliable of narrative opening *formulae*, immediately places the tale in an undefined literary past, an *in illo tempore* that can also be equivalent to an absolute, or "timeless," present. Spatially, the rural simplicity of cottage, grove, and dale suggests, as in *The Clerk's Tale*, the salt-of-the-earth semiotics of the Christian pastoral. Not only are the details of the humble scene described in this first sentence fittingly spare, they appear to be controlled by a subtle yet shifting pattern of physical attitude and situation: first by angle (the widow is somewhat bent over), then by size (the cottage is "narwe"), then by contiguity (the cottage is "biside" a grove), and then by centrality of place (it is "stondynge" in a dale). These and subsequent details accord neatly, perhaps too neatly, with Aristotle's ten categories (substance, quantity, quality, relation, place, time, position, state, action, affection).[24] And they certainly appear to be arranging themselves into a stable pattern of interpretable significance even though no external norm, such as the marquis's palace in *The Clerk's Tale*, stands as a determiner of contrastive meaning.

Moving to the second sentence, then, we are told of the widow's life of patient simplicity—a restrained life initiated on the day of her husband's death: "Syn thilke day that she was last a wyf." Here, perhaps, in the narrator's intimation of the widow's former life, is the determiner of contrastive meaning we need. But are we really meant to imagine in any detail the widow's pre-widowed existence as a life of various and pointed pleasure? (The Clerk, we recall, provided his readers little opportunity to imagine an alternative Griselda—given, say, to self-indulgent mood swings.) Having implied that the cause of the widow's present stalwart existence was her former husband's death, the Nun's Priest then explains that this "ful symple" life is also (or perhaps *rather*) the result of pressing economic circumstance: "For litel was hir catel and hir rente." Although the widow's crimped vocation does not yet resonate with the Christian virtues of stoic labor and heroic poverty, like Griselda she shares her life communally with her fellow creatures:

> By housbondrie of swich as God hire sente
> She foond hirself and eek hir doghtren two.
> Thre large sowes hadde she, and namo,
> Three keen, and eek a sheep that highte Malle.

Her daughters, her only living flesh and blood, might be expected to figure as important supporting characters in the manner of Janicula, Griselda's exemplary father. Thus it comes as a bit of a surprise that the narrator chooses not to gather us around the hearth to share with these three women their bond of familial *caritas* and Christian devotion. Instead, we move hastily past the undescribed and unnamed "doghtren two" (never to be seen again) and emerge into the barnyard to meet the live-stock, whom we then count with census-taking precision. These animals (all of them female) immediately gain more importance than the widow's daughters, as we measure the size of the pigs (large) and learn that the sheep's name is Malle—a plebian name (Molly), Beryl Rowland informs us, but not unusual for a fourteenth-century English domestic animal.[25] Naming names in literature is always an important gesture, so we might wonder why the widow ("of which I telle yow my tale") has not been accorded the honor of even a familiar first name. But perhaps this is all part of a sustained modesty trope, reinforcing the edifying *topoi* of simplicity, poverty, piety, and virtue that are waiting to be figured forth through the details of this homely scene. Despite the narrator's assurances that he has accounted for the widow's meager livestock ("and namo"), the neatfold appears modestly sufficient rather than shockingly meager. Indeed, the widow's life seems so far to be an unexceptional representation of lower-class English subsistence farming. So it is hardly surprising that more than one scholar has chosen to disagree with the Nun's Priest's own assessment of the economic standing of his "povre" protagonist: "Her poverty," writes John M. Hill, "is fairly rich in farmyard products, so in her temperate diet and in her 'suffisaunce', she lives a materially pleasant life."[26] If this is the case, then pure poverty—with its potential attendant Christian virtues—does not yet appear to be an ideal exemplified within the Nun's Priest's *exemplum*. Indeed, to this point, the prevailing virtues of the widow's un-scintillating and joyless existence remain impressively underdefined.

So we now begin to retrace our steps, returning from the barnyard to the cottage interior, glimpsing along the way a sooty hall and bower (the scene's most anti-aesthetic detail so far, although "halle" and "bour" are socially upperclass designations), to find ourselves focusing intently on the widow's food:

> Ful sooty was hire bour and eek hir halle,
> In which she eet ful many a sklendre meel.
> Of poynaunt sauce hir neded never a deel.
> No deyntee morsel passed thurgh hir throte;
> Hir diete was accordant to hir cote.

Employing a variant of the rhetorical trope Derek Pearsall calls "idealisation by negatives,"[27] the narrator describes the rich foodstuffs—the "poynaunt sauce" and the "deyntee morsel"—that the widow did not eat. What we next learn, again to our slight disappointment, is that one reason the widow's diet is simple and her meals slender is they were "accordant to hir cote"—in accordance, that is, with what her small farm could provide. Any hope that the widow's simple diet was a voluntary act of corporeal mortification and spiritual self-actualization is further undone by the narrator's assertion that these rich foods "hir neded never a deel"— which could mean that rich foods did not appeal to her, or in the narrator's opinion she perhaps did not actually need them.

We have moved even further from the spiritual ideals with which it could have been presumed the opening *exemplum* of *The Nun's Priest's Tale* was initially concerned. It should perhaps be noted that we have not seen the widow offering her daily prayers; nor have we seen her nurturing her daughters with maternal affection; nor have we seen her communing with her animals in a state of Franciscan grace. Even a thin-broth version of such exemplary behavior would now seem inappropriate, for the widow's anemic spirituality has become almost antithetical to the virtues of Griselda's heroic life. What then, precisely, are the defining features of the widow's existence? Having readjusted our normative sights from matters spiritual to matters moral, we find ourselves readjusting them further from matters moral to matters physical. The primary virtue of the widow's life turns out to be her excellent physical health:

Repleccioun ne made hire nevere sik;
Attempre diete was al hir phisik,
And exercise, and hertes suffisaunce.

Rather like her modern-day aerobicizing and calorie-counting counterpart, the widow exercises, she eats right, and she enjoys her "hertes suffisaunce." This is a far cry from the norms of the Christian apologue where emblems of virtuous poverty, humble labor, stoic patience, and neighborly love grant generic steadiness to our literary vision. In place of Griselda's "rype and sad corage," we find ourselves celebrating three different kinds of physical "good." The first is the widow's moderate, well balanced, and "[a]ttempre" diet (her meals are no longer "sklendre"). The second is her physical fitness (does Chaucer anywhere else celebrate a character's dedication to the therapeutic values of physical exercise?). And the third is her "hertes suffisaunce," a phrase somewhat disturbing in its potential connotations. The semantic field of the one word "suffisaunce" stretches in Chaucer's poetry all the way from a generalized "good life" to the elevations of *fin amour* and the lineaments of gratified desire: "Welcome," sighs Criseyde as she draws Troilus into her arms, "my knyght, my pees, my suffisaunce!"[28] But since the two-word collocation "hertes suffisaunce" unambiguously resides inside the hothouse euphemisms of courtly love, the romantic parameters of the widow's well-being are something the circumspect reader will best avoid imagining. Let us therefore choose to understand the widow's physical activity as providing her tidy body with a high index of nonerotic cardiovascular fitness.

The widow's portrait concludes:

The goute lette hire nothyng for to daunce,
N'apoplexie shente nat hir heed.
No wyn ne drank she, neither whit ne reed;
Hir bord was served moost with whit and blak —
Milk and broun breed, in which she foond no lak,
Seynd bacoun, and somtyme an ey or tweye,
For she was, as it were, a maner deye.

Having assured us that overeating ("Repleccioun") never made her sick, the narrator insists that the gout has never prevented her from dancing nor has apoplexy succeeded in messing up her head. Preferring not to imagine an apoplectic widow swollen with gout, we replace this graphic misprision with a decorous alternative vision — that of a dancing widow with her brains intact. This merry widow *in compos mentis*, we sense, is also an errant configuration that needs to be set aside, but for what? Fortunately, the widow's meal is finally served.

If the controlling rhetorical strategy in this part of the widow's description, as Derek Pearsall insists, has been "idealisation by negatives,"

then negation has failed brilliantly to idealize. Rather, negation has succeeded in doing what Freud noted it is in the habit of doing: giving existence to that which is said not to exist, making present that which is
putatively absent. Perhaps for this reason when the widow's meal belatedly appears, it is a bit of a surprise. And indeed it proves to be a further
surprise since, for all its apparent simplicity, it is not all that simple to understand. Thanks to the narrator's obsession with unwonted explications,
the widow's diet seems to require a hermeneutic key in order to uncover
its meaning. In fact, there seem to be at least two keys—the first regulated by color symbolism, the second by some principle of numerology.
The widow drinks no wine, we are told, neither white nor red; rather,
her board is served pretty much ("moost") with white and black: that is,
milk and brown bread. Milk is white, we know, and brown bread, if not
exactly black, is nevertheless closer to the end of the color spectrum opposite white than most other colors of bread. But so what? Weirdly, these
propositions in color opposites recall those numerous medieval exercises
in Aristotelian logic where the premise term is white (*homo est albus*),
the subpremise term is black (*Sortes est negrus*), and then some kind of
syllogism or enthymeme is posited and extensively analyzed. But whatever syllogistic or sophistical problem subsists in the widow's nearly colorless diet would appear insoluble. (Are we faced with the preeminent problem of classical logic, the Law of the Excluded Middle? Should we ask
whether brown, subsisting somewhere between white and black, is a *tertium quid?*). If we still are trying to decipher this meal according to some
yet-to-be-explicated color code, perhaps it matters whether the color of
"Seynd" bacon is brown or black (some editors suggest "Seynd" means
smoked), and whether that single egg and its occasional mate are white,
speckled, or brown.

Surely it is time to abandon color altogether as a code of potentially
enabling hermeneutic power. In place of color, what may just as likely
serve as a ruling interpretative principle is number. Enumerating has obviously been a prominent activity throughout the portrait: we have been
told the number of the widow's daughters, the number of pigs, the number of cows, the number of sheep, and the number of eggs. As the philosopher Paul Kuntz remarks in *The Concept of Order,* numbers in various
patterns designate various principles of order: the principle of order of

1, 2, 3, 4, for example, is magnitude; the principle of order of 4, 3, 2, 1 is its opposite (Kuntz suggests "minitude"); the principle of order of 1, 2, 3, 3, 2, 1 is symmetry, and so on.[29] In the widow's world, we have the following number sequence: 1 (the widow), 2 (her daughters), 3 (the pigs), 3 (the cows), 1 (the sheep), and 1 or 2 (the eggs). An order of magnitude (1, 2, 3) thus gives way to a conjectured order of symmetry (1, 2, 3, 3, 2, 1), an expectation which is undone by skipping over 2 on the way back to 1, creating a disorder that is further confounded by the option of 1 egg or 2. (Need we count that piece of bacon, or is it merely a part of a whole? And does it matter that some of the creatures we are counting are human and the rest are animal, or that most are alive but the eggs are alive only *in potentia* and the bacon is dead?) The only scholars to find a pattern of significance in any of these numbers have been Levy and Adams. For them, the barnyard paradise is ruled over by three "threes"—the widow and her two daughters (3), the sows (3), and the cows (3). These three threes are not only numerically identical but also numerologically significant: that is, all symbolize the Trinity. Although the sheep is a ewe named Molly, Levy and Adams are determined to understand her to be a ram, and this ram in turn symbolizes Christ.[30] Counting and allegorizing the eggs is something Levy and Adams do not feel called upon to do.

Since numbers, like colors, lead in the direction of exegetical absurdity, what's left? One of the most obvious patterns throughout the portrait has been gender, for all living things considered in this scene (except possibly the eggs) are female—widow, daughters, sows, cows, and ewe. In a tale whose very title celebrates female preeminence, surely it is necessary to ask of its narrator-exegete what this absolute feminization of the *exemplum*'s community means. But, oddly, the narrator seems willfully to have "not seen" this all-female pattern, all the while attempting to impose rather abstract and ill-fitting patterns, like color and number, upon his original material. In other words, the *exemplum*'s celibate female aesthetic seems to be awaiting some kind of masculine imaginary that the *Tale* has yet to supply. In due time, the widow's prosaic world will stand in stark contrast to the variegated riches of Chauntecleer's life of high adventure. But how a poetics or politics of gender is instantiated in this shift in artistic register is a question that the *Tale*'s opening *exemplum* seems not to have included in any obvious way within its implicit hermeneutic system.

One final principle of narratorial control in the Nun's Priest's opening *exemplum* is causation. Early in the portrait the narrator had felt free
to provide several unnecessary explanations of why things in the widow's
life are as they now are. Should we therefore at the end of the portrait descry some continuing principle of causality connecting, say, the slab of
bacon, the widow, and those three fat pigs? Should we now infer some
principal producer of those eggs who for some reason has been left outside this framing fiction? If causation has been a dominant principle of
interpretation in this opening scene, why then does the portrait end with
such a flat-out parody of causal explanations? That is, the last line, introduced by a typically oblique Chaucerian conjunction ("For"), explains
that the real reason the widow's diet is made up of milk, bread, bacon,
and eggs, is: "For she was, as it were, a maner deye" (For she was, if you
will, some kind of dairymaid). The syntax of this line, as Pearsall notes,
is "characteristically elusive"; furthermore, "a maner deye" may possibly
mean a demesne servant, it may suggest she was not quite a "'proper'
dairymaid," or it may be "a merely conventional construction."[31] But do
we really care? Hasn't all the evidence for her mode of living been adequately presented in the preceding portrait itself, thus leaving this throw-
away causal explication nothing but a mildly irritating and slightly unnecessary anticlimax?

The unsatisfactoriness of the final line is entirely appropriate, I find,
for throughout the portrait of the widow the reader has time and again
been teased into a misleading sense of interpretative control. It is this presumption of interpretative control, or what Gélas calls "a theory of manifestation" ruling the connection between particulars and universals, that
is quite evidently being parodied throughout the Nun's Priest's mock-
exemplum. In *Authoritarian Fictions: The Ideological Novel as a Literary
Genre*, Susan Suleiman argues that all exemplary, or ideological, fiction
is determined by a specific end that exists "before" or "after" the story:

> The story calls for an unambiguous interpretation, which in turn
> implies a rule of action applicable (at least virtually) to the real life
> of the reader. The interpretation and the rule of action may be
> stated explicitly by a narrator who "speaks with the voice of Truth"
> and can therefore lay claim to absolute authority, or they may

be supplied, on the basis of textual and contextual indices, by the reader. The only necessary condition is that the interpretation and the rule of action be unambiguous—in other words, that the story lend itself as little as possible to a "plural" reading.[32]

The opening *exemplum* of *The Nun's Priest's Tale*, although it pretends to be an authoritarian fiction, lends itself to an embarrassing plurality of readings. Profoundly multifarious are both the "Truth" the *exemplum* purports to exemplify and the "rule of action" it expects its readers to apply to real life. In fact, Chaucer's *exemplum* egregiously commits the three crimes that Suleiman claims are most subversive to the teleology of any ideological narrative. These crimes are: (1) the multiplication of superfluous and distracting details; (2) "Saying Too Much"—that is, reifying a moral idea to such a degree that a negative character becomes attractive or an exemplary one becomes unattractive; and (3) "Not Saying Enough," by which Suleiman means a fiction's relativizing of all truths, even those it is explicitly committed to upholding.[33] The Nun's Priest's *exemplum* is thus a fine illustration of what not to do when writing in the *exemplum* format. It is chock-full of excrescent particulars, narratorial tangents, and unasked-for editorial asides (crime 1). It so particularizes, contextualizes, and narrativizes its exemplary character, the widow, that she and her lifestyle become increasingly less attractive (crime 2). And, finally, the portrait, after an initial attempt to foreground its controlling truths and virtues, succeeds only in submerging them in a welter of compromising alternative discourses, such as logic, food consumption, color, number, gender, and causation (crime 3).

Despite its many crimes against the *exemplum* genre, and in fact precisely because of these many crimes, there is nevertheless, I believe, in the experience of reading the Nun's Priest's exordium a developing sense of overall aesthetic control and purpose. Is it therefore possible to construct a nonunitary hermeneutics out of the many "theories of manifestation" at odds with each other in Chaucer's representation of the widow's life? In the remainder of this section I want to begin (but by no means conclude) the construction of such a hermeneutics. Although no single rule of interpretation will emerge, I hope such an undertaking will generate a renewed appreciation of the challenge of rereading Chaucer and a deeper understanding of the challenge of interpreting any kind of narrative fiction. I will begin by taking my impressionistic line-by-line responses to Chaucer's *exemplum* detailed in the foregoing pages and compressing them into seven very "minimalist" categories. These categories are: (1) the representative attitude of physical space and bodily position; (2) the possible relationship of marriage and widowhood to *sentence* and *solaas;* (3) the significance of various foodstuffs and their (non)consumption; (4) the logic of colors in fiction; (5) number sequences and the order of meaning; (6) female creatures, celibacy, and the generation of narrative; and (7) causation as a principle of narrative design. Crude as they are, each of these categories is obviously freighted with a great deal of ideological and methodological baggage. While each holds promise as a viable foundation for an overarching interpretative paradigm, each has already displaced other readings, and each promises eventually to be at odds with its paradigmatic peers.

My primary point is not to argue the greater rightness of any one of these overdetermined positions, but rather to claim the potential viability of all of them. And no matter how many interpretative foundations one constructs here, the next question is the same: is there a next step? Is it possible, that is, to ascend from these low-level categorical particulars in the direction of higher-level generalities, and then to universals? In testing out the possibility of such an ascent, I will continue to tilt my scheme in the direction of Chaucer's metapoetical concerns. (1) Like the opening scene's iconic representation of *exemplum* as a clearing in the woods, the widow's being "somdeel stape in age" suggests itself as an emblem of the moralized narrative's antique age and modest vigor. (2) Marriage, as borne out in Chaucer's Marriage Group, is not only a Christian sacrament but also a metonym for the poet's dream of the ideal union of Mercury (wisdom) and Philology (language), a dream scarcely realized in this opening piece of celibate verse. (3) The consumption of food, in beast fables as well as in other literature, is a traditional metaphor for the interpretation of fiction, be it salvific or toxic, bland or spicy. (4) The critical exfoliation of colors, from the Prologue to *The Legend of Good Women* on, is one of Chaucer's preeminent ways of examining the basic unit of his craft, the "colors" of metaphor. (5) A major element in the design of *The Nun's Priest's Tale,* as I suggested in chapter 2, is the deployment of the seven liberal arts—

the last four of which, the quadrivium, are mathematical arts measuring and numbering the order of all things in the universe as well as leading, in various curricular epics, to an illuminated vision of *novus homo,* or the New Reader. (6) The tension in this *exemplum* between enclosures and openings, the female and her restraint, may be illustrative of what Patricia Parker has called the male narrator's failed attempts at "mastering or controlling the implicitly female, and perhaps hence wayward, body of the text itself."[34] Finally, (7) the narrator's awkward attempts to rationalize the wayward body of his text by supplying gratuitous cause-and-effect explications may highlight the often irresolvable tensions that subsist between the two activities of fiction-making, *exemplare et narrare.*

In beginning to amplify these seven readings, it may appear that I am beginning to move in the direction of harmonizing all the *exemplum's* disparate parts. But in this attempt to move from the Many toward the One, it may also appear that I am ascending in the direction of even more overt interpretative bullying. Some part of us would like to believe that everything in criticism that rises must eventually converge; some part of us suspects that all things that transcend the particular are forms of ideological cooptation. The epistemological debates between the nominalists and realists are thus philosophical analogues to our own disputes concerning the generic rules versus the particular instances of any literary work. In recognition of the complexity of this debate, I do not intend to undertake the extension of these seven interpretative realms into an overarching critical synthesis.[35] For even if such a synthesis were possible,[36] my focus here has been on a close reading of the idea of a narrative's beginning, the originary foundation of Chaucer's *ars poetica,* and the methods we employ as we assemble a series of conflicted meanings out of one exemplary narrative.

Positing a beginning for any master narrative is an unusual act of self-assertion. "One rarely searches for beginnings unless the present matters a great deal," notes Edward Said in *Beginnings;* "It is my present urgency, the here and now, that will enable me to establish the sequence of beginning-middle-end and to transform it from a distant object—located 'there'—into the subject of my reasoning."[37] By beginning his *ars poetica* with a high-resolution exercise in literary parody, Chaucer is clearly testing our habits of imposing a stable significance upon the *materia* of any recalcitrant text. Of course this does not mean that the propriety of a didactic reading is ever absolutely erased: in the stoicism of the widow's existence a moral concreteness remains firmly intact.[38] However, in the interplay between the parodic levels of this *moralitas* a newly inflected collaboration between author and reader might begin to effect a more innovative reading practice. If so, then Chaucer's *exemplum* could be seen as posing a variety of generic questions from which the aesthetic arguments of his *ars poetica* gradually emerge.

In *Narrative, Authority, and Power,* Scanlon traces the power relations fought out between two medieval *exemplum* traditions in the fourteenth century. The first he identifies as the sermon tradition, which represents the "Church's broad-based attempts to increase its institutional control of secular life." The second is the classical and "public" *exemplum,* through which the so-called Chaucerian tradition of poetry attempted to "establish its own authority."[39] Some tension between these two powerful traditions may resonate in the Nun's Priest's *exemplum,* although it is scarcely self-evident with which tradition Chaucer identifies more fully, the arts of Christian poetry as championed by Geoffrey of Vinsauf or the arts of classical poetry as championed by Horace. What is much more striking is how Chaucer's *exemplum* advertises itself as an act of artistic supersession: here is a poet who wants to fashion his own clearing in the woods, to be at the origins of his own poetry, to compose his own master-narrative *ab ovo.* So it is not surprising that Chaucer's opening assertions of artistic liberation are clinched by his unique resolution of the aestheticians' *in medias res/ab ovo* debate. The famous lines from Horace need to be recalled in full:

> Nec reditum Diomedis ab intertu Meleagri,
> nec gemino bellum Troianum orditur ab ovo:
> semper ad eventum festinat et in medias res
> non secus ac notas auditorem rapit.

> ———

> Nor does he [the poet] begin the return of Diomedes from the
> death of Meleager nor the Trojan War from the twin egg. He
> always moves swiftly to the issue at hand and rushes his listener
> into the middle of the action just as if it were already known.[40]

Like Sterne in *Tristram Shandy,* Chaucer impishly disobeys Horace's classical prescriptive advice. Tristram, telling of his biological conception by his parents at the beginning of his life story, praises his own narrative genius: "right glad I am, that I have begun the history of myself in the way I have done; and that I am able to go on tracing every thing in it, as *Horace* says, *ab Ovo.*"[41] Chaucer, unlike Tristram, does not explicitly celebrate his narrative skills nor does he name his classical authority. But he nevertheless manages to round off his opening *exemplum* in a quite eggy fashion. Whereas Horace had seen the epic of Trojan history as beginning *ab gemino ovo,* from a unique twin egg produced by the violent union of a mortal woman and a bird-god, Chaucer starts off his avian beast fable with the most casual allusion to "somtyme an ey or tweye." This momentary authorial aside—in its insouciant underscoring of unity and doubleness, certainty and vagueness, creation and consumption—is a subtle metapoetic gesture. As a pseudo-classical ovoid overture, it serves as an apt beginning to the *vita* of a hero who is little more, but nothing less, than a somewhat tragic medieval chicken. And if any uncertainty remains about this as an exemplary beginning, then we are left contemplating one more parodic issue of mock-epic origins: in the best of all fictions, which should come first, the chicken or the egg?

MOCK-*MORALITAS,* OR THE *FOLYE* OF CLOSE READING

How to end? Guiding a story to narrative closure is a task at least as daunting as devising an appropriate narrative beginning. One challenge among many is generated by the presumed genre of the work itself, although—and this seems especially true of Chaucer's fictions—it could be a writer's intent *not* to fulfill a reader's developing expectations, preferring rather to subvert and thus further complicate the generic identity of the unfolding text.[42] Since *The Nun's Priest's Tale* indubitably belongs to the beast fable genre, we might anticipate few "terminal" difficulties, since the endings of medieval beast fables are traditionally pretty much all of a kind: an authoritative *moralitas* sums up the wisdom—be it practical, moral, or spiritual—extrapolated from the preceding *narratio.*[43] In fact, Chaucer

anticipates the monitory spirit of the typical beast fable ending by offering not only one but three pithy apothegms just before he moves into his
post-narrative *finale*. Chauntecleer's last words, "For he that wynketh,
whan he sholde see, / Al wilfully, God lat him nevere thee!" (VI.3421–22),
are immediately countered by the fox's acerbic response, "Nay, . . . but
God yeve hym meschaunce, / That is so undiscreet of governaunce, /
That jangleth whan he sholde holde his pees" (VI.3433–35), to which
the narrator adds his own concluding bromide, "Lo, swich it is for to be
recchelees, / And necligent, and truste on flaterye" (VI.3436–37). Following these three *seriatim* bits of proverbial lore—they in fact constitute the *narrative* conclusion to *The Nun's Priest's Tale*—Chaucer brings
the entire fable to its generic conclusion with a *moralitas* ending with a
timely "Amen":

> But ye that holden this tale a folye,
> As of a fox or of a cock and hen,
> Taketh the moralite, goode men.
> For Seint Paul seith that al that writen is
> To our doctrine it is ywrite, ywis;
> Taketh the fruyt, and lat the chaf be stille.
> Now goode God, if that it be thy wille,
> As seith my lord, so make us alle goode men,
> And brynge us to his heighe blisse! Amen.
>   (VI.3438–46)

Many scholars have felt reassured by this coda, in no small part because at
its center Chaucer employs a hermeneutical image familiar to all medievalists: every text, be it sacred or secular, has an outer cortex that needs
to be winnowed away in order to arrive at a privileged understanding
of the work's deeper meaning. The *Tale's* closing directives have pleased
scholars for other reasons as well, for it is fairly apparent that Chaucer has
chosen *not* to decode the fable's implicit *sententia* with a finalizing *expli-
catio,* but rather to leave that discovery to his reader's own designs: "Taketh the fruyt," the narrator advises, "and lat the chaf be stille" (VI.3440).
Of course, as I noted in the Introduction, this is not an easy assignment,
for in a tale of only 646 lines there are numerous fruitful generalizations

scattered throughout the *Tale* decrypting the import of ongoing events. And, as we have just witnessed, Chaucer ups the monitory ante at the very end of his narrative by piling on three concluding morals—his intent perhaps being to emphasize how the *Tale*'s many philosophemes resist coalescing into anything close to a sentential universal.

But what, then, is the fable's *moralitas* actually saying or doing? If *The Nun's Priest's Tale* is Chaucer's signature *ars poetica,* and if its *moralitas* is designed to provide guidance on how best to read a piece of literature, at a very basic level we should expect that there would be some agreement among Chaucerians in defining what this *moralitas* simply says and quite literally means. But such is not the case, as Derek Pearsall's synopses of variegated readings of the *moralitas* amply attest. In part because the tale refuses to perform the straightforward exegetical services provided by the traditional beast-fable ending, Pearsall finds that no adequate critical interpretation of the *moralitas* has yet been provided. The message Pearsall eventually extracts from this situation bears repeating: there is simply no point in searching for the ultimate meaning of *The Nun's Priest's Tale* because "the fact that the tale has no point is the point of the tale."[44]

Buried within Pearsall's skeptical hermeneutics, I wish to suggest, lies the germ of a quite radical critical theory that acknowledges the essential resistance of all literature to any form of interpretation, ideological or otherwise. Pearsall's negative caveat could be viewed, in other words, as a promising first step leading toward a rereading of the *Tale*'s *moralitas* as a self-deconstructing literary artifact. The Nun's Priest's *moralitas* is obviously a quite complex verbal collocation that deserves to be studied with extreme care. Yet what I find most challenging about the *Tale*'s ending is not so much *what* it appears to be saying to the reader (although that is problematic enough), but rather the *way* it deploys language to carry its various, and perhaps contradictory, messages. Whereas the *Tale*'s opening *exemplum* asks to be read as a carefully designed parodic deconstruction of conflicting generic registers, the Nun's Priest's closing *moralitas,* I now intend to illustrate, asks to be read as a carefully designed deconstructive parody of conflicting linguistic semiologies. The Nun's Priest's *moralitas,* in a nutshell, embodies and foregrounds the potentially self-paralyzing linguistic modalities at work in any literary text. From classical times to the twenty-first century, these linguistic modalities have always been defined as the trivium—grammar, logic, and rhetoric. Additionally, throughout the Middle Ages these three *artes* were also understood to be central to *enarratio,* the *techne* of reading and interpreting works of literature. What I hope to prove by chapter's end is that the *moralitas* of *The Nun's Priest's Tale* is actually putting under scrutiny the very act of reading itself. Via its own "trivial" resistance to critical extrapolation, the *moralitas* demonstrates how the linguistic essence of a piece of literature short-circuits all attempts to arrive at a stable and nonconflicting set of interpretative meanings.

To provide a theoretical framework for understanding Chaucer's parodic interrogation of the *praxis* of reading I will be drawing intermittently upon a postmodern theory of reading that also centers on the trivium. In *The Resistance to Theory,* Paul de Man argues that since all traditional literary criticism is ideologically (that is, grammatically) pre-inflected, the essential rhetoricity of literature, its "literariness," has yet to be given a theoretically close reading.[45] A rigorously disinterested way of approaching an understanding of what de Man calls the act of "mere reading" is by prizing apart the internal conflicts among the constituent parts of the trivium in any text. If a purely grammatical reading practice were actually possible, de Man asserts, the continuity between theory (which is already embedded in the language of literature) and phenomenalism (refracted by the mathematical arts of the quadrivium) would appear unbroken, and there would be relatively few problems. When logic is added to the grammatical program of study, de Man continues, there is still nothing essentially threatening to a theory of reading, for in their symbiotic affinity (grammar being "an isotope of logic")[46] as well as in their discursive rigor, these two *artes* match up with the four quadrivial sciences: via this discursive linkage between logic and the mathematical sciences, *verba* and *res* appear ultimately connected. It is only when the third element of the trivium is brought into play that reading finds itself dramatically disequilibrated, because rhetoric, the fundamental constituent of literary language, reveals itself as the "wild card" that queers all the hands in the deck. The act of reading, in other words, runs into difficulty when it is no longer possible to keep rhetoric in its place as a mere ornament within the semantic functions of language. De Man's favored example is the title of Keats' unfinished epic "The Fall of Hyperion," a title that invites at least two conflicting readings: each is grammatically correct, each is rhetorically possible—*but these two readings, one grammatical and the other rhetorical, are entirely and absolutely incompatible.* Furthermore, not only does rhetoric undo the claims of language to be an epistemologically stable construct, rhetoric is itself divided, suspended between a system of self-referring tropes and a system of extrareferential/performative speech acts. Unable to bridge the aporia between these two rhetorics, equally unable to bridge the aporia between grammar and rhetoric, reading is a rhetorical activity that invariably deconstructs its own efforts to access meaning. Rodolphe Gasché, in *The Wild Card of Reading*, provides a distillation of de Man's core thesis that language in its essence is entirely unreadable: "mere reading destroys . . . all the sediments of meaning by which the grammatical has covered language, to exhibit language in its pristine state of unintelligibility, before all epistemological and aesthetic commodification."[47]

There is little doubt that the medieval liberal arts curriculum provided Chaucer's readers with an ample understanding of the differences among the three linguistic arts, both as semiological systems as well as contentious academic persuasions. Throughout the Middle Ages, trivium wars were carried out in the academy, as one *ars* sought to appropriate or weaken the terrain of one or both of its sibling rivals. Grammar, as Jeffrey Hunstman notes, was "at times during the Middle Ages unthroned as the preeminent art when dialectic or rhetoric gained the ascendancy within the trivium," yet it "never lost its most fundamental position as the basis of all liberal learning."[48] Rhetoric, viewed by Aristotle in his *De rhetorica* as merely a branch of dialectics, occasionally enjoyed pride of intellectual place, as when the twelfth-century Chartrians honored rhetoric as "the integrating factor of all education";[49] but by the thirteenth century, rhetoric had descended to a "theoretical low point" even though, as Martin Camargo notes, this same century was "a highpoint for its practical use."[50] Logic tended to be valued throughout the Middle Ages as the most advanced art in the trivium (Aquinas celebrates logic as the gateway to the quadrivium), and in the twelfth and thirteenth centuries it dominated the intellectual climate of the universities; in Chaucer's time, however, logic's prestige was beginning to wane, and by the fifteenth century it was seen again as subordinate to rhetoric because of rhetoric's perceived political utility.[51] Partial syntheses between and among these arts were occasionally achieved at a quite high level of intellection, a prime example being the works of the twelfth century speculative grammarians, or Modistae, who assimilated logical terms into their linguistic studies as a way of further understanding the grammar of the mind and its relation to the real.[52] But over the centuries intense turf wars among the three linguistic *artes* were the norm.[53]

Obviously these academic power struggles are squabbles typical of scholars in adjacent fields seeking to increase their prestige within their university culture. But these battles are also profoundly symptomatic of the contestatory and self-conflicting characteristics of language, be it literary or nonliterary. Every verbal proposition, no matter in which language it is framed, requires decoding, and the only means of determining the significance of that proposition are the three linguistic disciplines that are constitutive of language itself—grammar, rhetoric, and logic. What characterizes each of these linguistic disciplines, how one might determine the boundary lines between them, and how one should employ the three *artes,* especially grammar and rhetoric, as mainstays in *enarratio,* or literary criticism, were issues fully addressed in the early years of a typical medieval education. As we have seen in chapter 2, students began their study of language with an analysis of sounds, syllables, letters, words, parts of speech, and the rules of morphology and syntax. Acquiring a basic understanding of grammar through a close reading of Donatus's *Ars Minor,* progressing next to Cato's *Distichs* and to a collection of Aesopian fables, young grammarians moved with remarkable speed toward a disciplined reading of the authors of ancient Rome, most notably Statius, Virgil, Lucan, Juvenal, Horace, and Ovid. Poring over these texts—translating, paraphrasing, explicating, and imitating significant passages—students were expected above all to focus on perfecting their knowledge of the inner workings of the Latin language itself. After completing these extensive literary-linguistic assignments (including Priscian's *preexercitamina*), students returned to a more detailed study of the technicalities of Latin grammar, the standard texts being part 4 of Donatus's *Ars Major,* known as the *Barbarismus* (tellingly, a study of figures and tropes), Priscian's instruction on the parts of speech and syntax in *Institutiones Grammaticae* and *Partitiones,* and works on meter.[54] As Suzanne Reynolds remarks in *Medieval Reading,* her illuminating study of twelfth-century academic reading practices, there is "no room for doubt; literary authors, and principally classical authors, were an essential part of grammatical instruction, of instruction in the earlier stages of learning Latin." [55]

There is likewise no room for doubt that this early introduction to the classical *auctores* was equally essential to the schoolroom study and application of the second trivium art, rhetoric. The two standard rhetorical primers, Cicero's *De Inventione* and pseudo-Cicero's *Ad Herennium,* characterized rhetoric as an art embracing two quite different kinds of language activity. As defined in the *De Inventione,* rhetoric is the art of public persuasion, formal oratory divided by Cicero into three subcategories: epideictic rhetoric, which concerns praising or blaming individual persons; deliberative rhetoric, which involves expressing an opinion in a political debate; and judicial or forensic rhetoric, which encompasses the prosecution or defense of a case in a court of law. However, rhetoric is classified quite differently in *Ad Herennium,* part 4, where it is seen as comprising a set of distinctive verbal skills with which a speaker or writer modulates his or her linguistic diction, register, or style for the sake of achieving a "rhetorical" or "poetic" effect, the most notable of these techniques being the use of "figurative" language (the *Ad Herennium* gives examples of ten different tropes and nineteen different figures of thought). Having been trained to identify a variety of figures and tropes, equally well instructed to appreciate the ways language might be manipulated for suasive effects, students preparing to read the classics were in for a bracing experience because the assigned literary texts are obviously "rhetorical" through and through. Yet these authoritative texts are also to be read at the very same time as exemplars of classical Latin illustrating the rules of proper grammar in action. How, then, is one actually to know, with anything close to real certainty, when a word in a certain context is being used grammatically and when it is being used rhetorically? Grammarians and rhetoricians both taught the *auctores,* and both laid claim to figures and tropes as appropriate objects of study for their disciplines. While this crossing of pedagogical boundaries is one of many indications of the indistinct separation between the two verbal arts, it is also symptomatic of a deeper uncertainty concerning the semiological stability of lexical signs generally, a problem that the liberal arts curriculum dealt with by eventually granting the student-reader considerable authority in determining the truth concerning an author's "real intent." Reynolds explains:

> Many of the linguistic features so dear to the rhetorician or to the poet were considered to be faults from a formal grammatical point of view. . . . There is, of course, a way round this. The faults occur either at the level of the word (barbarisms: *barbarismi*) or at the level of the combination of words (solecisms: *solecismi*), and grammarians and rhetoricians agreed that it was part of the grammarian's task to warn against these faults. However, if they were found in poetry, they became acceptable on the grounds of metre or ornamentation, and earned new names: figures (*metaplasmi* and *schemata*) and tropes (*tropi*). It was the authority of the utterer— *puer* or poet—that determined whether using the "wrong" case was a grammatical error or a stylistic embellishment.[56]

With the emergence of the *artes poetriae* at the end of the twelfth century—works such as Eberhard of Béthune's *Grecismus,* Matthew of Vendôme's *Ars Versificatoria,* and Geoffrey of Vinsauf's *Poetria Nova*— the fraught intersection between grammar and rhetoric within literary works became even more pronounced. While *enarratio* was still generally understood to be a grammatical application seeking to determine the "literal" meaning of the author's words, in these preceptive grammars *enarratio* was revealed to be a sophisticated *rhetorical* activity as well, in that students were asked to identify, imitate, and emulate the author's figurative maneuvers. Furthermore, in their glosses, commentaries, and paraphrases, students were expected to go far beyond the "literal" surface of the work in order to discover, and, in truth, to *invent,* the real meaning embedded in the words in the text. As Reynolds further explains:

> [I]f we accept that the text is a rhetorical construction, and that exposition is a grammatical activity, then this movement of "grasping" [the thought behind the verbal surface] constitutes the appro-

priation by *grammatica* of rhetoric's productive structures and, once again, reading practice defies the division of the two arts.

 This dissolution of the boundary between grammar and rhetoric in reading depends on a single hermeneutic notion— authorial intention.... The recovery of intention, which is of course one of the most important categories in the twelfth-century *accessus ad auctores,* underpins the exposition of the figures and tropes, and represents the most profound erosion of the boundary between grammar and rhetoric.[57]

In other words, "authorial intent" proves to be the supreme fiction ultimately necessary in the successful "grammatical" interpretation of a work of literature because, without this intentionalist placeholder, it would be impossible to determine whether a word, phrase, or sentence is to be taken literally (grammatically) or figuratively (rhetorically). Reynolds's careful documentation of the ways medieval readers decoded or encoded authorial intent in order to overcome the grammar/rhetoric divide leads her linguistic and critical theorizing in the general direction of de Man's more explicit and much more radical analysis of language as an interpretative cul-de-sac. While *Medieval Reading* scarcely arrives at de Man's conclusion that a work of literature is ultimately "unreadable," Reynolds's study of medieval reading practices demonstrates how the grammatical decoding of a text inevitably left a residue of indetermination that had to be resolved, but could not legitimately be resolved, by grammatical means.

 In his *moralitas* to *The Nun's Priest's Tale* Chaucer addresses these issues, but in point of fact he takes matters one step further than both Reynolds and de Man by engaging his readers' detailed knowledge, not only of grammar and rhetoric, but of the third and most prestigious of the medieval trivium arts, that is, logic. Chaucer does this by deploying a small set of logical words known as *syncategoremata*—namely, the four words "al," "but," "and," and "or"—each of which his well-educated readers would have spent hours analyzing in and out of the university classroom. By the late thirteenth century the *logica moderna* had two main branches, the first focused on accounting for the properties of *categoremata* (adjectives, pronouns, nouns, and verbs), the second on accounting for the signification and function of *syncategoremata* (normally conjunctions, adverbs, and prepositions). Whereas *categoremata* were seen as carrying the major semantic signification of a proposition, *syncategoremata* were understood by and large to create its syntactic structure and logical significance. Many late medieval logicians wrote syncategorematic treatises, including Peter of Spain, Nicholas of Paris, Henry of Ghent, William of Ockham, Walter Burleigh, William Heytesbury, Albert of Saxony, Paul of Venice, and William of Sherwood.[58]

Now in our general practice of reading literature, we scarcely stop to think about the way we decode the basic meaning of quite ordinary words. And when, as practicing literary critics, we choose to prioritize a word's figural significance over its literal significance, or vice-versa, in making such a choice we tend to rely upon our second-nature intuitions of the felt differences between rhetoric and grammar. And were we ever to find ourselves interpreting a literary passage as though it were a "logical" proposition, in all likelihood our sense of what we mean by logic as an intellectual discipline would be quite general. In other words, the intelligentsia who made up an important part of Chaucer's audience were, quite frankly, better trained than are we in the disciplines of the trivium. And most especially, they were well trained in logic, considered in Chaucer's time to be the trivium's most powerful instrument. There is of course no way of compressing Oxford's vast *curriculum logicae* into a few paragraphs. However, because I believe the Nun's Priest's *moralitas* depends upon an awareness of the critical methods and intellectual issues of medieval dialectics, it will be necessary at this point to fill in just a few of the blanks.

I have selected William of Sherwood's thirteenth-century *Treatise on Syncategorematic Words* as an illustration of syncategorematic studies because it is "written in a rather informal scholastic style and evidently derives fairly closely from a course conducted by Sherwood at Paris or at Oxford."[59] Sherwood's *Treatise* is quite typical of its kind in that each of its chapters, focusing exclusively on one word or on one pair of logically interrelated words, is organized around a standard sequence of expository and critical elements: (1) definitions and analyses of the syncategorematic word under analysis; (2) classifications of its uses; (3) grammatical, semantic, and logical rules governing its use in propositions; (4) examples illustrating the classifications and rules of parts 2 and 3;

(5) *sophismata* involving the syncategorematic word; (6) expositions of propositions in which this word appears; and (7) questions arising from parts 1 through 6.[60] Of these, a most instructive element are the *sophismata* included in part 5 because, as we shall see shortly, each of the *syncategoremata*-embedded sentences in Chaucer's *moralitas* is constructed as if it were a *sophisma,* that is, as a problematic proposition "puzzling in its own right or on the basis of a certain assumption, [yet] designed to bring some abstract issue into sharper focus."[61] Classifiable under certain overarching rubrics, such as inclusion, exception, conjunction, and alterity, these abstract issues in the Nun's Priest's *moralitas* address metapoetic concerns raised in Chaucer's closing instructions on how to read his own *ars poetica.*

Sherwood's *Treatise* opens with *syncategoremata* that determine the "disposition of a subject" of a proposition (17). Of these, there are those that determine the supposition of a subject in the affirmative—the words "every," "whole," number words, "infinitely many," and "both." Next there are the negative distributive signs associated with the subject—"no," "nothing," and "neither." The subsequent category is the exceptive and exclusive signs—"but," "alone," and "only." Following these are those words "pertaining to the composition of a predicate with a subject" (91)—"is," "not," "necessarily," and "contingently." A lengthy chapter considers the special case of the two verbs "begins" and "ceases" (we will learn much more about this pair in chapter 6). The remainder of the treatise is given over to syncategorematic words pertaining to "one subject in respect of another, or to one predicate in respect of another, or to one composition in respect of another" (116). These words are the consecutive conjunctions "if," "unless," and "but that," the copulative conjunction "and," the disjunctive conjunctions "or," "whether" and "or," the particle "*ne,*" and "whether . . . or."[62] Of these three dozen or so *syncategoremata,* as I have noted, Chaucer employs four in a crucial way in the Nun's Priest's *moralitas*—"al," "but," "and," and "or"—and these four match up with four or five words in Sherwood's *Treatise*: "al" with *omnis* or *totum;* "but" with *praeter;* "and" with "*et*"; and "or" with "*vel.*" While I am not insisting that each of Chaucer's words is absolutely identical to each of these Latin *syncategoremata* (for instance, *sed* is closer to "but" used as a conjunction than is the preposition *praeter*),[63] an appreciation of the intellectual energies at work in medieval syncategorematic studies should help nurture a tolerance for the finicky linguistic discriminations the Nun's Priest's *moralitas* invites us to make.

Sherwood opens his *Treatise* with an extended study of *omnis* and *totum* (chapters 1 and 2, totaling twenty-three pages). *Omnis* is known to signify universality, Sherwood writes. But sometimes it signifies universality "as the disposition of a thing" (17); in that case, it is not in fact a syncategorematic word, which is logical, but rather is equivalent to *totum* (whole), which is grammatical. At other times, however, it is a syncategorematic word because it signifies universality "as a disposition of a subject" (17). Thus, for example, in the proposition "'every man is running' the word 'every' [*omnis*] signifies that the word 'man' is universal in respect of serving as a subject" (17). Thus the *substance* belonging to *omnis* is "infinite" substance "spoken of finitely through its subject, but the *quality* belonging to it is universality" (18). A major characteristic of *omnis* is that it sometimes is "taken properly and divides for specific parts, and at other times [is] taken commonly and divides for numerical parts" (20). On the basis of this principle, Sherwood reasons, the following *sophisma* can be posed and solved:

> Suppose there are only asses. Then [*a*] every (*omnis*) animal is an ass, but [*b*] every man is an animal; therefore every man is an ass.
>
> [Proof:] [*a*] is true by hypothesis; [*b*] is necessary, because in it the genus is predicated of a species.
>
> Solution: If the word "every" is taken properly in [*a*], [*a*] is false, for it means that the animal conditionally in Socrates and in Plato and in all the others conditionally is the ass, which is false.
>
> If, however, it is taken commonly, [*a*] is true and [*b*] is false, since a distribution occurs for the actually extant parts of man, and by hypothesis there are none. If, however, the minor [*b*] is taken in the sense in which it is true, there will be a *figura dictionis* (figure of speech) in the argument, for the word "animal" is taken for numerical parts in [*a*] and for specific parts in [*b*]. From another point of view there will be a paralogism of accident, for "animal" is not predicated of "man" in the way in which "ass" is predicated of "animal." (21–22)

A second major syncategorematic word in the *Treatise* is *praeter,* a preposition meaning "but," "except," or "besides" (chapter 10, totaling ten pages).[64] Sherwood argues that there are two ways that "but" can take exception from the whole. First, "diminutionally," as in "Socrates has eleven fingers but one": here "but" signifies that "a diminution from some whole occurs as regards the thing itself" (58). Second, "counter-instantively," as in "Every man but Socrates is running." In this case "but" excepts "a part from a whole in respect of a predicate" (58); in other words, it sets aside the proposition that Socrates is running, "which counter-instantiates 'every man is running'" (59). From this essential distinction there proceed, however, various *sophismata* that confuse the distinction between taking exception from the whole diminutionally and taking it counter-instantively. For example, suggests Sherwood, let the whole (*totum*) of Socrates be called *a* and the whole (*totum*) of Socrates but his foot be called *b*. It would seem to follow that *a* is an animal and *b* is an animal, since *totum* in *b* must be taken distributively, or else the exception "but his foot" could not be made. But since *b* is part of *a,* what seems to follow is the paradoxical assertion: an animal (*b*) is part of an animal (*a*). Some logicians, Sherwood explains, maintain that "*b* is an animal" is false in the same way that "Every part of an animal but its foot is an animal" is false. Others, however, maintain that "*b* is an animal" is true because, if a foot were cut off, "it will be said truly that *b* is an animal," and since "nothing is still an animal that was not earlier an animal, therefore '*b* is an animal' is true" (60–61). Sherwood goes on to solve this *sophisma* through a "paralogism of accident," which discriminates between being a part of the body, and being a part of a body that is an animal that in turn is made complete by the soul (61).

The third syncategorematic word crucial to reading Chaucer's *moralitas* is the conjunction "and" (*et* is the subject of chapter 20, totaling six pages). In contradistinction to Priscian, who implies that the copulative conjunction "and"—signifying "being together" (*simul esse*)—is not a syncategorematic word, Sherwood insists that it is. He explains that the *simul esse* signified is sometimes two predicates in one subject, sometimes two predicates in two subjects, sometimes two subjects in one predicate, and sometimes two subjects in two predicates (134). Thus it is clear that "and" is a syncategorematic word, for it "copulates" ambiguously and in different ways. One of the most critical ways it copulates ambiguously is illustrated in the difference between its being taken "divisively" and its being taken "conjunctively." When one takes "and" divisively, the statement "Two and three are five" yields the grammatically correct but logically false propositions "Two are five, and three are five" (137). But when one takes "and" conjunctively in such a sentence as "Socrates and Plato are running," it yields the two logically valid propositions "Socrates [is] running, and Plato [is] running" (137). Another illustrative *sophisma* is " 'Socrates and Plato are brothers', which can be taken conjunctively only, and 'Socrates and Plato are dead', which can be taken divisively only" (138, n. 17).

The final major syncategorematic word parodically foregrounded in Chaucer's *moralitas* is "or" (*vel* is the subject of Sherwood's chapter 21, totaling eight pages). Like "and," "or" is a conjunction, but a "disjunctive" conjunction rather than a copulative conjunction. And, again like "and," it can work in two quite different ways. As a disjunctive it conjoins two terms indicating that one is true and the other is false. But as a "subdisjunctive," it "indicates solely that one is true while touching on nothing regarding the other part" (141). For example, the proposition "Every animal is rational or nonrational" is a *sophisma* because it appears to contain two mutually contradictory propositions: proposition A is "Every animal is rational," but since this is not true, it must follow that its contradictory, proposition B, "Every animal is nonrational," is true, although that is also not true. So Sherwood explains that a distinction must be drawn between how "or" can disjoin either between terms or between propositions. The determination "or nonrational" can be compounded with what precedes it (so that the whole "rational or nonrational" is in every animal). Or the determination "or nonrational" can be divided from what precedes it—so that either "rational" is in every individual animal, or "nonrational" is in every individual animal (145).

With this cursory introduction to the logical analysis of four key *syncategoremata*—one of inclusion (all), one of exception (but), one of conjunction (and), and one of alterity (or)—we are finally prepared to set about reading the "sophismatic" directives the Nun's Priest's *moralitas* offers concerning the art of reading. Not surprisingly, these directives are themselves involved with inclusion and exception (such as defining the membership of the narrator's audience) as well as with conjunction and alterity (such as determining the figural or grammatical essence of the beast fable's linguistic identity). What this means, in part, is that the grammatical/figural tension at the core of medieval literary studies will also prove central to the work of defining the precise meaning of each injunction. Furthermore, since the four sentences constituting the complete *moralitas* are intended to achieve some kind of suasive effect, the success or failure of this speech act as a rhetorical performance as well as the grammatical, logical, and figural valences of each of its key words all require our disciplined attention as close readers.

Here is the Nun's Priest's *moralitas* once again, now with three different fonts—GRAMMAR, *Rhetoric*, and **Logic**—foregrounding the first-impression semiological valence of a few key words:

> **But** *ye* that holden this tale a folye,
> As of a fox, **or** of a cok **and** hen,
> Taketh the moralite, goode men.
> For Seint Paul seith that **al** that writen is,
> To oure doctrine it is ywrite, ywis;
> Taketh the *fruyt* and lat the *chaf* be stille.
> Now goode God, if that it be thy wille,
> As seith MY LORD, so make us alle goode men,
> And brynge us to his highe blisse! *Amen.*
> (VII.3438–46)

If we were in a medieval classroom, the number of trivial questions that could be addressed to this one text would take many days of study. What follows, then, is but the initial steps of a fully realized scholastic interrogation. The first word, the syncategorematic "But," is an adversative conjunction that depends upon an implied "prejacent universal" (as the logicians express it),[65] a universal from which whatever follows is some kind of exceptive. Now if the logic of this "but" operates diminutionally, it may be seen as marking off the *moralitas* from the tale itself (of which it is *not* a part); yet if it works counter-instantively, then the *moralitas* would have to be a part of the total (*totus*) from which in some sense it is nevertheless able to be excepted.[66] But of course this "but" also appears to be doing *rhetorical* work even as it is doing logical work, by addressing an indeterminate audience whose "grammatical" identity is awaiting definition even as it is being partially located by the performative maneuverings of the adversative conjunction "but." Let us now turn to "ye." Is this categorematic "ye" the totality of Chaucer's audience, is it the totality of the Nun's Priest's audience, or does the preceding logical exceptive "but" succeed in delimiting the referential scope of "ye"? (In his Variorum edition Pearsall observes that "This exhortation is often interpreted as if it were addressed to all uninstructed readers or auditors, with the implication that appropriate instruction will follow"; but he adds that the narrator might be "speaking directly to people like the Parson, who rebukes such telling of fables."[67]) Obviously in striving to locate or to construct that population who are the *Tale's* putative audience, a crucial "consignificant" word ("something in respect of which the exception is made")[68] is "folye." And here the narrator provides quite exacting assistance, explaining that the *Tale* is a "folye" (that is, according to the *MED*, something foolish, idle, empty, or nonsensical) when it is understood to be "As of a fox, or of a cok and hen."

At this point we need to proceed with unusual logico-linguistic care. It is rather surprising that the narrator does not employ the exceptive syncategorematic word "only": "as of *only* a fox and a cock and hen." Instead, he does something strange. Why, the dialectician might ask, does he insert "or" into his list of three animals: "As of a fox *or* a cok and hen"? And why does he further complicate this list by inserting that other troublesome syncategorematic word "and": "As of a fox, or a cok *and* hen"? Why not simply "*a* and *b* and *c*" or else simply "*a* or *b* or *c*"? In light of the several ways we have seen that "or" and "and" can signify inside a *sophisma*, what logical work are these two *syncategoremata* actually performing here? Is "or" meant to be taken disjunctively, so that one term that it conjoins is valid and the other invalid: either "fox" obtains to "folye," or "cok and hen" obtain, but not both? Or is "or" here meant to be taken subdisjunctively, so that "fox" obtains and "cok and hen" *might also* obtain? Consider as well the "and" conjoining "cok" and "hen": is this copulative intended to be taken divisively or conjunctively? That is, is a tale a "folye" if it is a tale only of a cock? Is a tale a "folye" if it is a tale only of a hen? Either of these options, in William of Sherwood's terms, would be an instance where there are two predicates in two subjects. On the other hand, if the being together (*simul esse*) signified by "and" is an instance of two predicates in one subject, then the tale apparently has to be both of a cock *and* of a hen in order that it be a "folye."

This is all of course bordering on the absolutely ludicrous: are we really meant to ask, in a state of dialectical bewilderment, if one logico-literary fox is equivalent to one logico-literary cock plus one logico-literary hen? At some point we might hope that these problems are merely the result of scribal misunderstandings which over time have blanked out the author's original intent. But the two most authoritative manuscripts of *The Canterbury Tales,* Ellesmere and Hengwrt, authenticate "as of a fox or a cock and hen," and all modern editions publish this line without editorial demurral.[69] Therefore, and especially in light of the extremely significant roles played by "or" and "and" in late medieval syncategorematic and sophismatic treatises, we need to step back for a moment to consider what Chaucer's authorial intent might be. An enabling approach surfaces as soon as we invoke a poetic strategy Chaucer employs throughout *The Nun's Priest's Tale,* and that, of course, is parody. I do not mean to suggest that Chaucer is intent here on parodying medieval logic itself, satirizing its penchant for microlinguistic discriminations and playfully absurd *sophismata* ("Socrates has eleven fingers but one," and so forth). Instead, I think Chaucer in this problematic logical/grammatical/rhetorical collocation has constructed a subtly instructive pseudo-*sophisma:* "puzzling in its own right or on the basis of a certain assumption, [yet] designed to bring some abstract issue into sharper focus."[70] Of course what is most important here are the abstract issues brought into sharper focus: one of these, I believe, concerns precisely the grammar/rhetoric frontier highlighted in both Suzanne Reynolds's and Paul de Man's studies. In other words, as a fable that gives credence to the fiction of talking animals, *The Nun's Priest's Tale* crisscrosses the aporia between grammar and rhetoric at every moment. To put it another way, the interplay of possible but contradictory meanings inside these two *syncategoremata,* "or" and "and," is a chiastic exchange that mimics the truly significant border crossings between the *Tale*'s two major ways of being read: either as a constative grammatical statement or else as a sustained figure of thought.

It is inviting at this point to begin exploring the *metaphorical* structure of such border-crossings (this will be the focus of chapter 4), but we
need to move forward since we have not even finished the text's first sentence, which concludes with a pointed directive: "Taketh the moralite,
goode men." Now we might well infer that that element of the audience
who hold the tale to be a "folye" are in fact "goode men," and that it be-
hooves them to extract the narrative's "moralite," the implication being
that reading for the "moralitee" and reading "as of a fox, or a cok and hen"
are mutually exclusive enterprises. But just having been ensnarled in the
many logical complexities embedded in "and" and "or," whether or not we
are justified in cleanly discriminating between reading literature ideologically, that is, for its "moralite," and reading literature at the level of
the letter—or more precisely, at the level of the "half-letter," since the *Tale*
might be viewed either "as of a fox" or "of a cock and hen"—is a question
not easily answered.

But no matter, for at the outset of the next three lines, the reader is
asked to make a logical U-turn on a syllogistic "For":

> For Seint Paul seith that al that writen is,
> To oure doctrine it is ywrite, ywis;
> Taketh the fruyt, and lat the chaf be stille.

The crucial syncategorematic word here is "al." What precisely does Chaucer, citing Saint Paul, mean by "al"? Today most scriptural scholars believe that in Romans 15:4 Paul was probably designating only the Old
Testament when he refers to "Quaecumque enim scripta sunt" (note that
he does not employ either *totus* or *omnis*). However, A. J. Minnis, in his useful survey of slight variants of Romans 15:4 invoked in medieval literary
texts, illustrates how this passage was regularly used as an *apologia* for
the doctrinal value of secular texts. Whereas some medieval authors understood Paul's words as defending *some* nonscriptural writings as being
instructive (such as that of the classical pagans), others used his words
to support an extremely liberal defense of *all* texts, a reading designed,
as Minnis puts it, "to justify practically everything."[71] The author of the
Ovide Moralisé, to cite but one example, argues that because all litera-

ture may contain elements of both good and evil, all literature contributes to our moral improvement: "Alle scriptures and wrytyngis ben they good or evyll ben wreton for our proufyt and doctrine. The good to thende to take ensample by them to doo well. And the evyll to thende that we shoulde kepe and absteyne vs to do evyll."[72] So then, what does Chaucer mean here by "al"? If he means *every* work of literature (*omnis*), then it must logically follow that every single work—every fabliau, every song, and every lecherous lay—is written "for our doctrine." But if by "al" Chaucer means the totality (*totus*) of all that is written, that is, every part of every work of literature, then it must follow that every discrete element of every single text is written "for our doctrine." To assert that every work of literature is written for our instruction is to embrace an extremely liberal critical creed, especially in the Middle Ages, but to maintain that even the smallest piece of every work of literature is written "for our doctrine" is to embrace an astonishingly radical and totalizing aesthetic.[73] Applied locally, what this aesthetic means is *not* that *The Nun's Priest's Tale* has no point; rather, the point of *The Nun's Priest's Tale* is that it is *all* point, since its totality, including its *moralitas*, cannot but have been written for "our doctrine."

But whether we opt for the first or the second meaning of "al," there seems no way of interpreting what immediately follows, "Taketh the fruyt, and lat the chaf be stille," other than as a stunning *non sequitur*, another logical U-turn. For if, as the narrator has just asserted, everything is written for our instruction, it surely must follow that all texts are invariably "fruyt" and there is no "chaff." What then is the point of being enjoined to take the "fruyt," if the "fruyt" is everywhere in a text and the "chaff" is apparently nowhere? Of course, to interpret "fruyt" this way, as a signifier whose significance is equivalent to the significances of "moralite" and "doctrine," requires that one wrench a metaphorical expression out of its rhetorical register and transpose it into a grammatical register. And, as we have seen, at least according to Suzanne Reynolds and Paul de Man, *this cannot legitimately be done*—unless we choose to justify such a maneuver by placing it inside the critical category of "authorial intent."

The niggling critical difficulties parodically foregrounded to this point—difficulties relating to reading a text grammatically, figuratively, logically, and performatively—are now so numerous that it is not surprising the narrator concludes his counsel on literary criticism with a heartfelt prayer to God:

Now goode God, if that it be thy wille,
As seith my lord, so make us alle goode men,
And brynge us to his heighe blisse! Amen.

The field of pronouns introduced by "ye" at the beginning of the *moralitas* unfolds now into "thy" and "my" and "us" and "his." Embracing the demarcations of inclusion, exclusion, alterity, and conjunction in one grand rhetorical gesture, the narrator begs that all of us be delivered, by the power of his prayer and by the grace of God, in the direction of "his heighe blisse. Amen."

My trivial reading of the *moralitas* is not quite complete, however, for there remain two unwonted locutions that still need to be accounted for. Considering the interplay between the issues of exception, alterity, conjunction, and universality that has been exercised throughout the *moralitas,* the fact that *The Nun's Priest's Tale* is Chaucer's only poem to incorporate a closing "Amen" within its prosodic frame, that is, rhyming "Amen" with the last word of its penultimate line, is surely an important gesture. As an integral part of the poem as poem, the sacred interjection "Amen" appears to give semiotic capital to the *Tale* as a rhetorical performance that strives to connect literary fiction with the real. Directly addressing the divine Other, even as he is directly addressing his own audience, the narrator prays that the words of his fable's *moralitas* will do the suasive work of helping move "goode men" toward their own salvation. Of course, whether or not the text of the *moralitas* or of the entire *Tale* is a successful speech act in this regard is something only Chaucer's readers could resolve "performatively," that is, in their own lives.

There is one other moment at *Tale's* end that attempts to connect literary language with the real: the narrator's sudden invocation "as seith my lord" in the poem's penultimate line. This casual, out-of-the-blue appellation is in fact an egregious semantic howler. Who in the wide world of fact and fiction is "my lord"? Since it has been proven that "my lord" cannot possibly mean Christ, a few scholars have halfheartedly searched through lists of fourteenth-century bishops and archbishops to locate an historical referent.[74] But the denotative meaning of "my lord" remains as perplexing as Chaucer's similar and equally mystifying allusion in the very last line of *The House of Fame* to the "man of gret auctoritee." That there is no extra-diegetic referent for either of these mysterious semantic intruders is, I believe, precisely Chaucer's point. A categorematic nominal, an ostensive and constative and personal signifier, "my lord" is a sign that carries a limited connotative meaning, or *Sinn*, but it enjoys no phenomenal reference, or *Bedeutung*. And the implication here, I believe, is that the indeterminate relation of this isolate lexical sign may be symptomatic more generally of the indeterminate relationship of literary language to the real. To put it one more way, the question "my lord" implicitly raises is whether our customary habits of reading literature "grammatically" and thus referentially ever succeed in truly connecting its "trivial" language with the phenomenal world.

So what does this extremely labor-intensive analysis of the *moralitas* of *The Nun's Priest's Tale* finally leave us with? Grammar, Nietzsche once wrote, is the metaphysics of the people.[75] It surely is an important part of our metaphysics as readers, since we tend to assume that in some complex fashion a "stable cognitive field" exists in literature "that extends from grammar to logic to a general science of man and of the phenomenal world."[76] But by so complexly foregrounding in his *moralitas* all three elements of the trivium, it appears Chaucer puts the "metaphysics" of all three under considerable scrutiny. Rhetoric, in both its performative and figurative modes, proves — unsurprisingly — to be a wild card in language's semiological deck. As a speech act, Chaucer's beast fable may fail to connect "rhetorically" to the world, and as a sustained human/animal metaphor its figurative/grammatical border-crossings obviously deprivilege any stable category of meaning. Dialectic, as evidenced in the several logical points of arrest in this *moralitas*, likewise exhibits surprisingly deconstructive qualities. Fashioned out of three or four pseudo-sophisms containing three or four unresolvable syncategorematic puzzles, the *moralitas* appears to be adamantly resistant to any univocal system of logical interpretation. Finally, although not spotlighted until the end of the *moralitas*, grammar is revealed to be an equally problematic linguistic art. "[T]he grammatical decoding of a text," as de Man explains the matter in a slightly different context, "leaves a residue of indetermination that has to be, but cannot be, resolved by grammatical means, however extensively conceived."[77] Thus, strategically placed at the very end of the *Tale,* the problematic question "Who *is* 'my lord'?" serves as an arresting semantic conundrum that quite pointedly underscores the instability of the *Tale*'s entire literary/linguistic enterprise.

Now, if we were ever fully to embrace the "ultraskeptical radicality"[78] of Paul de Man's theory of "mere reading," it appears we would have to conclude that the Nun's Priest's *moralitas* is, in fact, quite "unreadable." But is this conclusion inevitable? And do we ourselves need to mean precisely the same thing when we use the term "unreadable"? To unpackage de Man's radical theory somewhat further, "mere reading" for him is an activity that "proceeds by demonstrating that (a) the figural potential of language is disruptive of grammatical univocity and conversely that (b) the grammatical or conceptual rigor of texts is disruptive of . . . 'rhetorical mystifications.'"[79] Accordingly, a de Manian "mere reading" proves invariably to be a "negative process" that ultimately "exhibits the illusory nature of all comprehension."[80] Or, as Gasché explains, "[I]f '*to read*' is to understand a text and if '*to understand*' means thematically, aesthetically, or conceptually to totalize a text, then the production of insights into the mechanics of the text will certainly render that text opaque and unreadable."[81]

However, merely to conclude that Chaucer's *moralitas* is "opaque and unreadable" seems willfully perverse. The final nine lines to Chaucer's beast fable are obviously a unique treasure. Nowhere else in his entire *oeuvre* does Chaucer set out a list of explicit directives on how to read a work of literature; and even if it were little more than a fourteenth-century *Idiot's Guide to Reading Literature,* such critical counsel would need to be valued for whatever it says in its own right as well as for whatever traces of Chaucer's purpose may therein be descried. Surely, in the spirit of salvageability, we could belatedly tease out various "positive" reading protocols, such as: (1) let us read "grammatically," that is, "literally"—"as of a fox or a cok and hen"; (2) let us read "figuratively"—wherein metaphorical "fruyt" means metaphorical "fruyt"; (3) let us read "ideologically"—encoding a transcendent "moralite"; or (4) let us read "rhetorically"—embracing the text as a suasive artifact. But even the subtlest refinements of these heavy-handed protocols, rather like the seven methods I confected in response to the hermeneutic schemas implicit in the tale's opening *exemplum*, are very likely to prove self-contradictory and unharmonizable. In summary, then, I have intercalated Chaucer's parodic intensification of medieval reading practices and de Man's deconstruction of contemporary reading practices because I find that each reinforces the other, most notably in their mutual reliance upon the trivium as the foundation of literary production and literary criticism. But are these two reading theories, one implicit and the other explicit, identical? In other words, is Chaucer's "unreadability thesis" as radically skeptical as de Man's? My answer, finally, is "No." Having reread Chaucer's *moralitas* with gimlet-eyed linguistic attention, we have discovered in its grammatical, logical, and rhetorical constructions a host of oddities, ambiguities, and contradictions. And having reread with equal attention the advice of the *moralitas* concerning the proper methods for discovering the meaning of a literary text, we have discovered even more oddities, ambiguities, and contradictions. There is no question that as readers we are here challenged with a host of undecideabilities, and that these undecideablilites, at least in the de Manian sense, demonstrate how the text is itself "unreadable."[82]

But here, finally, I want to rebut de Man's "radical skepticism" with a dash of Chaucerian optimism. That is, I believe it is the undecideabilities themelves that comprise the precise import of Chaucer's literary-critical instruction. Because a disinterested analysis of the *moralitas* leads into a series of interpretative culs-de-sac, it certainly appears that no unified extrapolatable meaning exists. Nevertheless, the very *experience* of rereading Chaucer's conclusion both as a disseminal verbal artifact and as a self-reflexive literary text proves to be a profoundly instructive education in its own right. As we have experienced in the preceding pages, this kind of close reading requires us to think aggressively about the way language is fashioned into patterns of signification, about how we are traditionally instructed to read a text, and about the exemplary resistance of that text to the totalizing regimes of our understanding. Therefore, to conclude this chapter's interrogation of Chaucer's interrogation of the art of reading, we might agree there is much to be learned from the Nun's Priest's final words. Quite specifically, we have learned that the point of Chaucer's *moralitas* is that it has no "point." But we also now know there are other ways of making the same point, most notably by endorsing the "radical" critical proposition that the entirety of Chaucer's *ars poetica,* including its *moralitas,* has indeed been "written for our doctrine."

A CLOSE READING OF CLOSE READING

Since the reading protocols I have employed in this chapter are exaggerations and parodies of what we normally understand "close reading" to be, a brief coda on close reading itself may be in order. As I noted in the Introduction, the large number of close reading sessions included in the 2006 New Chaucer Society conference may be symptomatic of a renewed interest in close reading. Yet in the conference's final discussion it became obvious that each of us had a quite different take on what the term "close reading" means. What is close reading? Is it simply an ardent reapplication of the formalist persuasions of New Criticism, or has it morphed into something else? The recent anthology *Close Reading: The Reader,* published in 2003, is designed to provide an answer.[83] Dividing an array of already published essays under two general rubrics, "Formalism (Plus)" and "After Formalism?" its first group includes essays by Ransom, Brooks, Burke, Krieger, Blackmur, Lentricchia, Vendler, and Fish; its second group includes essays by de Man, Barthes, Jameson, Gallagher and Greenblatt, Gilbert and Gubar, Sedgwick, Moretti, Baker, and Bhabha. As the collection's co-editor Frank Lentricchia explains, the purpose of gathering together these well-established works (first appearing between 1947 and 2000) is to "emphasize the continuity" between "the formalists" and "the nonformalists" and to underscore the centrality of close reading in their critical endeavors. Although the nonformalists, in Lentricchia's opinion, have "dominated literary criticism and theory over the last decades of the twentieth century," they "do their most persuasive work by attending closely to the artistic character of the text before them. The common ground [between the two groups] is a commitment to close attention to literary texture and what is embodied there."[84] Now if by "close reading" we mean simply "close attention to literary texture and what is embodied there," then the studies included in this anthology have a great deal in common. But if one were to reread these essays, one might eventually conclude that these various studies are actually engaged in rather dissimilar activities. And obviously there are other studies, such as Derrida's "Ulysses Gramophone," a lengthy analysis of the single word "Yes" in Joyce's *Ulysses*, that raise further questions about whether there exist any satisfactorily "close" definitions of close reading.[85] Is it possible that the reading of a certain text is so brilliantly and obsessively myopic as to disqualify it as an acceptable example of close reading?

The close readings in this chapter have remained so very close to the texts under scrutiny that the patience of some readers is certain to have been sorely tested. I hope, however, that inspecting Chaucer's *exemplum* and *moralitas* with a literary/linguistic/logical magnifying glass has proven to be an appropriate response to Chaucer's art. I recall walking through a gallery of paintings by the neorealist artist Chuck Close. The typical Close painting is a much-larger-than-life representation of a human face whose most impressive quality is its astonishing realism—every pore, strand of hair, and fleck of pigmentation is represented with a magnified exactitude. But to what purpose? According to art critic Robert Storr, "Close [explores] the dynamics and connotations of enlargement in two distinct but complementary ways. On the one hand, the scale of his paintings amplifies the image so that, at a distance, it confronts us with an almost overwhelming presence. On the other hand, by painstakingly accounting for the smallest details of form, texture, and color within the expanded field, Close's paintings invite the most careful inspection."[86] Typically, the viewer's first response is to stand far back in order to take in the entire work. But the viewer is then drawn forward. Moving gradually "into" the painting, the viewer's initial appreciation of the painting's "naturalism" subtly morphs into a close-up recognition of painting's artifice—a realistic earlobe is now a thousand nano-specks of paint. This cognitive transformation appears to have been part of Close's intent. "The only way that I can accomplish what I want," he has said, "is to understand not the reality of what I am dealing with, but the artificiality of what it is. So perhaps I would feel more comfortable with 'new artificialist' than with 'new realist.'"[87] It was with a similar purpose in mind that I undertook the two close reading exercises in this chapter. After viewing each text briefly from afar, I have then drawn extremely close to the work to examine its myriad "artificial" details, tracing out the parodic interplay of genres in Chaucer's opening *exemplum,* parsing the parodic instabilities of language in the closing *moralitas.* That these two close readings, even while complementary, differ remarkably from each other, both methodologically and theoretically, is explained in part by the vantage points from which I chose to view the two works themselves. That is, I studied Chaucer's *exemplum* standing a few inches away from the canvas, so to speak, while I read his *moralitas* in cross-eyed contact with the text itself. At least some modern readers are likely to resist the invitation to read medieval works of literature this closely, or through the lens of formal logic, as I have done with Chaucer's *moralitas.* Nevertheless, there is no doubt that certain medieval poems called upon a quite precise training in logic, and that medieval readers enjoyed approaching these poems as if they were sophismatic puzzles. In "Medieval Fora: The Logic of the Work," D. Vance Smith provides a brilliantly "logical" close reading of the very short Middle English poem "Erthe toc of erthe erthe with wo." Employing many of the terms I have outlined in the preceding pages, he concludes his essay with this relevant assertion:

> The play of terms and references, the forms that supposition theory trained readers to parse, suggest a mode like that of close reading. But its rules were even more elaborate and intricate, themselves often the focus of aesthetic attention in the popular form of the *sophisma.* The rigorous order in which these rules were to be applied, and their centrality in the curriculum, meant that every educated reader could be expected to read in the same manner. Reading in such a complex and intricate fashion may seem like mere virtuosity, the demonstration of individual skill, talent, or genius. But such rules were a part of the communal experience of educated reading in the English Middle Ages, a reading for form that proceeded out of a common discipline and that ultimately formed the community of readers.[88]

Thus, even a brief consideration of the critical activity we call close reading appears to lead toward the conclusion that an overarching definition of the term is probably an impossibility. In the English Middle Ages, a set of specific rules for the close reading of texts may well have been practiced by a community of like-minded readers. But now, because our conceptions of "closeness" may be premised upon a more *individual* sense of appropriate spatial proximity and aesthetic boundaries, different levels of critical comfort with different degrees of textual intimacy are bound to produce different modes of interpretation as well as different expressions of theoretical understanding.

FOUR

Chaucer's Heliotropes
and the Poetics of Metaphor

> *What is proper to the sun? . . . Unceasingly,*
> *unwillingly, we have been carried along by the*
> *movement which brings the sun to turn in metaphor; or have been*
> *attracted by what turned the philosophical metaphor toward the sun.*
> *Is not this flower of rhetoric (like) a sunflower? That is—*
> *but this is not exactly a synonym—analogous to the heliotrope?*
> —JACQUES DERRIDA

One possible way of dealing with the strange art of rhetoric is to claim one knows nothing about it. This is the tack taken by Chaucer's Franklin in his prologue to his Canterbury tale:

> I lerned nevere rethorik, certeyn;
>
> . . . .
>
> Colours ne knowe I none, withouten drede,
> But swiche colours as growen in the mede,
> Or elles swiche as men dye or peynte.
> Colours of rethoryk been to me queynte.
>
> (V.719, 723–26)

Here the Franklin pretends to be an ignoramus when it comes to understanding the *figurae*—the colors, or flowers, of poetry—taught in the rhetorical handbooks. The Franklin's antipoetic sentiments are of course problematic, for his four-line demurral concerning the proper understanding of "colours" contains a subtle illustration not only of the word "colour" being put to good metaphorical use but of metaphor's complex linguistic, ontological, and indeed epistemological nature. Here, in the Franklin's modesty trope, "colour" is a word that seems to have so many metaphorical meanings that it is difficult to descry its proper or original significance. Transported from what we might assume is its realm of original, literal meaning (the colors of pigment) into another linguistic realm as a name for poetic tropes (the "colours" of rhetoric), it is translated by the Franklin back to the domain of nature to serve as a synecdochic name for flowers ("swiche colours as growen in the mede"), even though "flowers" is a traditional medieval name for verbal tropes, the "flowers" of poetry.

A host of philosophical questions relating to the nature of metaphor is compressed into these quicksilver category shifts and semantic exchanges. What in fact is denoted by the name "colour"? Is there an absolute divide between "colour" meaning flower, "colour" meaning a quality in paint, and "colour" meaning a poetic trope? Does paint belong to nature or to art? Are the pigments of paints the properties of things, are they actually substances, or are they some kind of *prima materia* upon which nature itself is predicated? Is it possible that all the Franklin's "colours" are metaphorical names for things, and, if so, does this mean that all literal language is fundamentally metaphorical or, contrariwise, that all metaphorical statements are ultimately literal propositions? Indeed, what is meant when we say we "knowe" colors in this world: do we know the world first, before learning its "colours," or do "colours" bring us knowledge of the world?

All of these questions concerning metaphor—its denotive functions, truth-value, ontological character, and epistemic powers—are questions that derive from an animated aesthetic debate that can be traced back at least to the twelfth century. A seminal contribution to this debate is Alanus de Insulis's characterization of rhetoric as painting in his twelfth-century epic of the seven liberal arts, the *Anticlaudianus*. At the center of Nature's paradisiacal garden in the *Anticlaudianus,* a *hortus conclusus* which Alanus terms a "place apart,"[1] stands a mural of magnificent paintings. "Oh painting with your new wonders!" Alanus exclaims: by "turn[ing] the shadows of things into things and chang[ing] every lie to truth," painting "checks logic's arguments and triumphs over logic's sophisms."[2] Whereas painting appears here to symbolize all of the creative arts, later in the epic it is the allegorical figure of Rhetoric that proves to be painting's linguistic equivalent.[3] "[E]nfold[ing] in her bosom the complete art of the painter," Rhetoric's verbal elegances are palpable in the very colors of her person: "Her countenance is steeped in radiant colour: a brilliant red glow tints her face with roseate luster." "But," adds Alanus by way of anxious qualification, "a foreign glitter haunts her face to some extent and tries to combine with the native hue."[4] Despite his exuberant praise, Alanus is clearly troubled by the oddity of linguistic tropes, by the unnatural "foreign glitter" that attempts to intermix with Rhetoric's "native hue." In fact, the colors of rhetoric are painted ambiguously throughout the *Anticlaudianus*: they are both natural and artificial, creative and counterfeit, comforting and uncanny. This is a "strange art," Alanus concludes, which "divert[s] itself" by "aping reality" and bringing into being something that "can have no real existence."[5]

Alanus's artifice of painted Rhetoric surrounded by the garden of Nature and the Franklin's intricate intercalation of flowers, paint, poetry, and color are two semidiscursive contributions to an energetic metapoetical exchange concerning the "strange art" of poetry and its most fundamental trope—which is, of course, metaphor.[6] In this chapter, I intend to focus upon the poetics of metaphor as figured forth in a popular, antidiscursive, and powerfully foregrounded meta-metaphor: the heliotrope. Compressed into this medieval poetic icon are a variety of issues concerning metaphor including those inhabiting the Franklin's meadow and Alanus's garden. There were in fact two kinds of heliotropes, one mineral and the other vegetable, that medieval poets used as symbols for their craft. *Heliotropia* was the medieval Latin name for a diaphanous gem to which lapidaries attributed the power not only of reflecting the sun's light but also of generating its own light so that it was capable of rivaling, even occluding, the light of the sun. *Heliotropium,* on the other hand, was the medieval Latin name for a flowering plant (normally described in the lapidaries alongside the *heliotropia*) that is unusually sympathetic to the rays of the sun, opening at dawn, bending in the sun's direction throughout the day, and closing at night.[7] Because my main concern is defining the poetics of Chaucer's heliotropes, in the following pages I accord primary attention to the herbal heliotropic tradition, even though the gem's special power also sheds light on the complex characteristics of metaphor, including those already cited: metaphor's figural residence in a "place apart," its natural brilliance and artificial beauty, its antagonism to the rigors of logic, its vexed relationship to material reality and to the generative powers of nature, its uncanny and exotic otherness.

To sketch in the cultural environment of Chaucer's poetics of metaphor, I open with Ovid's originary heliotropic myth and then turn to Machaut's heliotropes (with a brief side-glance at Froissart). To facilitate a further appreciation of the integrity of these poetic icons, I interweave insights taken from philosophical studies of metaphor, ranging from classical to postmodern. A major purpose in my integrating philosophical analysis with poetic semiotics is to suggest that the heliotropic readings of metaphor provided by medieval poets, and most notably by Chaucer, are at least as rigorous as those advanced in philosophical treatises. Both figural discourse and speculative discourse are in fact essential to understanding the unusually sophisticated defense of metaphor that Chaucer contains within his two great heliotropes: first, the daisy at the center of his poetological dream-vision, the Prologue to *The Legend of Good Women*; and second, Chauntecleer, the rooster-hero of his most achieved *ars poetica, The Nun's Priest's Tale.* In a colorful heliotropic flower and in an even more colorful heliotropic chicken, Chaucer not only embodies the dynamics of metaphor emphasized by his continental predecessors and peers, he details his personal vision of metaphor's unique power to interrogate the hierarchical and analogical categories of our minds. While demonstrating metaphor's ability to define the nature both of poetry and of the intellectual world his readers inhabit, the theoretical light emanating from Chaucer's two heliotropes is of such scope that metaphor, that is, poetry, proves capable of transforming its readers into heliotropes themselves.

THE HELIOTROPE AS META-METAPHOR

In his story of Clytie in the *Metamorphoses,* Ovid composed an etiological myth for the flowering heliotrope. A maiden loved and then rejected by the sun, Clytie is changed into a sunflower as a punishment for her jealousy. But both during and after her transformation, her gaze remains fixed upon her lost lover as she traces the course of his progress through the skies:

> tantum spectabat euntis
> ora dei vultusque suos flectebat ad illum.
> membra ferunt haesisse solo, partemque coloris
> luridus exsangues pallor convertit in herbas:
> est in parte rubor, violaeque simillimus ora
> flos tegit. illa suum, quamvis radice tenetur,
> vertitur ad Solem mutataque servat amorem.
>
> > (*Metamorphoses* 4.264–70)

> ——
>
> She only gazed at the sun as it went, turned her head to the face
> of the god. They say her limbs adhered to the ground, and her
> pallid bloodless color turned partly the color of grass, remained
> in part red; her face is hidden by a flower almost like a violet.
> Though held at the root, she turned her love to the sun and,
> though changed, maintained her love.[8]

Ovid's major interest lies in the extraordinary poetry Clytie's tragic story helps him to create, as he captures, in polymorphic slow motion, the astonishing transmogrification of human form into floral form. Ovid's narrative thus represents two tropic movements at once: while Clytie is turning into a flower, the girl/flower is turning herself in response to the sun. Both of these turnings, I believe, are essential to the way metaphor makes meaning. That is, Ovid's narrative takes the absolute equals sign of metaphor (Clytie *is* a flower) and explores the graduated process of selection involved in metaphoric translation: the dissimilar features between girl and flower are suppressed; their analogous features are made more nearly identical, even though (and very importantly) at translation's end traces of the girl's physical and emotional identity remain firmly intact. Regarding this remaining trace, the fact that the heliotrope remains firmly rooted in one place is especially significant: the poet Paul Valéry once described metaphor as a "stationary movement" because, even while taking another's place, a word used metaphorically never deserts its radical place of original meaning.[9] Being rooted in one place (a), reaching toward the sun (b), and turning with the sun's movement across the sky (c): each of these characteristics, I intend to demonstrate, is essential in the symbolic dynamics of the heliotrope's metaphorical behavior.

Between the 1360s and the 1380s in France, a new and powerful artistic movement took shape around the poetry of Guillaume Machaut, Jean Froissart, and Eustache Deschamps and their mutually shared icon, the marguerite, or French daisy.[10] In many of their marguerite poems this daisy is described in considerable botanical detail even though its human morphology as the female beloved is often not far beneath its leafy surface. Situated in its characteristic *locus amoenus* (a paradisiacal place apart), the marguerite of Machaut's "Le dit de la Fleur de Lis et de la Marguerite," for example, has four distinct parts: a very green stem; a cincture of white petals; a red crown; and a vermillion and seemingly gilded center, or *greinne*, whose treasure the flower locks tightly in its petals at night.[11] While conceptualizing the various properties of this French marguerite (which, I should note, is not the same species as the white-petaled American daisy), the reader attempts to translate, as much as possible, the flower's physical parts (stem, petals, crown, *greinne*) into the physical person or apparel of the female beloved. This many-layered exercise in floramorphic/andromorphic analogizing is an example of the complex filtering process involved in any metaphor-translation. Here, the *in*complete success of certain equations (does a green stem really equal a green dress?) foregrounds an important underlying principle in the way metaphor works: although often overlooked in analytic studies, metaphor thrives as much upon dissonance as upon similarities in kind or part. However, while Machaut's readers are in the process of personifying the marguerite at one level of analogy by "painting" her body or her clothing in four colors, Machaut unexpectedly shifts categories. Rather than her physical attributes and vestments, two of the flower's external colors prove to be signs of the woman's interior qualities: the white petals of her cincture signify joy, and the red crown symbolizes her modesty. The green stalk, meanwhile, remains unglossed, and the eroticism of the unallegorized *greinne* is only heightened by the poet's "literal" warning that no one should seize, spoil, steal, or ravish it. Machaut's French daisy thus illustrates the complexity of metaphor-translation: as readers we must sort out the implicit hermeneutics of every specific marguerite while honoring the fertility of the generic marguerite as a signifier of the poet's creative imagination.

The quality of the heliotrope most admired by the medieval French poets is the daisy's exquisitely choreographed movements throughout the daylight hours. In the beginning of Machaut's "Dit de la Marguerite," the narrator proclaims:

> J'aim une fleur qui s'uevre et qui s'encline
> Vers le soleil, de jour quant il chemine;
> Et quant il est couchiez soubz sa courtine
> > Par nuit obscure,
> Elle se clost, ainsois que li jours fine.

> ———

> I love a flower who opens and bends
> Toward the sun, when it slowly travels through the day;
> And when it is embedded under its covers
> > By the dark night,
> She closes herself, before the day ends.[12]

So great is their admiration of the daisy's motion that all three poets find their cerebral faculties nearly paralyzed by their rapturous gaze. None of them attempts to explicate or allegorize the marguerite's uncanny empathy with the sun—not erotically, mythically, philosophically, or metapoetically. Machaut gestures briefly in this direction by suggesting that his marguerite is gifted with a special knowledge of the sun and its power ("Et samble qu'elle ait cognoissance / Dou soleil et de sa poissance" ["And it seems that she has knowledge of the sun and of its power"]),[13] but the nature of this knowledge is something Machaut appears unable, or unwilling, to put into words.

What these poets do enjoy putting into words, or more precisely, putting inside words, are names hidden in anagrams: in *L'espinette amoureuse*

Froissart tantalizes his readers by explaining that he has hidden the name of both the poet and his lady in four lines of verse. These names have been discovered and identified: JEHAN FROISSART and VIOLETTES/ MARGUERITES.[14] But who are these Violettes and these Marguerites: are they one woman, and is she a real lady or a poetic flower? In her study of the role of the marguerite in Froissart's poetry, Sylvia Huot eventually leans toward the final option: most often it appears that the marguerite-woman for Froissasrt is a self-referential icon, a "poetic flower," a "reified image, a work of art."[15] A similar cryptogram has been discovered in Machaut, where, in one of his minor poems, an acrostic spells out two names: MARGUERITE/PIERRE.[16] James Wimsatt is certain that Pierre is Pierre of Lusignan, king of Cyprus, and Marguerite, although a very popular French name, may be Marguerite of Flanders, a woman known to Peter of Cyprus and "unquestionably the most important heiress of the day."[17] Wimsatt's equation of conventional literary names with proper historical names is a problematic maneuver, but by no means is it entirely inappropriate.[18] As with the Platonized and emblazoned female archetype of so much early-modern poetry, be she called *midons, donna,* or "my mistress," or named Laura (Petrarch), Stella (Sidney), or Olive (du Bellay), "marguerite" in these French poems embodies the complexity of poetry's extrafictive referentiality even while underscoring poetry's narcissistic claims to being a purely self-contained image, an autotelic work of art.

These heliotropic flowers—like Alanus's depiction of painted rhetoric in nature's garden and the Franklin's clever riff on the colors of poetic and natural flowers—raise a number of questions about metaphor's curious qualities. An issue of primary importance is the transgressive relationship metaphor creates between signifier and signified, that is, between *verba* (words) and *res* (physical objects and mental concepts). All mimetic theories of language appear to honor proper language over figurative language because the latter is seen as swerving, or troping, from the norm. The normative function of proper language is, of course, that of maintaining a "natural" or at least a "conventional" relationship between name and the thing thus named. Metaphor, on the other hand, as its Latin name *translatio* indicates, moves away from the *res* it points to and appropriates another, and "improper," referent. According to Cicero, metaphor is a word put into an alien place as if it were its own ("in alieno loco tanquam in suo positum").[19] According to Isidore of Seville, metaphor's displacement of another word is a form of semantic usurpation ("metaphora est verbi alicuius usurpata translatio").[20] And according to Bede, metaphor involves not only a transference of words but a transposition of words and things ("metaphora est rerum verborumque translatio").[21] Yet even as they recognize the revolutionary improprieties of figurative language, most philosophers acknowledge that human discourse would be a bland affair if it were entirely devoid of metaphor's transgressive pleasures.

Aristotle, for example, believed metaphor to be "the greatest thing by far" when used as part of rhetorical and poetical (but not philosophical) discourse. The orator's ability to create pleasing metaphors is in fact "a sign of genius," "the one thing that cannot be learnt from others" (*Poetics* 1459a).[22] At the same time, Aristotle (like Alanus) was also quite leery of metaphors. Metaphors for him are very similar to a foreign language and are thus strange and alien: if the poet writes "a whole statement in such words [it] will be either a riddle or a barbarism" (*Poetics* 1458b). Thus, in themselves, metaphors are wild and enigmatic, a threat to rational discourse because they violate the principles of semantic propriety. Not only does metaphor violate Aristotle's own law of the excluded middle (a proposition must be either true or false), but it oftentimes seems to claim a more fundamental relationship to its newly appropriated referent than that enjoyed by the referent's prior, or original, name. Aristotle's paradoxical attitude, as Paul Gordon has shown, is dramatized by his inconsistent use of one adjective, *allotrios*. In the *Poetics* Aristotle defines metaphor as *allotrios* ("strange, belonging to another"), but in the *Rhetoric* metaphors are said to be popular only if they are not *allotrion* ("strange, belonging to another"). "Metaphor is truly uncanny and enigmatical," writes Gordon, "for it must be something other than itself in order to be itself."[23] Aristotle's reading of metaphor, concludes Gordon, is much like Freud's reading of the uncanny: foreign but familiar, threatening but delightful, falsifying but validating, supplemental but essential.

Of all the major classical writers on metaphor, it was Augustine who most powerfully associated metaphor's otherness, its linguistic displacement of proper signification, with the state of human existence itself. For Augustine, humankind has fallen away from the atemporal essence of true signification to wander in exile through an alien region of semiotic confusion called the place of dissimilitude (*regio dissimilitudinis*), or the land of unlikeness. Not only does human language fail to represent adequately things essentially unlike itself, which is everything in this world and in our minds, but it also fails to share in the essence of the only true *res,* which is God. God's being, the *est* of his identity, constitutes an ontological unity of essences: "Ego sum qui sum." But the *est* of human exile is a failed equation because it cannot express the essence of perfect sameness but only the predication of attributes. Unity of being thus exists only in God's being, where his transcendent *est* simply is, or, as Augustine puts it, "EST EST." As Margaret W. Ferguson has observed, this means that there is no such thing as proper language available to human speakers: for Augustine, therefore, all propositions are already figurative, displaced, and fraught with (dis)similitudes.[24]

Although the medieval poets I have mentioned—Chaucer, Alanus, Machaut, and Froissart—are obviously more comfortable than was Augustine with the fallenness of language, they are nevertheless aware of the "alien" nature of metaphor as it has been perceived within both philosophical and religious traditions of thought. It is thus a profoundly important gesture, I believe, that these poets all situate their prized poetic figures in a special "other" world, a world that Alanus terms "a place apart." This place of poetic removal is linguistically and hermeneutically significant. As several modern theorists have remarked at length, metaphor tends to "retire" or "retreat" from the field of proper semantics into a space of its own. Paul Ricoeur refers in *The Rule of Metaphor* to "the space of the figure."[25] Jacques Derrida's extensive gloss to "White Mythology" is entitled "The *Retrait* of Metaphor."[26] And Patricia Parker has suggested that this space is akin to the liminal place of creative meaning that an interpreter constructs between metaphor's two dialectical poles.[27]

At the very center of this place apart is the powerful reality of the metaphorical icon itself. While its significance radiates in many directions, the icon's first function seems to be simply to reify itself. The existential reality of the icon, in other words, is something these poets insist the reader give full credence to: my poetry places before you this flower, which is a flower, is a flower is a flower. Thus as a physical sign of its own materiality, the quintessential poetic metaphor appears to be retreating as far as possible toward a domain where words and things are one, or even further toward a preverbal and prelogical iconicity where *res* simply represents *res*.[28]

Analytical studies of metaphor have recently caught up with the iconic intuitions of the poets. In a brief but important article entitled "Metaphor as Matter," Darrel Mansell argues, "Language in metaphor is on the way back toward becoming the object again."[29] What Mansell means is that metaphors resist the logical predications of interpretation and align themselves instead with the "mind-boggling plentitude" of nature. For example, "Man is a wolf" may be accorded a "meaning" whereby a few qualities of the wolf are attributed to man, such as "Man is a fierce and powerful predator." But this reductive extrapolation, Mansell strenuously argues, is not what the metaphor actually *is* or *says:* in metaphor, *all* that belongs to the wolf and *all* that belongs to man are included in a fiercely nonlogical equation that can only be found, or imagined to exist, in the material world before its translation into the predications of rationalized language. Every metaphor is thus "a throwback to a more primitive and earthbound way of thinking,"[30] satisfying, at least partially, the mythic yearning for an "imagined original state when the referent and sign were actually one."[31]

Even while thrusting its roots deep into a world of prelogical materiality, metaphor is involved in an equally strenuous movement in the direction of postlogical transcendency. That is, all metaphors strive toward the sun. Like their iconicity, their solar ambitions inspire their authors' idolatrous reverence. But the significance of these solar yearnings, even though they would seem to invite some form of interpretative grammar, are yearnings the poets typically leave for others to explain. The most celebrated study of metaphor's solar aspirations is Derrida's "White Mythology," an essay that takes as its central text a passage in Aristotle's *Poetics* in which Aristotle provides an example of what he calls a "qualified metaphor": "It may be that some of the terms thus related have no special name of their own, but for all that they will be metaphorically described in just the same way. Thus to cast forth seed-corn is called 'sowing'; but to cast forth its flame, as said of the sun, has no special name. This nameless act (B), however, stands in just the same relation to its object, sunlight (A), as sowing (D) to the seed-corn (C). Hence the expression in the poet, 'sowing around a god-created flame' (D + A)" (*Poetics* 1457b). What Aristotle illustrates here is metaphor's ability to create an identity of two motions—the farmer's sowing of seeds, the sun's projecting its rays of light—even though one half of the identity (the sun's movement) is "nameless" because no proper verb exists to designate that activity. In filling this semantic gap, the broad-casting trope of the poet may also be providing an understanding of the circumambient movement of the rays of the sun. But Derrida is persuaded that Aristotle is mistaken on more than one count. First, although some readers may understand Aristotle to be drawing on analogy between two motions, Derrida is certain he is positing an identity. Second, Derrida insists that the sun's "nameless act," which Aristotle accepts as no more than a catachrestic gap, is something constituting an epistemological abyss. "Where," he asks, "has one ever *seen* that there is the same relationship between the sun and its rays as between sowing and seeds?"[32] Where, in other words, do we have any evidence that we "know" the sun, and know what to name its activities, its qualities, and most importantly its essence?

For Derrida, if there is anything within our experience that serves as a transcendent signifier it is the name of the sun, or else of course the sun itself, and therefore what is proper to the sun must define the essence of its unique, substantive, and unmetaphoric being. But because we do not "know" the sun, the sun cannot serve as an unmoved prime mover; rather, in its own turning, in its amenability to metaphor, the name of the sun is already inscribed in a metaphorical system and is thus no different from the heliotropes that turn toward it as their ultimate stable signifier. In its tropings, therefore, in its "sowing of seeds," the sun participates in the same imperfect system of relations as do all other heliotropes, which is the name Derrida gives to those "philosophic" metaphors that dramatically turn with the turnings of the sun: "Heliotropic metaphors are always imperfect metaphors. They provide us with too little knowledge, because one of the terms directly or indirectly implied in the substitution (the sensory sun) cannot be known in what is proper to it. . . . But as the best metaphor is never absolutely good, without which it would not be a metaphor, does not the bad metaphor always yield the best example? Thus, metaphor means heliotrope, both a movement toward the sun and the turning movement of the sun."[33]

There are undoubtedly many reasons why the poetic heliotropes I have examined are designed not to become one with the sun. If the sun in these poems is Being, or a sign of the transcendent, then anything truly identified with Being would no longer be a metaphor. Or, to put it another way, it would be a too successful metaphor, its EST achieving the ideal verbal and ontological copulative, the hypostatic union of EST EST. But since the turning sun is a heliotrope itself, all metaphors, including the sun, keep a "metaphoric" distance from the Idea of any transcendent signified—just as they do from the *materia* of nature. Striving toward yet resisting natural materiality, striving toward yet resisting the Logos, the idea of metaphoricity, according to one of Derrida's best explicators, Rodolphe Gasché, is that of a "non-phenomenalizable quasi-transcendental."[34] This double-barreled name, "non-phenomenalizable quasi-transcendental," may seem rather much for one poetic flower to bear. But such is the significance borne by a trope that gracefully threatens to subvert some of the most fundamental assumptions of logical and metaphysical speculation.

Thus there are three basic movements in the poetic heliotropes briefly examined above, and these behaviors appear to signify the fundamental ways in which metaphor reveals its own meaning. The first motion is one of retreat into a paradisiacal place apart, whereby the heliotrope roots itself even more deeply into its hypernatural environment. While there are many linguistic, philosophical, and epistemological implications to this radical gesture, it serves primarily as a symbol of metaphor's iconic desire to become purely autotelic, self-defining, and self-reifying. The second movement is a constant striving toward the sun. While there are many implications to these solar aspirations, the heliotrope's nostalgic longing for the sun figures forth metaphor's desire to discover a transcendent signifier in whose being its own essential meaning may be found and shared. I have given considerable attention to the philosophical ramifications of these two motions—the self-reifying and the self-transcending—because it is rare to find a culturally shared poeseme such as the heliotrope that so economically dramatizes the metaphysical outer limits of metaphoricity itself. However, before I turn to Chaucer, there is one more metaphorical behavior that demands further sustained attention. The heliotrope's lateral movement from east to west, the arc of its back-and-forth motion in subsolar space, I take to be a sign of metaphor's process of analogy, whereby one system of correspondences is fused with another system of correspondences in accordance with categories of likeness and unlikeness made possible by an overall taxonomy of kinds. Because we are so accustomed to domesticating metaphor (making "proper" sense out of such odd locutions as "Clytie is a flower"), it is important to underscore the "wild" analogies that metaphor constructs between radically different classifications of being. Once examined, metaphor's analogy systems have a way of exposing the quasi-artificiality of those hierarchical categories that traditionally have been understood as the organizing principles of the world.[35]

Aristotle based the first part of his famous definition of metaphor upon a distinctive hierarchical arrangement of classes, the subordination of species to genus, and the rest of his definition upon the principle of analogy: "Metaphor consists in giving the thing a name that belongs to something else; the transference being either from genus to species, or from species to genus, or from species to species, or on grounds of analogy" (*Poetics* 1457b). It is clear that metaphors move easily from one category level to another (for example, from "flower" to "woman") inside what has been called an "ordonnance of ontological classes."[36] One major difficulty, however, devolves from there being many distinct ordonnances of ontological classes (in addition to genus and species), each with different, yet overlapping, hierarchical categories, each powerfully resistant to being unified into a single cosmological paradigm. By moving freely from taxonomy to taxonomy, metaphors have a way of exposing the friction and dissonance among ontological models.

This feature leads to a second major problem exposed by metaphor. Since metaphor draws "wild" analogies not only within a single ordonnance but among several ordonnances at once, one must ask if analogy is a unifying principle to the ontological classes themselves and, if so, whether these analogy principles are as "wild," or fictive, as those employed by metaphor. On the one hand, because they test our deepest understanding of how different things share comparable qualities, it makes sense that metaphors have been called "a basic cognitive model for understanding one's own mind and culture."[37] To understand why modesty is an acceptable analogue to white petals, or a vermillion *greinne* an acceptable analogue to sexual treasure, is to learn, or relearn, some deep-seated values of Western culture. But since we know that white petals and sexual treasures may be analogized to many another thing, what can be done with the proposition that ultimately anything can be analogized to anything else? Consider the following examples: "man is an animal"; "a poem is a pheasant"; and "life is a bowl of cherries." If these analogues are acceptable, then could it also be said that "man is a pheasant," "a poem is a bowl of cherries," and "life is an animal"? And if these equations are also acceptable, could the terms of subject and predicate actually be reversed, so that "an animal is a poem," "a bowl of cherries is a man," and "a pheasant is life"? If it is possible, as has been claimed, that the entire "theory of analogy is nothing but a pseudo-science,"[38] then at the heart of every metaphor lurks the danger that our views of the world (scientific, theological, rational, a priori, or whatever) will *not* be reconfirmed by metaphor's system of analogies. Rather, some kind of "calculated category mistake"[39] contained in metaphor might lead toward another perspective, toward another way of judging and knowing the world. As I shall now show, Chaucer shared with his forebears a deep interest both in the iconicity and in the solar affinities of metaphor. But it is metaphor's third and most mysterious behavior, the arc of its back-and-forth motion through analogical space, that proves to be the central focus of Chaucer's aesthetic gaze.

"OF ALLE FLOURES FLOUR": METAPHOR AS CATEGORY MISTAKE

In the Prologue to *The Legend of Good Women* the object of the narrator's all-consuming adoration is a common English daisy. Although during the rest of the year the poet-narrator surrounds himself with his "olde bokes," every morning in the month of May he has no choice but to leave his study and retreat into "the smale, softe, swote gras" where he is able to worship his beloved flower to his soul's content:

Adoun ful softely I gan to synke,
And, lenynge on myn elbowe and my syde,
The longe day I shoop me for t'abide
For nothing elles, and I shal nat lye,
But for to loke upon the dayesie.

(F.178–82)

As soon as the flower closes at night, the poet immediately rushes home so that he may sleep, in imitation of his beloved, in a specially constructed "herbere," a natural bed of green turf strewn with flowers.

Because of the depths of his belief in the daisy's perfection, the narrator on occasion addresses "it" as "she": "she" is "my gide" (F.94), my "lady sovereyne" (F.94), "myn erthly god" (F.95), "Fulfilled of al vertu and honour" (F.54), equally fair "in winter as in somer newe" (G.58). Perceived intermittently as feminizable and semitranscendent, the daisy nevertheless remains first and foremost "of alle floures flour" (F.53)—the paragon of its natural genus, the quiddity of its kind. The reality of the flower's botanical presence is enhanced by the narrator's admiration for the same heliotropic movement that had so mesmerized his continental peers: its gradual diurnal movements in response to the sun. In fact, the absolute perfection of the daisy's daisyhood is so stunning that the narrator almost turns into a daisy himself: his crepuscular stirrings at dawn and dusk, his subsolar motions to and from the daisy's bower, and the floral habitation of his own "natural" bed translate him into a heliotrope, an andromorphic flower sensitive to the sun.

A good bit later, in the second half of the Prologue, the narrator is told explicitly by his poetic patron, the God of Love, that his daisy is the epitome of all rhetorical tropes: "this flour . . . bereth our alder pris in figurynge" (F.297–98; "this flower . . . takes our most esteemed prize in the art of figuration"). But the only explicit attestation in the early part of the Prologue to the daisy's primacy as a metaphoric icon is the etymology of its name: "That wel by reson men it calle may / The 'dayesye,' or elles the 'ye of day'" (F.183–84). In striking contrast to the marguerite of the French poets, whose name might point toward an extrafictive woman, the English "daisy" is a word that points directly to the sun. The "eye of the day" is thus simultaneously a proper (even though common) name pointing toward a flower and a metaphorical name, or heliotrope, pointing toward the sun.[40]

With the exception of its name, however, Chaucer provides no direct authorial assistance in decoding this flower, even though the daisy's name and its heliotropic leanings invite the reader to draw analogies with the sun. Like the sun, the daisy is bright and colorful; it appears in the morning and closes up at night; its petals look like rays of light; and its round center looks rather like the orb we see in the sky. Yet nonanalogies also abound, both on the level of predication (the daisy is not a hot star; the sun has no green stem, etc.) as well as on the level of essences (what *is* the interiority of this flower? what *is* the spiritual essence of the sun?). What, then, can be said or not said about the daisy as it relates to the sun? In the only published attempt to understand Chaucer's daisy as a meta-metaphor, Lisa Kiser answers this question with impressive certitude: "the daisy 'means' the sun, both *in verbo* and *in re*."[41] Further, in asking what the sun means, Kiser answers that "it stands for God."[42] This *allegoresis*, like many forms of spiritual exegesis, appears to me to be rather willfully imposed, yet Kiser's initial inspiration to read Chaucer's daisy as a philosophical metaphor, *in verbo* and *in re*, points toward a mode of critical thinking that I believe Chaucer encouraged his readers to explore.[43]

As guidance in this exploration, Chaucer does something remarkable in the second half of the Prologue. Falling asleep, the narrator dreams a dream, and this dream provides an extensive commentary upon the metaphoricity of his poetic flower. The poet dreams he is lying in his May-morning meadow, but in place of his daisy he is met by one floramorphic human figure and then another. First to approach is Queen Alceste, whose appearance the dreamer recalls in exacting detail:

> And she was clad in real habit grene.
> A fret of gold she hadde next her heer,
> And upon that a white corowne she beer
> With flourouns smale, and I shal nat lye;
> For al the world, right as a dayesye
> Ycorouned ys with white leves lyte,

So were the flowrouns of hire coroune white.
For of o perle fyn, oriental,
Hire white coroune was ymaked al;
For which the white coroune above the grene
Made hire lyk a daysie for to sene,
Considered eke hir fret of gold above.
                    (F.214–25)[44]

Chaucer leaves no doubt that Queen Alceste is "as" and "lyk" the daisy: her hairnet ("hir fret of gold"), her white-petaled crown, her regal green habit, and all the other attributes of her attire make her into a human, and royal, flower. While her name indicates that she is a historical person from the classical past recorded in Chaucer's "olde bokes," she is nevertheless a discrete figure generated out of the poet's imagination. She is, in short, a dreamed-up metaphor, an idealized floral/female equation, closely aligned with, but not the same as, Chaucer's daisy.

By adding Alceste to his field of flowers, Chaucer might be thought to be embracing what is now called an "interactionist" theory of metaphor.[45] This theory contends that the equation of a metaphor's two terms, $A = B$, necessarily generates a third term, C, a newly created domain by which the metaphorical exchange is understood. Between the daisy (A), a non-human flower, and the sun (B), a nonhuman and perhaps transcendent entity to which the daisy most pointedly refers, Chaucer has constructed an idealized human female (C), who is both a flower and (apparently) a demidivinity. This demidivine female, while a metaphor in her own right, may constitute the human characteristics, ideal virtues, and classical historicity that Chaucer would wish to discover within his special daisy. So the dream-vision appearance of Alceste in all her hybrid glory is a compact reification of all the flower/woman/sun analogies construed not only inside the narrator's perfervid mind but inside the reader's creative imagination as well.

If this interactionist gloss is part of Chaucer's purpose in adding Alceste as an explanatory tertium quid, he immediately confuses matters by adding a fourth element, Alceste's consort and companion, the God of Love:

Yclothed was this myghty god of Love
In silk, enbrouded ful of grene greves,
In-with a fret of rede rose-leves,
The freshest syn the world was first bygonne.
His gilte heer was corowned with a sonne
Instede of gold, for hevynesse and wyghte.
Therwith me thoghte his face shoon so bryghte
That wel unnethes myghte I him beholde;
And in his hand me thoughte I saugh him holde
Twoo firy dartes as the gledes rede,
And aungelyke hys wynges saugh I sprede.

(F.226–36)

Male, floral, heliotropic, and divine, the God of Love is dressed in green silk; he carries two fiery darts; his hair is gilded; he is crowned with nothing less that "a sonne." Moreover, his face is so bright that the poet-dreamer cannot bear to look at him. Clearly, the God of Love is an actual divinity (albeit pagan), and much more proximate to the sun that his kindred heliotropes, even though he is like Alceste in many aspects, including his sartorial similarities to the daisy. We now find ourselves with an embarrassment of heliotropes—the daisy, Queen Alceste, and the God of Love. All three are allotropes intimately related to each other (two—Alceste and the God of Love—may even be married), and all three are responsive to the sun's governing presence. If we were to imagine a Venn diagram classifying as PROPER or as *figural* just three characteristics of these three figures, we could make the following assertions: the daisy is FLORAL, *human*, and *divine*; Queen Alceste is HUMAN, *floral*, and *divine*; and the God of Love is DIVINE, *floral*, and *human*. Now unless the sun is also properly HUMAN, or FLORAL, or DIVINE, it may be that none of the metaphors in Chaucer's meadow equates with anything proper to the sun. Kiser is firmly convinced that the God of Love "*is not* the sun" (emphasis added), while Alceste is "both the daisy and sun *at once*" (emphasis added).[46] But surely there is a major philosophical problem here. This problem is contained in the meaning of "is": how can Alceste "be" the sun, let alone "be" the daisy and the sun at once? And if Alceste "is" the sun, why should anything else that is also sunlike, such as the daisy or the God of Love, "not be" the sun?

What the innumerable analogical similarities and dissimilarities among these three heliotropes demonstrate is that there is no self-evident principle readily available for prioritizing their properties and qualities. In the single most influential modern study of metaphor, Max Black asserts that there is almost always a principal subject and a subsidiary subject in metaphor, such that every "metaphor selects, emphasizes, suppresses, and organizes features of the principal subject by implying statements about it that normally apply to the subsidiary subject."[47] This prioritizing is apparently what the narrator attempts to sort out in the opening part of the prologue with his flower and his lady. But what the dreamer discovers in his dream is that distinguishing between a principal subject and a subsidiary one is such a fuzzy proposition that is it impossible to determine if the daisy's features are to be selected, emphasized, suppressed, and organized according to the beloved's, or Alceste's according to the daisy's, or the sun's according to the God of Love's, and so on. What we experience in this pinwheeling of correspondences, therefore, is what many have called the "calculated category mistakes" of metaphor, whereby prior classifications are undone in order to bring to light new resemblances and establish new frontiers of possible knowledge.[48] These category mistakes begin with the narrator's traditional metaphorizings of his flower into a woman but continue, in his dream, by spawning wilder and even wilder analogies. What the dream suggests is this: if a genderless flower that "gazes" at the genderless sun may be perceived by a viewer to share qualities and essences with a female beloved, then this initial metaphoric translation is capable of expanding further, not only into a heliotropic, female, floral, and properly named queen of history, and not only into a heliotropic, male, floral, and generically named pagan deity, but into an infinitude of further analogues. This infinitude of analogues leads to one of the prologue's most important insights concerning metaphor: while deconstructing the "logic" by which we are wont to discriminate between "principal" and "subsidiary" subjects, metaphor parodies our own aprioritizing of ontological classes in order that we may arrive at a more resilient, creative, and self-aware understanding of the importance of metaphorical categories themselves as modes of reality construction and interpretation.

In partial summary, then: I have tried to show how the category mistake attributed by Derrida to Aristotle and attributed by several medieval poets to their heliotropic icons leads to the central question: what, if anything, is proper to the sun? The category mistake attributed by Chaucer to his own narrator's imagination in the Prologue to *The Legend of Good Women*, exfoliating as it does into a confused flurry of kindred metaphors, leads inevitably to another central question: what, if anything, is proper to metaphor? As I now move to a consideration of Chaucer's second great heliotrope, Chauntecleer, these issues take on even greater urgency, for here Chaucer incorporates the dynamics of metaphor in the person and character of a "human" animal. This animal/human equation brings into bold relief the most fundamental question implicit in the activity of translating any metaphor: what, if anything, is proper to humankind? The figure of Chauntecleer, a walking and talking metaphor, represents Chaucer's crystallized summa of the foregoing heliotropic controversies concerning the relationship of art to nature and to truth. Moreover, Chauntecleer embodies evidence not only that metaphor is the defining feature of the creative arts but that metaphor is the defining feature both of human kind and of the knowable world.

HOMO EST ANIMAL FIGURANS

The Nun's Priest's Tale opens with a mock-*exemplum* portraying a prosaic life eked out by a nameless widow and her two nameless daughters. This scene gives way to Chauntecleer, a figure who takes center stage with such poetic élan that the widow's gray existence is emphatically occluded by the variegated riches of his exotic barnyard universe. As in *The Wizard of Oz*, having begun in black-and-white Kansas, the viewer wakes up inside a phantasmagorical dream-vision of technicolor wonder:

> A yeerd she hadde, enclosed al aboute
> With stikkes, and a drye dych withoute,

In which she hadde a cok, hight Chauntecleer.
In al the land, of crowing nas his peer.
His voys was murier than the murie orgon
On messe-dayes that in the chirche gon.
Wel sikerer was his crowing in his logge
Than is a clokke or an abbey orlogge.
By nature he knew ech ascencioun
Of the equynoxial in thilke toun;
For whan degrees fifteen weren ascended,
Thanne crew he that it myghte nat been amended.
His coomb was redder than the fyn coral,
And batailled as it were a castel wal;
His byle was blak, and as the jeet it shoon;
Lyk asure were his legges and his toon;
His nayles whitter than the lylye flour,
And lyk the burned gold was his colour.

                                             (VII.2847–64)

In this eighteen-line *blazon*, all the major qualities of metaphor covered
so far in this chapter are compactly contained. Because many of the aesthetic implications of these qualities have already been assessed, I intend
to comment briefly upon each in order to conclude with an exploration
of the new challenges Chauntecleer-as-metaphor poses. These challenges
are directed, first, toward our philosophical understanding of the place
of human nature within the ordonnance of ontological kinds and, second, toward our acquiring a deeper understanding of metaphor, and thus
poetry, as the primary element in the proper definition of our own con-
stitution as human beings.

Chauntecleer's first distinctive metaphorical feature is embodied
in his very chickenness. More than fifty years ago at a convention of the
Modern Language Association (as I have noted in my Introduction), Lalia
Boone read a paper whose title, "Chauntecleer and Partlet Identified,"
attracted a flock of curious scholars. Demonstrating, by a scrupulous examination of the color and form of their bills, legs, toes, nails, plumage,
and crenelated comb notchings, that the tale's hero and heroine were actually Golden Spangled Hamburgs, Boone appears to have left her au-

dience critically agape. Yet by investigating the identity of Chauntecleer and Pertelote at this down-to-earth level, Boone succeeded in demonstrating an important dimension of metaphor itself. Metaphor, as Darrel Mansell has explained, draws toward the materiality of its referent and as an icon of that materiality stands resistant to all interpretation.[49] Thus the more Chauntecleer insists on being a Golden Spangled Hamburg, the more he is a metaphor behaving as a metaphor should.

Chauntecleer's chickenyard, attached as it is to the widow's dour homestead, embraces a second feature of metaphor, which is its *heimlich/ unheimlich* interdependence with the realms of the proper. Like Augustine's region of dissimilitudes and Alanus's place apart, Chauntecleer's kingdom of poetic extravagance threatens to subvert the rectitude of truthful discourse: it is fabulous, exotic, and "other." Seen either as a low mimetic *hortus inconclusus* walled with sticks[50] or a crenelated castle with a dry moat, this chicken run exemplifies metaphor's liminal position wherein the proper and the figural, the domestic and the alien, the plain and the pleasurable contend for priority of linguistic place.

The third element of metaphoricity actualized in Chauntecleer's world is found in the figural semiotics of his personal colors. His comb is "redder than the fyn coral"; his bill is "blak and as the jeet it shoon":

Lyk asure were hise legges and his toon,
His nayles whitter than the lylye flour,
And lyk the burned gold was his colour.

These brilliant colors have impressed different readers as being aesthetically meaningful, as indeed they are: Derek Pearsall remarks on the "lofty and periphrastic quality" of the language in which the colors are themselves presented;[51] Elizabeth Salter finds that the colors' admixture of "formalism and realism" reminds her of "courtly painting of elaborate French style";[52] and Claes Schaar, while remarking on the repeated use of simile in Chauntecleer's description, suggests that his emblazoned colors are evocative of the heraldic colors of the French *roman*.[53] Within the parameters of this chapter, I suggest that the bejeweled colors of Chauntecleer's native regalia hark all the way back to the allegorical figure of Rhetoric in the *Anticlaudianus* and to the verbal elegances embodied in her person: "Her locks reflecting the gloss of gold lie adorned with wondrous artistry. . . . Her countenance is steeped in radiant colour: a brilliant red glow tints her face with roseate luster but a foreign glitter haunts her face to some extent and tries to combine with the native hue."[54] Thus Chaucer, in his painterly portrait of Chauntecleer, has recontextualized in a few brush strokes a long-lasting aesthetic debate concerning the superiority or inferiority of the colors of nature to the colors of rhetorical art.

The response of Alanus de Insulis to the murals in Nature's garden was one of pure ecstasy: "Oh painting with your new wonders!" Machaut and Chaucer respond to the glorious beauty of their own poetic flowers in forms of similar rapture. Chauntecleer's fourth metaphorical characteristic is thus the internalization of the poet's ecstatic admiration of his own work of art. In part because he is closely aligned, as we shall see, with the mineral heliotrope—which not only refracts the sun's light but radiates an internal light potentially capable of occluding the sun's— Chauntecleer so fully contains the brilliance of his own creation that he requires no explicit reverence from his author. Although Chauntecleer's cocky hubris has been commented on by many moralists, his narcissistic self-assurance is preeminently a celebration of poetry's luminescent and self-generating beauty.

Chauntecleer's fifth characteristic as meta-metaphor is the figural propriety of his cryptogrammatic name. Names, situated in their proper and improper places, have proved crucial in understanding the way that metaphor works. In the medieval poetry I have briefly reviewed, not only did the names of the poem's foregrounded metaphors, such as "marguerite" and "daisy," raise questions about their proper referents, but the names of their authors on occasion (as with Froissart) were found to be encrypted in their verse. What Chaucer has chosen to do here is to inscribe both his pure art of poetry (of singing clearly) and his own occulted surname inside the name CHAUnteCleER itself.[55] Thus Chaucer's self-advertising name candidly acknowledges that the primary extrafictive referent of the medieval poetic heliotrope, no matter what its name, is not some historical woman but rather the male poet, who wishes to be at one with his own, feminizable, art.[56]

The sixth and most striking sign of Chauntecleer's metaphoricity is his uncanny affinity with the sun:

> By nature he knew ech ascencioun
> Of the equynoxial in thilke toun;
> For whan degrees fiftene weren ascended,
> Thanne crew he that it myghte nat been amended.

The ability of roosters to tell the precise time (thus embarrassing all clockmakers, astrolabists, and astronomers) and their privileged understanding of the movements of the sun were two superhuman powers much admired in the Middle Ages.[57] Elsewhere in *The Nun's Priest's Tale* Chauntecleer is able to measure the ascension of the sun in degrees and minutes so accurately that he knows the right time to the nanosecond; moreover, this time is that of absolute hours, rather than the expanding and contracting hours of liturgical time.[58] Chauntecleer's ability to know the sun, to know what fourteenth-century philosophers called the Absolute Clock,[59] is about as close as a late-medieval cock could get to approaching the transcendent Logos. Derrida thus might wish to consult Chauntecleer on how, as a philosophical metaphor, he knows what is proper to the sun. And Wallace Stevens, a poet very much interested in the epistemology of metaphor, could likewise address his command in "Credences of Summer" to Chaucer's avian and metapoetic signifier:

> Trace the gold sun about the whitened sky
> Without evasion by a single metaphor.
> Look at it in its essential barrenness
> And say this, this is the centre that I seek.[60]

These six dimensions of Chauntecleer's metaphoricity—his iconicity, semantic liminality, semiotic colors, self-glorification, authorial self-naming, and solar wisdom—lead to what I believe is Chauntecleer's final and most important quality as Chaucer's signature heliotrope: his categorical humanity. As a living metaphor, a feathered cluster of compressed analogies, Chauntecleer is a category mistake writ large. He is writ so large, in fact, that Chaucer manages to suggest that his anomalous existence challenges all our orderly paradigms, including those that attempt to define the essence of human nature. To appreciate this challenge, we need to take one further step toward understanding metaphor's disequilibrating powers.

As noted above, at the heart of every metaphor lie certain principles of analogy that work within, among, and against those principles of analogy that are understood to govern the world. These a priori world-governing principles authorize the legitimacy of our discovering relations between quite different things positioned in quite different places along the great chain of being. The danger, however, to any such system of correspondences is that its principles of analogy may at times be diffi cult to differentiate from the principles of poetic conceits: rather than the metaphysical foundation of the world, the shared essence of earthly phenomena may seem to reside only in the "false" equals sign of metaphorical equations.

A critical study that maps out some of the doctrines at work in the philosophical construction of an analogy-based but apparently non-metaphorical order of being is Paul Ricoeur's *Rule of Metaphor*. In his concluding chapter, "Metaphor and Philosophic Discourse," Ricoeur focuses upon the medieval development of the Aristotelian doctrine of the "analogical unity of the multiple meanings of being" (258). Put rather simply, philosophers such as Aristotle and Aquinas felt it necessary to unify, through some mediating principle of correspondence, several discrete and radically different doctrines. First, there is the "horizontal" relation of the categories of substance, which honors the "equivocal" and species-specific differences among natural kinds. Second, there is the "vertical" relation of created things to the Creator, which honors the "univocal" (generic) principle of the metaphysics of essence. A third doctrine, born of the desire to encompass both of these schemes, Ricoeur calls *analogia entis*, or the analogy of being. But one problem with any such onto-theological scheme of analogy, Ricoeur's study reveals, is that analogical predication functions at the level of names and predicates and thus belongs to the conceptual order, while the condition that makes analogy possible must of necessity belong elsewhere, in "the communication of being itself" (274).

Philosophers often dealt with this difficulty by constructing a meta-level theory of interanimating participation, wherein one thing is understood as possessing partially what anther thing possesses fully, but never as fully as God. "The struggle for an adequate concept of participation," Ricoeur explains, "underpins the struggle for an adequate concept of analogy. But then, is not participation evidence that metaphysics has turned to poetry through its lamentable recourse to metaphor . . . ?" (274). Aquinas took an unusually bold step in refining the concept of analogy, creating "composite modalities of discourse" by using the metaphorics of proportionality so that, at the intersection point of the descending order of being and the ascending order of signification, "the meaning effects of proportional metaphor and transcendental analogy are added together." At this point of "chiasmus," Ricoeur admits, it might appear that "the speculative [merely] verticalizes metaphor, while the poetic dresses speculative analogy in iconic garb" (279). Nevertheless, Ricoeur argues forcefully that Aquinas's ontological doctrine of analogical participation, despite its enabling utilization of metaphor, succeeds as a speculative discourse untainted by the figural discourse of poetry.

Even after many readings, Chaucer's portrait of Chauntecleer would seem to be far removed from the arcana of all this metaphysics. For here is a rooster whose existential anxieties appear entirely divorced from any analogical problems subsisting inside an ontotheological doctrine of participation in Being. Conventional reading experiences notwithstanding, I contend that Chauntecleer's carefully crafted portrait constitutes Chaucer's poetic deployment of the very same philosophical problems addressed by Ricoeur—with one obvious difference. While philosophical treatises are intent on purging their ontological schemata of the taint of metaphoricity, Chaucer's portrait, with the active assistance of his readers, is intent upon proving that metaphoricity is essential, and perhaps foundational, to all discourses. Chaucer constructs his bold defense of metaphor by involving his readers in a three-stage exercise of analogy analysis: the first exercise involves at least eight specific analogies drawn between a rooster's qualities and the qualities of certain nonhuman things; the second exercise involves an indeterminate number of analogues drawn between a rooster's being and a human being; and the third exercise involves analogues drawn between beast-fable fiction and the narrative domain of nonmetaphorical "truth."

In the passage cited above from *The Nun's Priest's Tale* (VII.2847–64), Chaucer invites his readers to move self-critically into the field of analogical discourse by making no fewer than eight explicit analogies in a row. Five examples will here suffice, four in the comparative degree ("better than"), one in the positive degree ("the same as"). Chauntecleer's voice, the narrator asserts, is "murier" than the merry church organ; his crowing is more accurate ("sikerer") than a clock; his comb in "redder" than the coral; his nails are "whitter" than the lily; and his color is "lyk" that of burnished gold. Two of these similes are set in the direction of inanimate mechanical instruments made by humankind; three are set in the direction of things in nature—two vegetable and one mineral. While each comparison appears innocent enough, taken together they begin to put pressure on the process of analogy itself. How, in fact, do these analogies work?[61] We are told that merriness is a defining quality of Chauntecleer's crowing. But is merriness a defining quality at the same level for the church organ—whose sound should perhaps not be overly merry to begin with? Next we are told that accuracy is another defining quality of Chauntecleer's song. But is accuracy a defining quality *at the same level* for the fourteenth-century mechanical clock—which was always notoriously inaccurate? Then there are the inner workings of the three color analogies: if coral red (which may or may not epitomize the category of perfect redness) is here outdone, and if lily whiteness (which may or may not epitomize the category of perfect whiteness) is here outdone, why is it only gold that is not outdone? Is it because in this case the name for quality and substance happens to be identical: gold is "gold"? Or is it because this is not merely gold, but "burned [burnished] gold"? Or is it because gold is an absolute—"than which," as the philosophers say, "nothing is more gold"? But even if gold itself is an absolute, are gold's properties (such as its color) equivalent to its substance or essence? As Paul de Man has shown in "The Epistemology of Metaphor," this question was addressed by John Locke in his meditation on the arbitrary relation between the properties and presumed essence of gold: Locke's reluctant conclusion is that "no one has authority to determine the significance of the word *gold.*"[62] In the five foregoing analogies, the reader is faced with problems similar to Locke's: who has the authority to determine the relative or absolute value—in substance, qualities, and properties—of those things to which Chauntecleer's excellent characteristics are being compared?

Having drawn our attention to some of analogy's ontological complexities, Chaucer's next step is to provide an extended demonstration of the difficulty of distinguishing between metaphorical and nonmetaphorical analogies. In the second part of his portrait, Chauntecleer's features are no longer explicitly compared to the features of inanimate things. Rather, his entire person and being (physiological, intellectual, linguistic, erotic, musical, social) is now positioned in an implicit analogical relationship to that of a human counterpart, his own alter ego. The reader is thus asked to consider the degree to which the defining features of Chauntecleer's rooster domain are equivalent to the defining features of his human domain. Are his inner chicken essence, requisite chicken qualities, and external chicken properties superior to, inferior to, or simply different from those of a human being? How far does his chickenness participate in our humanity? How far does our humanity transcend or subtend his chickenness? Most importantly, where do the animal/human analogies of Chauntecleer's person derive from: are they grounded in ontological realities, speculative categories, or metaphorical conceits?[63] The humor in the conclusion to Chauntecleer's portrait illustrates the difficulty of answering these questions:

> This gentil cok hadde in his governaunce
> Sevene hennes for to doon al his plesaunce,
> Whiche were his sustres and his paramours,
> And wonder lyk to hym, as of colours;
> Of whiche the faireste hewed on hir throte
> Was cleped faire damoysele Pertelote.
> Curteys she was, discreet, and debonaire,
> And compaignable, and bar hyrself so faire
> Syn thilke day that she was seven nyght oold
> That trewely she hath the herte in hoold
> Of Chauntecleer, loken in every lith;
> He loved hire so that wel was hym therwith.
> But swich a joye was it to here hem synge,

Whan that the brighte sonne gan to sprynge,
In sweete accord, "My life is faren in londe!"—
For thilke tyme, as I have understonde,
Beestes and brides koude speke and synge.

                              (VII.2865–81)

As we read through this passage, our amusement turns to bemusement because at a certain level of consciousness we are aware of category transgressions alternating with category overlaps and confluences. In the wide world of fact and fiction, how does one know where the bird ends and the human begins? How does a rooster (not) sing like a human? How does a rooster (not) have a wife? How may a hen (not) have a proper name? How may a hen (not) be married to her brother? How do chickens (not) love like humans? How do chickens (not) think, feel, hope, speak, remember, and dream like humans? What kind of soul do chickens (not) have? While Western philosophy has always striven to articulate an adequate concept of participation between the animal and the human even while carefully discriminating their differences, the sum effect of this portrait is to expose the inevitable metaphoricity that binds together all such hierarchical and "logical" categories.[64] Perched upon that "chiasmus" where "the meaning effects of proportional metaphor and transcendent analogy are added together,"[65] Chauntecleer and Pertelote provide vital testimony that the analogical discourse in which all phenomena are conceived is the discourse about which philosophers have been most anxious: the figural. Thus, in response to the categorical question of the philosophers, "what is proper to humankind?" Chaucer's answer seems unequivocal. It is the improper that is most proper: "homo est animal figurans."

The ultimate metaphor problem incorporated into Chauntecleer's portrait concerns the analogy between narrative fiction itself (as represented by the Nun's Priest's beast fable) and any alternative form of narrative that claims to be properly related to extrafictive truth. How could it be, the narrator seems to hear his distrustful reader ask, that a rooster and hen are able, for instance, to sing a popular English ballad?

In other words, does the metaphor of articulate animals relate in any proper way to reality? The Nun's Priest provides his own answer: "For thilke tyme, as I have understonde, / Beestes and brides koude speke and synge." As in so many of Chaucer's off-hand pronouncements, the chop-logic of this defense constitutes a special kind of philosophical conun-drum. On first reading, the narrator's assurance may seem to make proper sense, as we willfully believe, once upon a time, that this fiction was ac-tually true. However, on further reflection, the counterfactuality of the narrator's explication becomes increasingly evident, so that finally both verbal constructs—the narrator's description of talking animals and the narrator's assertion that at one point in history animals talked—reside at nearly the same level as figurative, or metaphorical, propositions. Similar in design to the Cretan-liar paradoxes so popular in fourteenth-century logical treatises, the Nun's Priest's figural justification of his figural art suggests that the premise upon which every metaphorical construct is grounded is, simply, another metaphor.

Thus in a variety of ways Chaucer's poetics of metaphor argues the foundationality of the figural: metaphor is the absolute category within which we construct reality, poetry, and ourselves. Like the heliotropic gem that outshines the sun, Chaucer's advertisement of his art appears to claim that poetry is blessed with a unique and world-illuminating power. Yet this *apologia pro arte sua* is so audaciously hubristic that it may well be designed to effect in readers at least a modicum of critical resistance. A final issue thus remains to be addressed: Does a poet's defense of metaphor stand as a rhetorical gesture no different in kind from the philosopher's urgent insistence on the primacy of the proper? Or (slightly differently) does Chaucer grant himself full confidence in the figural only because he and his peers retain some fundamental belief in the realm of the proper? In the literature we have been considering, we can find two closely related responses to these questions, one embedded in the Nun's Priest's defense of fiction, the other embedded in medieval heliotropic lore.

The medieval lapidaries firmly held to an extraordinary belief con-cerning the magical power of heliotropes: if a heliotropic gem were ever situated under the plant of the same name in such a fashion that the for-mer could not be seen, the "owner" of this weird configuration would be-come invisible or, worse, suddenly disappear! Robert M. Durling and Ron-ald L. Martinez explore some of the implications of Dante's fertile use of this *petra sott'erba* image in their study of the *Rime petrose*.[66] Chau-cer of course does not deploy the *heliotropia/heliotropium* configuration itself.[67] Rather, I suggest, he weaves certain of its philosophical implications into the Nun's Priest's paradoxical defense of poetry. Consider that defense once again: "For thilke tyme, as I have understonde, / Beestes and briddes koude speke and synge." At a very minimum, this utterance differs as a proposition from its surrounding verbal fictions because it clearly invokes the concepts of the proper, if only in absentia. In addition, possible-world narratologists argue that verbal gestures such as "I have understonde" mark, beyond the proper and the improper, an imagined tertium quid, an "ontologically hybrid textual world."[68] The Nun's Priest's paradox therefore suggests, among other things, that the category of the figural cannot possibly be known without a countercategory from which it might be "set apart." Thus not only is the figural absolutely essential to metaphor, but (surprisingly) so is the proper. An analogy can now be drawn between the Nun's Priest's caution against reducing everything to the level of "improper" equivalencies and the lapidaries' caution concerning the perfect superimposition of one heliotrope upon another. What if a metaphor were totally identified with, or displaced by, another? What if a metaphor were so powerful that it blocked entirely the subsumed signifier? In short, what if every name, every proposition, every narrative were an equally figural element in an absolutely fictive metadiscourse? How could we then distinguish heliotropes from heliotropes, pheasants from bowls of cherries, and crowing cocks from the poets who make them sing?

It is at this level of interrogation that our understanding of metaphor as a "category mistake" comes full circle. For if metaphor's identification with everything else were not a rhetorical conceit, were not, that is, some kind of mistake about the category of metaphor itself, then the world would have already imploded into the tautological domain of EST EST. The effects of this subsolar hypostatic union, as readers of Chaucer have the right to conclude, would be disastrous.[69] In a hermetically sealed simulacrum of absolute equivalence, Chaucer would have found nothing but a world of metaphor to illuminate and "cover" with rhetorical flowers. And the reader of his poetry would be equally incapacitated. As the privileged "owner" of a perfect imposition of metaphor upon metaphor, such a reader would—simply, suddenly, and properly—disappear.

FIVE

The Noise of History

*Consonance is a mixture of high and low
sound falling pleasantly and uniformly on the ears.
Dissonance, on the other hand, is a harsh and unpleasant percussion
of two sounds coming to the ear intermingled with each other.
For as long as they are unwilling to blend together and each
somehow strives to be heard unimpaired, and since one interferes
with the other, each is transmitted to the sense unpleasantly.*
—BOETHIUS

*[Music] is a herald, for change is inscribed in noise faster than it transforms
society. . . . Listening to music is listening to all noise, realizing that its
appropriation and control is a reflection of power, that it is essentially political.*
—JACQUES ATTALI

When we listen to the poetry of Chaucer's words, we listen to meaning-ful sounds as well as to sounds that are culturally coded to carry little or no meaning. As medieval grammarians explained it, when we attend to *vox articulata literata*, to transcribable and humanly understandable speech, we are also committed to suppressing various kinds of *sonus*—nonverbal and thus not fully meaningful sounds. A similar form of discrimination, repression, and purification happens when we listen to music. Music, as medieval and modern theoreticians have maintained, is essentially dissonance harmonized, sounds mathematically arranged into an order of ultimately concordant significance. But this concordance is always achieved by a form of cultural proscription, by determining that certain sounds are insignificant noises that if unrepressed would otherwise disrupt the decorum of harmonic design. It is perhaps not surprising that these same prescriptive discriminations between meaningful and antimeaningful sounds in language and in music are also found in traditional models of the body politic, where dissonance generated by a discordant element is likely to be classified as a violation of the authorized harmonics of the orderly state.

The dialectic between order and disorder in the realms of music, language, history, and social politics is powerfully dramatized in the classical myth of Harmonia. The child of Venus and Mars, Harmonia is conceived as the realization of *concors discordia,* the well-tempered union of erotic love and martial power. And Harmonia's marriage to Cadmus, the inventor of the Greek alphabet, might well have translated these principles of order into civilized institutions such as writing. However, Cadmus established Thebes, a city where the collision of savage desire and feral aggression—incest, fratricide, parricide, and internecine war—ultimately defines civilization at its most tragic and self-defeating. After the final battle among the sons of the Seven against Thebes, the city is razed, the only surviving object in its silent rubble proving to be Harmonia's necklace, the city's originary symbol of order. Chaucer, choosing to center Statius's *Thebaiad* as a foundational historical text in *The Knight's Tale,* obviously understood the symptomatic "noise" of Theban history as a cautionary narrative of human civilization run amok. However, Chaucer was absolutely fascinated by noise throughout his career, and by the possible significance, political and otherwise, of sounds that are traditionally understood to be devoid of meaning.

A number of musical models that directly influenced Chaucer's thoughts about the politics of sound hark back to Cicero's seminal work, *De Re Publica.* For Cicero, the political state is analogous to a musical body wherein a pleasing consonance is produced by maintaining fit intervals between highest, lowest, and middle tones and highest, lowest, and middle classes:

> For, as in the music of lyre and flute and as even in singing and spoken discourse there is a certain melody [*concentus*] which must be preserved in the different sounds—and if this is altered or discordant it becomes intolerable to the ears of a connoisseur—and as this melody is made concordant and harmonious in spite of the dissimilar sounds of which it is composed, so the state achieves harmony by the agreement [*consensu*] of unlike individuals, when there is a wise blending of the highest, the lowest and the intervening middle classes in the manner of tones. And what musicians call harmony in song is concord in a state.[1]

Cicero's audition of the harmonics of the state is obviously classical and conservative—it is unimaginable that melodies could be produced outside the order of preexisting tones. Yet Cicero's awareness of political realities is nevertheless sufficiently acute to recognize that "dissimilar sounds" are in fact endemic to the sonic city and that in order to achieve an aesthetically pleasing harmony some agreement needs to be arrived at among "unlike individuals." Powerfully impressed by Cicero's well-tempered political/musical analogy, Augustine in *De Civitate Dei* first cites the same Ciceronian passage and then strives to improve upon Cicero's resolution of the contestation between *concordia* and *discors* in human society. Ameliorating the musical aesthetics of Cicero's secular paradigm, Augustine so harmonizes the sonics of the city-state that he succeeds in all but silencing the fractiousness of social dissent:

> The peace of the political community is an ordered harmony [*concordia*] of authority and obedience between citizens. The peace of the heavenly City lies in a perfectly ordered and harmonious communion of those who find their joy in God and in one another in God. Peace, in its final sense, is the calm that comes of order. Order is an arrangement of like and unlike things whereby each of them is disposed in its proper place.[2]

What Augustine willfully achieves here, under the generalized influences of "authority and obedience between citizens," is the salvific absorption of all symptoms of political and social discord into a transcendent realm of exquisite peace. Augustine's ability to hear the music of the heavenly city within the dissonance of the city of man stands as a resolute rebuttal to the most discordant political models of his pre-Christian forebears. "Whereas the Stoics (like Heraclitus) had thought of harmony as forcing together the inimical," writes Leo Spitzer in his important study of classical and Christian ideas of world harmony, "Augustine has in mind rather the ability of harmony to smooth out apparent discord—as the 'inner ear' of the believer hears the unity underlying diversity. Thus the *concordia discors* foreshadows the differentiated harmony of the saints."[3]

Chaucer's "inner ear," fashioned by politicomusical textbooks such as Macrobius's *Commentary on the Dream of Scipio,* fully internalized the hierarchical auditory politics of classical and medieval thinkers and paid homage to their harmonics within the sonic landscape of his own poetry. Yet Chaucer was also intent on paying homage to the dissonance of history and to the noise of political turmoil with an "inner ear" that appears to be radically different from the auditory practices of his peers. Throughout his career Chaucer focuses his critical attention on noise, not only as a signifier of social discord but also as a potential site of epistemological transformation, poetic pleasure, and the liberating opportunities of social change. Or, to put the matter much more carefully, Chaucer is fascinated by the resistance of noise to our understanding. Noise thrives outside the pleasing paradigms of human discourse. Noise is a militant intervention in our lives—it parodies our models of comprehension, and its percussive force is often a threat to civilization. Yet noise remains integral to our world and to our selves. It may in fact be entirely of our own construction. For these discrete reasons and many more, Chaucer is persuaded that the confusion of noise must be respected and somehow interpreted "on its own terms." In fact, as we shall see, noise's resistance to our understanding is strikingly similar to poetry's resistance to our traditional modes of literary explication.[4]

Chaucer's readers were well prepared to attend to the many kinds of sounds and noises amplified in his work. Linguistically, they had been trained in their studies of Donatus and Priscian to theorize about *sonus* and *vox*, phones and phonemes, in an unusually sophisticated fashion. Musically, they had been educated, especially in their readings of Boethius's *De musica*, to ponder the social as well as the mathematical principles of harmonic and unharmonic sounds. And politically, they had been indoctrinated by such works as Macrobius's *Commentary on the Dream of Scipio* to conceive of the order of the cosmos, the order of the state, and the order of the human psyche in sonic terms. While invoking features of these three traditions, Chaucer was equally committed to exploring the historical and social significance of *discordia*. Rather than simply the antithesis of aesthetic harmony and social order, noise in Chaucer would appear to contain its own counter-harmonics.

To attune our inner ear to these counter-harmonics, it is helpful to open up the field of auditory aesthetics by acknowledging from the outset that all sounds, even the most dissonant, are culturally coded and humanly significant. A persuasive demonstration of this general proposition is Richard Leppert's *The Sight of Sound: Music, Representation, and the History of the Body*,[5] a study of musical instruments and music-making represented in various eighteenth- and nineteenth-century paintings. In his first chapter Leppert sets out four premises:

(1) sounds surround us, helping to construct us as human subjects and to locate us in particular social and cultural environments;

(2) sounds produced or manipulated by humans result from conscious acts and hence carry a semantic and discursive charge;

(3) all sounds—even those not produced by humans but "merely" heard by them—can be read or interpreted;

(4) sounds are a means by which people account for their versions of reality: as it was, is, or might be. That is, people do not employ sounds arbitrarily, haphazardly, or unintentionally—though the "intentionally" haphazard may itself constitute an important sort of sonoric discourse.[6]

Leppert's major contention is that the paintings examined in his study are all works of art depicting "the alliances between human desire, on the one hand, and the manipulations of power, on the other"; as such, these paintings instantiate class-inflected social tensions within "sonoric landscape over stakes that are in every sense always already political."[7] Drawing upon Leppert's premises, my contentions in this chapter are similar: I believe that Chaucer's poems are "sonoric landscapes" wherein sound carries a discursive, and indeed political, charge. In certain works Chaucer dramatically foregrounds the noise of history as well as the politics of noisy rebellion in order to provide his readers a variety of "auditory" positions from which to appreciate the dissemination of noise as a possible herald for change.

The most explicitly musical of Chaucer's early poems is certainly *The Parliament of Fowls,* where the harmony of the nine spheres is heard as the source of all music in the sublunary world. Although obviously influenced by Macrobius's *Commentary on the Dream of Scipio,* the major source of Chaucer's knowledge concerning the principles of music remained the standard text in the medieval quadrivial curriculum, Boethius's *De musica.* From the *De musica* Chaucer had learned that musical harmony was based on the tones produced by the intervals between the planets revolving at different velocities, and these intervals correspond perfectly to the seven strings of the heptachord, with Saturn producing the highest note and the Moon the lowest. Deriving from the ratios of God's cosmic harmony, music thus constitutes all rational proportioning and in the universe is made manifest in three different forms: *musica mundana, musica humana,* and *musica instrumentalis.* Each of these three musics is in turn threefold. *Musica mundana* consists of the melody and motion of the heavenly bodies, the harmonious mingling of the four elements, and the variations of the four seasons. *Musica humana* consists of the harmonious proportioning of members of the body, the mixing of the rational and irrational parts of the soul, and the joining of soul and body. Finally, *musica instrumentalis* is found in string, wind, and percussive instruments or in blowing, striking, and giving voice.[8] Not only are all these nine forms operative in Chaucer's poem, as David Chamberlain has persuasively demonstrated, but those principles of mathematical harmony upon which music is founded are also embedded in the very structure and numerology of the poem's rime royal stanzas.[9]

Framed by circles of music-making harmony—opening, that is, with the *musica mundana* of the heavenly spheres and closing with the "roundel" sung by the mating birds at poem's end—*The Parliament of Fowls* is a serious inquiry into the possibility of realizing the *harmonia* of heaven inside the erotic polity of earthly existence. Yet at the poem's center there is a "huge . . . noyse" (*PF* 312), the source of which turns out to be a raucous parley held on St. Valentine's Day among a community of birds. Approaching this earth-shattering noise, Chaucer gradually discovers that there are several sociolects audible in the debate, ranging from the animaloid squawks of the lowest orders—"kek kek! kokkow! quek quek!" go the goose, the cuckoo, and the duck—to the bourgeoisie parlance of the middle classes (turtledove, merlin, and sparrow-hawk), to the elegant *poesie* of the aristocrats. But which class and whose desires are in fact least disruptive of the harmony, the "commune profyt," of the state? The lower-class birds may be "more loudly discordant and more gross," writes David Chamberlain, but nevertheless "the tercels are the center of interest, they are socially more obliged to create 'pes' and 'accord,' and yet they are the 'welle' of discord, *the contrary of the spheres*."[10] A critical position that hears the *voces populi* as if they were positively aligned with the music of the spheres would thus seem to place the poem's political sympathies, at least in part, with the commoners. And indeed, because the lower-class birds' noisy complaints verge on active rebellion, several recent studies have suggested that the class debate in *The Parliament of Fowls* alludes directly although perhaps ambivalently to the social discontent that gave rise to the Peasants' Revolt of 1381.[11]

Of the many explosive political events occurring in Chaucer's lifetime, the Uprising of 1381 may well have been the most traumatic for the English nation. Yet whatever views Chaucer held concerning this trauma are famously difficult to pin down—even when he actually cites a specific event from the Uprising itself, as he does in *The Nun's Priest's Tale*. Of course for much of the twentieth century this historical obliqueness had been considered a virtue. A poet's poet, Chaucer is to be honored in part because his personal politics are not to be descried in his verse: a noncommittal "Laodicean" or else gracefully hand-in-glove with the dominant ideologies of the seigneural class, Chaucer's politics are either "moot" or "transcendent." However, in the most recent generation of Chaucer criticism, depoliticizing and dehistoricizing Chaucer in this fashion has come to be seen as indefensible—a political dodge in its own right. Influenced by Marxism, new historicism, and cultural materialism, a number of major critiques written in the past twenty-five years have committed themselves to reading Chaucer's poems as nuanced political statements that need to be judged at the same level as one judges the other micro- and macronarratives of late medieval British history.

In their foci, critical methodologies, and conclusions, these historicist readings differ one from the other. In *Chaucer*, for example, David Aers argues that while "texts, immersed in history, are social acts," and while "[a]ny attempt to understand literature must include the attempt to re-place it in the web of discourses, social relations and practices where it was produced," we must always remember that "surviving evidence about the medieval past . . . represents the dominant classes' versions of significant reality."[12] In *Social Chaucer*, Paul Strohm asserts that Chaucer's *Canterbury Tales* are themselves political sites of "unresolved contention, of a struggle between hegemony and counter-hegemony, . . . crowded with many voices representing many centers of social authority."[13] In *Chaucer and the Subject of History*, Lee Patterson contends that while *Troilus and Criseyde* shows Chaucer attempting to "expand the cultic language of the court beyond its prescribed limits, thus examining and implicitly challenging the largest presuppositions of aristocratic culture," *The Canterbury Tales*, on the other hand, "shows a writer of coterie verse expressing values that now seem quintessentially literary, and it traces the route by which a court poet came to be the father of English poetry."[14] And in *Chaucerian Polity*, David Wallace explains that the aim of his historicist methods "is not to create a vantage point above the text from which the text—and the struggles of its protagonists—can be explained, or explained away," but rather "to restore the text to the movement of history; to recognize its own sense of precariousness in occupying a time and place that shifts even at the instant of its own articulation."[15] Despite their different critical perspectives and methods, each of these important studies (and there are others) has contributed profoundly to our understanding of how Chaucer's poetry is fully immersed in the social, economic, and political complexities of his age.

It is not my intention to emulate these historicist studies, either in their methods or their findings. Rather, my major goal is to illustrate how Chaucer himself holds up to scrutiny many of the very same *historiographical* issues these historicists self-consciously interrogate. That is, rather than carefully representing the actual events of history, past or present, I find that Chaucer instead explores the essence of history via his experimental interrogations of the semiotics of noise, even as he explores with equal intensity the resistance of noise to our understanding. In *The House of Fame,* as we shall see, Chaucer listens to the orchestrated bedlam of the *longue durée*—the earliest recorded sounds to the most recent—and finds that the noise of history writ large avails itself to no historiographical, or "harmonic," interpretation. Next, in *The Summoner's Tale,* he invites his readers to decipher a single percussive noise, one so dense and complex that, although it may well serve as a compressed stand-in for the 1381 Uprising, proves to be as challenging to our interpretative faculties as is the entirety of world history. Finally, into the fox chase of *The Nun's Priest's Tale,* a carnival celebration of myriad sounds produced at every level of the barnyard world, Chaucer splices strident noises from the Uprising itself—namely, the murderous shouts of rebels as they brutally slaughter their Flemish scapegoats. The effect, for many of Chaucer's readers, is profoundly disturbing. Why has Chaucer done this? What does he expect us to learn here, as our literary pleasure is suddenly arrested by historical slaughter? The early part of this chapter is thus a "noisy" prolegomenon leading to one extremely challenging question: if *The Nun's Priest's Tale* is Chaucer's *ars poetica* parodically foregrounding the major metapoetic concerns of his career, what does his beast fable's violent integration of fictional and historical sounds have to say in terms of our ability to hear Chaucer's voice as a political presence living at a specific time in history? Or, to put it differently, why is Chaucer's clearest articulation of the relation of his own poetry to the percussive events of his time expressed through the "disseminal" hermeneutics of noise?

HISTORIOGRAPHICAL NOISE IN *THE HOUSE OF FAME*

The House of Fame is a poem of a thousand noises. Ascending into the ethereal regions in his tutor's grasp, Chaucer anticipates a privileged audition of the ineffable music of the spheres—if, that is, the space journeys reported in Martianus Capella's *Marriage of Mercury and Philology,* Macrobius's *Commentary on the Dream of Scipio,* Alanus de Insulis's *Anticlaudianus,* and Dante's *Commedia* are to be trusted. But the only sonic reward for his adventurous ascent is ultimately a noise of such dreadful magnitude that even at a mile's distance Chaucer finds its impact deafening. "[W]hat soun is it lyk?" asks the testy Eagle, and Chaucer answers:

> "Peter, lyk betynge of the see,"
> Quod y, "ayen the roches holowe,
> Whan tempest doth the shippes swalowe,
> And lat a man stonde, out of doute,
> A myle thens, and here hyt route;
> Or elles lyk the last humblynge
> After the clappe of a thundringe,
> Whan Joves hath the air ybete.
> But yt doth me for fere swete."
>   (*HF* 1034–42)

Fearful and sweaty, Chaucer eventually enters into the House of Fame, only to find therein a pandemonium of raucous petitioners seeking celebrity from those classical purveyors of history whose accounts of past events prove to be totally arbitrary—in part because all words spoken on earth as they arrive in the House of Fame, Chaucer learns, are instantly homogenized into a single *vox confusa,* in part because the goddess Fama is herself perfectly illogical in determining which tidings then go forth from her house. As William S. Wilson has emphasized in "Scholastic Logic in Chaucer's *House of Fame,*" Fama's nine different groups of petitioners, asking for good fame or ill fame or no fame, are treated in one of three "irrational" ways: either they are granted what they wish, or they are granted the opposite of what they wish, or—in violation of the truth-tables of logic and the law of the excluded middle—they are granted something else, a *tertium quid.*[16]

Disconcerted by the illogicality and indecipherability of all this noise, Chaucer eventually leaves the House of Fame only to light upon an ancillary house, a wickerworld of innumerable speech-acts that might nevertheless succeed in harmonizing the noise of history's tidings. But the House of Rumour proves to be a sixty-mile-long word-processor running amok, a spinning labyrinth of sonic signifiers that together make such a volume of collective noise that the concentrated impact feels, even to the distant auditor, like a massive ballistic missile rushing past:

> And therout com so gret a noyse
> That, had hyt stonden upon Oyse,
> Men myghte hyt han herd esely
> To Rome, y trowe sikerly.
> And the noyse which that I herde,
> For al the world ryght so hyt ferde
> As dooth the rowtynge of the ston
> That from th'engyn ys leten gon..
> (*HF* 1927–34)

Piero Boitani has suggested that for Chaucer the House of Fame constitutes the literary representation of the past, whereas the House of Rumour represents present reality, "the whole world of man and nature," "not reality as such, as it *exists* in the sublunary world . . . but as it is *told*."[17] Boitani's distinction is impressive in its implications, but what remains remarkable is the similarity of the two worlds: rather than reflecting the actuality of historical events (whose unmediated reality Chaucer implies we can never know), both houses are made up of warring words, or, more precisely, the percussive repercussions of stridently militant sounds. Thus if all history is an arbitrary mix of *vox* and *sonus* and a complete confusion of truth ("sad soth") and falsehood ("lesyng"), how can any writer—Homer, Virgil, Ovid, Lucan, Claudian, or any of Fama's other "auctoritees"—harmonize past events and make sense of them? And if the factuality of history is indistinguishable from the rhetoric of its historiographical representation, that is, if the noise of *res* is made up of exactly the same sounds that also constitute *sonus* and *vox,* does this in fact mean it is impossible for a fourteenth-century poet such as Chaucer to arrive at a "logical" and "harmonic" principle of interpretative order to make some sense of the world? Is it not the case that the *vox confusa* that is history comprises such an unabated racket that any attempts to make sense of the chaos of chronicled events, past or present, will prove to be little more than an absolute mockery of the music of the spheres?

What is ironic about all this historiographical skepticism is that language, the medium of history and poetry alike, is in its essence perfectly ordered—as Chaucer's readers had learned early in their liberal arts education and as Chaucer has no choice but to relearn on his way to the House of Fame. The primary "substaunce" of every word is sound, the Eagle declaims to the student in his talons, created by an initial act of percussion the effects of which then amplify into space like the concentric circles formed by a stone thrown in water. The points the Eagle makes in his somewhat logorrheic explication are so essential to our understanding of Chaucer's hermeneutics of noise that I quote him at length:

> Thou wost wel this, that spech is soun,
> Or elles no man myghte hyt here;
> Now herke what y wol the lere.
>   Soun ys noght but eyr ybroken;
> And every speche that ys spoken,
> Lowd or pryvee, foul or fair,
> In his substaunce ys but air;
> For as flaumbe ys but lyghted smoke,
> Ryght soo soun ys air ybroke.
> But this may be in many wyse,
> As soun that cometh of pipe or harpe.
> For whan a pipe is blowen sharpe
> The air ys twyst with violence
> And rent—loo, thys ys my sentence.
> Eke whan men harpe-strynges smyte,
> Whether hyt be moche or lyte,

Loo, with the strok the ayr tobreketh;
And ryght so breketh it when men speketh.
Thus wost thou wel what thing is speche.
    Now hennesforth y wol the teche
How every speche, or noyse, or soun,
Thurgh hys multiplicacioun,
Thogh hyt were piped of a mous,
Mot nede come to Fames Hous.
I preve hyt thus—take hede now—
Be experience; for yf that thow
Throwe on water now a stoon,
Wel wost thou hyt wol make anoon
A litel roundell as a sercle,
Paraunter brod as a covercle;
And ryght anoon thow shalt see wel,
That whel wol cause another whel,
And that the thridde, and so forth, brother,
Every sercle causynge other
Wydder than hymselve was;
And thus fro roundel to compas,
Ech aboute other goynge
Causeth of othres sterynge
And multiplyinge ever moo,
Til that hyt be so fer ygoo,
That hyt at bothe brynkes bee . . .
And ryght thus every word, ywys,
That lowd or pryvee spoken ys,
Moveth first an ayr aboute,
And of thy movynge, out of doute,
Another ayr anoon ys meved;
As I have of the watir preved,
That every cercle causeth other,
Ryght so of ayr, my leve brother:
Everych ayr another stereth
More and more, and speche up bereth,
Or voys, or noyse, or word, or soun,

Ay through multiplicacioun,
Til hyt be atte Hous of Fame—
Take yt in ernest or in game.
                    (*HF* 761–822)

As Martin Irvine has helpfully revealed in "Medieval Grammatical Theory and Chaucer's *House of Fame*," the Eagle's lecture is in fact a series of serio-comic citations taken nearly *verbatim* from medieval commentaries upon Priscian's *Institutione grammaticae*.[18] A remarkable proportion of these popular texts (the Eagle's "wel wost thou" is an accurate assessment) is devoted to glossing Priscian's very brief opening chapter, *De voce*, and its definitions of the phonetic, phonemic, and semantic properties of language as *vox*.[19] Physically, these grammarians agreed, *vox* is actually indistinguishable from *sonus:* every word, like every sound, is a vibration of air whose transmission conforms to the same orderly and universal laws of motion. And these sounds are no different in their physical properties from other, nonverbalized sounds. Thus when Priscian economically remarks, "[p]hilosophers define spoken utterance (*vox*) as very thin struck air or its property perceptible to hearing," his commentators elaborate on how a variety of instruments, in addition to the human throat, are able to move or strike air in order to make *sonus*. Isidore of Seville, to take one example, explains in his *Etymologiae* how air can be passed through a horn trumpet (*tuba*) or a bone pipe (*tibia*), or it can be moved by striking something like the strings of a harp (*cithara*), or "by anything else that is melodious by percussion."[20] In light of the fact that Priscian's glossators viewed the formation and transmission of verbal sound, musical sound, and other kinds of sound as nearly identical, it is not surprisingly that their major non-Priscian source proves to be none other than Boethius's *De musica*. In *De musica* Boethius had already defined sound as the "percussion of air remaining undissolved all the way to the hearing."[21] Similarly, he had already expatiated upon the roles of tension, stress, and percussion in *musica instrumentalis:* "This music is governed either by tension, as in strings, or by breath, as in the aulos or those instruments activated by water, or by a certain percussion, as in those which are cast in concave brass, and various sounds are produced from these."[22] And, most famously, in a brief chapter entitled "How We Hear,"

Boethius compares the production and dispersion of every form of sound to the movement of concentric circles in a pond formed by a stone thrown into its center:[23]

> First it causes a wave in a very small circle; then it disperses clusters of waves into larger circles, and so on until the motion, exhausted by the spreading out of waves, dies away. The latter, wider wave is always diffused by a weaker impulse. Now if something should impede the spreading waves, the same motion rebounds immediately, and it makes new circles by the same undulations as at the center whence it originated.
>
> In the same way, then, when air that is struck creates sound, it affects other air nearby and in this way sets in motion a circular wave of air; and so it is diffused and reaches the hearing of all standing around at the same time. The sound is fainter to someone standing at a distance, since the wave of activated air approaches him more weakly.[24]

It is not surprising that Chaucer was not the only "historiographical" poet in the Middle Ages to ring changes on Boethius's foundational image. Dante, most notably, in the opening lines of *Paradiso* 14, describes the sound waves of St. Thomas's voice repercussing from the center of his mind to its rim and then back again:

> Dal centro al cerchio, e sì dal cerchio al centro
> movesi l'acqua in un ritondo vaso,
> secondo ch'è percosso fuori o dentro:
> ne' la mia mente fé sùbito caso
> questo ch'io dico, sì come si tacque
> la glorïosa vita di Tommaso . . .
> (*Paradiso* 14.1–6)

———

> From the center to the rim, and so from the rim to the center, the water in a round vessel moves, according as it is struck from without or within. This which I say fell suddenly into my mind as the glorious life of Thomas became silent . . . [25]

While the collision of waves produced by percussions both "from without and from within" might have resulted in a tempest of rough waters, the effect of these sanctified sounds blending in the "ritondo vaso" of Dante's mind proves to be the purest of spiritual harmonies. Topographically, such harmony is appropriate, for St. Thomas and Dante are presently within the sphere of the sun, the site of mathematical order, reason, and harmony. However, Dante next ascends to the heaven of Mars, the planet of discord par excellence. But even here harmony ultimately reigns. While these martial cantos are rich with allusions to historical dissonance, most notably the discordances of Florentine urban violence recounted in Canto 16, Dante manages to hear, quite amazingly, an ineffable melody "which held me rapt, though I followed not the hymn" (*Paradiso* 14.122–23). The music's ultimate source proves to be Christ's crucified body imposed upon a cross of stars intersecting the dome of heaven, a "sweet lyre" whose "holy strings" are invisibly strummed by the "right hand of Heaven" (*Paradiso* 15.5–6). As Jeffrey Schnapp explains in his erudite study of these "historical" cantos, *The Transfiguration of History in the Center of Dante's Paradise,* the invisible instrument of Christ's body serves as "a scandalous countersign to anarchic discord of the human city," staging a utopian integration of the "heterogeneous strings of the city of man into the transcendent unity of the sign of Christ in anticipation of history's end."[26] Counterposing the gently percussive words of St. Thomas with the percussive instrument of Christ's sweet passion, and the "ritondo vaso" of Dante's mind with the circles of the heavenly spheres, Dante's Christian faith manages to hear, even in the din of urban revolt and in the clamor of historical discord, the harmonies of divine love.

But in *The House of Fame* Chaucer hears nothing of the kind. It is an obvious understatement to assert that Chaucer refuses to embrace Dante's unifying eschatological perspective, that his "inner ear" is not attuned to the universal harmonies of eternity, that he accords no credence to the "harmonious logic which pervades the text of history," and that he finds dissonance rather than consonance to be the dominant chromatic of the body politic. Whereas Dante strives in the *Paradiso* to repress and distance the sounds of history until their discordance serves as a providential minor key to the symphony of God's love, one major way Chaucer parodies Dante's great work is by refusing to ameliorate, aestheticize, or

Christianize the cacophonous explosions of the world. Yet it is through variations and intensifications of Boethius's basic stone-in-water image that Chaucer expresses his own appreciation of history's sonic force. Contra Boethius, for Chaucer the sonic volume caused by these explosions does *not* dissipate the further they carry, but rather increases. What this means is that no matter where one stands, the charge of historical noise is as dangerous as a missile shot from a supersonic cannon. Accordingly, as he attends to history's noise, Chaucer is fortunate not to be flattened by one of its projectiles whizzing past. And he is just as fortunate not to slip out of his mentor's grasp on the way to fame, for his plummeting *corpus* would have served as but another illustration of the Boethian laws of audiodynamics.

The Boethian laws of audiodynamics, of "how we hear," are thus demonstrated in every corner of the world of *The House of Fame,* and each example confirms Chaucer's persuasion that history is an indiscriminate chaos of sounds. And it is not only the force, but also the sordid quality of these sounds that is intensely disorienting, as Aeolus's trump of brass, from which ill fame emanates, unpleasantly demonstrates:

> And [Aelous] gan this trumpe for to blowe,
> As al the world shulde overthrowe,
> That thrughout every regioun
> Wente this foule trumpes soun,
> As swifte as pelet out of gonne
> Whan fyr is in the poudre ronne.
> And such a smoke gan out wende
> Out of his foule trumpes ende,
> Blak, bloo, grenyssh, swartish red,
> As doth where that men melte led,
> Loo, al on high fro the tuel.
> And therto oo thing saugh I wel,
> That the ferther that hit ran,
> The gretter wexen hit began,
> As dooth the ryver from a welle,
> And hyt stank as the pit of helle.
>
> (*HF* 1638–54)

Throughout his career, as we can see symptomatically in the odiferous and militant explosions emanating from ill fame's trump of brass, Chaucer's parodic redeployments of Boethius's stone-in-water trope have a disequilibrating yet potentially instructive edge. From his textbooks, from his *auctoritates,* and from his discriminating auditions of the deeds and words of the past, Chaucer finds that every historical event is an instance of "ayr ybroke." To human ears some of these sounds are meaningful, others are not. And yet—be they music or words, animals sounds or the sounds of men beating upon the bodies of other men—they are all produced by an original act of percussion. In the brief hearing I have given the sonic performances in *The Parliament of Fowls* and *The House of Fame,* I have not attempted to progress very far from honoring the noise itself toward an understanding of its possible import. However, in *The Summoner's Tale* and then finally in *The Nun's Priest's Tale,* I intend to do just that: to invent an auditory hermeneutics that might do justice to the dense and confusing sounds emanating from the body of the text.

THIRTEEN WAYS OF LISTENING TO A FART

My major purpose in undertaking an extensive analysis of the fart detonated at the center of *The Summoner's Tale* is to celebrate the fart's impact on its auditors as a complex political sign. At the same time I intend to argue against a narrow historicist decryption of the fart. Shifting away from what I call premature historicist/allegorical closure, I hope to expand the fart's hermeneutic circle so that the "meaning" of this distinctive noise is understood to contain all the contradictory responses and associations that come to the critic's mind.

   As is well known, in *The Summoner's Tale* a friar named John has for many years been bilking a sick freeholder named Thomas, all the while promising to restore him to good health via the ardent prayers of his brethren in the friary. Midway through the tale, Thomas's long-repressed ire is so ready to explode that he finally promises the friar he will give him a treasured gift, but only on one condition: that he divide the gift evenly among all the members of his convent. Groping eagerly into Thomas's sickbed under the "clifte" of Thomas's "buttok" until he reaches Thomas's "tuwel," Friar John receives the gift directly into his hand: "Ther nys no capul, drawynge in a cart, / That myghte have lete a fart of swich a soun" (III.2150–51). The friar is instantly nonplussed—not, as one would expect, by the material gift itself, but rather by the impossibility of its equal division. Intent on keeping his word, however, he anxiously carries his metaphysical conundrum from Thomas's house all the way to the manor house of the "lord of that village" (III.2165). Presented with this baffling sophistical problem in "ars-metrike[s]" (III.2222), everyone in the seigniorial household—lord, wife, squire, and "ech man" (III.2287)—is invited to gloss the churl's *impossibilium.*

The lord proceeds to process the difficulties of the dilemma at length, both intensively and extensively. That is, his thoughts begin in a prelinguistic silence of internal deliberation (III.2218–27); they then suddenly explode into public discourse with the locution "Lo . . . !" (III.2228); thereafter, expanding into open air, his words amplify to such a pitch that each of his last three utterances is graced by editors with an exclamation mark (III.2228–42):

> The lord sat stille as he were in a traunce,
> And in his herte he rolled up and doun,
> "How hadde this cherl ymaginacioun
> To shewe swich a probleme to the frere?
> Nevere erst er now herde I of swich mateere.
> I trowe the devel putte it in his mynde.
> In ars-metrike shal ther no man fynde,
> Biforn this day, of swich a question.
> Who sholde make a demonstracioun
> That every man shold have yliche his part
> As of the soun or savour of a fart?
> O nyce, proude cherle, I shrewe his face!
> Lo, sires," quod the lord, "with hard grace!
> Who evere herde of swiche a thyng er now?
> To every man ylike? Tel me how.
> It is an inpossible; it may nat be.
> Ey, nyce cherl, God lete him never thee!
> The rumblynge of a fart, and every soun,

Nis but of eir reverberacioun,
And evere it wasteth litel and litel awey.
Ther is no man kan deemen, by my fey,
If that it were departed equally.
What, lo, my cherl, lo, yet how shrewedly
Unto my confessour to-day he spak!
I holde hym certeyn a demonyak!
Now ete youre mete, and lat the cherl go pleye;
Lat hym go honge hymself a devel weye!"
                                        (III.2216–42)

Duplicating the interior/exterior production of Thomas's rude *sonus* at the level of *vox,* the lord's corporeal rumblings and vocal ventilations eventually come to naught, and so it is left to his ingenious squire to find a solution to the friar's perplexing problem. A twelve-spoked cartwheel, he suggests, needs to be positioned under the nostrils of the friary's twelve brothers spaced equidistantly around its rim. With Thomas donating his sonic gift at the wheel's hub, the twelve fraternal scholars will be able to receive equally the fart's sound and odor. But, the squire insists, Friar John in all fairness should be placed directly under the "nave" and there receive the fart's "first fruyt, as resoun is" (III.2277). And on this note *The Summoner's Tale* comes to its end, leaving the image of the actualization of the equitable division of this devilish gift to resonate in the reader's mind.

For many decades of Chaucer criticism *The Summoner's Tale* has been appreciated as a brilliant example of antimendicant satire, which of course it is. However, after the publication of Lee Patterson's *Chaucer and the Subject of History* in 1991, it has become apparent that the closing scenes of the tale also give expression to certain political agendas that violently confronted each other in the 1381 Uprising. Audible in the language attending Thomas's ironized gift, Patterson discovers, is the rebels' cry for material equality: "every man sholde have yliche his part" (III.2225). Similarly, the lord's response to Thomas's demand reiterates upper-class incomprehension and disbelief: "To every man ylike? Tel me how. / It is an inpossible; it may nat be" (III.2230–31). Just as a fart cannot be "departed equally," neither, according to the dominant social classes, can the goods of this world. For Patterson, this scene provides a "brief allegory" of the seigniorial reactions to peasant demands articulated in the Uprising. However, once Chaucer takes cognizance of these demands, he apparently retreats from considering their implications. That is, once the squire offers his ingenious cartwheel solution, we are witnessing, according to Patterson, the "translation of Thomas's challenge back into the dehistoricizing language of antifraternal discourse."[27] This translation works at two levels: it dramatizes the historical phenomenon of the rebels' political demands being "displaced and finally appropriated to the traditional structure of medieval society,"[28] and it serves as "an allegory of Chaucer's own practice of articulating but finally containing the voice of political protest."[29] And this containment, Patterson insists, is final. As he did at the end of *The Miller's Tale* (Chaucer's boldest foray into radical politics, according to Patterson), at the end of *The Summoner's Tale* the poet retreats into a position he never again leaves: a politically unmarked and "socially undetermined subjectivity . . . that stands apart from *all* forms of class consciousness."[30]

Patterson's argument that *The Summoner's Tale* contains a rare moment where Chaucer can be observed, if not directly naming the most disquieting historical event in his lifetime, at least evoking that rebellion by citing key words in its political manifestos, marks a significant turn in the general *mentalité* of Chaucer criticism. Traditionally seen as either timelessly apolitical or politically indistinguishable from his conservative acquaintances, Chaucer may indeed be revealing within these scenes a moment of "radical" political sympathy. But, then again, he may not. Instead of revealing his own singularly personal reading of the Revolt, he may be more interested as a poet in transforming the fart's sonoric environs into a cornucopian text embodying a rich array of interpretative positions.

Persuaded entirely by Patterson's insistence that the ending of *The Summoner's Tale* directly evokes dominant discourses surrounding the Revolt, I want to amplify the range of critical audition by tuning into a wider variety of locutions that may all be encoded in this dense noise. To understand the fart in as nuanced a fashion as possible, in other words, it is helpful to recall that in *The House of Fame* history is disclosed to be nothing but sounds — percussive sounds emanating from history's actors mingled with percussive sounds emanating from history's reporters. Indeed, the sonic chaos of the House of Fame combined with the sonic chaos of the House of Rumour proves that all those who declaim the meaning of history are also contributors to history's making; consequently, history itself is nothing more nor less than a contestation of conflicting voices, a concatenation of sounds. In a strikingly similar fashion, Steven Justice in his excellent study *Writing and Rebellion: England in 1381* arrives at a determination parallel to that advanced by Chaucer in *The House of Fame*. The Peasants' Revolt of 1381, Justice finds, was in no small part an extended battle over the meaning of verbal utterances, with the peasants striving to make their voices audible and recordable as human voices, and the chroniclers managing wherever possible to reduce the rebels' locutions to the level of noise and inarticulate sounds. The chroniclers' "trope of noise," writes Justice, was "there to deny, take away, obscure, and otherwise render inaudible anything the rebels might have *said*—by speech, script, or purposeful action—and jumble all their words and actions into undifferentiated *sound*."[31] Similarly, I suggest, the central problem in *The Summoner's Tale* is not simply the political intention of a rebellious sound, but, as with the Revolt itself, the politics of its aural reception and aural repression.

Thus a major part of the interpretative task posed by Thomas's fart is to appreciate its complexity as a noise that invokes, contains, and projects a concatenation of historical words, sounds, and actions. And also embedded in the significance of this noise, I insist, are the explanatory glosses provided by Thomas, Friar John, and the village lord. These glozing activities encircling the fart continue to radiate outward, embracing the figure of the squire, the figures of the twelve friars, and then (beyond the rim of the *Tale*) all those who strive to interpret the great noise at its center. The general critical strategies I am advancing thus differ from Patterson's methods of historical and biographical *allegoresis*. In its presumption that Chaucer takes one "radical" look at "history" and then returns to "literature" and the safe haven of a "socially undetermined subjectivity," Patterson's allegory, while insightful, remains cautiously circumscribed and self-contained. Or, to put it another way, Patterson compresses the signifying parameters of the fart in *The Summoner's Tale* into what we can infer to be true about Chaucer's political persuasions as they relate to specifically cited social agendas contested in the Revolt. My own con-

cerns are in fact not focused upon Chaucer's privately held political beliefs (which may well be impossible to locate), but rather upon the shared
hermeneutics of historical dissonance provided by this publicly repeated
fart, a hermeneutics, I have suggested, that is embodied in the noise itself as well as in the circular image of the wheel that contains it.

The cartwheel surrounding the fart is semiotically as important as
the noise released at its center. Throughout the Middle Ages the circle's
geometric perfection served as an icon of the harmonic perfections of
music, human or divine. In *De musica,* as we have already noted, Boethius compares the production and dispersion of a sound to the movement of concentric circles in a pond. In Martianus Capella's *The Marriage of Mercury and Philology,* the liberal arts figure of Harmony (or
Music) carries a shield that is "circular overall, with many inner circles,"
and from these circles emanates the enchanting music of the spheres.[32]
In *The Parliament of Fowls,* as we have seen, Chaucer counterpoints the
poem's many harmonic circles against the explosive noise at its center, and
in *The House of Fame* it is the circular "tuel," or end-hole, of Sklaundre, the
black trumpet of brass that contains the direction of the sonic explosion
emanating from its bowels. Accordingly, in *The Summoner's Tale* it is the
particular variant of this circular icon, namely the cartwheel, that I wish
to honor critically even as I attempt to decrypt the explosive noise resonating from its center. The cartwheel obviously works somewhat like the
margins of Boethius's pool and the "cerchio" of Dante's mind; it invokes
the outermost rim of the heavenly spheres, the *primum mobile;* and it attempts to contain the centrifugal circles of "air ybroke," returning its own
centripetal locutions back toward the center. Yet what is perhaps most distinctive about this wheel is its twelve-spoked design (Dante's star-crossed
orb of heaven is a distant analogue), and the position of twelve friar-
scholars as exegetical recipients of its great rushing of wind.

Thus, in deference to Chaucer's iconic and subphonemic instructions, I will provide in the next few pages the same number of contending positions vis-à-vis the fart that the image of the twelve-spoked cartwheel invites and parodies. My major purpose in defining these twelve
positions is to demonstrate how the *vox confusa* of the Revolt, resisting
the codifications of any single-minded *allegoresis,* discovers much of its

meaning in the dissonance among its multifarious interpreters, including the rebel-actors themselves. The result, inevitably, is a wide variety of locutions, all of them potentially "political," all pertaining to Thomas's disruptive fart. After completing the hermeneutic circle of these twelve readings, I will then attempt to answer a question that seems to hover at the cartwheel's very center: is there any central thematics that succeeds in harmonizing the dissonant readings of a noise which by its very nature resists the hegemonic politics of critical harmony? In other words, is there a thirteenth way of listening to a fart?

Spoke One. Thomas, the fart's originator, appears to be a peasant: at least he is called a "cherl" a total of ten times in the *Tale.* But what is his actual social status, and does it matter? All material evidence indicates that he is neither poor nor indentured, but rather an independent and rather wealthy freeholder who has his own "meynee" (III.2156). Initially, therefore, it seems unlikely that Thomas would identify himself with the demands expressed in the Peasants' Revolt for personal freedom and material equality. However, as Justice illustrates in *Writing and Rebellion,* a great many of the insurgents were already freeholders whose public insistence that peasants be given *libertas* was in certain ways a symbolic rallying cry rather than an economic program.[33] In an act of free self-naming, the rebels collectively identified themselves as peasants, choosing, Justice explains, "the rural laboring class . . . as a focus around which they could arrange diverse ambitions."[34] Thus some of the tensions at the center of the Peasant's Revolt are dramatically reflected in the political/linguistic issue of Thomas's being properly, or improperly, called a "cherl."

Spoke Two. As Anne Hudson has argued in *The Premature Reformation,* twentieth-century readings of Wycliffite thought as providing a proto-communist theory of property are readings based on scant evidence. Assuredly, Wyclif believed that "the just" would wish to share their spiritual or temporal goods with others, but these "just" are for Wyclif otherworldly conceptions of perfect charity rather than human individuals living on earth.[35] Thus, to smell a Marxist in the Lollard wind of *The Summoner's Tale* appears to be an act of creative misprision. Nevertheless, Wyclif's critique of the materialism of the endowed church coincided with the rebels' belief, recorded in the *Anonimalle Chronicle,* that "the goods of holy church should not be in the hands of . . . any churchmen, but that they should have their sustenance alone, and the rest of their goods should be divided among parishioners."[36] Thus the ideal of a redistribution of goods from church to parish could easily have been generalized, in the minds of some rebels, into a more radical equalization of *all* material wealth.

Spoke Three.   As Wendy Scase has demonstrated in *Piers Plowman and the New Anti-Clericalism,* extremely heated debates raged between monks, friars, and seculars in the late fourteenth century as to whether or not the ideal of commonly held property forbade or legitimized a religious order's accumulation of wealth.[37] Chaucer's satire not only addresses this urgent contemporary issue, I suggest, but also gives voice to one of the rebels' major complaints, ecclesiastical materialism. Calling the first partition of Thomas's fart the "firste fruyt" is, of course, an indelicate allusion to the long tradition of tithing. Thus Patterson may well be mistaken in assuming that the ending of *The Summoner's Tale* effects a "translation of Thomas's challenge back into the dehistoricizing language of antifraternal discourse." Only a purely formalist sensibility (which Patterson strenuously eschews) should be able to view all forms of antimendicant satire as belonging to a "literary," "dehistoricizing," and "apolitical" genre. In certain local contexts, in other words, pieces of antifraternal satire such as *The Summoner's Tale* may well be targeted against specific abuses, such as those ecclesiastical excesses that were seen as one cause catalyzing the Peasants' Revolt.

Spoke Four.   In an excellent study of the social classes of *The Summoner's Tale,* Linda Georgianna reveals how the friar's attempt to sustain with Thomas a "horizontal," cash-nexus, and secular "brotherhood" is a modernizing social gesture. This self-serving attempt at bourgeois social leveling is itself a sullying of the penitential association to which both Thomas and his wife belong, a lay confraternity attached to Friar John's convent.[38] By *Tale's* end, however, both spiritual and social economies are turned inside out: first, by the hierarchical positioning of the fart (the "cherl" on top); and then by "the vertical relations of older feudal practices" in the lord's manor, where, for example, gifts are given instead of money as signs of personal esteem.[39] Thus vertical, horizontal, spiritual, material, collective, personal, feudal, and capitalist dynamics are all mingled inside the social exegetics and body language of this increasingly complicated "political" fart.

Spoke Five.   For more than thirty years, the twelve-part division of the fart has been interpreted as a profanation of the iconographic representations of the descent of the Holy Spirit to the twelve apostles at Pentecost.[40] The lower-body language of the fart is undoubtedly a parody of the Holy Spirit's ghostly afflatus, that great rushing of wind with tongues of fire. But to what degree are the two utterances, one sacred (*vox dei*) and the other profane (*vox populi*), actually opposed to each other? And to what degree is the parody a top-down critique of the material by the spiritual? For some auditors, it may indeed be possible to hear in Thomas's *sermo humilis* the voice of one utopian ideal of *communitas* speaking to another, the community of saints unified in the body of Christ. In Thomas's great rushing of wind, it may even be possible to hear reverberations of John Ball's famous revolutionary question: "Whanne Adam dalfe and Eve span, / Who was þanne a gentil man?"[41] At any rate, because the discourses of doubting Thomas and the Holy Spirit are equally nonverbal and glossolalic, both utterances require an unusual degree of auditory creativity to calibrate the parodic interplay between their political and their anagogic meanings.

Spoke Six.   Although it may at first seem blasphemous, the polyvalence of Thomas's fart in this regard is strikingly similar to the polyvalence of Christ's body as it was represented and understood in the late Middle Ages. In her study of the role of Christ's body in the city of York and especially in the York mystery plays, Sarah Beckwith provides a compressed outline of its many competing registers:

> [T]he body of Christ . . . does not simply operate according to static binary opposition: divinity versus humanity. Rather it catches in its

network of association a range of oppositions that, because they are mutually constructed through the way the body of Christ conflates them, provide nuance, add to, and so defer any final signification. Christ's body alludes to numerous oppositions: inner and outer, transcendent and immanent, spirit and flesh, male and female, left and right, up and down, noisy and silent, just and unjust, passive and active, noumenal and phenomenal, public and private, hierarchical and collective, unified and multiplicitous, and so on.[42]

Similarly, it could be argued that the network of associations inhering in and adhering to the fart of *The Summoner's Tale* is a complex semiotic site embracing oppositions whose relative significance is constantly being contested and revalorized.

Spoke Seven.   Now that we are halfway around the hermeneutical circle, we should honor the intellectual lightheadedness of the entire enterprise, for part of the fart-and-cartwheel's satiric thrust is obviously directed against *any* form of elevated discourse. The "demonstratioun" of the solution to this "probleme" in posterior analytics is clearly a send-up of scholastic choplogic, of all manner of "ars-metrike[s]," and of liberal arts learning in general. The lord's squire is a "kervere" who, like Plato's philosopher-king, believes it is possible to cut reality at the joints: thus the lord's educated household praises him for speaking "As wel as Euclide [dide] or Ptholomee" (III.2289). English peasants, however, would typically have responded by using less abstract, but equally expressive, language. Among the medieval *illiterati,* as Aron Guverich has shown, the "disinclination for abstract concepts" was by no means a deficiency, but rather a conscious way of organizing experience within a less generalized and socially elevated discourse.[43] The fart thus can be seen as a noise organizing peasant experience and expressing their revolutionary sentiments in a lower yet extremely powerful linguistic register.

Spoke Eight.   The fart's rhetorical strains of opposition between material substance and immaterial essence are also embodied in the linguistic logic of the tale's central pun. A medieval French verbal game helps make the point:

Demande.

Comment partiroit on une vesse en douze parties?

Response.

Faittes une vesse sur le moieul d'une roe, et douze personnes ayent chascun son nez aux xii trous, et par ainsi chascun en ara sa part.

————

[Question: How can one divide a fart into twelve parts? Answer: Make the fart in the middle of a wheel, with twelve people, each with his nose between the twelve spokes (lit: in the twelve holes), so that each shall thus get his share.][44]

In *The Summoner's Tale*, as Richard Firth Green has insightfully suggested, Chaucer may be using a similar English riddle, "How do you part a farthing into twelve?"[45] Mindful that a farthing is next to worthless — literally a penny cut into fourths — the traditional respondent is expected to have no answer. Thomas, however, responds to Friar John's question "What is a ferthyng worth parted in twelve?" (III.1967) by brilliantly transposing the meaning of "ferthyng" from the economic to the metaphysical. The English courtly audience, undoubtedly familiar with the riddle (the French analogue is found in a collection of courtly verbal games), would have appreciated the cleverness of this intellectual joke. But would they also have appreciated the novel "ymaginacioun" of its churlish author, who "shrewedly" has created a "question" which no one had heard "Biforn this day"? Chaucer is careful to model at least two responses for his readers: either the so-called peasant is stupid, or he is extremely intelligent. The village lord's first explanation is that Thomas was momentarily possessed by a demon: "I trowe the devel putte it in his mynde." But once the peasant's problem is solved, all (except for the silent friar) agree that "subtiltee / And heigh wit made hym speken as he spak; / He nys no fool, ne no demonyak" (III.2290–92). Thomas, the churlish freeholder, ultimately comes across as a devilishly clever intellectual.

Spoke Nine. If this landed freeholder has the intellectual subtlety to pose a highly sophisticated problem concerning the equal division of a sound, we should recall that Chaucer himself had been extensively trained, as had all his reasonably well-educated readers, in precisely how to determine whether a musical tone (which is, admittedly, different from a single sound) is evenly divisible. This problem and its rational, mathematical solution constitute the entirety of book 3 of Boethius's *De musica,* of which I quote a very small part:

> The first numbers containing the tone are 8 and 9. But since these follow each other in natural sequence in such a way that there is no mean number between them, I multiply both these numbers by two, which, of course, is the smallest I can use. This makes 16 and 18. Between these a number, 17, falls naturally. Thus 18:16 is a tone, but 18 compared to 17 contains the latter wholly plus 1/17 part of it. Now 1/17 part is naturally smaller than 1/16 part, so the ratio contained in the numbers 16 and 17 is larger than that between 17 and 18. Let these numbers be set out in this manner: let 16 be A, 17 C, and 18 B. . . .
>
> But since the ratio 18:17 follows next after 17:16, we should see whether, multiplied by two, it will not fill a tone. The term 18 contains 17 plus one part of 17. So if we produce another number in relation to 18 with the same ratio that 18 has to 17, it will be 19 and 1/17 part. But if we produce a number situated in the sesquioctave ratio in relation to the term 17, it will make 19 and 1/8 part. An eighth part is larger than a seventeenth part, so the ratio of numbers 17 and 19 1/8 is larger than that comprised of 17 and 19 1/17 (which, of course, consists of two continuous 18:17 ratios). Thus, two continuous ratios of 18:17 are seen not to complete one tone. Therefore, 18:17 is not a half tone, since these terms, when duplicated, do not fill a whole; they do not form halves, for a half, when doubled, is always equal to that of which it is half.[46]

Considering the difficulty of determining whether a single tone can be divided equally, it is no wonder that dividing into twelve equal parts the discontinuous ratios of an atonal, or multitonal, noise would seem an *impossibilium* to all but the most brilliant, and perhaps hubristic, medieval scholars.

Spoke Ten.   But, a fourteenth-century intellectual interested in parts and wholes might ask, would any sound so divided be *part* of a sound or a *full* sound? The branch of medieval philosophy known as mereology, the study of parts and wholes, would take such an issue into the deepest recesses of logic, and then into physics, metaphysics, and theology. To keep matters uncomplicated, let us simply turn to *The Consolation of Philosophy.* Lady Philosophy, by way of emphasizing that worldly wealth is a finite good as opposed to the limitless nature of the *summum bonum,* asserts that it is impossible to distribute one's riches perfectly. She illustrates her precept by using a familiar analogy: "And certes a voys al hool (that is to seyn, withouten amenusynge [diminution]) fulfilleth togydre the herynge of moche folk. But certes your rychesses ne mowen noght passen unto moche folk withouten amenusynge; and whan they ben apassed [have passed away], nedes they maken hem pore that forgoon tho rychesses."[47] In other words, whereas worldly wealth is diminished in proportion to the number of individuals who divide it, this is not true of the Platonic Absolute, the *summum bonum:* just as all auditors hear equally "a voys al hool," so may all share equally in the Idea of the Good.[48]

Spoke Eleven.   As requital to Boethius's Platonic defense of his family property, it is useful to recall that it is the "savour" of Thomas's fart, as well as the "soun," that must be divided equally. Mindful of the economic and political symbolism of eating in literature (and in life), the emphasis in *The Summoner's Tale* upon the provision and consumption of food, as the friar moves from Thomas's table to his lord's table, is significant. The lord of the village dismisses the posed question of social and material equality by calling the friar to his meal: "Now ete youre mete, and lat the cherl go pleye" (III.2241). The relationship of the squire to his lord is also expressed via food: the squire's foremost duty is to "karf[en] his [lordes] mete" (III.2244). With all of this concentration on the social semiotics of the service of food, the *qualitas* of the fart's "savour" may be an incontrovertible sign of its owner's ill health or well-being. Since Thomas's major complaint is that he has been physically sick for years, the symptomatic "stynk" of his fart provides a qualitative critique of the process of economic consumption, distribution, and expulsion within the English body politic.

Spoke Twelve. After circling through these eleven theoretical positions, we need to reemphasize the fart's powers of self-reification: the fart is a fart is a fart, and as a literal fart it asks that it be read literally. Yet it is difficult, perhaps impossible, to interpret even a fart exclusively *ad litteram.* As Richard Leppert reminds us, "sounds produced or manipulated by humans result from conscious acts and hence carry a semantic and discursive charge."[49] The discursive charge of this fart is especially redolent because it is conceived within a literary register, that of the Christian pilgrimage, which is ideally fart-free. In an interview dwelling on the genre of the Western, Mel Brooks was asked about his movie *Blazing Saddles*: "What was the point of the vulgarity—the farting scene, for example?" Brooks answers, "The farts were the point of the farting scene":

> For 75 years these big, hairy brutes have been smashing their fists into each other's faces and blasting each other full of holes with six-guns, but in all that time, not one has had the courage to produce a fart. I think that's funny. I think the farting scene in *Blazing Saddles* is funny because farts in our world are funny. Farts are a repressed minority. The mouth gets to say all kinds of things, but the other place is supposed to keep quiet. But maybe our lower colons have something interesting to say. Farts are human, more human than a lot of people I know. I think we should bring them out of the water closet and into the parlor, and that's what I did in *Blazing Saddles.*[50]

By bringing his political fart to the lord's parlor and the scholars' critical wheel, Chaucer thus appears to be saying many things—or, more precisely, he is providing a complex sonoric environment wherein many things may be said at once about this lower-order speech act. As in *The House of Fame,* where the sounds of history are glossed by secondary sounds whose admixtures then appear as the chronicled tidings of the *auctoritates,* so here a dozen viable glosses interchange with Thomas's authorial intent, which is itself a gloss, a fusion of *sonus* and *vox.* Resonating at such length in the tale (a total of 148 lines), Thomas's long-winded fart thus refuses any univocal significance—be it physiological, characterological, musicological, satiric, Marxian, folkloric, iconographic, parodistic, or historicist. In its resistance to monotonal analysis, it provokes the construction of a nuanced acoustics hypersensitive to a multitude of sounds intermeshed with a multitude of other sounds—linguistic and sublinguistic, musical and cacophonous, classical and contemporary, social, political, artistic, religious and scholarly. Yet for all this dissonance, Chaucer, I maintain, is committed to positioning his readers so that they not only may hear the many individual and overlapping sounds compressed into this noise but also to critique the counterharmonic significance of disruptive social dissonance wherever it may be heard.

One of Mikhail Bakhtin's primary purposes in his extensive explorations of "heteroglossia," a term with which he attempts to define a culture's discourse at any moment in its history, was to understand the political forces that are always at play in language:

> [A]t any given moment of its historical existence, language is heteroglot from top to bottom: it represents the coexistence of socio-ideological contradictions between the present and the past, between differing epochs of the past, between different socio-ideological groups in the present, between tendencies, schools, circles and so forth, all given a bodily form.[51]

Given in bodily form, the fart in *The Summoner's Tale* is heteroglot from top to bottom, a complex and contentious mixture of physical, political, social, clerical, and intellectual sounds. Or, to be more precise, it is heteroglot from bottom to top, for as Bakhtin is careful to emphasize, as it exists in *history* heteroglossia is rarely an egalitarian, horizontal continuum of contending speech forms, but rather a dialogic interaction among socially unequal registers in which prestige languages are persistently attempting to maintain and extend their control. In some forms of *literature,* however, and in certain social behaviors ranging from carnival celebration to political revolution, lower-order discourse at least momentarily contests the dominant forms of political hegemony and provides a rereading of reality from a perspective often proscribed from speaking.[52]

A rereading of contemporary political realities, I believe, is what Chaucer's literary fart allows. The fart is eloquent in part because it is a proscribed *sonus* whose nether-orifice origin parodies all the higher-orifice *voces* that normally control and determine its meaning.[53] Equally important, the heteroglot fart undercuts the power of any single discourse to dominate the significance of *any* historical event, and of *any* political rebellion, for this speech-act is the site of so many "socio-ideological contradictions" that it may well be the contradictions themselves that Chaucer is most intent upon foregrounding.[54] Because Chaucer does not unwaveringly align himself with the ideologies of the rebels, Patterson comes close to charging him with political fecklessness for ultimately muting and containing "the voice of political protest": retreating into a bourgeois subjectivity, Chaucer is caught in a Foucauldian loop of class power which inevitably circulates back to the top. I have already indicated how my own critical position differs from Patterson's: Chaucer I believe is much less committed to defining his personal politics than he is committed to providing his readers a circumambient arena of varied critical discourses that collectively bring interpretative pressure upon the percussions of history, both in the present and in the past. Rather than suppressing or retreating from the sounds of overt political protest, as Patterson suggests, Chaucer instead collides them against the sounds of other expressive systems so that readers might construct for themselves a more "dissonant" and disseminal set of auditory and interpretative strategies to determine the tidings of these and other historical/literary events.

Chaucer's disseminal hermeneutics would thus appear to be measurably different from the historical consciousnesses of his contemporaries who commented directly on the Revolt. Derek Pearsall has shown how all fourteenth- and fifteenth-century poets and historians who wrote about the Uprising constructed their narratives to conform to an *a priori* set of time-honored generic models; by any positivist standards, these texts are all forms of propagandistic fiction rather than reliable "history."[55] Furthermore, even the so-called documentary records of the Revolt are transparently subjective and self-serving: they too "must be understood in terms of the assumptions, prejudices, beliefs, and ingrained habits of mind that color them."[56] What is distinctive about Chaucer's strategy of oblique historical representation is the degree to which he does *not* coerce his readers into any single model, *a priori* or otherwise, but rather provides them with a host of enabling strategies whose collective turbulence is meant, I believe, to subvert "the assumptions, prejudices, beliefs, and ingrained habits of mind" by which medieval literary and political events are characteristically glossed and understood. Ideally, this interpretative dissonance is designed to create in each reader a heteroglossic hermeneutics that is sensitive and "material" yet at the same time theoretical and self-critical. It may also serve as a thirteenth way of listening to a fart, wherein the politics of explosive noise is heard as a promising herald for change. But then again, it may not. The safest position, as long as you are not in the direct line of fire, is to hear this noise for what it most materially and literally is: nothing more nor less than a very loud and very politically charged fart.

CHAUCER'S TRIVIAL FOX CHASE AND
THE PEASANTS' REVOLT OF 1381

> Here is the house. It is green and white. It has a red door. It is very pretty. Here is the family. Mother, Father, Dick, and Jane live in the green-and-white house. They are very happy. See Jane. She has a red dress. She wants to play. Who will play with Jane? See the cat. It goes meow-meow. Come and play. Come play with Jane. The kitten will not play. See mother. Mother is very nice. Mother, will you play with Jane? Mother laughs. Laugh, Mother, laugh. See Father. He is big and strong. Father, will you play with Jane? Father is smiling. Smile, Father, smile. See the dog. Bowwow goes the dog. Do you want to play with Jane? See the dog run. Run, dog, run. Look, look. Here comes a friend. The friend will play with Jane. They will play a good game. Play, Jane, play.

Once heard and once read, the Dick and Jane primer is never forgotten. Its simple one-syllable words, the distinctive rhythm of its short sentences, the artificial parataxis of its imperative, interrogative, and declarative propositions, the almost surreal indeterminacy of its authorial voice are all part of the cultural consciousness of generations of American readers. Recollected with fond nostalgia, the Dick and Jane reader epitomizes that moment in our early education when so many recently mastered semiotic systems are triumphantly melded together: the graphic signs of the alphabet, the vocalic principles of syllabification, the integrity of written words as they correspond to things in the mind and to images upon the page, the syntactical unit of meaning called a sentence.

Each time we read these sentences we are taught again about the nature of language, and especially about nouns, verbs, and adjectives and what they represent. Dick and Jane are nearly generic names for boy and girl; Father and Mother are words that both denote and name their bearers; cat and dog are apparently not names, although Spot (if he were here) would be a proper noun. These creatures define the essence of their species. Mother is very nice; she laughs. Father is big and strong; he smiles. Dick, once named, disappears; Jane, in her red dress, wants to play. The cat, which goes "meow-meow," does not want play; the dog, which goes "bowwow," runs with dog-like eagerness. Jane's world is a bright and orderly world: there is a place for every thing and everything is happily in its place. Like a comedy, the narrative ends in bliss, as the friend, defining the essence of play, gratifies Jane's and the reader's desire.

When the Dick and Jane narrative serves as the opening paragraph to Toni Morrison's *The Bluest Eye*—a novel that depicts a world of misery and injustice populated by characters with names like Pecola and Bay Boy and Cholly Breedlove—it takes on further significance. Morrison's second paragraph produces the Dick and Jane narrative again, this time denuded of its punctuation; the integrity of each of its sentences disappears:

> Here is the house it is green and white it has a red door it is very pretty here is the family mother father dick and jane live in the green-and-white house they are very happy see jane she has a red dress she wants to play who will play with jane see the cat it goes meow-meow come and play come play with jane the kitten will not play see mother mother is very nice mother will you play with jane mother laughs laugh mother laugh see father he is big and strong father will you play with jane father is smiling smile father smile see the dog bowwow goes the dog do you want to play do you want to play with jane see the dog run run dog run look look here comes a friend the friend will play with jane they will play a good game play jane play[57]

In her third paragraph Morrison runs all the letters together (which is something Miss Fidditch in the first grade told us not to do); the integrity of each word disappears:

> Hereisthehouseitisgreenandwhiteithasareddooritisveryprettyhere
> isthefamilymotherfatherdickandjaneliveinthegreenandwhitehouse
> theyareveryhappyseejaneshehasareddressshewantstoplaywhowill
> playwithjaneseethecatitgoesmeowmeowcomeandplaycomeplay
> withmethekittenwillnotplayseemothermotherisverynicemother
> willyouplaywithjanemotherlaughslaughmotherlaughseefatherheis
> bigandstrongfatherwillyouplaywithjanefatherissmilingsmilefather
> smileseethedogbowwowgoesthedogdoyouwanttoplaydoyouwantto
> playwithjaneseethedogrunrundogrunlooklookherecomesafriend
> thefriendwillplaywithjanetheywillplayagoodgameplayjaneplay[58]

Morrison's final act of aggression is to slice the text into pieces, using its fragments as rubrics to various chapters inside the novel. One reason Morrison makes the Dick and Jane reader unreadable, crushing it in the fist of her own fiction, is to provoke a reconsideration, a rereading, of the politics of one's own education. The world of letters is, from the beginning, informed by a cultural construct that privileges certain colors, sounds, words, dialects, names, character types, and models of behavior. A product of this education, yet excluded from the ethnocentric world it depicts and sustains, Toni Morrison, in her graphic deconstruction of this text, says, in effect: the Dick and Jane reader is patently unfair; it is a story in fact about injustice.

When Dante Alighieri reaches the sphere of the just in Canto 18 of *Paradiso,* he is privileged to be the sole reader of what is perhaps the most spectacular display of letters in all literature. The warrior-saints of God, each of them a spark springing forth from Jove's torch, trace out in the heavens, one letter at a time, the injunction from the Book of Wisdom: *DILIGITE IUSTITIAM QUI IUDICATIS TERRAM* [Love justice, ye that judge the earth]. This phantasmagoric skywriting, accompanied by the singing voices of the saints, is a study of several things: the semiotics of writing, the psychology of reading comprehension, and the nature of divine justice as it is administered on earth. As each of these thirty-five letters is formed Dante records that "I took note of the parts as they appeared in utterance to me" until, as individual letters combine in his mind to be sounded into syllables, Dante finally perceives that "*DILIGITE IUSTITIAM* . . . were the first verb and noun of the whole design."[59] What is initially a sequence of meaningless letters Dante is eventually able to read, understand, and then recognize as the words of God.

The next lesson in Dante's tutorial session is a close-up audio-visual demonstration of the two elements that constitute linguistic communication: the graphic sign and the oral sound. While the fiery souls maintain their final configuration as the letter M in *terram,* other souls join them, superimposing a lily upon the M, and gradually transforming it into the shape of an eagle (figure 5.1).

Figure 5.1. The Transformation of an M to an Eagle: *Paradiso* 18[60]

The significance of this single-letter text appears to work on two levels. One is a demonstration of the graphemic power of the literal letter that maintains its essential "M-ness" even while it signifies, as an icon or a hieroglyph, first a flower and then a bird. The second level is that of historical allegory: while the essence of M, which stands apparently for *MONARCHIA,* remains steadfast, the lily (a French-Guelph Florentine emblem) yields to the heraldic eagle (an emblem of the Italian Empire)—a prophetic narration of the "consummated unity of all peoples in a just world-order and common obedience"[61] realized here on earth.

This polysemiotic eagle, in addition to reifying language as *écriture,* provides a close-up demonstration of language's phonetic nature as well. In Canto 20 Dante traces with deft precision the generation of inchoate sound and its physiological pilgrimage up the Eagle's throat as it gradually takes on the characteristics of significant human utterance: "[A]s the sound *(suono)* takes its form at the neck of the lute and the wind at the vent of the pipe it fills," so "that murmur *(mormorar)* of the Eagle rose up through the neck as if it were hollow. There it became a voice *(voce)* that came forth thence by the beak in the form of words *(in forma di parole)* such as my heart, where I wrote them down, awaited."[62] From murmur, to sound, to voice, to word, to writing, Dante quickly ascends the ladder of locution, from subphonemic rumble to lexical units arranged and recorded in a complex syntactical proposition. Progressing from confused noise to the harmony of clear and wished-for understanding, the Eagle's voice is also an allegorical analogue to our changing perceptions of earthly justice. The injustices in human history about which Dante had been so troubled—its wars, treachery, and oppressions—even the injustice of God's denying salvation to that unbaptized yet perfectly virtuous pagan born on the bank of the Indus: all these, the Eagle has explained to Dante, are the workings-out of God's divine justice on earth.[63] Imbued with grace, the truth of this transcendent justice must be accepted and revered, even though it lies beyond the reach of human comprehension. And so ends Dante's lesson.

The ABCs of reading, the basic elements of language, the principles of identity and difference that accord meaning to letters, words, and sentences: both Toni Morrison and Dante Alighieri are committed to revalorizing these elements of our early education even as they address the seemingly unrelated matter of human suffering on earth. Morrison begins by emptying Dick and Jane's letters, words, and sentences of their familiar associations, stripping them of referential value, in the hope of somehow redefining language and the interplay between literary narration and human history. Dante's earth-bound vision of the injustice of human suffering is similar to Morrison's: both recognize the horrors of history, past and present. Like Morrison, Dante returns to the propaedeutics of his literary education in the hope of revalorizing its symbols and redefining the interplay between inscribed text and human history. However, through an effort of supreme will, he transvalues written language by literally sanctifying its symbols: those saints who defined justice in their lives are the very figures who give ontological reality to the scriptural injunction in heaven to pursue justice while on earth.

In *The Nun's Priest's Tale,* Chaucer parodically foregrounds many of the basic exercises in his readers' literary-linguistic education. And although his purposes in doing so are varied, like Morrison and Dante he enjoins his readers to reexamine their earliest classroom experiences in order that they might develop into more responsive critics of their culture. To this point I have been tracing the development of Chaucerian noise as a sign of historical impenetrability and political dissonance whose counter-harmonics might yet be discerned within the reader's "inner ear." In the three works examined—*The Parliament of Fowls, The House of Fame,* and *The Summoner's Tale*—we have seen how Chaucer has chosen to *describe* these noises extensively: their thickness, density, volume, and disquieting percussive power. However, in the *The Nun's Priest's Tale* Chaucer suddenly ups the ante by actually *embodying* the chaos and power of noise inside his own poetic language, even while maintaining his poetry's aural pleasures *as poetry.* One reason the fox chase is one of the most admired passages in Chaucer's *oeuvre* is that it is a *sonic* tour-de-force. Its auditory pleasures are so wildly extravagant that in reading it one experiences something approximating unbounded *jouissance;* at the same time, however, Chaucer invites a quasi-rational response to this carnivalized noise by invoking the standard classroom taxonomy of the "substaunce" of all language, which is sound. The fox chase is also a *poetic* tour-de-force: as the central narrative in Chaucer's *ars poetica,* in its rhythmic, percussive, and noisy splendor the fox chase is a bravura demonstration of rhetoric's functioning at its highest level of creative energy. Finally, and very importantly, the fox chase is also a *trivial* tour-de-force: within his verbal performance of the chase itself Chaucer integrates parodic exercises involving the three linguistic arts, especially logic, an integration that helps construct a critical frame for decrypting all these sounds. Thus, for all its liberating ludic pleasures, we should not be surprised that the poem's sonoric landscape embodies strains of the same historical and political issues Chaucer has consistently identified with the chaos of noise. A fundamental question the fox chase asks is one that Chaucer has been addressing since the beginning of his career: do the sonorities of poetry bear any resemblance to, and do they bear any responsibilities toward, the noisy realities of the world? Much more pointedly, does poetry have anything to say about the (dis)harmonics of human justice?

Sonic Mimology

The most revered grammar in the Middle Ages was Priscian's *Institutiones grammaticae*, a work normally studied with the assistance of one or more popular commentaries, such as the early twelfth century *Glosule super Priscianum maiorem*, William of Conches's *Glose super Priscianum*, Peter Helias's *Summa super Priscianum*, and a work incorporating all of these earlier glosses, the mid-thirteenth century *Tractatus super Priscianum maiorem* usually attributed to Robert Kilwardby, Archbishop of Canterbury.[64] As I have already noted, a remarkable proportion of each of these commentaries is devoted to glossing Priscian's brief opening chapter, *De voce*, and to exploring the phonetic, phonemic, and semantic properties of language as *vox*. According to Priscian, there are in fact four classes of *vox: vox inarticulata illiterata* (noises not resolvable into distinct phonetic units), *vox literata inarticulata* ("meaningless" animal sounds, which can nevertheless be represented by letters), *vox articulata illiterata* (human sounds, like murmuring, which have meaning but have no phonetic units), and *vox articulata literata* (articulate speech and literary language).[65] Although it is only the final category, that of articulate and literary speech, that grammarians selected as their prime subject of study, commentaries on Priscian's first chapter nevertheless elaborated extensively upon all four kinds of sounds. Priscian gives a few examples of "meaningless" animal noises—the frog (in Latin) makes the sound *co-ax* and the crow says *cra*. But commentators, such as Papias in his *Vocabulista*, took pleasure in offering extensive lists of animal *voces*: eagles make their noise (*aquilas clangere*), hawks chirp (*accipitres pipilare*), vultures cry (*vultures pulpulare*), and crows crow (*coruos cruxare vel crocitare*).[66] Thus one of Dante's small triumphs in *Paradiso* 20 is his transformation of the eagle's grammar school clangor into *vox articulata literata*, inscribable human discourse capable of articulating revealed truth.

Whereas Priscian tersely remarks, "philosophers define spoken utterance (*vox*) as very thin struck air or its property perceptible to hearing,"[67] his commentators elaborate extensively on how a variety of instruments, in addition to the human throat, are able to move or strike air in order to make sound. A principal task for medieval students of grammar was learning how to distinguish insignificant sound from significant sound.

The standard axiom was that "every *vox* is a *sonus,* but not vice versa"[68]—although delineating these boundaries, as we shall see, is actually no easy matter. Once defined, however, *vox* serves as the first in a series of ascending linguistic signifiers. *Littera,* which means both a graphic and a phonetic unit, follows *vox* and is divisible into a unit of sound called *elementum* and into its appropriate graphic character, called *figura.* After an extensive analysis of all the letters in the Greek and Roman alphabets, and the vocalic, semivocalic, and consonantal phonemes of which they are figures, Priscian proceeds to a study of the syllable, then of the word (*dictio*), then of the complete statement (*oratio*), and then of the *partes orationis,* the semantic and syntactic components of a sentence. Intimately related to the theory of *vox* in the *artes grammaticae* is the art of interpretive reading called *lectio,* an oral reconstruction of a text that leads naturally to *enarratio,* the art of textual exegesis. It is this complex process of the generation and interpretation of spoken language and written discourse that Dante foregrounds in the sphere of the just.

But rather than ascend the ladder of locution like Dante, Chaucer favors what we might call the art of linguistic regression, following graphemes, lexemes, and phonemes "downwards" into the realm of sonic vibrations and apparently subsignificant noises. Chaucer's favorite sublinguistic domain is animal sounds, those "natural" utterances whose orthographic representation he explores with comic brilliance both in *The Parliament of Fowls* and in the fox chase of *The Nun's Priest's Tale.* "Kek kek! kokkow! quek quek!" go the goose, the cuckow, and the duck in *The Parliament of Fowls.* Of course, in obedience to Priscian, one should assert that each of these is a clear-cut instance of *vox literata inarticulata*—a "meaningless" animal sound that nevertheless can be represented by letters. However, on second thought it could be argued that each of these sounds is actually meaningful rather than meaningless. The onomatopoetic word "kek" is both a signifier (the *vox* representing the *sonus*) and a signified (the *sonus* itself). "Kokkow" is obviously a *sonus* that has two meanings: it is both a bird call (*vox literata inarticulata*) as well as the name (*vox articulata literata*) of the very bird that makes that call. And then, as the goose helpfully reminds us, "quek quek" is both an animal locution and a privileged Middle English verb meaning "to quack": "Ye queke ful wel and fayre!" he brays at the turtledove.[69] One need not be a trained philosopher to sense that the signifying modalities of a "quek" *qua* "quek" constitute a complex linguistic conundrum.[70]

Well before Chaucer's time, most notably in Plato's *Cratylus,* and well after Chaucer's time, as Gérard Genette's monumental *Mimologiques: Voyage en Cratylie* brilliantly illustrates, the relationship between words and their referents, between a "quek" and a "quek," has prompted a great deal of poetic creativity, theoretical speculation, and critical analysis. As Thaïs E. Morgan notes in her introduction to Genette's *Mimologics,* "[t]he wish to make words resemble things in a variety of ways—by sound, by shape, and even by smell and taste—has repeatedly manifested itself in the works of philosophers, theologians, rhetoricians, grammarians, philologists, poets, novelists, and linguists."[71] So what is mimologics? Basically, according to Genette, it is the belief, and determination to prove, that there must be "a relation of reflective analogy (imitation) between 'word' and 'thing' that motivates, or justifies, the existence and the choice of the former."[72] Chaucer's opting in the *General Prologue* for the slippery signifier "cosyn" while asserting, albeit in Plato's name, "[t]he wordes moote be cosyn to the dede" (I.742) suggests that he, like Socrates, might well be skeptical of both the Cratylist position (language enjoys a natural relationship to its referents) and the Hermogenist position (linguistic signs are pure convention). Yet Chaucer is nevertheless intensely fascinated with the ways language, and especially the language of poetry, relates to its referents in the world. His most concentrated interrogation of the matter is in fact contained in his onomatopoetic words, and most notably in those mimological locutions that are meant to represent animal sounds. Theoretically, of course, a *vox* spoken by humans imitating a *sonus* uttered by animals should exemplify language's most perfect integration of *verba* and *res:* one locution equals the other. But are these two sounds in fact identical? And if they are not, is there at least a vestigial element of the referent immanent in every linguistic signifier, mimetic or otherwise?[73]

A closely related question is whether or not the putative boundary between various classifications of sounds is a categorical fiction. Is *vox inarticulata illiterata* (a noise not resolvable into distinct phonetic units) absolutely distinct from *vox literata inarticulata* (such as a "meaningless" animal sound that can nevertheless be somehow represented by letters)? And what in turn are the commonalities between these "meaningless" sounds and *vox articulata illiterata* (a human sound, like murmuring, which has "meaning" but no phonetic units) and *vox articulata literata* (articulate speech and literary language)? Since these *voces* are all sounds, how is it that some are eventually accorded meaning and others are not? Isn't every sound always and already invested with meaning? Is it ever possible to successfully "translate" all the sonic elements of a linguistic unit, or do we ultimately fail in these acts of audition, displacing a host of sounds back into the realm of sheer noise?

In his chapter on onomatopoeia, Genette focuses on a group of nineteenth-century mimologists whose theories may sensitize our auditory appreciation of Chaucer's sonic craft in the soundscape of the fox chase. Genette's star philologist is Charles Nodier, whose *Dictionnaire des onomatopées* and *Notions élémentaires de linguistique* advance the thesis that only "a slight effort" is needed "in order to arrive . . . at the belief that the imitation of animal noises was the main element in the beginning of natural languages."[74] Nodier's theory of the formation of speech begins (rather like Dante's) by analogizing the vocal organ to a musical instrument: the speech organ is a

> keyboard, a string and wind instrument [that possesses] . . . in its lungs an intelligent and sensitive bellows; in its lips, an outward-curving, mobile, extensible, retractable rim that projects the sound, modifies it, reinforces it, makes it supple, constrains it, veils it, quells it; in its tongue a supple, flexible, sinuous hammer that curls itself up, shortens itself, stretches itself out, that moves around and interposes itself between its valves, depending on whether the voice is to be held back or poured forth, that attacks its keys fiercely or skims over them idly; in its teeth a solid, pointed, strident keyboard; in its palate, a low-pitched and resonant tympanum.[75]

For Nodier, the child's maturation toward articulate speech repeats the growth of the species, which in each case begins with the vowel: "His linguistic expression was at first simply vocal, like that of the animals . . . bellowing, mooing, bleating, cooing, hissing."[76] The vowel, the nearest thing to man's animal instincts, also develops into the cry of admiration and similar expressions of "veneration, contemplative prescience, spiritualism, worship and religion."[77] Still in his infancy, this little "Cadmus in swaddling clothes" progresses to the "age of the first consonant," or [b], and "by extension all the labials." Thus

> The *bambino*, the babe-in-arms, the brat has discovered the three labials: he broods, he pouts, he mopes; he babbles, blabbers, prattles, blathers, bleats, blabs, bawls, broods, smacks his lips; he grumbles over a bauble, a bagatelle . . . a baby, a bon-bon, a booboo.[78]

Mankind's next stage is that of dental articulation, marking an advance toward maturity and a "solidity and toughness" that is "[m]ainly proper to sounds that are tenacious, tonic, tumultuous, to keystrokes, to sustained notes, to intonations, to twitterings, to tinklings, to stirring sounds that require a pronunciation that is strong, loud, strident, and firmly stopped; . . . the firmest key, and the most solid keyboard of speech, consists of the teeth."[79] Finally, a whole range of phonothematic patterns clusters around the remaining consonants. The aspirated [h], for instance, is often "related to the activity of seizing or of stealing."[80] The rolling palatal [r] "has become the written character of all signs through which the idea of continuity, of repetition, of renewal has been rendered."[81] And of the lingual consonant [l] Nodier notes: "This liquid, limpid, fluid and flowing, flexible and flattering articulation had to lend its pliable elocutionary nature to the elucidation of lexicons. . . . [A]s the principal lever of the language system, as that of logic, of dialectic, and of law, the letter *l* has left its name to language itself."[82]

In conformity with its nineteenth-century usage, "mimologism" for Nodier is not entirely synonymous with onomatopoeia. In his *Dictionnaire* he argues that "the majority of the words of primitive man were formed in imitation of the noises that struck his hearing. This is what we call *onomatopoeia*."[83] However, primitive man also "figuratively represented his own vocal noises, his cries, his interjections. This is what we call mimologism."[84] Nodier's wonderful example is the French (and English) word *haha*, which is a "mimologism of an exclamation of surprise and, by extension, the name of a barrier or ditch [sunk fence] that appears

unexpectedly and wrenches this exclamation from the travelers. There is
no other word in the language that so well captures what is understood by
mimology."[85] Other illustrative instances prized by Nodier are *haro* (harrow, hue and cry), *huée* (boo!), and *brouhaha*.

Like many of his fellow theorists, Nodier believed that the link between *verba* and *res* is not only in the words' sounds but also in the words
themselves. While this conviction places him in the most progressive wing
of the Cratylist party, Nodier remains a "secondary mimologist," in Genette's terms, because he is also persuaded that natural language has tragi-
cally fallen away from its mimological origins. It is thus the poets' charge
to invent new words and to redeploy existing words in such a way as to
restore to language its occluded symbolic powers. Yet even as we wait for
writers to repair the link between words and things, we must as readers
"welcome into our mother tongue the distant echoes that reverberate in
the hollow centers of words. . . . When reading words we see them and
no longer hear them."[86] Genette's deep pleasure in discovering Nodier's
"nearly unobtainable book" dissuades him from negatively critiquing
Nodier's fabulous theory, his *rêve des mots*. "What a revelation the good
Nodier's *Dictionnaire des onomatopées* was for me!" he concludes. "It
taught me how to explore with my ear those syllabic cavities that constitute the sound structure of a word."[87]

I am not of course suggesting that Chaucer is a Cratylist *manqué*, or
that he is intent on his readers' embracing highly romantic *rêves des mots*
at all akin to Nodier's. But a heightened awareness of the universal ability
of sounds to carry meaning, mimological and onomatopoetic, should refine our powers of audition as we seek out "the syllabic cavities that constitute the sound structure of [words]." In the sonic commotion that constitutes the fox chase, Chaucer invites us to associate its different sounds
with different domains of signification, personal and cultural. These include the Priscianic commentaries learned from early grammar school
instruction, but also those childhood noises, animal noises, "natural"
sounds, "literate" sounds, musical notes, percussive explosions, and an
orchestration of other sounds all freely associating in the mind. There is
obviously no cognitive boundary between our abilities as readers to *see*
the meaning of a word and to *hear* the implications of its sonic resonance.
But in the fox chase, Chaucer takes such pleasure in colliding these two

modes of cognition against each other that we willingly suspend our critical faculties, at least for a few moments of astonished, sonic pleasure.

Sounds in Motion

Chauntecleer, the fable's prolix hero, has just been "hente" in the "gargat" by Russell the fox. Priming himself for the upcoming fox chase, the narrator takes a deep and very rhetorical breath. As noted earlier, the narrator's declamations are a bravura performance of piled-up apostrophes each attempting to out-apostrophize their rhetorical rivals: first he apostrophizes Destiny, then Venus, and then Fridays—all in the course of apostrophizing Geoffrey of Vinsauf, the master-rhetor whose *Poetria nova* taught him how best to apostrophize. Catching his wind, the narrator then concentrates on the decibel rating of the noises made by the keening chickens lamenting the imminent demise of their hero-husband, Chauntecleer. Compared to the sounds of the Trojan women lamenting Priam's death, compared to the sounds of Hasdrubal's grieving wife in burning Carthage, compared to the sounds of the mournful Roman wives whose husbands died in Nero's mad fire, compared to all these expressions of classical grief, the sounds of the hens' barnyard ululations, the narrator assures us, are much the louder and more shrill:

> Certes, swich cry ne lamentacion
> Was nevere of ladyes maad whan Ylion
> Was wonne, and Pirrus with his streite swerd,
> Whan he hadde hent kyng Priam by the berd,
> And slayn hym, as seith us *Eneydos,*
> As maden alle the hennes in the clos,
> Whan they had seyn of Chauntecleer the sighte.
> But sovereynly dame Pertelote shrighte
> Ful louder than dide Hasdrubales wyf,
> Whan that hir housbonde hadde lost his lyf
> And that the Romayns hadde brend Cartage.
> She was so ful of torment and of rage
> That wilfully into the fyr she sterte
> And brende hirselven with a stedefast herte.

O woful hennes, right so criden ye
As whan that Nero brende the citee
Of Rome cryden senatoures wyves
For that hir husbondes losten alle hir lyves—
Withouten gilt this Nero hath hem slayn.
Now wole I turne to my tale agayn.

　　　　　　　　　　(VII.3355–74)

While a full critical commentary teasing out the mock-heroic dispropor-
tionalities in the narrator's celebration of human and animal expressions of grief would here be in order, the poem's forward momentum—
riding upon the every-expanding waves of percussive ululations and
ejaculations—invites us to stay in sync with its sounds without slowing
down for any kind of rational *explication de texte.* And so let us continue
with the poem's sonar, onomatopoetic, and mimological pleasures:

Now wole I turne to my tale agayn.
　This sely wydwe and eek hir doghtres two
Herden thise hennes crie and maken wo,
And out at dores stirten they anon,
And syen the fox toward the grove gon,
And bar upon his bak the cok away,
And cryden, "Out! harrow! and weylaway!
Ha! ha! the fox!" and after hym they ran,
And eek with staves many another man.
Ran Colle our dogge, and Talbot and Gerland,
And Malkyn, with a dystaf in hir hand;
Ran cow and calf, and eek the verray hogges,
So fered for the berkyng of the dogges
And shoutyng of the men and wommen eeke
They ronne so hem thoughte hire herte breeke.
They yollenden as feendes doon in helle;
The dokes cryden as men wolde hem quelle;
The gees for feere flowen over the trees;
Out of the hyve cam the swarm of bees.
So hydous was the noyse—a, benedicitee!—

Certes, he Jakke Straw and his meynee
Ne made nevere shoutes half so shrille
Whan that they wolden any Flemyng kille,
As thilke day was maad upon the fox.
Of bras they broghten bemes, and of box,
Of horn, of boon, in whiche they blewe and powped,
And therewithal they skriked and they howped.
It semed as that hevene sholde falle.
(VII.3374–3401)

All sounds imaginable, *vox inarticulata literata, vox articulata illiterata, vox articulata literata,* and even perhaps *vox inarticulata illiterata,* are here— barked, blown, screamed, yelled, struck, grunted, buzzed, skriked, hooped, and pooped, a brouhaha of phonemes and morphemes and lewed and learned locutions combining into one raucously apocalyptic hullaba- loo. And what is one to do with all of this noise? We can surely appreci- ate how, for Chaucer's contemporary readers, this sonic *amplificatio ad ab- surdum* would at some level have triggered a comically rueful evocation of those carefully memorized taxonomies of animal-versus-human sounds, human-versus-instrumental sounds, and instrumental-versus-animal sounds classified in Priscian's *De voce* and its commentaries. The Nun's Priest's parodic citations of these taxonomies certainly have a way of ad- vertising their own deconstructive cleverness. "Out! harrow! . . . weyl- away! Ha ha!"—these human noises sound as inhuman as those animal noises "Kek kek! kokkow! quek quek!" recorded by Chaucer in *The Parlia- ment of Fowls* or the *cra* and *coax* mimologically mimicked by Priscian. And it is surely quite uncanny that *harrow!* Nodier's example of "one of those secondary-formation onomatopoeias called mimologisms be- cause they were made in imitation of the spoken word itself," and *haha!* should both surface in Chaucer's self-reflexive soundscape more than five centuries before the publication of the mimologist's *Dictionnaire.* Ob- viously those wind instruments bugled in hot pursuit—the "bemes" of brass, of horn, and of bone—brilliantly refunction the authoritative *tuba* and *tibia* of Priscian's grammatical commentators, even as they antici- pate Nodier's description of the human speech organ as "a wind instru- ment [that possesses] . . . in its lungs an intelligent and sensitive bellows."

These brassy, horny, and boney noisemakers once again have a way of subverting our trust in any classification of sounds that knows how to discriminate between a human hoop and a musical poop. Finally, because of the limitations imposed by the chase's presumed narrative verisimilitude, no stringed or skin-covered musical instruments are plucked or struck to honor the commentaries' *cithara* "and anything else that is melodious by percussion." Thus it is the fate of the frantic ducks to serve as timorous understudies in percussion, their anxious fear of future beating sufficient to make them scream: they "cryden as men wolde hem quelle."

The fox chase is thus a wonderfully complex gloss on the production of every kind of *vox*, putting to parodic use the standard examples of Priscian's commentaries, crisscrossing categories with such dazzling aplomb that the passage deconstructs the very designs by which we normally discriminate phonemic from subphonemic sound. The heuristic agenda inside all these parodic citations, however, is by no means immediately decodable. All that is clear so far is that Chaucer is intent upon celebrating and problematizing the ways we have been instructed to think about language and about literature's relationship to what we normally call the world of nature, or reality, or history.

One response provoked by the passage's admixture of natural and lexical sounds is to meditate more intently upon the interplay between conventional words and those sounds we understand to be "real." As Derek Attridge has remarked in his excellent study of onomatopoeia and its choreography of sounds as proof of its unusual powers of *mimesis*:

> The common feeling that the words of a favorite literary passage have an unusually strong purchase on reality, a peculiarly intimate bond with the nonlinguistic phenomena to which they refer, is often accounted for . . . by finding ways in which it can be said that the properties of the objects or events in question are represented, independently of the conventional semantic system, by the physical properties of the language, its sound and their sequential arrangement. [Thus] literary criticism abounds in phrases such as "mimetic syntax," "appropriate sound-patterns," "rhythmic enactment," "aural embodiment," and other related terms.[88]

After appreciating the fox chase for its mimetic syntax, rhythmic enactments, mimological inventiveness, and sonic naturalism, we may eventually be forced to concede that the sounds and movements of this passage, like the sounds of any poem, are finally only *substitutions* for the noises and actions of the real world. This being so, the fox chase's aural pyrotechnics call equal attention to Chaucer's poetic language in the act of becoming even more linguistically formal—a controlled, contrived, and self-contained medley of rhetorical flourishes. Thus Chaucer's variegated sounds accentuate in a number of ways the riven nature of literary allegiance. Literary language, we need to believe, shares a certain kinship with truth and reality; yet we must concurrently recognize that all literary fiction, since it is fabulous, also falsifies reality. Thus not only are all the Priscianic categorical imperatives deconstructed in the hoops and poops of the cacophonous fox chase, but the paradoxes of linguistic referentiality at the heart of the Hermogenes/Cratylus debate are spun about in a sonic kaleidoscope whose labile determiners of meaning are as shifty as those in the spinning labyrinth of Chaucer's House of Rumour.

I am nevertheless persuaded that all of this disequilibrating sonic activity is meant ultimately not to muffle thinking but to heighten our awareness of what goes on when we think *about* language, and when we think *in* language about language and thought. That is, while celebrating the noise and motion of the chase, the frenetic busyness of people and animals all hustling "on the viritoot," Chaucer appears to be celebrating the kinetic spirit and visceral élan of the act of thinking itself. Because reading texts in the Middle Ages was the out-loud performance of oral interpretation (*lectio*), the corollary act of thinking interpretively about literature (*enarratio*) was very similar to *lectio* and thus very close to being a form of verbal and oral activity. Even today, despite our having lost the art of reading aloud, our thinking process is a remarkably kinetic and sensuous exercise. In a passage that attempts to reify this very thought, Stephen A. Tyler has defined the act of thinking as:

> motion and activity, the upward *movement* of sensory information from the senses to the higher cognitive faculties; it is the *movement* from sensory particulars to conceptual generalization; it is

the *movement* from the concrete to the abstract; it is the *move-ment* from unconscious to conscious; it is the *movement* of feeling from impression to expression; it is the *movement* from sense to sensibility, of sentient sensitivity in the sensorium that assents to sense, dissents from nonsense, consents to common sense, and is sensitized to sensuality. It is in this sense that thinking makes sense of sense, thought of sense, and sense of thought, for thinking is sense sentenced.[89]

In the fox chase, as we attempt to make sense of its thought and thought of its sense, by following its medley of sounds and words as they move up and out and to and around and fro, it is clear we have been granted a special license to play freely in the fields of semantic significa-tion. This freedom from the customary restraints of analytic discourse can be intoxicating. Stephen A. Barney, for example, characterizes the ani-mals in the chase as a group that "hustles and bustles pell-mell, helter-skelter, hurry-scurry, in a huggermugger hodgepodge higgledy-piggledy, a topsy-turvy arsy-versy mishmash hurly-burly hoo-ha of hitherand-thithering."[90] Yet it should also be evident that we are not meant simply to neutralize our cerebral powers, but rather to reengage them in what we provisionally can only call a more sensitized and sentient fashion. In our attempts to make some progress from the level of *sonus* in the direc-tion of the critical activities of *enarratio,* towards what Tyler calls "the senses to the higher interpretive faculties," we find ourselves constantly returning to the basics of grammar and to the materiality of sound. Seem-ingly far removed from the art of *enarratio,* theorizing *de voce* in this way may possibly have been designed to serve as a synecdoche of the *artes grammaticae* in their entirety. What is absolutely clear, at any rate, is that Chaucer is not going to lead his readers straight up Dante's grammati-cal ladder of education from *sonus* to *vox* to *elementum* to *dictio* to *oratio* to *lectio* to *enarratio* and from there to a pronouncement engraved in the heavens and accompanied by the music of the saints explicating the work-ings of divine justice in human history. Rather, Chaucer keeps his readers thinking, with little guidance, but at least independently and energeti-cally, about the low-level elements of language, and about how the sounds and sense of words are processed and created in the mind.

To this point, then, I have examined the fox chase on a presyntactic level, as if its words were not arranged into statements or propositions. To gain further purchase on Chaucer's heuristic strategies, it is appropriate now to consider the fundamentals of propositional language by turning to the medieval art of formal thinking called logic, for the basic exercises of this second trivial art are as deeply imbedded in the activities of the fox chase as are those of the first.

The Logic of the Peasants' Revolt

Medieval logicians divided all words into two classes: *syncategoremata,* parts of speech such as conjunctions and prepositions that structure the meaning of a proposition but do not have extramental significance of their own; and *categoremata,* all nouns and verbs, which signify an extramental something in the world, and are thus the formal terms, the predicables, of any sentence. The way a noun such as the word "man" determines its categorematic meaning depends, medieval logicians realized, on dozens of different rules: whether it is unmodified, or modified by a definite article, an indefinite article, or a demonstrative adjective like "this" or "that," or by words like "some," "any," "only," "all," or whether it is replaced by a pronoun or demonstrative pronoun or proper name.[91]

When a verb, the other categorematic term, was combined with a noun, the result was a proposition, the logical rules of which medieval scholars explored with both zeal and brilliance. A number of basic propositions, all of them appearing originally in the opening pages of Aristotle's *De interpretatione,* reappear in infinitely varied forms in the medieval logical texts studied by Chaucer and his contemporaries. *Homo est animal* (man is an animal) was one of the most productive and interesting basic propositions—although a man is an animal, and an animal is an animal, an animal is not a man. Under the influence of three other Aristotelian propositions—"man is rational" (that is, capable of reason), "man is risible" (capable of laughter), and "man is grammatical" (capable of speech)—medieval logicians delighted in inventing propositions and syllogisms remarkable for their apparent illogicality. Here are a few, taken haphazardly from medieval logical textbooks: "Every man is an animal, everything risible is a man; therefore everything risible is an animal";

"Some animal is a man; therefore some non-man is a non-animal"; "Socrates is a risible animal; therefore he is a man"; "A mortal rational animal is not an ass; therefore a man is not an ass"; "God is, and therefore man is an ass."

The proposition that Aristotle himself chose to emphasize most is *homo est iustus* (man is just), using it for his three squares of opposition in chapter 10 of *De interpretatione*—graphic tables that help illustrate all the possible pairs of contradictory propositions in logical language. In the first, "is" and "is not" are added either to "just" or "not-just" to square off as:[92]

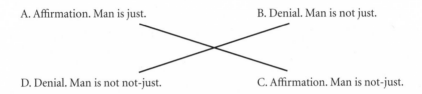

A. Affirmation. Man is just.   B. Denial. Man is not just.

D. Denial. Man is not not-just.   C. Affirmation. Man is not-just.

In the second, the subject is "distributed" by the modifier "Every," yielding:

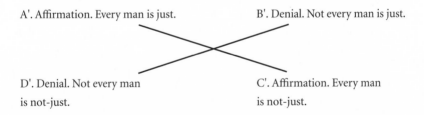

A'. Affirmation. Every man is just.   B'. Denial. Not every man is just.

D'. Denial. Not every man   C'. Affirmation. Every man
is not-just.   is not-just.

In the third square of opposition, the subject is negated, yielding:

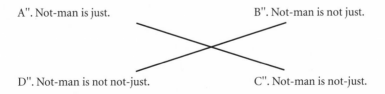

A''. Not-man is just.   B''. Not-man is not just.

D''. Not-man is not not-just. C''. Not-man is not-just.

Although most medieval students would have memorized these sub-alterns, contradictories, and subcontraries, another of Aristotle's con-structions, *homo currit* (man runs), absolutely captured the imagination of logicians because it is in fact a much better archetypal sentence. This simple sentence spawned a long run of hypothetical propositions and syllogisms, such as: "If a man runs, an animal runs"; "Man runs, but noth-ing risible runs"; "No man is running except that ass"; "Every ass, except Socrates, runs"; "If Socrates is running, there is something that is white and is running"; "Every man or his ass is running, but every man or his ass is a non-runner; therefore some non-runner is running."

Boethius appears to be a major cause of the popularity of *currit* propositions, for in his translation of the *De interpretatione* he added to Aristotle's three *est iustus homo* squares of opposition a fourth square based on *currit omnis homo*.[93] William of Sherwood in his influential *Introduction to Logic* decided to use "man runs" as the basic logical propo-sition of all three of his squares of opposition. Further variations of this proposition produce what Norman Kretzmann has diagrammed as Wil-liam of Sherwood's "hexagon of opposition" (figure 5.2).

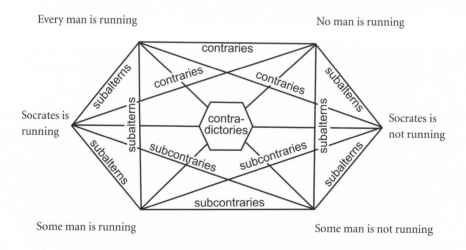

Figure 5.2. William of Sherwood's "Hexagon of Opposition"[94]

William of Sherwood continues to use variant forms of "man runs" in his more advanced *Treatise on Syncategorematic Words*.[95] Part of the opening chapter of this treatise, which we have already studied in chapter 3, should remind us of the refined metalinguistic world Chaucer is evoking. Consider *omnis* once again. When used categorematically (that is, when *omnis* assists in defining a noun's semantic or essential significance), then *omnis* is equipollent (equivalent in function) to such words as *totum* (whole) and *perfectum* (complete); an example of *omnis* used categorematically in a proposition is *mundus est omne* (the world is complete). In other instances, however, *omnis* functions syncategorematically (syntactically as an adjective that "signifies universality as a disposition of a subject insofar as it is a subject"). Sherwood's example of *omnis* used syncategorematically is "every man is running."

Sherwood then examines the various ways *omnis* may determine the meaning of the subject and the predicate of a proposition. In section four, dealing with "proximate and remote parts," he hypothesizes the situation where exactly one individual of each species of animal is running; thus it may be said that (a) "every animal is running," for "A man is running, a lion is running, a goat is running, and so on with respect to single things; therefore every animal is running. But (b) every man is an animal; therefore every man is running."[96] This fallacious inference leads, however, to the self-contradictory *sophisma* "every man is running and only one man is running," or the equally absurd "every animal is running but not every man is running."[97] Sherwood then attempts to demolish this fallacy of reasoning, which he designates as a *figura dictionis,* by applying the logical rule determining how *omnis* sometimes "distributes a subject for the single things belonging to the genera under the subject, and at other times for the genera of the single things under the subject."[98]

My point, obviously, is that any reader with even a minimal post-elementary education would have enjoyed the logical palimpsest of running propositions in *The Nun's Priest's Tale* with special intellectual relish. What is wonderful about these propositions is that nobody and nothing is denied the chance to run. Not only is man running, but men are running; not only is man running, but woman is running; not only is woman running, but women are running; not only are animals running, but every animal is running; not only is every animal running, but all animals are running. And even those animals who can't run are running through the air as fast as they can so that the whole world may be gloriously exercised in a universal celebration of the illogical joys of running.

As we shift our appreciation from predication to categorematic denotation, however, it rapidly becomes unclear what it is the names and nouns and pronouns in this running passage signify or denote. Take the proper names, none of which has appeared before in the tale. Chaucer provides assistance with the first: Colle is a dog; not only that, he is ours—"our dogge." Malkyn in the next line is also a proper name. She, we are certain, is a woman—the distaff confirms her gender; but since she appears only in this one line, her name doesn't seem to "mean" as much as a proper name in literature should. And then what about the two creatures stuck in between Colle and Malkyn named Talbot and Gerland? Hinckley, way back in 1918, argued that, like Colle, Talbot and Gerland are common Middle English names for dogs;[99] but Pearsall in his Variorum edition notes that they are also common Middle English surnames for human beings.[100] Like the hybridized sounds filling the air, I think we have to allow these names to stand as ambiguous signifiers, denoting perhaps two human beings, or perhaps two dogs, or perhaps one of each. The noun substitutes and the noun modifiers also have problems during the chase getting their feet under them and stabilizing their significance. Consider "they" in "after hym they ran": "they" refers some seven lines back to the beginning of the chase, to "This sely widwe and eek hire doghtres two"—which is some help, even though the narrator more than five hundred lines back, at the very beginning of the tale, had unceremoniously dropped these three female creatures into extradiegetic oblivion. But because "they" are female in the statement "after hym they ran, / And eek with staves many another man," Chaucer appears to be using "many another man" in a rather special way. Not only is "many another" a complex linguistic construction that excludes the universal and the singular and unites plurality with both the indefinite and the particular, "man" in this instance would seem to be gender specific (since staves are a "male" attribute). However, even though "they" are feminine and "man" in this context cannot be used as a universal (as meaning "mankind"), it apparently has to mean something in between. I think we have to call this remarkable him-them-her collocation a neutrally gendered and slightly pluralized dissemination of multigendered being and leave it at that.

What then does all this linguistic and logical falderal demonstrate? As with Chaucer's evocations of the basic exercises in Priscianic grammar, his parodic citations of these time-honored Aristotelian propositions of running do not appear to lead directly toward any self-evident interpretative position. Rather, they lead first, as with all successful parody, in the direction of highlighting the most subtle and distinctive features of the target text, which in this case is the metalinguistic essence of medieval logic itself. By parodying logic, Chaucer is quickly teaching logic to his readers all over again—some of its basic propositions, its syllogisms, its squares of opposition, its excruciatingly finicky philosophical categories and linguistic discriminations. The effect, as we have seen, is both to carnivalize these basic categories (such as animal/man, male/female, singular/plural, some/many, and so forth) and to construct a comic vision of a universe that, for all its parts, is somehow whole: *mundus est omne.* Yet, as with our initial grammatical reading of the chase, this initial logical response is scarcely adequate, so I will proceed to the last of the trivial arts, rhetoric, to consider the passage from one more perspective.

When the Nun's Priest abruptly announces at the beginning of the fox chase, "Now wol I turn to my tale again," we might wonder for a moment where the devil we have been if not somewhere inside *The Nun's Priest's Tale.* But what is alluded to here is of course the traditional medieval perception that poetry divides itself into different parts, an aesthetic taste acquired at an early age by a series of elementary exercises in literary composition we have already considered at some length, the *pre-exercitamina.* The second exercise, narration, as we have also noted, proves there are, at a minimum, four different kinds of narrative: the fabulous (*fabularis*), the plausible (*fictilis*), the historical (*historica*), and the legal (*civilis*). The fox chase is clearly three of these: fabulous (it *is* a beast fable), plausible (foxes in fact do steal chickens), and legal (the peasants are doing what they are legally obliged to do—crying harrow, raising the hue and cry to enforce criminal arrest). But it is more, as well. By the sixteenth century a special class of narration was called, by Puttenham and others, *pragmatographia*—the main purpose of which is to represent an action in language achieving a high degree of physical immediacy and sensuous accuracy, onomatopoeia being recognized as an especially appropriate scheme. Peacham suggests, in addition, useful embellishments such as archaisms, verbal compoundings, and what Ronsard and Du Bellay called *provignement*—the composition of special words by adding suffixes or prefixes or by wrenching their grammatical nature.[101] With its narrative energy, onomatopoetic flourishes, sensuous immediacy, and eye for descriptive detail, Chaucer's fox chase is a masterful example of this genre. He even constructs two or three nonce words: "powped" he uses only once elsewhere; "howped" and the Danish-looking "skriked" are each a *hapax legomenon*. The familiar "this" in "This sely wydwe," the domestic "our" in "Colle oure dogge," and the linguistically conservative "he" construction of "he Jakke Strawe" all add an avuncular touch of old-fangled, lower-class familiarity.[102]

However, in this otherwise brilliantly choreographed arabesque of thought and action, there is one maladroit moment. This is the inclusion of a rhetorical figure that compares the sensuous features of the chase with those of an event outside the tale. The Nun's Priest has just used this topos three times in his ironic praise of the unprecedented volume of his chickens' screams. Inside the fox chase he uses it once again:

> So hydous was the noyse—a benedicitee!—
> Certes, he Jakke Strawe and his meynee
> Ne made nevere shoutes half so shrille
> Whan that they wolden any Flemyng kille,
> As thilke day was maad upon the fox.

This rhetorical maneuver fits awkwardly into that category of tropes Curtius calls the "panegyrical topos of outdoing."[103] Used by Statius, Claudian, Lucan, Dante, and Chaucer himself, its purpose is to praise a contemporary person, place, thing, or even one's own artistic achievement by contrasting it to a less fully accomplished classical forebear. It thus turns the anxiety of influence inside out, implying that if we see farther than the ancients it is because as giants we are standing on the shoulders of midgets. But the "outdoing topos" here is unfortunately inept, conforming neither to its figural category nor to its literary context. Rather than a moment from the classical past, what is wrenched into the poem and given an unasked-for hearing is the Peasant's Revolt of 1381, the most earth-shaking and decentering event in English history during Chaucer's lifetime. For seven days in the city of London and in the towns and countryside of East Anglia, it seemed like the world would end. In a sudden paroxysm of social disaffection, thousands of peasants and townspeople subverted authority, issued ultimatums, possessed private property, burnt down buildings, rampaged through the city streets, slaughtered citizens and noblemen alike, until their leaders, meeting with Richard II in Smithfield outside the city, were duped, apprehended, and summarily beheaded by the king's henchmen.[104]

Modern liberal historians tend to find a *cause célèbre* in this dramatic image of a spontaneous uprising of the oppressed but contemporary chroniclers such as Thomas Walsingham, Henry Knighton, Jean Froissart, and the author of the *Anonimalle Chronicle* felt not a drop of sympathy for the revolutionaries' aspirations. Even the great radical John Wycliffe was certain that they were grievously wrong: "all things not to the will of the Lord must end miserably. . . . As all suffering results from sin, it cannot be denied that in this case the sin of the people was the cause."[105] Chaucer very rarely alludes to contemporary historical events, as we have noted, and many readers would perhaps be relieved had he not chosen to situate his only overt allusion to the Peasants' Revolt in such a farcical context. Unless one finds human slaughter to be a sprightly witticism, no matter what one's political persuasion there is an unsettling dissonance in this casual juxtaposition of comic alarums and grotesque brutality.

One can of course say that the Nun's Priest, or Chaucer, is not in full control of his material. One can also contend that he is satirizing someone else's ineptness—a schoolboy who wants to stuff an historical *narratio* inside his already fabulous, plausible, and legal *narratio*. But these suggestions are scarcely adequate. Recognizing now that the fox chase is a powerfully parodic evocation of the trivium, and that the trivium in turn not only was the heart and soul of every medieval reader's liberal arts education but comprised as well the totality of those linguistic skills that made possible the art of *enarratio*, the interpretation of literary discourse, we must agree that this passage cries "Out! harrow! and weylaway!" for some kind of deliberative judgment. Modern readers should in fact have an easier job of it from one perspective, for the intrusion of this bit of "reality" into the artifice of literature is comparable to those self-referential gestures found in metafiction and in so much modern art—like the sound of jackhammers in a string quartet, the inscription inside a painting that this pipe is not a pipe, or the author's apology that his paragraph describing a departing train has been partially obscured by its smoke.[106] But the generic and aesthetic subversion of *The Nun's Priest's Tale* is of a different magnitude. It is a subtle piece of professional violence—as if a film editor had neatly sliced out a few frames of the My Lai episode in the movie *Platoon* and spliced them into the middle of a Wile E. Coyote and Road Runner chase scene.

But I am fairly confident it is also an intelligent and carefully considered use of a violent slice of history. Why, for instance, from among the hundreds of recorded incidents in the Revolt, did Chaucer choose this one? Jack Straw's name undoubtedly had something to do with it. The French peasants were pejoratively and collectively named *li Jacques Bonhomme* and their uprising in the Ile-de-France in 1358 was called the *Jacquerie*. In his chronicle of the English Peasants' Revolt, Henry Knighton gives the names of the revolutionary leaders as, first, Thomas Baker, and then Jakke Strawe, Jakke Mylner, Jakke Carter, and Jakke Crewman.[107] These names are suspiciously, and cleverly, generic, authored quite possibly by the peasants themselves. At any rate, Jakke Straw—half nurture and half nature—is a descriptive literary type-name that fits into the pastoral landscape of *The Nun's Priest's Tale* much more readily than do those historical-sounding names Talbot, Malkyn, and Gerland.

Historical and literary names—or more precisely, name-calling—interpenetrate at another level as well. As Lee Patterson has reminded us, throughout the Middle Ages the "ubiquitous vilification" of the peasant was that he is nothing but an animal—an irrational (even insane) and inarticulate beast.[108] Pressed into service by several chroniclers as they attempted to explain the causes of the Peasants' Revolt, the axiomatic equation of peasants with animals is given a special turn, a kind of optative modality, in Chaucer's sustained confusion of animal and human denotations. But the most obvious way Chaucer yokes everything together—animal and human, literary and historical, high and low, powerful and powerless, English and foreign, pursuers and pursued, reader and text—is by the powerful bond of sound. Sound, as we have seen throughout this chapter, is Chaucer's disseminal symbol for the disharmonics of history and for the harmonics of our powers of audition. How, then, are we able to hear and understand the *musica humana* of this noisy percussive chase?

There are several options already available in existing Chaucer criticism that identify Chaucer's way of hearing the noise of the Uprising as indistinguishable from that of his contemporaries. In "*Vox populi* and the Literature of 1381," David Aers agrees with Derek Pearsall, Stephen Knight, and others, that Chaucer, like his contemporary Gower, saw the rebels "as farmyard animals gone berserk"; thus this sudden allusion to the Uprising in *The Nun's Priest's Tale* is "very characteristic of the way he experiences political and social conflict, converting it into material for anecdotal humor, private and personal competition and literary games."[109] In support of this position, we could turn to contemporary chroniclers who with remarkable consistency complain not so much about the peasants revolting or the revolting peasants, but rather about their "hideous cries and horrible tumult," an offence to civilized ears: they created "a most horrible shouting . . . not like the clamour normally produced by men, but of a sort which enormously exceeded all human noise," writes one witness; another complains of their "threatening words and disorderly shouts"; a third of their "enormous wailing"; a fourth of their "horrible shrieks"; and a fifth chronicler remarks, "[T]hese unhappy people shouted and cried so loud, as though all the devils of hell had been among them."[110] The question of course remains: is Chaucer's audition of the sounds of history absolutely identical to that of his contemporaries?

To construct a counter-hermeneutics of noise, it is perhaps necessary to break away from all traditions of harmonic order. Jacques Attali, a French economist and advisor to François Mitterand, in a book entitled *Noise: The Political Economy of Music,* strives to do just that. As Attali sees it, and here he is relying upon the prior works of Webern, Spengler, and Adorno, "Every code of music is rooted in the ideologies and technologies of its age, and at the same time produces them."[111] Thus "[w]ith music is born power and its opposite: subversion," and "[w]ith noise is born disorder and its opposite," which Attali calls "the world."[112] In music resides the triple agenda of those for whom that music is produced: make people forget, make them believe, and silence them. Specifically, music, which Attali believes was originally conceived as a part of human sacrifice, is produced first in a *ritual zone* of power to make people forget the general violence; in the second, or *representative zone* of power, it is employed to make people believe in the harmony of the world, that "there is order in exchange and legitimacy in commercial power"; and in the third, the *bureaucratic zone* of power uses a deafening, syncretic kind of music to silence alterity, censoring all other human noises.[113] Thus music localizes and specifies power, because it marks and regiments the rare noises that a culture, in its normalization of behavior, sees fit to authorize. Nevertheless, noise is able to create meaning on its own: because interrupting any message signifies the interdiction of the transmitted meaning, noise signifies "censorship and rarity," and because pure noise is the very absence of meaning, by "unchanneling auditory sensations," noise has a way of liberating the listener's imagination. Noise's absence of meaning thus evokes a construction outside meaning—either absolute ambiguity or "the presence of all meanings."[114] Indeed, Attali believes, both noise and the noise out of which music is made are politically prophetic, auguring change in the state and enabling the creation of a new social order.

Attali's rereading of the noises of history is a welcome antidote to the transcendental metaphors of the classical and humanist musical paradigms, and despite its utopian agenda it may connect with Chaucer's fox chase in some surprising ways. Perhaps most compelling is Chaucer's having chosen, as a synecdoche of the entire Uprising, the sound made by Jakke Strawe and his "meynee." This chronicled piece of historical noise seeks, yet resists, some kind of understanding. Is it a sound full of fury? Does it signify nothing? Does it cry out for justice? Does it cry out for revenge? Although Chaucer does not answer any of these questions, the dissonance of the revolutionaries' screams have a way, as Attali puts it, of "liberating the listener's imagination." And so, in turn, do the voices of silence. That is, what is the significance of that not-sound, or no-sound, of the persecuted Flemings whose screams in their foreign tongue as they run from imminent death are not even audible inside this English beast fable? If, in Attali's representative zone of power, music is employed to make people believe in the harmony of the world, what power is it that silences these foreign merchants and entrepreneurs? Is it the subversive noise of the English radical "meynee," or is it the bureaucratic "music" of Chaucer's literary and social class?

Since the narrator has pretended to a tin ear, perhaps the only way we might ultimately decode/encode his tone of voice is by attempting to stabilize all the other elements of his literary/historical analogies. When the keening hens were compared to the mourning women of Troy, Carthage, and Rome, we heard the tone of mock-heroic irony because we believe that the present is not equal to the classicized past, that animals are not equal to humans, and that volume is not the measure of grief. Here, however, a bunch of shouting human beings and animals both in pursuit of a single fox are compared to a bunch of shouting peasants in pursuit of an indeterminate number of urban Flemish immigrants. The central question is: Which element in this trope of outdoing is outdoing the other? Since there are so many nonstable valences in this world of outdoing, it seems appropriate to break things down to their basic syllogistic terms by arranging them into a pattern of subalterns, contraries, contradictories, and subcontraries. Using a mode of analysis which was second nature to all of Chaucer's educated readers, the central concerns in the fox-chase conundrum can be patterned into a logical square of opposition and still remain a series of open-ended questions. Therefore: Are the human beings inside this comic chase greater than, lesser than, or equivalent in value to Jakke Straw and his "meynee"? Are the animals inside this comic chase (all but the fox, I mean) greater than, lesser than, or equivalent in value to Jakke Straw and his "meynee"? Is the fox, looting and killing in order to survive, as innocent as the Flemings about to be slaughtered in a shudder of xenophobic fury? Are these Flemish foreigners in turn greater than, lesser than, or equivalent in value to the English peasant underclass? And are the English peasant underclass—that is, Talbot, Malkyn, and Gerland—greater than, lesser than, or equivalent in value to the fox, looting and killing as need be in order to survive?

What I have done, in my progress through these interrogative Ps and Qs, is to use as my implicit propositional base, rather than *homo currit*, two of Aristotle's equally famous propositions: "man is just" and "man is an animal." My justification for doing so is by analogy with Chaucer's use of the other trivial arts: just as the disciplines of grammar and rhetoric are evoked in the fox chase by Chaucer's citing one of their elementary parts, so do the chase's running propositions evoke kindred propositions frequently found contiguous to *homo currit* in the medieval logical primers. The fox chase is thus fashioned to bring to consciousness a palimpsest of once memorized and never entirely forgotten hypothetical definitions. All of these propositions, like "man is just" and "man is an animal," are concerned with defining what it means to be human: "man is rational," "man is grammatical," "man is risible," and "man is mortal." And all of these propositions, once plotted out as subalterns, contraries, contradictories, and subcontraries in the square of opposition, bring our dialectical faculties to bear upon the moral and social issues of this historical/literary passage. This strategy of logical recollection, I believe, is one of Chaucer's major ways of assisting his readers toward a more sophisticated level of critical thinking without attempting to coerce them into a predetermined set of true-and-false equivalences.

But once again, Chaucer provides no still point in this turning world of political and social values. What he does do, late in his long career as a poet of Richard II's court, is to fine-tune the reader's powers of audition so that the Peasants' Revolt, an historical event dangerous to recount in any way other than by hegemonic condemnation, serves as the subject of sustained critical interrogation. This interrogation begins with percussive sound, the foundation of language and music and history, and progresses from there to embrace much that language and music symbolize, contain, and repress. So in addition to the logical square of opposition and the rhetorical tropes of outdoing, it is the grammatical dissemination of sounds that contributes most profoundly to the heuristics of the chase. Where, finally, does Chaucer stand in terms of all this noise? I think the answer is that he stands where his readers might stand—in the middle and a bit to the side. We have noted that Priscian's grammatical commentators meditated at length upon *musica instrumentalis,* one example of which is the creation of sound by striking a skin-covered instrument. This trope Dante elevates all the way to heaven as a metaphor for the striking of Christ's body, which is the music of salvation. Chaucer stays on earth, in the ruckus of contemporary life, close to the squawking ducks, the shouting combatants, and the stricken peasants about to strike the Flemings. So it is perhaps understandable that Chaucer allows his readers, via literary comedy, to take a step or two sideways, so that the thunderous missile of revolution does not drive directly into our ears.

I opened this final section by remarking that we recall our Dick and Jane primers with fond, if slightly bittersweet, nostalgia. The parodic update of this primer, *More Fun with Dick and Jane*—where Jane, now a thirty-eight-year-old yuppie mother, enjoins her daughter, "Look, Robin, look. It is easy to make a quiche!"[115]—embraces this nostalgia with only the mildest touch of irony or satire. So it may be a shock to be reminded that there is a significant part of American culture who recall their Dick and Jane readers with loathing and self-hatred. H. Rap Brown in his autobiographical work significantly entitled *Die Nigger Die!* writes that "if you leave school hating yourself, then it doesn't matter how much you know. . . . The street is where young bloods get their education. I learned how to talk in the street, not from reading Dick and Jane."[116] In light of Toni Morrison's *The Bluest Eye,* in light of other novels that take their own kind of revenge upon poor Dick and Jane,[117] the syntax of such locutions as "burn, baby, burn" reveals the special power of one kind of parody, as American inner city after American inner city is engulfed in flames.

Without question, Chaucer's parodic citations of the trivium are affectionate; he wants not to satirize these liberal arts, but to refunction them in ways that effect a more refined awareness of our linguistic construction, representation, manipulation, and interpretation of reality. The urgency of this refunctioning is intensified by the intrusion of the political will to violence into the world of academic discourse—a world scarcely innocent of violence itself. The vehicle of this intrusion, a rhetorical trope, reveals ironically that history has already parodied art: the trope of outdoing recounts an event where disempowered men are fiercely intent on outdoing, and doing in, other men with even less power. The expressed effect of these political confrontations is a series of percussive sounds that invoke and contest the musical models of society, history, and the entire universe surveyed earlier in this chapter. Against all this cosmic high seriousness, the comic brilliance of the fox chase asserts its own kind of counterpressure, so that only a Chicken Little could read Chaucer's carnival apocalypse entirely straight. Yet amidst all the literary and historical dissonance, images of the promised end persist, the trumps of doom pooping, the narration stretching toward some kind of closure and final judgment concerning the nature of men and women and their political actions. One of the most relevant logical contexts within which to pursue the analysis of these political actions is that of "arguments from causes" ("as the efficient cause is, such is its effect"), deriving from Boethius's *De differentiis topicis:* "Every human society that gives rise to justice is natural, justice derives from a human society that gives rise to justice; therefore justice is natural." But if this is reaching too deeply into the old textbooks, let me conclude this chapter's study of Chaucerian noise with one of the first logical propositions drawn to our attention. In a trivial chase that has mixed humankind with animals, sense with nonsense, harmony with dissonance, and risibility with irrisibility, the single cock-eyed judgment *Non-homo est non-justus* will have to suffice.

SIX

Chaucerian Horologics
and the Confounded Reader

> *What, then, is time? I know well enough*
> *what it is, provided that nobody asks me; but if*
> *I am asked what it is and try to explain, I am baffled.*
>
> —ST. AUGUSTINE

Just a few hours out of London on the pilgrimage to Canterbury, Harry Bailly, the pilgrims' leader, suddenly decides to determine precisely what time of the day it is. He does this not by reading a portable mechanical clock, since these lightweight coiled-spring instruments were not invented until the fifteenth-century.[1] Nor does he determine that it was the hour of ten *ante meridian* by consulting what was called a "chlyndre," a portable dangling sundial such as that sported by the lecherous monk in *The Shipman's Tale*.[2] Nor, as was most common in the Middle Ages, does he almost accidentally learn of the time by hearing bells rung from a tower in a nearby town or abbey. Rather, Harry uses his own extraordinary powers of discrimination to determine that, for this precise latitude, since the sun had run a bit more than a half hour more than the fourth part of its course through the artificial day, and since the shadow of every tree at this very moment was absolutely equal in length to the tree's height, and since the date of this day could be inferred or known to be the eighteenth day of April, and since the sun had ascended precisely forty-five degrees into the sky, it could readily be asserted that, beyond all shadow of a doubt, it was exactly "ten of the clokke" (II.14). And by "clokke," a word first recorded in English in 1371,[3] Harry does not mean an old-fashioned sundial or water clock, but rather the newly invented mechanical clock that indicates sixty-minute, or equinoctial, hours whose length and *termini* remained constant throughout the day and year.

This is an astonishing moment, not only in the entirety of Chaucer's literary corpus, but in all of medieval literature. To my knowledge, nowhere in Western literature before Harry's calculation does a literary figure determine the exact, equinoctial hour of the day. Rather, in all medieval literature until at least the last quarter of the fourteenth century, time remained essentially what it had always been: natural and cursive, hours changing in length as the seasons expanded and contracted through the agricultural and liturgical year.[4]

Harry's time-telling on the first day of the pilgrimage is in fact not the only moment when Chaucer's conventional markings of time are ruptured by a technically convoluted temporal periphrasis. A second instance occurs at the very end of the pilgrimage, just before *The Parson's Tale,* when Chaucer determines that the sun is descended from the meridian not quite twenty-nine degrees, that a man's shadow is at this moment eleven times one-sixth the height of his body, that the zodiacal sign Libra is beginning to ascend above the horizon, and that it is precisely four of the clock. Such an egregiously complicated and technical time-measurement occurs in only one other place on the pilgrimage, this time inside a tale, namely, *The Nun's Priest's Tale.* Chauntecleer, the tale's rooster-protagonist, determines the precise equinoctial hour of the day since he knows "by nature" the degrees of the sun's ascension; and the Nun's Priest, the tale's horologically challenged narrator, attempts to determine the month and date of that day via a calculation so convoluted that most readers refuse to go through the mental contortions necessary to arrive at anything close to the actual day upon which the events of this beast fable putatively happen.

There are several extraordinary things about these three passages. The first oddity is that they are very rarely discussed by scholars other than editors. Until very recently, the only two scholars to have paid sustained attention to the scientific technicalities of these passages, Sigmund Eisner and John D. North, are both astronomers by training.[5] But literary critics are not immediately to be faulted for their reluctance to engage in such scientific calculations, for the second unusual element concerning these time-telling episodes is that Chaucer's ideal contemporary interpreter had to know how to use either an astrolabe or a complex scientific almanac in order to corroborate the hour of the day, the date of the day, and the ascension of the sun at the Canterbury pilgrims' precise geographic latitude. Although a highly allusive and intertextual poet, Chaucer nowhere else in his poetic corpus requires that his readers hold a scientific text in hand in order to determine the accuracy and rightness of a passage of poetry. But the most challenging feature of all three *chronographiae* is also the most frustrating and confusing: when the scientifically inclined reader goes through all the necessary calculations to verify Chaucer's data, it turns out that each and every one of Chaucer's three determinations of time is somehow wrong!

In this chapter I intend to examine Chaucer's three "wrong" *chronographiae* by calling upon both sides of the reader's bicameral brain. For humanists this means developing a high tolerance for scientific and philosophical lore: mathematical tables, physio-kinetic diagrams, metalinguistic word problems, an astronomical syzygy, and logical speculations about change, motion, and time, as well as about the kinematics of beginnings and endings. Because I am persuaded that the significance of Chaucer's *chronographiae* cannot be understood by merely reading them in a formalist fashion, any more than the significance of time can be comprehended by staring at the heavens (or a calendar, an astrolabe, a sundial, or a mechanical clock), I begin by considering five modes of understanding and representing time in the fourteenth century. While these five modes do not provide all the information necessary to assessing Chaucer's chronographic art, all five are called into play as Chaucer's readers attempt to determine that phenomenon we offhandedly call the time of day.

FIVE MEDIEVAL WAYS OF LOOKING AT TIME

One mode of time measurement in the Middle Ages was computistical. *Computus* was the science by which medieval scholars sought to forecast the correct date for Easter and thus the precise dates of all the other movable feasts in the liturgical year. Although eight full days of Oxford University's liberal arts astronomy syllabus were given over to studying a dizzying array of tables, charts, diagrams, and mathematical formulas, and although all medieval Western Christians were in agreement that Easter day should be the Sunday after (but not on) the fourteenth day of the Paschal moon—that is, the calendar moon whose fourteenth day, reckoned from the new moon inclusive, falls on, or is the next following, the vernal equinox—in Chaucer's time the computus had proved strikingly inadequate. Nature, failing to conform to humanly prescribed divisions of sidereal, solar, and lunar movement, was obdurately lifting into the fourteenth-century heavens a sun and a moon whose motions mocked all the authoritative tables of solar positions and lunar phases, as well as ushering in a true vernal equinox roughly a week before the orthodox date of March 21.[6] Irreducible even in the eighteenth century to a comprehensible algorithm,[7] the principles of mathematical and astronomical calculation for determining Easter day were in the fourteenth-century a constant reminder of the extraordinary complexities and mysteries of mastering and measuring time.[8]

A second mode of analyzing time in the later Middle Ages was philosophical. The urgency of the most prominent fourteenth-century metaphysical speculations on time devolved from two major condemnations that had been pronounced by Bishop Stephen Tempier in 1277. In one condemnation Tempier anathematized the extreme Aristotelian proposition: "If heaven stood still, fire would not burn flax, because time would not exist."[9] But in a second condemnation he evenhandedly anathematized the extreme Augustinian assertion: "Time and eternity have no existence in reality but only in the mind."[10] Because of Tempier's condemnations, fourteenth-century philosophers had to hypothesize an understanding of time that although deriving from the works of their two great temporal authorities, Aristotle and Augustine, fully embraced the position of neither. Duns Scotus and Peter Aureole, for example, invented a phenomenon called *potential time*—which inheres inside the mind when understood as a continuous succession without parts, but which inheres in some substance outside the mind when understood as "measured time," a composite of continuous or discontinuous arithmetical magnitude.[11]

Ockham's extensive treatise on time was even subtler. For Ockham, the word "time" like the word "motion" principally signifies the ninth heavenly sphere, the *primum mobile,* moving with maximum speed and uniformity; but the word "time" unlike the word "motion" also consignifies the soul numbering or observing that heavenly sphere. Ockham intermittently implies that the diurnal movement of the *primum mobile* is in fact the ultimate clock, but he just as regularly retracts this Aristotelian position by arguing that the very idea of regular movement is a human conception generated to conform to a purely ideal clock that our mind constructs as soon as it perceives any movement or change whatsoever. So where then does this ideal of temporal measurement, this Absolute Clock, exist? Ockham never satisfactorily answers this question. And neither do Walter Burleigh, John Buridan, Albert of Saxony, or Marsilius of Inghen, all of whom nevertheless attempt to determine the nature of the Absolute Clock, its relationship to the *primum mobile* as well as to the motions of our minds.[12]

The third salient mode of analyzing time was mechanical. Until the invention of a block-and-release mechanism, or escapement, which made use of oscillatory motion to divide time into countable beats, the nature of civilized timekeeping had been in the West essentially the sound of bells rung by human beings at certain unfixed times during the day in response to the movement of a shadow across a sundial. This was all dramatically modified by the mechanical clock, a late thirteenth-century invention, which many historians believe constituted "one of the most important turning-points in the history of science and technology."[13] Despite the advent of mechanical clocks, the old ways of "knowing time" remained dominant, that is, either sensing time by an intuitive feel or attending to monastery or church bells that divided the day into seven uneven liturgical *horae:* lauds, prime, tierce, sext, none, vespers, and compline. But the appearance of so many magnificent and elaborate block-and-release clocks in the center of city squares—such as the tower clock of Norwich Cathedral (1325), the St. Albans clock (1330), and the famous de' Dondi clock of Padua completed in 1364—not only inspired further urban horological competition, but, in the judgment of Jacques Le-Goff, effected a violent collision between the old and the new meanings of time.[14] Used in some cities as *werglocken* to regulate the length of working days no matter how long or short the natural day, these clocks, uniquely designed to measure equal and unchanging hours twenty-four hours a "day," created a new consciousness which LeGoff calls "merchant's time"—where time is seen as something secular, measurable, mechanized, commodifiable, wasteable, exploiting as well as exploitable.[15] To balance LeGoff's vision of crisis, however, I think we must also emphasize that these clocks in their very designs expressed a social pride in humankind's ability to imitate and venerate the designs of divine creation: "The hourly parade of saints and patriarchs; the ponderous strokes of the hammer-wielding jacks, the angel turning with the sun, the rooster crowing at sunrise; the lunar disk waxing and waning with the moon—all these movements and sounds," writes David Landes, "offered lessons in theology and astronomy to the up-gazing multitude that gathered to watch and wonder."[16]

The fourth way of determining time in the Middle Ages was astrolabic. As the author of the *Treatise on the Astrolabe,* a treatise that in North's view is "the first competent work in English on such a subject,"[17] Chaucer was clearly fascinated with the workings of one of the most remarkable instruments of the Middle Ages. A handheld brass instrument consisting of a graduated circle and a sighting rule that pivoted about a central pin held in place by another pin, often decorated with a horse's head, the astrolabe allowed observations of the altitude of any star or planet. What enabled the astrolabe to serve as astronomical computer was its set of circular brass plates: the uppermost plate, the "rete," represented the rotating heavens and contained a star map and an eccentric circle representing the ecliptic; this was superimposed upon a second plate called the *climate,* or *tympanum,* which bore the projection of a fixed coordinate system defined for the latitude of the user; the upper plates (there could be multiple, interchangeable *climatae* for different latitudes) were held in a circular depression in the larger *mater* plate, which was usually engraved on the back with various astronomical and mathematical tools. The *climate* consisted of an horizon line, circles of equal altitude, and lines of equal azimuth, as well as the celestial equator, Tropic of Cancer, and Tropic of Capricorn. The rete would be rotated over the *climate* in order to make a variety of calculations concerning such matters as the rotation of the

heavens, the position of the sun, and the time of day. As Marijane Osborn
has shown, Chaucer's fascination with this instrument may be seen in a
number of places in the poetry of the latter part of his career, most notably in the magical steed of brass in *The Squire's Tale,* which is fashioned
as a larger-than-life model of an astrolabe.[18]

The fifth and final way of assessing time in the late Middle Ages was
kalendric. It is this mode which is most important in the study of Chaucer's *chronographiae,* not only because Chaucer expects his most attentive readers to consult a *kalendarium,* but because the *kalendarium* incorporates into its measurements at least three of the four other modes
of temporal analysis I have so far discussed. If on an English country road
one did not have an astrolabe in hand and for some unnatural reason
wished to know the precise time of day, what could one do? The answer
is to be found in Chaucer's *Treatise on the Astrolabe,* where he cites two
English contemporaries, John Somers and Nicholas of Lynn, each the author of a *kalendarium*—that is, an ingenious and highly rationalized system of determining mechanical clock time without the use of mechanical
clocks (which were notoriously inaccurate anyway). John Somer's *Kalendarium* (1380) and Nicholas of Lynn's *Kalendarium* (1386) both reveal
the many different ways time could be reckoned in the fourteenth century. The latter is of more immediate relevance because it is this almanac
that Chaucer relies upon in all three *chronographiae.*[19] It is the almanac,
in other words, that Chaucer's readers had to know how to use *if* they
wished to emulate, and verify, Chaucer's own calculations of time. The
following description of this *kalendarium* is thus meant to stand in for
Chaucer's readers' direct experience of reading it—of poring over its instructions, learning how to decipher its tables, corroborating its data with
their own astrolabic calculations, and putting these corroborations to ex-
periential use.

Nicholas of Lynn's *Kalendarium* opens with a month-by-month calendar from the year 1387 to the year 1462. Each page consists of a series
of vertical columns. The left-most column, labeled *Numerus dierum,* contains a vertical line of numbers running from 1 to 28, 29, 30, or 31, de-
pending upon the month. Next is a column of numbers ranging from 1
to 19, indicating each day's Metonic cycle (that is, the order in which the

moon nearly returns to the position it held in the nineteenth year before
the given year). Next follows a column for the Roman calendar, designating each date by ides, nones, and kalends. Next is a column assigning
saints' days, after which follows a double column labeled *Verus locus solis,*
indicating the degree and minutes of a degree of the sun in a given sign
of the zodiac at noon for each day of the year. After this there follows a
double column labeled *Quantitates diei artificialis,* which catalogues the
length of each "artificial day," given in hours and minutes, from the point
of the sun's rising above the horizon to the point of the sun's setting below
the horizon. This is followed by a second double column labeled *Quantitates diei vulgaris,* the "vulgar" or "natural" day being the artificial day
plus the morning and evening twilights. For our purposes, the next important column is something unique to Nicholas of Lynn's *Kalendarium,*
a shadow scale, in degrees and minutes, entitled "The altitudes of the sun
and the lengths of the shadows of any man six feet high in hours of equal
distance [in other words, hours as measured by a mechanical clock] at
51 degrees, 50 minutes," which is the latitude of Oxford, England. The column is in fact double, divided into *altitudines solis* and *umbre hominis,*
so that, for instance, at 5 p.m. on October 1 the sun is 4 degrees above the
horizon and the length of the shadow of a six-foot man is 85 feet and
51/60ths of a foot.

　　Following these pages of columns there is another section that includes a table of solar eclipses, lunar eclipses, the ascendant and beginnings of the celestial houses, the reign of each planet, a table of moveable
feasts, tables tracing the motion of the sun and the dignities of the planets, and a chart indicating which zodiacal sign the moon is in each day
of the year. In light of the many ways of measuring time represented in
the *Kalendarium*—solar, lunar, Roman, liturgical, astrolabic, and mathe-
matical/scientific—Nicholas's concluding manual placed at the very end
of his almanac is all-important: it serves as a guide to the use of its disparate tables and points in the direction of deeper questions concerning
the nature and measurement of time itself.

　　What is collectively indicated by this introductory survey of five medieval ways of assessing time—computistical, philosophical, mechanical, astrolabic, and kalendric—is the increasing awareness of the prob-

lematics of time developing within certain communities in the late fourteenth century. Of course the majority of rural Europeans continued to live within the same time continuum as had their ancestors—working and resting in harmony with the expanding and contracting daylight hours during seasons that were given sacred definition by the fixed and movable feast-days of the liturgical year. It was primarily in the cities that a self-conscious awareness of time's rationalized divisibility was taking hold: this fascination with measuring and meting out units of "mercantile" time is something that Chaucer's London audience was very much in the process of assimilating. But that part of Chaucer's potential readership that participated most fully in all five ways of assessing time was without question the scholarly community. In *Schools and Scholars in Fourteenth-Century England*, William J. Courtenay notes, "At the opening of the fourteenth century students shared with their nonacademic contemporaries the same sense of time: solar time."[20] Like rural laborers, scholars divided their day into twelve liturgical hours that shrank or expanded to fill up the time from sunrise to sunset no matter the day's length. In northern latitudes this guaranteed that the length of classes and class-days fluctuated greatly with the seasons, the result being that a "lecture in early June in England might be almost twice as long as one given in mid-December."[21] However, by the end of the fourteenth century, university life in places like Oxford had been so affected by the mechanical clock that daily academic exercises were now measured in equal units of time. Thus in less than one century England's intellectual community had shifted the scheduling of its daily life from medieval solar time to modern clock time. In fact, Courtenay goes so far as to speculate that the great number of fourteenth-century Oxford treatises on the phenomenology of time may be traced directly to the influence of "one of the wonders of that age," the large mechanical astronomical clock at the monastery of St. Albans. Whichever way the influence worked, Courtenay continues,

> the development of the mechanical clock in England is contemporary with a growing fascination at Oxford with units of time and with measurement, which by 1340 had produced a mathematical

physics as well as a quantitative theology. The problem of the divisibility of temporal and spatial *continua,* which was a fundamental issue within the philosophy, science, and theology of fourteenth-century Oxford, may have caught the interest of so many because it corresponded to changes in their daily experience.[22]

As an intellectual attuned to the philosophical concerns of Oxford, as an authority on the technical and scientific intricacies of the astrolabe, and as a cosmopolitan civil servant working long but "regular" hours, Chaucer was clearly engaged in the many ways contemporary time could be measured and assessed. Without doubt, Chaucer's personal fascination with the different modes of ascertaining the time of day influenced his decision to include in *The Canterbury Tales* three state-of-the-art horological calculations. However, it is not so much the literary egregiousness of these technical calculations themselves but rather the unique way Chaucer presents them to his readers that needs most carefully to be explored. The majority of Chaucer's contemporary readers would of course never have troubled themselves with extra homework assignments to determine the right time of his literary days. And modern scholars of Chaucer, because of the shortcut "solutions" and correct "answers" supplied by editors of *The Canterbury Tales,* fail to experience anything close to the complicated *process* of intellectual inquiry that each of Chaucer's *chronographiae* invites and makes possible. It is only by simulating the analytic experiences of any one of Chaucer's well-educated, "clergial," and contemporary readers that the philosophical significance of these passages begins slowly to emerge. Working back and forth between Chaucer's text, Nicholas of Lynn's *Kalendarium,* and other modes of measuring and thinking about time, Chaucer's inquisitive reader runs into a series of puzzlements and intellectual cul-de-sacs. It is only after these scholarly frustrations modulate in the direction of a necessary but peculiar heuristic strategy that the confounded reader begins to make progress; that is, in due time, having contemplated the many errors in calculation presented in these *chronographiae,* and then having reflected at length upon the concept of "error" itself, Chaucer's reader will be able to arrive at a more sophisticated understanding of the temporal anxieties of the late fourteenth century. And because the interplay of ideas inside the zone of literary-critical "error" is one of the distinguishing features of *The Nun's Priest's Tale*, the "quadrivial" questions its *chronographia* knowingly parodies are questions that address with equal force its own "trivial" claims concerning literary truth.

TEMPUS EST HOMINIS CONFUSIO

Fragment II of *The Canterbury Tales* opens the Introduction to *The Man of Law's Tale* with Chaucer's first technical *chronographia*:

> Oure Hooste saugh wel that the brighte sonne
> The ark of his artificial day hath ronne
> The ferthe part, and half an houre and moore,
> And though he were nat depe ystert in loore,
> He wiste it was the eightetethe day
> Of Aprill, that is messager to May;
> And saugh wel that the shadwe of every tree
> Was as in lengthe the same quantitee
> That was the body erect that caused it.
> And therfore by the shadwe he took his wit
> That Phebus, which that shoon so clere and brighte,
> Degrees was fyve and fourty clombe on highte,
> And for that day, as in that latitude,
> It was ten of the clokke, he gan conclude,
> And sodeynly he plighte his horse aboute . . .
>
> (II.1–15)

The means of arriving at the time of day by "Oure Hooste" is quite a feat for someone with neither astrolabe nor *kalendarium* in hand, for, by some natural gift, he is able to make four interrelated calculations. First, he perceives that the artificial day, that is, the passage of time from the exact point of the sun's rising above the horizon to the exact point of the sun's setting below the horizon, is more than one-fourth gone. In fact, relying upon some interior chronometer, he has been able to divide the artificial day into quarters and then add the amount of time that has passed since the completion of that first fourth: the sun has "ronne / The ferthe part, and half an houre and moore." The next calculation Harry makes is the equally extraordinary determination that the day's date is April 18—which, being a numerical designation, is also unusual in the Middle Ages especially when made by one "nat depe ystert in loore." Harry's third calculation is perhaps not so astonishing, for it is a mode of affixing "natural" time that can be traced at least as far back as Anax-agoras.[23] Although Harry apparently does not get off his horse and ac-tually measure any shadows, he determines that because all shadows at this moment are equal in length to the objects that cast them, the sun "[d]egrees was fyve and fourty clombe on highte." The final measure-ment, putting together all of this information, is the scientific induction that the precise time "for that day, as in that latitude, / . . . was ten of the clokke." And this clock, we should be reminded, is a mechanical clock, measuring "equal," or sixty-minute hours, rather than a sundial that mea-sures "unequal hours."

Harry's temporal calculations are obviously informed by an expert-ise that no human being could master without the assistance of an astro-labe or *kalendarium*. Although most readers do not stop to ponder the impossibilities, it is obvious that one cannot intuit, one can only learn of the measured length of the artificial day one is presently living in; one cannot know, one can only discover from some text or instrument how many hours, at a specific moment, have passed beyond the first fourth of that artificial day; without the use of an astrolabe, one cannot with absolute certainty ascertain that the sun is precisely forty-five degrees ascended; and, finally, if one were to use the less precise, shadow-scale method of measurement, without the help of a *kalendarium* one could not translate its natural hours into regular clock-hours.

Now, if we do choose to check Harry's measurements by turning to the tables in Nicholas of Lynn's *Kalendarium* for the month of April, we see that Harry has got some matters quite right. April 18, for instance, is the only time in the entire month when at a regular hour (actually, at both 10 a.m. and 2 p.m.) the sun is precisely forty-five degrees in the sky, and thus the shadow of a six-foot man (or tree) is six feet long. But even so, as Sigmund Eisner has noted, Harry's first, "astrolabic" calculation is not entirely accurate. For according to Nicholas of Lynn, the artificial day of April 18 (that is, from sunrise at 4:47 a.m. to sunset at 7:13 p.m.) is 14 hours and 26 minutes long. One fourth of this artificial day, 3 hours and 36 minutes, yields 8:23 a.m.; add another "half an houre" and we arrive at 8:53—which is still a rather long time away from 10 a.m. So what does Harry, or Chaucer, mean by "and moore" in "half an houre and moore"? Eisner, feeling that "and moore" has to "signify an inappropriately long stretch to bring the time to 10:00 a.m.,"[24] concludes that this faulty computation is not Chaucer's, but the Host's, who was "nat depe ystert in loore." However, Eisner is pleased to report that Harry's shadow-calculation is right, not only because it agrees with the *Kalendarium,* but because he, Eisner, "standing in the rare sunshine of Chaucer's island and latitude," took the same shadow measurement with the same results, although it had to be taken on April 27, which is the Gregorian equivalent to Chaucer's Julian April 18.[25]

Eisner's explanation of Harry's scientific errors is based on his analysis of Harry's character: Harry is not very well educated. Nevertheless, throughout the pilgrimage Harry suffers from a very modern obsession with the passage of time, an obsession that is an instantiation of the mercantile mentality characterized by LeGoff. Harry is thus very much a man of the hour, epitomizing the burgeoning bourgeois fascination with the process of gaining and losing the measurable *minutiae* of time. Yet what is to be made of Harry's intuitive ability to measure and enumerate these *minutiae?* It is as if a calculator, astrolabe, clock, *kalendarium,* and GPS device had all been programmed into the microchip of Harry's brain. Harry thus remains an unusually strained poetic conceit, his a priori abilities to measure clock-time "by nature" placing him in a peculiar relationship to the realistic surface of Chaucer's fiction.[26] And just as peculiar is his relationship to Chaucer's readers, who are invited to make their own calculations. While most readers will countenance Harry's time-telling powers as so much poetic license, a few "clergial" readers, conversant as Chaucer was with contemporary almanacs, will take it upon themselves to look into a *kalendarium*—checking out the relevant columns, making the appropriate calculations, and double-checking their arithmetic— only to discover, finally, that Harry's calculations were wrong. Although the fiction of Harry's improbable powers provides an invitation to duplicate Harry's calculations, the reader's reward for dutifully undertaking

such extratextual research is to arrive at a small but significant miscalculation. But whose miscalculation is it? Harry's? Chaucer's? Nicholas of
Lynn's? The reader's? Or two, or more, of the above?

To address the significance of this miscalculation will ultimately involve addressing the issue of error itself. At the moment, however, it is
instructive to consider the second instance of technical measurement of
"non-fictive" time taken on the road to Canterbury. In the Prologue to *The
Parson's Tale*, near the very end of the pilgrimage, the narrator informs his
readers in a roundabout way that it is getting late in the afternoon:

> By that the Maunciple hadde his tale al ended,
> The sonne fro the south lyne was descended
> So lowe that he nas nat, to my sighte,
> Degreës nyne and twenty as in highte.
> Foure of the clokke it was tho, as I gesse,
> For ellevene foot, or litel moore or lesse,
> My shadwe was at thilke tyme, as there
> Of swiche feet as my lengthe parted were
> In sixe feet equal of proporcioun.
> Therwith the moones exaltacioun—
> I meene Libra—alwey gan ascende
> As we were entryng at a thropes ende . . .
>
> (X.1–12)

Although very much a part of the same tradition, the perspective of Chaucer's *chronographia* is quite different from Harry's. Whereas Harry's provides a secular measurement of quotidian time *in medias res,* Chaucer's
vision of time is numinous with signs of finality, judgment, and death.
The twenty-nine degrees of the descending sun may symbolically renu-
merate the twenty-nine original tale-telling pilgrims; the impossibly long
and carefully measured shadow cast by the narrator's idealized six-foot
body seems profoundly spiritual in its demarcations;[27] the sun's descending, the moon's rising, and Libra, the scales of judgment, suspended above
the pilgrims' entrance into a nameless town's end, all suggest time's yearning for eternity. The eschatological tenor of these images has in fact led
one scholar into the far reaches of numerological allegory: for Russell

Peck the four of "four of the clokke" is the "number of Fortune, a number which is intimately associated with the world"; twenty-nine is the number of "transgression, spiritual decrepitude, sterility, [and] concupiscence"; eleven is also a number of sin and transgression; while six is a number of the perfect soul and a sign of earthly perfection.[28]

Were the text not so obviously concerned, even here at the end of the pilgrimage, with the scientific measurement of human time in the here-and-now, it would be tempting to elevate all of these arithmetical calculations far away from the literal and into typological, tropological, and mystical *allegoresis*. But the empirical nature of these matters and their obvious obsession with the accuracies of scientific measurement simply cannot be denied—even though the narrator's measurements are even more inaccurate than were the Host's. The first difficulty is that while *The Riverside Chaucer* prints "foure of the clokke," all manuscripts but one (MS Ch) give the time of day as "ten of the clokke." If "ten of the clokke" has to be a scribal error (as all Chaucer's editors presume), its correction appears rationalizable in one of two ways. Eisner argues that since the Roman sign for ten was an X and the Arabic sign for four was an X with an arc over the top, modern editors are justified in emending a mistaken ten to four.[29] Peck, from a different angle, argues that Chaucer is using one of the several modes of hourly numeration employed in the Middle Ages: "ten of the clokke" means ten hours after liturgical prime; and since prime (Peck presumes) is equivalent to 6 a.m., the tenth hour of the day is, actually, four p.m. But even after this textual crux (if it is such) is amended, two other difficulties remain. At 4 p.m. in mid-April, as Nicholas of Lynn's *Kalendarium* makes absolutely clear, it is Saturn, rather than Libra, which is the moon's exaltation. How could Chaucer manage to get this very basic piece of information so wrong? The other egregious time-telling problem concerns the day itself. Unlike Harry, Chaucer does not provide the date of the day whose hours he is measuring. So it is left to the reader to turn once again to Nicholas's *Kalendarium,* and then to focus upon the *altitudines solis* column and the *umbre hominis* column for the month of April, and eventually to determine that the only possible date for the last day of the Canterbury pilgrimage is April 17. That is, on April 17 the sun's altitude at 4 p.m. is 28° 57'—or, "nat, to my sighte, / Degreës nyne and twenty as in highte." And the length of a six foot man's shadow at 4 p.m.

is ten feet, ten inches (51/60) long—or, "ellevene foot, or litel moore or lesse." Thus, working with both Chaucer's and Nicholas of Lynn's texts, readers and editors must eventually conclude that April 17 is the last day of Chaucer's pilgrimage to Canterbury.

But determining the day's date, rather than settling all matters, only succeeds in creating more time-telling problems: as we recall, the Host's *chronographia* has already determined that the first day of the pilgrimage was April 18. By these calculations, the Canterbury pilgrimage—setting out from London on the morning of April 18 and nearing Canterbury on the afternoon of April 17—ends one day before it begins. What is the reader to make of this paradox? In the prototypical medieval literary journey, the *Divine Comedy,* it makes perfect sense that time at a certain point should leap backward: that Dante, moving from the northern to the southern hemisphere as he leaves Inferno and arrives at the base of Purgatorio, should actually gain twelve hours, the result being that he is able to live through the same Holy Saturday for a second time in the same year. But in Chaucer's earthbound pilgrimage within the same latitude, unless time is itself moving backward, the chronically earthbound interpreter is left, once again, in a quandary.[30] Eisner's solution to all these difficulties is to proclaim that they are "not significant" because Chaucer uses these dates only for "symbolic purposes." The one symbolic purpose Eisner advances is this: "[T]he tone of the Parson's Tale is fitting for Good Friday. The joyous arrival in Canterbury would be fitting for Easter. In 1394 Good Friday was 17 April."[31] Such "symbolic" explanations are attractive, and as one form of literary exegesis need not be "wrong," but in my judgment they nevertheless refuse to confront the issue of "error" head-on, for surely Chaucer could have used a symbolic mode that did not get tangled in such convoluted scientific conflicts.

What, therefore, are we to do with this plethora of arithmetical and astronomical miscalculations? First, even though the purpose of the resulting confusion is not entirely clear, I think we must acknowledge that Chaucer was aware he was inscribing errors of measurement into his *chronographiae:* these are errors of authorial intention, not of authorial ignorance or carelessness. Second, given that Nicholas of Lynn's diverse tables and explanatory canons provide encyclopedic instruction in the many ways time has been and may be measured, we must recognize that Chaucer has invited his careful readers to become equally careful readers of the *Kalendarium*. However, what Chaucer expects his readers finally to glean from their analysis of Nicholas of Lynn's various tables and from Chaucer's own "misreading" of these tables requires further thought. Third, despite the similarities between the two *chronographiae* examined to this point, it is clear that they embody two quite different relationships to time. Time for Harry is anxiously concentrated in the *hic et nunc* of the absolute present, whereas time for the Chaucerian narrator is both a phenomenon to be measured and a mystery to be pondered *sub specie eternitate*. The dialogue between these two different perspectives needs to be further articulated. Finally, unless we are able to accept Harry's uncanny time-telling instincts as merely so much poetic license, we need to consider how his superhuman powers raise questions not only about the narrator's presumed omniscience in telling "fictive" time but also about anyone's ability to scientifically know what the "right" time really is.

Together, these chronographic issues begin to suggest the possibility that a coherent inquiry may underlie Chaucer's exploration of the human interpretations of fourteenth-century time. In themselves, however, they do not provide adequate answers to the questions they obliquely raise. To more closely approximate these answers, we now must consider the most complex *chronographia* of *The Canterbury Tales*, which is that found in the middle of *The Nun's Priest's Tale*. To appreciate the intellectual context of the Nun's Priest's time-telling puzzle, it will in fact be necessary to trace out a very specific set of medieval logical studies pertaining to temporal beginnings and endings. But because of certain interpretative difficulties deeply embedded in the Nun's Priest's *chronographia*, a knowledge of these studies of time, motion, and change will (once again) not provide any "right" answers. Rather, the Nun's Priest's *chronographia* will have succeeded in foregrounding a set of conceptual questions that prove, finally, to be the backbone of his pedagogical agenda: that is, *understanding* some of the problematics of temporal calculation and *understanding* the potential significance of not arriving at right answers are what give ultimate coherence to Chaucer's explorations of the mysteries of time.

THE NUN'S PRIEST'S *SOPHISMA DE INCIPIT ET DESINIT*

More than halfway through *The Nun's Priest's Tale*, the narrator suddenly takes it upon himself to let his readers know when his fable putatively happened:

> Whan that the month in which the world bigan,
> That highte March, whan God first maked man,
> Was compleet, and passed were also
> Syn March bigan thritty dayes and two,
> Bifel that Chauntecler in al his pryde,
> His sevene wyves walkynge by his syde,
> Caste up his eyen to the brighte sonne,
> That in the signe of Taurus hadde yronne
> Twenty degrees and oon, and somwhat moore,
> And knew by kynde and by noon oother loore,
> That it was pryme, and crew with blisful stevene.
> "The sonne," he seyde, "is clomben up on hevene
> Fourty degrees and oon, and moore ywis...."
>
> (VII.3187–99)[32]

In this passage, Chauntecleer determines "by nature" that it is the liturgical hour of prime. And he is able, relying again on his native knowledge (like Harry he needs no astrolabe), to determine that the sun is forty degrees "and moore ywis" in the sky. The narrator supplies the information that the sun has ascended twenty-one degrees "and somwhat moore" in the sign of Taurus. With only this amount of information, the dutiful reader could go straight again to Nicholas of Lynn's *Kalendarium* and read down the first column until Taurus appears—to discover that the sun is in Taurus 21° 6' ("Twenty degrees and oon, and somwhat moore") on May 3. Further, at 9 a.m., which Eisner says is equivalent to "pryme," the sun is at an altitude of 41° 17' ("Fourty degrees and oon, and moore ywis"). And, if it matters at all, one could add that the shadow of a six-foot man (or six-foot chicken) at this moment is six feet, ten inches long. Finally, because 152 lines later the Nun's Priest notes in an aside that "on a Friday fil al this meschaunce," one could perhaps assert, as Eisner has done (using the *Kalendarium* once again), that the precise Friday on which *The Nun's Priest's Tale* occurs was either May 3, 1381, or May 3, 1392. For once, then, all the parts seem to fit, and Chaucer, the Nun's Priest, Chauntecleer, and the reader finally get everything right.[33]

However, in the opening four lines of the *chronographia* the narrator attempts to determine the month and day in quite a different way, and these lines complexify the reader's determination of the proper time of the tale's events:

> Whan that the month in which the world bigan,
> That highte March, whan God first maked man,
> Was compleet, and passed were also,
> Syn March bigan, thritty dayes and two,
> Bifel that Chauntecler in al his pryde . . .
>   (VII.3187–91)

Considering the unusual degree of syntactic and semantic complexity in this linguistic collocation, and its ambiguous overlappings of beginning points and ending points in time, it is not surprising that the passage's first four lines have succeeded in generating the longest single gloss in the Variorum edition of *The Nun's Priest's Tale*—a 152-line history of five centuries' worth of scribal emendations, editorial amendations, critical interpretations, and scholarly exegesis. It is also perhaps not surprising that almost every modern edition of Chaucer has gone entirely against the authority of all extant manuscripts and rewritten the phrase "Syn March bigan" as "Syn March was gon." Although we shall see eventually that these four lines parody a specific kind of medieval word-problem dealing with instants of beginnings and endings in time, the responses of scholars unaware of the tradition are nevertheless instructive in dramatizing the heuristic scope of the passage. The first point that needs to be underscored is that all readers are forced to follow the same general path at the outset. After first rereading the opening four lines several times, then muttering quietly to themselves a version of the fifteenth-century mnemonic poem—

> Thirty dayes hath November,
> April, June, and September;

Of XXVIII is but oon,
And all the remenaunt is XXX and I.[34]

—then counting carefully on their fingers (for, having got this far, it would be embarrassing to be wrong), and then wondering at least subliminally whether it makes any difference to measure from the ending of one unit of time (such as a day) or from the beginning of another unit of time (such as the next day), scholars have nevertheless managed to arrive at more than one apparently correct determination of the date Chaucer presumably "had in mind." Three of the most popular dates proffered have been April 1, April 2, and May 2, but the all-time favorite among Chaucerians is Chaucer's favorite day, the third day of the third month, May 3.[35] Yet even those who are certain their May 3 reading is right admit that the grammatical and syntactical construction of this sentence is extremely tortuous and even perhaps self-contradictory.

For many of Chaucer's scribes, editors, and readers, the way of solving these linguistic problems has simply been to correct or bracket the most irritating, illogical, or erroneous-looking parts of the sentence. The scribes of certain, less well-known, manuscripts were the first to take it upon themselves to straighten things out, by changing "thritty dayes and two" to their notion of the proper number of days that should have passed by. Thus "thritty dayes and two" becomes "twenty dayes and two" (MSS Cx2, G1, Pn, Wy), "thritty dayes and mo" (MSS Ph2, Ry1), "thritty dayes or two" (MS S11), "two monthes and dayes two" (MS Ha4), "seuene dayes and two" (MS Ii), or "seuen dayes and mo" (MS He).[36] Because these scribal emendations of the number of elapsed days create as many arithmetical problems as they seek to solve, various editors have taken it upon themselves to change, or reinterpret, what is clearly the crucial verb: "bigan" in the subordinate temporal clause "Syn March bigan." Thomas Tyrwhitt (1775) boldly emended "bigan" to "ended." Francis Thynne (1599), Andrew Brae (1870), and Mark Liddel (1930) all chose to interpret "bigan" as meaning "be gonne" as in "gone by or departed." Thus "Syn March began" actually means "March having passed by."[37] Robert Pratt in his 1974 edition confidently emends "bigan" to "was gon";[38] likewise, in *The Riverside Chaucer* (1987), Larry Benson replaces "bigan" with a bracketed "was gon," hypothesizing that originally "Chaucer wrote *was gon* and that scribal miscopying from [line] 3187 led to the mistaken repetition of *bigan* in [line] 3190."[39] The result of these decisions is that the majority of students now reading Chaucer will find:

> Whan that the month in which the world bigan,
> That highte March, whan God first maked man,
> Was compleet, and passed were also,
> Syn March [was gon], thritty dayes and two,
> Bifel that Chauntecleer in al his pryde . . .[40]

One rare exception to this spate of editorial emendations is the Variorum edition of *The Nun's Priest's Tale*, where Derek Pearsall allows "Syn March bigan" to stand unchanged. Although he concedes the meaning of the passage "is not transparently clear at first sight," Pearsall is nevertheless persuaded that "the text is clearly capable of unambiguous interpretation, and does not need emendation."[41] Pearsall's authority proves to be none other than William Skeat, who had contended in 1894 that "[t]he words 'since March bigan' are parenthetical" (which means, apparently, deletable or nonsignificant); thus, Skeat concludes, "we are, in fact, told that the whole of March, the whole of April, and two days of May were done with."[42]

At this point I wish to make a major assertion: Chaucer intended these lines to be written as they have been written. Any editorial correction is in fact a very grave error, because Chaucer's educated contemporaries would all have instantly recognized these four lines as a clever parody of one of the most persistent and popular intellectual problems in medieval logic and physics. Logically, this problem dealt with two verbs, "to begin" (*incipire*) and "to cease" (*desinire*). In formal propositions, these two verbs often proved to be ambiguous regarding their scope; they were seen to contain covert references to the past or the future despite their being in the present tense; and they were seen to involve covert negations despite their affirmative forms. As several historians of medieval philosophy have shown,[43] *incipit* and *desinit* were included in every late medieval logical textbook analyzing syncategorematic words—that is, those crucial little words in a proposition that determine the syntactical, rather than semantic, operations of a sentence, even though, properly speaking, as verbs they are *categoremantica*, that is, either nouns or verbs.[44] For example, consider this rather straightforward twelfth-century illustration of what is known as the logical "fallacy of division":

> Those two men cease to be.
> If anyone ceases to be, he dies.
> Therefore those two men die.[45]

The fallacy of the inference is this: since the two men as a pair may cease to be by way of the death of only one of them, it is erroneous to infer that both of them die. A more complicated form of logical scrutiny was represented in treatises that focused upon the fact that under certain conditions *incipit* and *desinit* involve covert negation and covert references to the past or future. Consider the fallacious inference in the next sophism:

> Socrates begins to be white.
> Therefore he begins to be colored.[46]

The covert negation and the covert temporal assertion are clearly interconnected: that is, in positing "Socrates begins to be white" the verb "begins" is also positing that immediately before now he was *not* white. The fallacy of the inference is that having been not white immediately before the present is not incompatible with having been some other color.

What moved *incipit* and *desinit* into the center of scholarly attention in the thirteenth and fourteenth centuries was the discovery of Aristotle's *Physics* and the gradual recognition that Aristotle's complex philosophy of limits—concerning the nature of the limits of motion, change, and time—was peculiarly receptive to a logico-linguistic reapplication within the receptive framework of fallacious syllogisms focusing upon the syncategorematic verbs of beginning and ceasing. In book 6 of the *Physics* Aristotle maintains that since time is a continuous phenomenon, temporal instants, rather like geometrical points on a geometrical line, are not actually real but are merely theoretical entities. Although time is infinitely divisible into instants, time is not made up of instants—which means that between two instants there exists an infinitude of further divisible instants. According to Aristotle, any change from one state to another must occur instantaneously, within a hypothetical instant of time; therefore, he writes, "that which has changed must at the moment when it has first changed be in that state to which it has changed" (*Physics* 6.5.235b6). In other words, the basic question is whether or not there *is* a first moment of change, or what Aristotle calls a "primary when." Common sense would assert that when a ball rolls down a ramp, there is a first instant of motion, call it T1, which follows immediately upon a last instant of nonmotion, call it T0. But Aristotle, hewing close to his fundamental belief in the infinite divisibility of time, would answer that between T1 and T0 there are an uncountable number of instants, and that for any given instant of change there exists a prior instant of change. Thus, he writes, "it is evident that every thing which is in motion must have moved before" (*Physics* 6.6.236b32). Equally important for Aristotle is the question of whether there is a first element of *completion,* an instant when it is true to say "this change is over." Aristotle's answer to this limit decision problem is that, although one must deny that there is no "primary when" at the beginning of continuous change, one must nevertheless affirm there is a "primary when" signifying that that change has been completed.

The medieval interpretation of Aristotle's position on limits was complicated by his treatment of another kind of change considered elsewhere in the *Physics.* In book 8, Aristotle contemplates what he calls "contradictory change," that instant when some subject changes within a given time interval from one state to another, such as from being nonwhite to being white. The question is, what is the status of the subject at the instant of change? Aristotle's answer, in contrast to that reached in book 6, is that the instant of change belongs to the time when the subject is white, rather than nonwhite. What this means, then, is that with contradictory change, and in direct contrast to continuous change, it is true to say there is a first moment when something *is* white, yet there is no last moment when one can say it is *not* white.

In attempting to develop a single doctrine that would unify these two passages in Aristotle, medieval thinkers decided that, in denying a "primary when" at the beginning of continuous change, Aristotle was denying a first instant of the existence of that change. Next, they determined that, in asserting a "primary when" at the completion of continuous change, Aristotle was in fact asserting a first instant of the nonexistence of that change. What this interpretation led to was a fairly complex definition

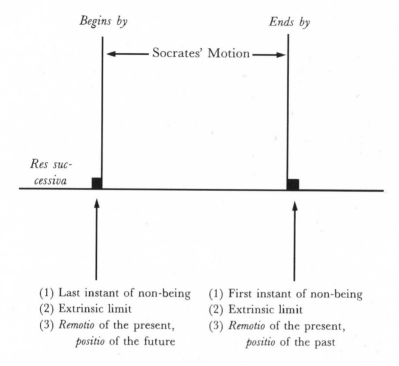

Figure 6.1. Beginning and Ending Limits: *Res successiva*[47]

of the nature of the beginnings and endings of continuous change. Since one must deny the existence of a first instant of a continuous change, one must perforce maintain that there is a last instant *before* the beginning of that change; likewise, since one must affirm the first instant of the change as no longer existing, one must perforce deny the existence of a last instant of the change itself. What this means is that every continuous change is *extrinsically* limited at both ends: it is limited at its beginning by its last instant of not-being and it is limited at its end by its first instant of not-being. A diagram supplied by the most ardent and informative student of these issues, John Murdoch, illustrates the extrinsic limits of continuous things, or *res successiva* (figure 6.1).

But, concerning contradictory change, matters were perceived by medieval logicians to be quite different, in light of Aristotle's definition of such change in book 8 of the *Physics*. Contradictory change (such as

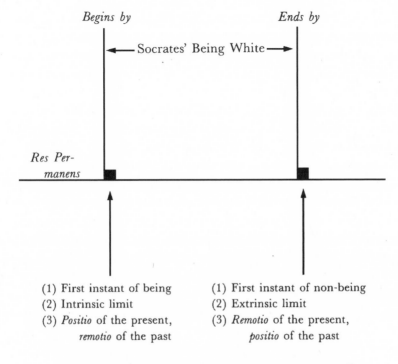

Figure 6.2. Beginning and Ending Limits: *Res permanens*[48]

Socrates' being white) differed from continuous change (such as Socrates' running) in that white was a *res permanens*, a permanent thing, all its parts existing at once, whereas Socrates' running was held to be a *res successiva*, its parts existing one after the other. It will be recalled that Aristotle maintained that the moment of change from nonwhite to white was contained within the time of his being white, which for the scholastics meant that there was a first instant of that change. Unlike continuous change, then, contradictory change is limited *intrinsically* at its beginning. But even though there is a *first* instant of that contradictory change, we recall that Aristotle allowed as to how no *final* instant of that state could be indivisibly posited. Therefore scholastic thinkers asserted that contradictory change at its ending was limited *extrinsically* (just like continuous change) and that its external limit was the first instant of its non-being. This analysis is illustrated by Murdoch's second figure (figure 6.2).

As scholastic interpretations of Aristotle's limit-decision positions developed, a number of treatises were written that focused upon the physical implications, or object-language analysis, of these matters, including Walter Burleigh's *De instanti* (c. 1340), John of Holland's *Tractatus de primo et ultimo instanti* (1369), and Peter of Mantua's (d. 1400) *De instanti*.[49] More popular, however, were those studies that remained essentially linguistic in nature, situating Aristotle's temporal theories into the preexisting logical tradition of *incipit/desinit* syncategorematic analysis. These studies included William of Sherwood's (d. 1272) *Treatise on Syncategorematic Words,* Peter of Spain's (d. 1277) even more influential *Tractatus syncategorematum,* and Thomas Bradwardine's (d. 1349) *Tractatus de incipit et desinit*.[50] By far the most important permutation of the Aristotelianized *incipit/desinit* phenomenon appeared in the second quarter of the fourteenth century and flourished for the next century in such works as Richard Kilvington's (d. 1361) *Sophismata,* William Heytesbury's *Regule solvendi sophismata* (ca. 1335), and Paul of Venice's (d. 1492) *Logica magna*.[51] This phenomenon was the rage for inventing irresolvable logical sophisms, or *sophismata,* wherein all the complicated issues of limit decision cases, including the discrimination of permanent versus successive things, were encapsulated in a highly compressed sophistical construction. In his survey of this form of limit-decision studies, Norman Kretzmann has counted almost 250 different examples of late medieval *incipit/ desinit sophismata*.[52] Here, by way of illustration, is one quite complex sophism posed by Chaucer's brilliant contemporary William Heytesbury:

> Assume that Socrates is now one foot tall, Plato two feet tall; and let each of them grow uniformly throughout the next hour, Socrates twice as fast as Plato, stipulating further that three feet is the smallest size that neither of them will have, since both cease to exist at the end of the hour at which moment both would have been three feet tall had they then existed.[53]

Although students of philosophy would have spent hours attempting to resolve a word problem such as this, the major point in their study was not to simply find a solution—because more often than not no solution was possible. In fact, time and again students discovered that a final and

correct answer had been thwarted or immobilized by a logical impasse—
something called in formal logic *vis confundendi,* and which I translate in-
formally as the "stymie principle."[54] Immobilizing the reader in a quandary, the irresolvable sophism is designed to force the reader into further
and deeper rumination both upon linguistic and logical issues at hand,
as well as upon phenomenological matters dealing with beginnings, endings, motion, change, and time.

   With all of this at least generally in mind, let us now return to Chaucer's crucial four lines:

> Whan that the month in which the world bigan,
> That highte March, whan God first maked man,
> Was compleet, and passed were also,
> Syn March bigan thritty dayes and two . . .

How might well-educated medieval readers have read this? In accordance
with their scholarly training in logic, they would first break down the
sophism into its *exponentes,* or exponible parts.[55] The *exponentes* are two
premises and one implied inference:

> The month of March has passed.
> Thirty-two days have passed.
> Therefore: A total of sixty-three days have passed.

Written out this way, the sophism's ambiguities are obvious, since it is perfectly possible that thirty-one of the thirty-two days which have passed
are contained inside the month of March itself. What gives special edge to
the sophism is Chaucer's combining its two premises with the innocent-
looking conjunction *and:* "and passed were also." As we have already seen
in chapter 3, one of the major words addressed in all medieval syncategorematic textbooks was "and" (*et*)—because it is an ambiguous delim-
iter, capable of serving either as a divisive conjunction or as a composite conjunction. For example, consider the radically different meanings
of "and" in these two sentences: "My son and my friend are here" versus
"My son and my friend is here." And consider the rules that make it al-
lowable to say "two and three are five" but never "two are five and three

are five." The pressure Chaucer places upon the ambiguity of "and" is dramatized equally well by "also," which is the intensifier of "and" in the phrase "*and* passed were *also.*" As in modern English, so in Middle English, "also" could be used as a simple additive, meaning "in addition, sequentially." However, it could be used with equal clarity of meaning to signalize a substitution for a preceding statement, meaning "likewise, concurrently." Thus we have the resulting ambiguity that appears to afford two equally right readings. One is sequential, adding thirty-two days to the end of March. The other is concurrent, adding thirty-two days to the beginning of March. The alternate syllogism is therefore:

> The month of March has passed.
> Thirty-two days have passed.
> Therefore: A total of thirty-two days have passed.

Because of the ambiguous nature of the two key syncategorematic words "and" and "also," two different readings seem to be equally available: sixty-three days have passed, or thirty-two days have passed. But are both readings equally valid? Clearly they are not. The second term of the syllogism is not simply "Thirty two days have passed," but rather "Thirty two days have passed *since March began* [passed were also, / *Syn March bigan thritty dayes and two*]." Therefore the two passages of time—concurrent rather than sequential—are in fact the *same* passage of time (plus one day), measured first in a month and then in days. Therefore, the valid solution to the *incipit/desinit* part of the Nun's Priest's *chronographia* cannot be either May 2 or May 3.[56] Rather, if there *is* a valid solution to the sophism (and of course there may not be), it has to be either April 1 or April 2.

But which is it? The sophism's evocation of medieval *incipit/desinit* scholarship would seem to imply that an application of that tradition might produce a definitively right answer. Having dealt with one *incipit* ("Syn March *bigan*") by using a quite straightforward logico-linguistic analysis, we are justified in hoping that the sophism's several beginnings ("When . . . the world *bigan,*" "whan God *first* maked man," "Syn March *bigan*") and ceasings ("*Was complet,*" "*passed* also"), as well as its various mixtures of different units of time (days, months, and perhaps years), could all be sorted out. Following good neo-Aristotelian thinking, what we find, however, is that time, at least in this case, cannot be neatly sorted out. A preliminary step in the medieval logical thinking process would be to determine that all these units of time are phenomena of continuous change rather than convertible change, *res successiva* rather than *res permanens*. Then, taking the precept that holds that every unit of continuous change is limited extrinsically at both ends, we see that the limits of the month of March are actually outside (rather than inside) the month of March. In other words, in order to measure from that point when "March bigan," we must measure from the last point before March actually becomes March; and in order to measure from the end of March, when it "was complet," we must measure from the first point when March is no longer March. Next, we must consider the termini of those two crucial days, day 31 and day 32 ("thritty dayes and *two*"). Day 31, as we have seen, has to be March 31, and thus it clearly occurs inside the month of March. However, the *incipit* of day 32 (April 1) must also occur *inside* the month of March, because the beginning-point of every unit of time is extrinsically limited. What this leads us to is the seemingly absurd proposition that the *incipit* of April 1 actually precedes the *desinit* of March 31. In other words, March ends in April, but April begins in March!

But how could it be that a *subsequent* unit of time (April) actually *begins* before the *preceding* unit of time (March) ceases? How could the beginning of the new day precede the ending of the old day? Our careful reasoning about time—according to the best medieval authorities— leads to a daunting and perhaps irresolvable paradox.[57] Let us put it one more way: if we measure thirty-two days from the *beginning* of March, we end up at the last instant inside April 1. However, if we measure one day from the *ending* of March, we end up at the first instant inside April 2. Thus the time of *The Nun's Priest's Tale*, its fictive present, seems to hover somewhere between the ending of one day (April 1) and the beginning of the next (April 2). But what is most weird is that this unit of time which we have determined to call the fictive present exists as an instant *before the ending of the past* and *after the beginning of the future*. While a resolution to this strange paradox remains a possibility, I leave its achievement to other readers, for it should by now be clear that Chaucer's major point is heuristic: that is, his parodic *incipit/desinit* sophism is meant first and foremost to raise questions about the nature of time and the complexities of its mensuration, rather than to posit a date upon which *The Nun's Priest's Tale* happens.

Thus, for Chaucer and his learned contemporaries, determining the *philosophical incipit-* or *desinit-*point of sequential temporal units was obviously no easy matter. However, determining the *conventional* termini of any "nonphilosophical" unit of time, such as an "everyday day," was *also* fraught with difficulties. As Linne Mooney has observed, there were five methods used in the Middle Ages to posit a day's *terminus a quo* (all five are incorporated into the *kalendaria* of John Somers and Nicholas of Lynn): the day could begin at midnight; it could begin at sunrise; it could begin at noon of the preceding day; it could begin at sundown of the preceding day; or, very importantly, it could begin at noon of the *stated* day.[58] Since the astronomical day was generally understood to begin at noon of the *stated* day (this, at any rate, is Nicholas of Lynn's practice), the forenoon of each calendar day actually belonged to the preceding astronomical day. It therefore follows in *The Nun's Priest's Tale* that the forenoon of April 2 (the calendar day) is actually contained within the diurnal confines of April 1 (the astronomical day).[59] Is it possible, then, that Chauntecleer escapes the jaws of death on the morning of the day before the day he escapes the jaws of death? Unless Chaucer's time is once again moving backwards, it may ultimately be best to recognize another "stymie principle" at work and accede to yet another paradox, namely, that the historical date of *The Nun's Priest's Tale* may in fact be two days, *both* April 1 *and* April 2. Indeed, this paradox may simply be a variation of the "philosophical" paradox arrived at above which places the tale between the ending of April 1 and the beginning of April 2.

But even if this ecumenical solution were entirely satisfactory, there is still the matter of "March." When Chaucer specifies "March" as "the month in which the world began," is he in fact saying that Chauntecleer's fall from grace actually occurred immediately after the very first month in which the world was created? Even though "literary" readers are unlikely to be troubled by this difficulty in semantic supposition, it is precisely this kind of *vis confundendi* that Chaucer's logical readers would expect to find embedded in an *incipit/desinit* sophism. Whereas our preceding analysis of "began," "was compleet," "and," and "also" focused on the sophism's key syncategorematic words, the ambiguities of "March" shift our attention to the sophism's most crucial categorematic word. It takes little training in logic to appreciate that "March," standing alone, could denote any month by that name in history; and it likewise takes little training to see that the doubly restrictive identification of this March as "the month in which the world bigan, . . . whan God first maked man" pulls its referential scope powerfully in the direction of the very beginning of human time. Of course what happens syntactically is that all three possible meanings of March play off against each other in the reader's mind: March is the proper name of the first month at the beginning of time; March is the common name of the first month of any and every year; and March is the proper name of the unique month of that specific year in which *The Nun's Priest's Tale* happened. Although some scholars, undaunted by Chaucer's sophistical springes, have confidently identified that year as 1392,[60] using the precepts of medieval logic should lead us away from such confidence. Rather, it is irresolution, paradox, ambiguity, and confusion that are the most important consequences of the heuristic strategies of Chaucer's brilliant *incipit/desinit* sophism. It is very doubtful, therefore, that Chaucer ever expected his careful reader to determine the sophism's "right" day—April 1 or April 2[61]—and it is just as doubtful that Chaucer ever expected that date to be successfully harmonized with the later date the remainder of the *chronographia* points toward—May 2 or May 3. Finally, even though it is extremely doubtful that Chaucer ever expected his reader to locate his beast fable in any specific year of human history, he certainly makes plausible the implausible inference that these events happen very near the beginning of time.

At what point, then, does time begin? No matter where we turn, it appears that the recurring question "What time is it?" continues to convert itself into Augustine's most famous question, "What then *is* time?"

INCOMMENSURABILITY IN CHAUCER'S TIME

Because he believed that time past and time future exist only in our subjective perceptions in the present, Augustine despaired that we could ever know the true nature of time. The only way we could possibly come to understand time is if we could somehow grasp the *in principio*, that mysterious moment where Eternity touches the *incipit*-point of time's beginning. Augustine's dream of reaching time's point of origin seems to have been realized by Dante the pilgrim in *Paradiso* 29. Arriving at the *primum mobile,* the ninth sphere of the universe, Dante observes the sun and the moon poised in perfect oppositional alignment, bisecting the earth by the plane of the same horizon. As Alison Cornish has argued, in pondering this extraordinary syzygy Dante is also observing the "primary when" of creation, that instant at the very beginning of time when the angels were created and when they fell.[62] Chaucer, in dramatic contrast, shares none of Augustine's anguish or Dante's hubris concerning the human desire to achieve a privileged *point d'appui* from which to view time's mysteries. Instead, Chaucer reminds us that, while grounded in the *hic et nunc* of the present, we are nevertheless empowered by quite advanced disciplines with which to measure the *minutiae* of time. These disciplines, although never fully in harmony with each other, embrace the five modes of assessing time outlined earlier—computistical, philosophical, mechanical, astrolabic, and kalendric. The human desires that our application of these disciplines may seek to satisfy are quite varied. As we have seen, the Host's calculations in the first *chronographia* on the pilgrimage are driven by his anxieties concerning the irrecoverable expenditure of time, and Chaucer's calculations at the end of the pilgrimage are informed by a human need to penetrate through time into the realm of eternity. In the last *chronographia* we examined, that of *The Nun's Priest's Tale,* it is the desire for a philosophical understanding of time that is most pronounced. This philosophical desire is foregrounded by Chaucer's careful use of formal logic, the liberal art that the later Middle Ages considered to be its most precise discipline for analyzing any phenomenon, be it theological, metaphysical, or physical. While the Nun's Priest's sophism invokes an extremely refined set of logical instruments for analyzing time, it also demonstrates how the thoughtful application of these instruments may nevertheless lead into uncertainty and confusion.

Chaucer's mixture of scientific professionalism, logical sophistication, and intellectual skepticism concerning our ability to understand time is unique in late medieval literature: there is simply nothing comparable to his technical *chronographiae* and the way they obliquely instantiate the epistemological fissures caused by the impact of the mechanical clock. Nonetheless, Chaucer's general perspective on the human parameters of "knowing" time is strikingly similar to the position advanced by one of the fourteenth century's greatest scientists, Nicole Oresme.[63] Oresme's magnum opus, *Tractatus de Commensurabilitate vel Incommensurabilitate Motuum Celi* (ca. 1351–62), examines an issue integral to the nature of time itself: the commensurability or incommensurability of the motions of celestial bodies. If the ratio between the motions of the celestial bodies is a rational number, Oresme explains, then the cosmos is controlled by a clear principle of order: as a consequence of this order, exact calendars and almanacs could be composed; future astronomical conjunctions could be confidently predicted; and the notion of the Great Year, in which all stars return to their original position, would be ratified. However, if the ratio between some of these celestial bodies is an irrational number, they are then incommensurable: in a cosmic system of even partial incommensurability, exact calendars and almanacs could not be composed; future astronomical conjunctions could not be predicted; and the Great Year would prove to have been a great myth. The first two books of the *Tractatus* constitute an extensive, highly technical, and fairly balanced defense of the potential validity of each of the opposing positions; the third book, which takes the unexpected form of an allegorical dream vision, is designed as a resolution to the debate. In this book, a dreamer-mathematician brings his concerns to Apollo, who, as "ruler of the Muses and Sciences," summons Arithmetic and Geometry to teach the dreamer what he wishes to know. But these two figures immediately start quarreling. Arithmetic, who espouses commensurability, argues that "[i]t seems unworthy and unreasonable that the divine mind should connect the celestial motions . . . in such a haphazard relationship."[64] Geometry, who champions incommensurability, finds a more beautiful pattern in a combination of regular and irregular ratios: "an harmonious union of them is more excellent than a separate [and independent] uniformity."[65] At the end of this unresolved disputation, Apollo feels "adequately informed"; the dreamer, however, finds himself "astonished and confounded." Although Apollo promises to provide the definitive answer once and for all, the dreamer reports what happens next:

"alas, the dream vanishes, the conclusion is left in doubt, and I am igno-
rant of what Apollo, the judge, has decreed on this matter."[66] On this note
of disappointment, the *Tractactus* come to an abrupt end.

Oresme's unsatisfactory ending is of course deliberate, for the entire *Tractatus* is premised upon Oresme's principled conviction that every
form of scientific inquiry is limited, imperfect, and subject to unavoidable
error. Even though his sympathies clearly lie on the side of incommensurability, Oresme repeatedly underscores the mere *probability* of each and
every thesis: in fact, he allows, "nothing prevents certain false propositions
from being more probable than certain true ones."[67] Thus, rather than
providing a definitive answer to its fundamental question, Oresme's *Tractatus*, as Steven Kruger notes, "focuses attention again and again on the
problem of attaining knowledge."[68] The frustrations built into the *Tractatus* eventually lead Oresme's confounded dreamer to cry out: "But, oh
immortal gods who know all things, why did you make the very nature
of men such that they desire to know, and then deceive or frustrate this
desire by concealing from us the most important truths?"[69] But Oresme
himself actually finds the existence of inscrutability cause for celebration
and hope: "it would be better that something should always be known
about [celestial revolutions], while, at the same time, something should
always remain unknown, so that it may be investigated further."[70]

Chaucer's strategies in his three *chronographiae*, I contend, are similar to Oresme's. Each *chronographia* encourages rigorous scientific inquiry, but each eventually throws into doubt the possibility of any veri-
fiably "truthful" conclusion.[71] Each requires the reader to integrate several
of the liberal arts (logic, astronomy, geometry, and arithmetic), while implying that the use of these liberal arts will not help us arrive at any form
of certitude. Each seems to promise the ardent scholar some kind of intellectual revelation at the very end, only to make that ending deeply disappointing. While Chaucer's stymied reader is quite justified in register-
ing various forms of frustration, it is clear that Chaucer's use of the *vis
confundendi* principle is meant to be enabling and instructive. The "wrong
answers" embedded in these *chronographiae* are designed neither to satirize intellectual inquiry nor to foster scientific paralysis. Precisely because
right and satisfactory solutions cannot be found to the problems of mensuration posed in the *chronographiae*—not only can they not be found,

they in all likelihood do not exist—when readers are confronted by these *insolubilia* they are forced to switch the focus of their attention to the very process of intellection itself. Certainly, a great deal of the reader's critical interrogations happens in the *process* of working through each calculation, as so many aspects of the ways we measure time are engaged, explored, and scrutinized. But just as much intellection may follow the completed investigation, when, having attained a certain level of knowledge, the reader is able to think more independently about our conceptualizations of time. What the *chronographia* in *The Nun's Priest's Tale* succeeds in doing is upping the ante by parodically foregrounding the linguistic, and especially the logical, dimensions of our scientific inquiries concerning time. Instructively, it also explicates the philosophical and scientific problems experienced in the scientific reading of his two other *chronographiae*. In the end, the most remarkable feature of all three *chronographiae* is, as forms of intellectual self-parody, they are essentially autodidactic exercises: in themselves they "say" little, because Chaucer grants the reader full freedom to fill in the interpretative spaces they make available. Ultimately, then, what we need to acknowledge about Chaucer's *chronographiae* is not that they fail to achieve closure but that they so brilliantly succeed in their open-endedness. This open-endedness is promising: one of these days we may indeed arrive at an adequate understanding of time, a matter about which none of us, as yet, is "depe ystert in loore."

SEVEN

The Parodistic Episteme: Learning to Behold the Fox

> *Dreams and beasts are two keys by which we*
> *are to find out the secrets of our own nature. All mystics*
> *use them. They are like comparative anatomy. They are test objects.*
>
> —RALPH WALDO EMERSON

Among the hundreds of scholarly books Rabelais lists as belonging to the mock-magnificent Parisian library of St. Victor is one *Quaestio subtilissima,* whose full title (in translation) is *A Most Subtle Question: whether the Chimera buzzing about in a vacuum can consume second intentions, it having been battered about for ten weeks at the Council of Constance.*[1] Rabelais' satire is aimed directly at the kinds of logical questions the later Middle Ages debated with uncommon energy and brilliance. For, although Rabelais' meaning of "battered about" was probably obscene, the debate posed by his most subtle question was a traditional one concerning the complex process of naming and describing—naming referents that exist in the world of things and ideas, naming referents that are words themselves (this is the meaning of "second intentions"), and naming referents that do not exist at all. "Chimera" was a staple medieval example of an

"empty name," a name referring to the purest figment of the poetic imagination; "vacuum" also is a name for nothing (can Nature abhor something that does not exist?), and so is the word "nothing" itself a name for
nothing, and therefore it seems, ironically, to mean something.[2] Rabelais'
Quaestio subtilissima is a learned satiric parody of those logico-linguistic
questions that philosophers have asked since the time of Aristotle's *On
Sophistical Refutations,* but Rabelais' scorn for such metalinguistic conundra was hardly shared by the intelligentsia of the fourteenth century, almost all of whom viewed the new terminist logic of Paris and Oxford as
the most exciting and far-reaching form of contemporary scholarly inquiry. Chaucer was no exception. Because of his own artistic interest in
the complexities of propositions as referential, nonreferential, and self-
referential structures, because of his careful reading of the popular logical treatises of his day (the majority of them generated by logicians at
Merton College), and because his well-educated readers were all thoroughly trained in the rules of logical deduction, Chaucer in his own poetry was able to explore with extraordinary subtlety numerous matters
obtaining to the way linguistic structures, fictional and otherwise, could
be understood to be significant or true.

Of course it is only on rare occasions that Chaucer actually casts logical and metapoetic issues such as these into the form of straightforward
propositions. However, quite unexpectedly, and at a moment of high
dramatic intensity, in *The Nun's Priest's Tale* he does precisely this. A few
seconds before Chauntecleer's good fortune goes bad, the narrator suddenly interrupts his narrative with a self-indulgent riff redolent with por-
tentous import:

> But sodeynly hym fil a sorweful cas,
> For evere the latter ende of joye is wo.
> God woot that worldly joye is soone ago;
> And if a rethor koude faire endite,
> He in a cronycle saufly myghte it write
> As for a sovereyn notabilitee.
> Now every wys man, lat him herkne me;
> This storie is also trewe, I undertake,
> As is the book of Launcelot de Lake,

That wommen holde in ful greet reverence.
Now wol I torne agayn to my sentence.
   A col-fox, ful of sly iniquitee . . .
                (VII.3204–15)

It is absolutely certain that Chaucer's educated readers would immediately have recognized the narrator's assertion concerning the truth-value of his own beast fable as belonging to that large category of propositions called *sophismata,* problematic sentences about which one can give plausible arguments both that they are true and that they are false. At Oxford and at Paris, disputations *de sophismatibus* were required of all undergraduates in order to test and improve their understanding of the more advanced forms of logical reasoning. Of the many different kinds of *sophismata,* it was *insolubilia* that were considered the most challenging and fascinating: these are the Cretan Liar paradoxes, so named in honor of St. Paul's account in his *Epistle to Titus* of the Cretan who swore that all Cretans always lied. More than any other kind of formal proposition, the *insolubilia* struck at the heart of logic itself, whose fundamental premise is that by incontrovertible rules any statement can be proved to be either true or false. The Liar Paradox is a profound threat to this premise. Let the sentence "What I am saying is false" be *a.* If *a* is true, then what it says must be so. But what it says is that *a* is false. Hence, if *a* is false, then it must not be the case that *a* is false—and so *a* has to be true, which would likewise be a self-contradiction.

Just about every medieval schoolman tried his hand at generating a variety of *insolubilia* and resolving them. Paul Vincent Spade lists over seventy extant medieval *insolubilia* treatises, many by anonymous and lesser-known philosophers, and many by the most famous, such as William of Ockham, Robert Grosseteste, Gregory of Rimini, Duns Scotus, Bonaventure, William of Sherwood, John Buridan, and Paul of Venice.[3] But it was a clutch of influential logicians, almost all of whom were fellows at Oxford in the fourteenth century, who made the *insolubilium* the most popular form of logico-linguistic puzzle in Chaucer's age. Among these were Robert Holcot, Roger Nottingham, Robert Fland, Richard Lavenham, Richard Swineshead, Thomas Bradwardine, Ralph Strode, John Wyclif, Richard of Campsall, Walter Burleigh, and William Heytesbury, whose *Regulae solvendi sophismata* was probably the single most influential specimen of medieval *insolubilia*-literature. Catch a fourteenth-century clerk in a meditative moment, in other words, and even Harry Bailly knows he is likely to be studying "som sophyme" (IV.5).

The possible solutions to these self-referential puzzles were as limited in number then as they are now: essentially, (1) they could be declared to be not genuine propositions at all; (2) they could be declared not to be really self-referential; (3) they could be determined not to be true or false but to possess some third truth-value distinct from truth and falsity (an early modal position); (4) some or all of them could be determined to be true; (5) some or all of them could be determined to be false; (6) they could be determined to have no truth-value at all.[4] For the purposes of resolving the Nun's Priest's *insolubilium,* what needs to be emphasized here is that it wasn't so much the solution itself but rather the rightness and tightness of logical argument that was understood to be the center of logical scrutiny. As one instructive example I cite John Buridan, Chaucer's brilliant contemporary, who in his *Sophismata* opens the eighth sophism (*What Plato is saying is false*) with a *précis* of his forthcoming argument:

> Let us posit a case in which Socrates says, "What Plato is saying is false," and nothing else, and Plato on the other hand says, "What Socrates is saying is false," and nothing else. Then the question is whether Socrates' proposition (which is the sophism itself) is true or false.[5]

After propounding arguments attempting to prove that the sophism is true, Buridan then outlines the arguments for the opposite view (the view he subscribes to) that the sophism is false:

> My [argument,] in brief, is that Socrates' proposition is false, not true. The argument for this has the following form: (a) Any proposition that in conjunction with something true entails something false, is itself false; (b) Socrates' proposition, in conjunction with something true, does entail something false; therefore (c) Socrates' proposition is false. Now (a) is an infallible rule; and (b) can

be proved as follows: The case we are discussing is a possible one, so let us assume that what we posited is in fact true. Now we can show that the posited case and Socrates' proposition taken together entail both (d) that Socrates' proposition is true, and also (e) that it is false. Since the conjunction of (d) and (e) is false (indeed impossible), this will establish (b). Hence all that remains is to show how Socrates' proposition and the case do not entail both (d) and (e). They entail (d) because the case posits that Socrates' proposition exists and, as we said earlier on, every proposition, together with the hypothesis that it exists, entails that it itself is true. They also clearly entail (e) by the argument given above, namely that if Socrates' proposition were true then Plato's would have to be true too, and this entails that Socrates' is false. It should be noted that by just the same reasoning Plato's proposition also turns out to be false.[6]

After this compressed preview, Buridan goes on to provide his full analysis—the sort of extensive *pro et contra disputatio* that university students were expected to emulate. Now as with my brief introductions in chapters 2 and 6 to medieval *syncategoremata* studies, the purpose of this brief introduction to *insolubilia* studies is to suggest how Chaucer's educated readers would have been deeply familiar with the methodologies and major issues of fourteenth-century sophismatic analysis. And while Chaucer surely is not expecting his beast fable to be read as if it were nothing but a series of air-tight logical propositions, he certainly expected a logical expertise would be brought to bear on passages that enjoy an unusually philosophical cast.

In the context of these expectations, let us now return to the Nun's Priest's *insolubilium:*

> This storie is also trewe, I undertake,
> As is the book of Launcelot de Lake,
> That wommen holde in ful greet reverence.

Is there any way the truth-value of this seemingly straightforward assertion can be determined? From the outset we need to appreciate that this is a fairly messy sophism, in part because it does not enjoy the clean framing devices of a philosophical text where only one or two utterances exist at a time. Be that as it may, we should first ask if these self-referential words are referring exclusively to themselves (an instance of second-intention material supposition) or if perhaps they are referring exclusively to certain past or future words? To put it another way, is the narrator's proposition propounded inside or outside his "storie"? The Nun's Priest, as we have already noted, has a disconcerting habit of saying "Now wol I turne to my tale agayn" (VII.3314), which invites one to ask where the narrator has been if not inside his own "storie." Is Chaucer possibly suggesting here that only when self-referential words such as "I" or proximal deictics such as "this" do *not* appear in one of his locutions that the narrator is actually "inside" the tale? Another matter of logical/literary ambiguity is that this sophism is also an enthymeme: it does not quite mind its formal Ps and Qs because its argument depends upon at least one suppressed premise. Suppressed premises are of course allowed in true enthymemes, but only if the truth of the premise is "obvious" and agreed upon.

The most "obvious" suppressed premise here is that *Lancelot de Lake* is patently untrue. This premise, which appears to be acceptable to modern readers without much demurral, was also accepted as a valid premise in the Middle Ages; at any rate, such was the considered opinion of Hugh of Rutland, who in the twelfth century wrote that Walter Map, the presumed author of the prose *Lancelot,* well "understands the art of lying."[7] Therefore, unless the Nun's Priest is possibly being "ironic," he appears to be making the following truth-claims: (1) the prose romance of *Lancelot* is untrue; and consequently (2) his own "storie" is also untrue. In addition, the narrator is also apparently asserting or assuming: (3) women are or tend to be naïve and credulous; and (4) some women are so credulous they would believe this beast fable to be as true as they believe the *Lancelot de Lake* is true—although this may be a fanciful extrapolation of the meaning of "ful greet reverence." Finally, and also importantly, the Nun's Priest may well expect his readers to note that (5) the above assertions and assumptions are all modified by his statement of *conditional* belief, "I undertake," where this subjectivized asseveration may have the effect of bracketing all his other declaratives inside the box of what medi-

eval logicians called a "mental proposition." According to Gabriel Nuchelmans, the "most controversial question of the medieval semantics of
propositions" is how mental propositions—that is, propositions involving "judging, assenting, dissenting, believing, and knowing"—differ or do
not differ in their truth value from simple declarative sentences.[8] Therefore "I undertake," at least in a strictly logical reading, might well com-
promise the truth value of all the other propositions and assumptions in
this one complex sentence. What then is one to make so far of this collocation of one assertion, at least two suppressed premises, and one mental proposition: are some or all of them true or false, and why?

Obviously it takes an enormous amount of credulity to believe that
Chaucer's beast fable is literally, referentially, or empirically "true." Priscian, as we have noted, in his refutation and confirmation exercises asserts that "those things which are unchallenged need no rebuttal or no
substantiation: such are the fables of Aesop or obviously false history."[9]
It therefore may be that the one truth the Nun's Priest is unequivocally
asserting is that his own beast fable is "untrue." But if that is the case, his
would be an exceedingly trivial proposition. "Think I none so simple
would say that *Esope* lyed in the tales of his beasts," declared Sir Philip
Sidney in *Apology for Poetry*, "for who thinks that *Esope* writ it for actually true were well worthy to haue his name cronicled among the beastes
hee writeth of."[10] For as Sidney notes, no poet should be accused of lying
(Plato notwithstanding) for the poet "nothing affirmes, and therefore
neuer lyeth."[11] In logical language, what this means is that fictional propositions are rather like formal propositions: they do not claim to be empirically veridical, to be describing the world as it is, but rather to be true
or false only insofar as they conform to their own formal and discursive
categories—the rules of logic and fiction respectively—where language
is not judged for its denotative rightness but preeminently for the va-
lidities of its signifying sense. So, then, one might possibly argue that
both *The Nun's Priest's Tale* and the *Lancelot de Lake* are both *significantly*
true, and as a consequence both might deserve to be held in "ful greet
reverence."

Indeed the most crucial element in these three lines may be contained
in another suppressed premise, this one involving the presumed credulity of women—even though it is impossible to know if by "wommen"

Chaucer means "all women," "some women," or "only women," since the level of supposition of "wommen" is semantically indeterminate. Even so, should it not be emphasized that Chaucer knew of one famous woman who held the *Lancelot* in full great reverence? She of course was Francesca of Rimini in Dante's *Inferno* 5, who read the *Lancelot* in the passionate company of her brother-in-law Paolo; at the moment Lancelot kisses Guinevere the two readers do so likewise, and begin their celebrated and short-lived adulterous affair. This story is told directly to Dante in the *Commedia* by Francesca herself, who calls the guilty book and its author by the name of one of its fictional characters, Lancelot's go-between: "A Gallehault was the book and he who wrote it; that day we read no farther in it."[12]

Since one of the issues debated by medieval schoolmen was "ampliation"—whether propositions are true only in the present, or true in the past and future as well—it could be argued that in the *Commedia* the prose *Lancelot* garners referential truth in the future as reality faithfully imitates literature and life verifies art: Francesca proves to be Guinevere and Paolo proves to be Lancelot. Thus, through an extended series of interlinking quasi-equations, Chaucer's story of Chauntecleer might be as true, or as false, as the story of Paolo and Francesca. But within a certain scholastic context is it not also appropriate to ask how "true" in fact their story is? Dante famously invites us to believe that his *Commedia* is the truth absolute: "The fiction of the *Divine Comedy*," Charles Singleton has emphasized, "is that it is not fiction. . . . [N]o work ever guarded that fundamental hypothesis more carefully."[13] But even if we were to demur, shouldn't we accept the historical actuality of Paolo and Francesca as a true narrative even if it was recorded inside an imaginative fiction?

In his early commentary on the *Commedia*, Boccaccio confirms the historicity of Paolo and Francesca's affair, chronicling a full account of what he knows actually happened. However, he allows he does not know how the love story *began* except for what Dante reveals in *Inferno* 5: "How she managed to get together with Paolo, one never hears tell, unless it really was as Dante writes. . . . But I believe rather that it was a fiction constructed in accord with what might possibly have happened, for I don't believe the author knew that it happened in this way."[14] If Boccaccio is right, then the truth tables shift in valence once again, and everything but Boccaccio's assertions may be rendered false: Chaucer's beast fable is fictional, the *Lancelot* is fictional, and Dante's account of the coming-together of Paolo and Francesca is likewise fictional. Disconcertingly, we seem well on our way into an epistemological *mise en abîme*, so it may be reassuring to discover Wesley Trimpi in *Muses of One Mind* declaring that their contemporary readers would have understood Boccaccio's and Dante's accounts to be equally but differently true: Boccaccio's truth is "historical," "external," and "quantitative"; Dante's truth is "ethical," "internal," and "qualitative."[15] But, turning to another part of Trimpi's study, we also learn, from Aristotle to John of Salisbury and beyond, that there was believed to subsist between history and fable an intermediate form of narrative called *argumentum,* a fictional rendering that has such a probable likeness to truth that it is much more "true" than crude historical fact.[16] Thus, the truth-table equations may flip once again: since Dante's verisimilar account may be "truer" than what might actually have happened, it follows with a certain degree of logical rigor that the *argumentum* of the Nun's Priest's beast fable is likewise "true."

What then are truth and fiction, what is truth-in-fiction, and how might they all be prized apart? After persuasively demonstrating that there is nothing intrinsic in words and in literary works that allows us to make any absolute distinction between "fact" and "fiction," Darrel Mansell in his study "Unsettling the Colonel's Hash: 'Fact' in Autobiography" nevertheless concedes that there is no other way in which the human mind can apprehend texts but to declare for one side or the other, truth or falsehood.[17] In "Feigning in Fiction," an essay read to the New Chaucer Society in 1984, Wolfgang Iser attempted to displace the false/true dualism with a triad: the real, the fictional, and the imaginary. The fictional, he writes, "might be called a 'transitional object,' always hovering between the real and the imaginary, linking the two together," although it does not itself exit.[18] Iser's "fictional," it appears, is itself a fictional category—or so it would seem in the eyes of any logical skeptic. Finally, and most instructively, the Bellman in Lewis Carroll's "The Hunting of the Snark" decides to settle all such matters concerning the true and the false by declaring simply: "I have said it thrice: / What I tell you three times is true."[19]

So where then does Chaucer stand inside this confusion of *pro et contra* truth tables, this metapoetic hall of mirrors? Or, more appropriately, where does he expect his readers to stand? Because of their extensive training in logic, Chaucer's educated contemporaries were well positioned to process this *insolubilium* with deft precision, entertaining a philosophical interplay among combinations of three or four or five true or false propositions in a sequence of hypotheses somewhat similar to the procedure employed by Buridan, the master of fourteenth-century *insolubilia* studies. While we modern readers would never expect ourselves to interrogate the Nun's Priest's *insolubilium* with similar philosophical rigor (my own analysis has been quite undisciplined), whenever we read a work of literature and especially whenever we teach a work of literature we are knowingly impacted—Rabelais might have said "battered about"—by an internal contestation among various valences of "fiction" and "truth." In the fourteenth century, *trowthe* was a "difficult word" of "enormous importance," as Richard Firth Green illustrates in *A Crisis of Truth*, its ever-shifting semantic field including a host of legal senses, ethical senses, theological senses, and intellectual senses.[20] As a work of fiction, an *ars poetica*, and a many-layered form of literary parody, *The Nun's Priest's Tale* is continually posing questions about the ontology of its own truth— be that truth intellectual, ethical, or even theological. "What is true and what is false in this tale of a 'cok,' his hen, and a fox," writes John M. Hill with considerable understatement in *Chaucerian Belief,* "has vexed Chaucerians for some time."[21] Yet rather than providing adequate answers to these vexing questions, as we have seen, Chaucer's fable instead simply advertises itself as an *insolubilium* writ large—a self-referential parody instantiating a series of paradoxes and focusing especially on the thoughts of its own inscribed reader who is invited, indeed challenged, to rearticulate and refine his or her own understanding of the meanings of truth-in-fiction.

In *Parody//Meta-Fiction,* Margaret A. Rose defines parody as a reflexive form of metafiction, a genre that sets up "'mirrors' to the processes of writing which tell us much about the aims and character of fiction, while also challenging the ability of art to 'mirror' the outer world."[22] Not only is the "mythos of realistic representation" parodied in literary parody, but so, typically, is the "naïve reader":

The naïve reader who, like Don Quixote, takes the fictional world to be "true" . . . has been seen to be the target of parody in meta-fictional works such as *Don Quixote* and *Tristram Shandy*. And such reader-satire may also reflect the author's fears of being mis-understood. But the parodist's foregrounding of the "mysterious" ability of literary statements to both evoke and suspend belief in their truth, in the parodistic juxtaposition of different perspec-tives, may also be seen as both an attempt to educate his reader to a more critical understanding of the workings of the literary text and an ironic game with the mysteries of fiction as such, which has as its aim not the total demystification of its secrets, but their refunctioning and renewal.[23]

Thus when the Nun's Priest chooses to assert inside his beast fable that his own "storie" is as true as some other work of fiction, he is equivalent to Cervantes who inside his novel *Don Quixote* criticizes another work of fiction because in no way is it believable. Both parodists enjoy the self-reflexive art of Cretan lying; both take pleasure indulging in what Rose calls a "Poetics of Contradiction" whereby "the illusion of reality given in fiction is used to analyse the peculiarities of the fictional world itself"; and both are intent on remystifying the mysteries of their art.[24] Thus Chaucer's "This storie is also trewe" is not only a literary-logical *insolu-bilium*, it is, I wish to emphasize, a metapoetic keystone to the parodic *argumentum* of the entirety of Chaucer's *ars poetica*. Or, to employ our theoretical terms more carefully, "This storie is also true" serves as the *Tale's parapoetic* keystone. In his examination of the Liar paradox, Michel Foucault proves to be one of many twentieth-century theorists who in-sist on deconstructing our access to any kind of "meta"-language. Not only is "I lie" a paradox, Foucault writes, but so is "I speak," because the language of any speaker's speaking cannot also serve as its own discur-sive referent. The language of the Liar paradox is thus like all language, postmodernists will argue: it is incapable of verifying its own truthful-ness because it cannot achieve a level of meta-discourse (for none ex-ists), and thus it may actually give the lie to the idea of Truth itself. *The Nun's Priest's Tale* may or may not give the lie to the idea of Truth, but that all the *Tale's* propositions are equally true and that all of them are equally false appear to be two equally logical and equally defensible assertions. Thus, once again, Chaucer is not expecting his readers to arrive at any ultimately "right answer" as a way of resolving these paradoxes. Instead, and in concert with his fable's other "scholarly" assignments, he here encourages his readers to refine their understanding of the parapoetic problems and enthymematic assumptions contained in their own evaluation of the veridical registers of Chaucer's fiction.

Rose's invocation of the "naïve reader" is obviously a shorthand way of foregrounding the role of the constructed reader in the heuristic stratagems of literary parody. In response to the Nun's Priest's continuously coy engagement with his own reader, I have alluded intermittently in this study to the central importance of Chaucer's inscribed reader in my analysis of Chaucer's parodic strategies. But in this chapter I intend to zero in on Chaucer's inscribed reader by tracing the interior workings of that reader's mind. One way of scrutinizing this mind's activities is by tracing the interplay between that reader's critical intelligence and the critical intelligence of the most ardent reader inside Chaucer's tale: Chauntecleer. By counterpointing a rooster's decoding powers, evidenced in his interpreting the text of his own dream, and a reader's decoding powers, interpreting the meaning of this dream inside and outside the fable's fictional frame, Chaucer plays off our epistemic faculties (those mental gifts with which we "read" the world) and our literary-critical faculties (with which we read imaginative fictions). To provide a fairly disciplined critical vocabulary with which to study the mental maneuvers of these two readers I will turn again to philosophy, this time to various sites of the mind as detailed in medieval faculty psychology. What steps does the reader's mind go through as it attempts to apprehend and then comprehend the image of a heretofore unknown and unnamed thing? Similarly, what steps does the reader's mind go through as it attempts to decode and then interpret the significance of an intensely expressive and yet apparently meaningless oral locution? In honor of the naïve reader's fairly close kinship with Chaucer's male hero, I will occasionally refer to the inscribed reader as "him"—but my intent is by no means to cast aspersions on the male gender. In this reader's occasional moments of critical naiveté we should discern a gently instructive parody of our own critical faculties when they are less than perfectly engaged. Because one of Chaucer's two inscribed readers is a rooster, I will also take into account his species by considering the intellectual and linguistic powers enjoyed by animals as these powers were understood in the late Middle Ages. Yet because Chaucer's primary inscribed reader is a parodic version of ourselves, my primary critical focus will be centered on certain operations of the human psyche. While tracing these operations, the core question posed at the outset of this chapter—we might call it this study's *Quaestio subtilissima*—remains as urgent as ever: from a congeries of self-reflexive paradoxes wherein every fiction appears to deconstruct every truth, is it ever possible to extrapolate an adequate form of meaning and some practice of living?

BEHOLDING THE FOX: "HEIGH YMAGINACIOUN" AND DREAM HERMENEUTICS

The first indication that Chauntecleer's dream is some kind of epistemological and literary-critical IQ quiz is its graphic realism. In Chaucer's closest source, *Le Roman de Renart, Branch II,* Chanteclere's dream is a nifty little puzzle. An animal appears wearing a red pelisse with a bone collar, which he forces over the dreamer's back. The neck of the coat proves to be painfully narrow, and the cock awakens fearful and trembling. Chanteclere's wife, Pinte, interprets the dream, and the reader follows with self-assured, even prescient, approval. The beast, she explains, is a fox (in fact, we are certain it is *the* fox lurking in the garden who has already been seen by husband, wife, writer, and reader). The red pelisse is the fox's sleek body; the collar is his mouth; the bone, his teeth. Over-determining the dream-text a bit, Pinte confidently predicts that before noon the fox will have the cock's head in his teeth. Chanteclere, however, despite the overwhelming evidence of the dream's proleptic significance, arrogantly rejects his wife's interpretation as foolish: "What's clear, Pinte, is you're out of your mind! . . . / Nothing you've said gives me concern."[25] Accordingly, Pinte, poet, and reader all watch Chanteclere's rejection of his wife's advice with an equal sense of knowing superiority.

In *The Nun's Priest's Tale*, Chauntecleer has a dream that is quite similar to Chanteclere's:

> "Now God," quod he, "my swevene recche aright,
> And kepe my body out of foul prisoun!
> Me mette how that I romed up and doun
> Withinne our yeerd, wheer as I saugh a beest
> Was lyk an hound, and wolde han maad areest
> Upon my body, and wolde han had me deed.
> His colour was bitwixe yelow and reed,
> And tipped was his tayl and bothe his eeris
> With black, unlyk the remenant of his heeris;
> His snowte smal, with glowynge eyen tweye.
> Yet of his look for feere almoost I deye;
> This caused me my gronyng, doutelees."
>   (VII.2896–2907)

Much of what we are given in Chauntecleer's recounting of his dream is an exacting description of the image itself, a series of what medieval philosophers of the mind called *phantasmata,* or *sensibilia.* With graphic clarity, we see the animal's color "bitwixe yelow and reed." We see the black tips of his ears, the black tip of his tail. We see his small snout and his glowing eyes. Surrounding the details of the empirical image is the dreamer's interpretation of the creature's intent. Although the creature remains motionless, the dreamer is able to infer that he "wolde han maad areest / Upon my body," and he "wolde han had me deed." Chauntecleer makes one more gesture toward interpretative understanding, moving from the particular image in the direction of its nominal form: he was a beast "lyk an hound." But he gets no further.

After this dream-report, there follow 250 lines (almost two-fifths of the entire fable) of extensive debate and dream exegesis, as Pertelote and Chauntecleer try to decipher the cryptic sign at the core of the rooster's dream. Pertelote is a naturalist who believes that dreams are only somapsychotically meaningful: the hound-like image in her judgment is nothing but a physiological symptom, its red and black colors importing her husband's melancholic-choleric imbalance, a humorous ailment urgently in need of a cure which she then prescribes—a potent series of vomits and laxatives. Chauntecleer, perhaps because he went to university, thinks that the art of interpretation needs to be much more lofty and learned. Accordingly, he turns to the *auctoritees,* retelling, interpreting, and not interpreting a variety of prophetic dreams found in "olde bokes." And like a good scholar, he gets so involved in the pages he is feathering through that he comes close to losing track of the issue at hand.

Chauntecleer's representations of his authoritative texts are scarcely the most scintillating narratives inside the entirety of *The Nun's Priest's Tale.* And that, surely, is part of their point. The first narrative (seventy-eight lines long) involves two pilgrims, one of whom appears three times in the other's dream, predicting that he himself will be killed that night and then hidden in a dung cart; the next day the dreamer sees the cart, the body is discovered, and the murderer is apprehended and hanged. The second narration is much shorter (thirty-seven lines): two companions are ready to set sail, one dreams their ship will sink, the other takes no account, he boards the ship, the ship founders and the skeptic drowns. The third (ten lines) is an anecdote about seven-year-old Saint Kenelm, whose bad dream his nurse is able to sense is predictive of his future murder. The fourth (four lines) alludes briefly to Macrobius's account of the dream of Scipio. The fifth (three lines) references Daniel, the sixth (three lines) references Joseph, the seventh (five lines) references Pharaoh, the eighth (three lines) references Croesus, and the ninth narrative (eight lines) briefly recounts Andromache's prophetic dream of Hector's death.

Throughout this protracted and one-sided disputation on the meaning of dreams the reader smugly sits. This is remarkably different from Chaucer's four dream-vision poems, with their errant meanderings through the liminal worlds of sleep and books and waking and life and gardens and love and death. Here there is no dreamer-inside-his-dream only a little more confused than the reader as to what the meaning of his dream-experience is. And here there is no authority figure to be partially trusted, like Nature in *The Parliament of Foules,* or the Black Knight in *The Book of the Duchess,* or the Eagle in *The House of Fame,* or the God of Love in the Prologue to *The Legend of Good Women.* Rather, it is the reader who is invited to assume the role of the "man of gret auctorite" (*HF* 2158), who looks down upon Chauntecleer's dream and says: "I know what it means; it's a fox, don't you see?" The reader is so confident that he also finds himself predicting the literary future. The fox will come, very soon. Upon waking from his dream, Chauntecleer had prayerfully whimpered, "Now God ... my swevene recche aright." Now it is the reader who assumes this privileged role, as his uncanny prescience renders him a self-assured prophet of future literary events.

One reason that the reader is so cocky in his interpretation of the dream is that he has one thing that the bird-brained protagonists of the tale lack: *experience.* It is both fortunate and unfortunate that Chauntecleer and Pertelote have never yet seen a fox (Russell does not appear until much later in the fable), so there is no way they can extrapolate a nominal form from the dream's phenomenal image. The reader parts company with his fine-feathered cousins at this point, because he is privileged to have had such an experience. Another reason that the reader so smugly sits is that he knows this animal's *name,* and knowing names, as Adam learned in paradise, is a way of knowing and controlling the world. Thus Chaucer's decision to deprive both his hero and his heroine of any prior experience of their archenemy, and of any knowledge of their archenemy's name, has potentially radical implications. Of course one question this radical decision brings to the fore is whether language, literary and otherwise, brings us knowledge of the world. It also brings to the fore two corollary questions: is our knowledge of the world merely confirmed by language, or does language—and the naming powers of fiction—actually enhance and deepen our understanding of reality? In short, Chaucer's decision to deprive his protagonists of a crucial *nomen* is a way of asking some of the most fundamental questions concerning the signifying functions of art: What does poetry tell us about the real world? Are we able to learn anything from literature? Does poetry make anything happen? Although, like the other parapoetic questions posed in *The Nun's Priest's Tale,* these too may be left entirely open-ended, I intend to take them on as a penultimate exercise in our critical reading of Chaucer's *ars poetica.*

Since the first mode of understanding addressed in Chaucer's IQ quiz is epistemology itself, we need briefly to review how the mind was generally understood to interiorize images emanating from the world. From Aristotle to Aquinas, the standard medieval vision of the brain is as follows. The first ventricle of the brain is the cell of the Imagination, where separate sensations, or images, are received and then combined by the Common Senses (*sensus communis*); in league with these senses, Imagination, or Fantasy, forms the mental images necessary for thought. The images produced in the first cell are then handed over to the powers located in the central cavity, the cell *rationalis,* wherein resides the *vis cogitativa;* here images by a complex process are transformed by Reason into ideas. The third and backmost cell, which is linked both to Reason and Imagination, is the *vis memorativa,* the storehouse of these images and ideas. Both Reason and Imagination call up images and ideas from Memory in order to judge new images gathered in by the common senses. To this basic tripartite model of the inward wits medieval philosophers added their own refinements. One of the most important was what Albertus Magnus called *aestimativa,* or the power of Opinion, which is able to discover the *intentiones* implicit in the image but not apparent to the common senses. The standard example, used by Albertus, Avicenna, Aquinas, and others, is the sheep who immediately recognizes its offspring as its own and who, upon seeing a wolf, instantly recognizes its murderous intent.[26] Chauntecleer, in his apprehension of his dreamimage, moves naturally, and quite predictably, from the common senses through imagination into the aestimative powers.

Now, one of the distinctive features of the fox-image presented in *The Nun's Priest's Tale* is that it was recorded in a dream; this dream is then recorded in Chaucer's fable via Chauntecleer's verbal description of the dream; and this verbal description is then recorded as images in the mind of the reader. Dreams are different from waking images—all dream psychologists of the Middle Ages noted—in that no immediate reality is prompting the images; rather, like poetic images, they are products of the imagination. What caused the imagination to create such images may have been some kind of past experience (Pertelote sensibly interprets the dream this way as a *somnium naturale*);[27] it may be some mysterious power in the dreamer's soul; it may be some spiritual power, divine or diabolical; it may be something unknown and unknowable. Most dreams, Macrobius and others warn, have no meaning; those that do are often highly enigmatic. But some dreams, history has shown, are apparently prophetic, although many authorities, like John of Salisbury, remained highly skeptical.[28]

The main reason the reader has no doubts this dream is a prophetic dream is that it is a *literary* dream. Real dreams, he knows, are weird images figured forth from the imagination, usually with no known cause and no readily discernible meaning. But literary dreams, especially when they are dreamt by major characters, are *always* significant. Has anyone read a dream in epic, tragedy, or romance that doesn't, somehow, come true? The reader first recognizes the image of the fox by relying upon his *experience,* stored in his cell of memory. But now he shifts to another category of memory, which Chaucer chooses to call *remembraunce,* the key to which is "olde bokes."[29] The reader's reaction is predictable: since in literature all dreams are meaningful, that is precisely the kind of dream we are asked to interpret here. But one of the major dramatic ironies of *The Nun's Priest's Tale* is that Chauntecleer, who reads his own dream as if it were a typical dream of literature, the *somnium coeleste,* isn't himself aware that he is actually living inside a piece of literature whose interpretative key is to be found only in life, in the *experience* of the reader. This would be a cruel dramatic irony if it were not for another irony. Although Chauntecleer is an imaginative literary hybrid, *gallus sapiens,* we eventually learn he really needn't worry overmuch about his dream's portents because the chicken part of himself will react naturally, and appropriately, as soon as he sees this hound-like animal in the flesh. Thomas Aquinas explains, as he discriminates between the aestimative powers of animals and of humans:

> For a sheep, seeing the wolf, judges it a thing to be shunned, from a natural, and not a free judgment, because it judges, not from reason, but from natural instinct.... But man acts from judgment, because by his apprehensive power he judges that something should be avoided or sought. But because this judgment, in the case of some particular act, is not from a natural instinct, but from some act of comparison in the reason, therefore he acts from free judgment and retains the power of being inclined to various things.[30]

It is precisely this animal aestimative power that Chaucer describes in Chauntecleer's first, instinctive, and totally *natural* reaction to the sight of the fox:

Nothyng ne liste hym thanne for to crowe,
But cride anon, "Cok! Cok!" and up he sterte
As man that was affrayed in his herte.
For natureelly a beest desireth flee
Fro his contrarie, if he may it see,
Though he never erst hadde seyn it with his ye.
(VII.3276–81)

Apparently, there was nothing Chauntecleer needed to have learned from his dream, or *could* have learned from his dream, that his Imagination and his aestimative powers would not at the appropriate moment immediately supply him with. This certainly seems to undercut that coterie of ethical allegorists, the Nun's Priest's parodic *persona* included, who have been very certain what course of action Chauntecleer should have followed this fateful day in order to avoid its tragic outcome. Stay on the beams, they preach; hunker in the henhouse. No sunshine; no food; no water; no singing; no loving; no looking after one's sisters, one's wives; no calling of humankind to their appointed labors; no *joie;* no *vivre.*[31] If the reader belatedly discovers that Chauntecleer might well have been advised *not* to take the reader's conservative advice based upon his "literary" interpretation of the dream-image, what should the reader now make of the meaning of this dream? A major amount of his energy should take place, I think Chaucer implies, in the center of his brain, where Reason abstracts images into ideas and, insofar as possible, even higher in the central ventricle, where Intellect contemplates universals. But before we get involved in the Intellect, the last and most abstract step in the epistemological process, we need to turn briefly to that most uncanny psychological faculty, the apparent ability of our imagination to "know" future events. The narrator seems to go out of his way, at the very moment the fox finally appears, to praise something in the text for its prescient powers:

A col-fox, ful of sly iniquitee,
That in the grove hadde woned yeres three,
By heigh ymaginacioun forncast,
The same nyght thurghout the hegges brast

Into the yerd ther Chauntecleer the faire
Was wont, and eek his wyves, to repaire . . .
                    (VII.3215–20)

That seemingly significant phrase, "By heigh ymaginacioun forncast,"
is—unsurprisingly—highly enigmatic. First, in a tale whose very title
raises questions about possessives, one has to ask to whom this free-
floating faculty belongs. The standard, but not quite universal, gloss assumes that it belongs to God, whose divine foreknowledge has forecast
this event.[32] This is highly doubtful, not only because imagination is a
human faculty that God's intellect absolutely transcends, but also because "forncast," the *Middle English Dictionary* reveals, is a rather sinis-
ter word normally associated with treasonous plots. While God is not a
dark schemer, the fox is, and for this reason two studies have chosen to attribute "heigh ymaginacioun" to him.[33] But what precisely *is* high imagination, and how did Chaucer perceive its powers to differ from those of
"low imagination"? Because the term occurs only once in Middle English
(here), we should consider what has been traditionally presumed to be
Chaucer's source—Dante's *alta fantasia,* as it appears in *Purgatorio* 17
and *Paradiso* 33.[34]

For Dante, *alta fantasia* is the human imagination working at its
most exalted level, as poetry borders on mystical vision. In the *Purgatorio,* through a dream, Dante's *alta fantasia* is able, suddenly and entirely
passively, to receive an image directly from heaven; in the *Paradiso,* however, the *alta fantasia* fails to conjure up an image through which it might
apprehend the mind of God. To return to *The Nun's Priest's Tale,* it would
seem less than fully appropriate to assign this poetic-mystical faculty to
anyone connected with the fable: Chauntecleer, the fox, the Nun's Priest,
Chaucer, God, or the reader. Unless, of course, its use is somehow ironic,
and we are involved in a subtle parody of a certain kind of predetermined
pattern of reading wherein our "heigh ymaginacioun" gets ensnared in a
dark plot of its own devising. If so, we should consider parting company
from that school of critics who blithely write of the *Tale,* "Everything happens just as Chauntecleer saw it in his dream."[35]

Having begun to develop a keener eye for the difficulties of decoding the phenomenal/oneiric/literary image, we must ask if the dream

ever predicted *when* the fox would arrive. (To a timekeeper as accurate as Chauntecleer, "the near future" is a terribly imprecise category.) Did this dream ever predict that *this* fox would arrive? (This fox is named Russell, a rather unusual name for a fox; apparently Reynard and his ilk are loping through other fictions today.) Did this dream predict that the fox would speak English, that he would cite Nigellus Wirecker, that he would have read Boethius's *De musica*? Above all, did this dire dream predict that everything would end happily, that Chauntecleer would escape, and that life, at least for today, would prove to be a sobering but scarcely catastrophic tragicomedy? At its highest, "heigh ymaginacioun" would seem capable of descrying only the most general kinds of truth. It is not very high after all.

It may be best, then, to return from high imagination to the central cavity of reason. In that cavity has been held our aestimation of the phantasmatic image which, relying upon experience, we have determined to call a fox. But in every medieval epistemology, there are additional steps to be made within the realm of reason before that external reality is fully known. What rests in our mind at the moment are merely the accidents of that material thing we have perceived. To understand its immanent form, to grasp the species in the particular, and to contemplate the spiritually intelligible meaning evoked by the material phenomenon, medieval philosophers from Avicenna to Aquinas called upon the *intellectus agens,* the supreme power of human understanding, which, although imperfect in man, is nevertheless that faculty he shares with God. The Agent Intellect is connatural to the human soul and is that power that enables the soul to transpose to a spiritual level the physical thing made immanent by the various sensory powers.[36] As literary reader and literary fox confront each other face to face, they are apprehending in their phantasmatic particulars and their singular accidents the materials necessary for a pilgrimage up the *via ascensus,* a ladder of translation that ends contemplating the quiddity and essence of immanent forms.

Yet a realist epistemological model such as this seems much more appropriate to Dante's poetics than to Chaucer's. Chaucer, as we have seen on several occasions, resists invoking any program of cognition that would immediately wrest readers away from material particulars into higher-order modes of interpretation. For Chaucer, literature is so disseminally resistant to such extrapolation that as a linguistic artifact it may well border on the uninterpretable. In fact, via ironic inversion, this salutary resistance appears to be one of the several parodic purposes of the nine illustrative texts that Chauntecleer reiterates. If the point of each narrative is to prove that dreams come true, in other words, what is the point of there being so many? What is the point of their being so differently designed? And what is the point of this extruded catalogue withering on the vine, getting more artless and exhausted the further it is strung out? The only things that makes these nine narratives fascinating as literature is their limited success as literature. Even though each manages to make the very same didactic "point," they are scarcely the stuff that will transport us toward self-knowledge, Canterbury, or the New Jerusalem—unless, inside their local literary context, we are invited to read them parodically.

In fact, if I may widen the lens for a moment, I would assert that the entirety of Fragment VII—variously called the "literature" fragment, the "language" fragment, or the "surprise" fragment—is Chaucer's parodic fragment *par excellence,* the fragment whose major commitment is to exploring the art of artistic unsuccess. At the height of his career Chaucer evidently lost interest in merely writing one masterpiece after another. Instead, he chose to construct a sequence of imperfect tales, each articulating a blinkered vision of literature's relation to the world, each leaving something most deeply to be desired by the reader. Thus, in Fragment VII *The Shipman's Tale* succeeds after a fashion—but only as a mirthless fabliau. The pieties of *The Prioress's Tale* teeter on the cusp of self-parody. *The Tale of Sir Thopas* trips over its own eagerness to provide *solaas.* The *Melibee* submerges itself under a compulsive need to provide undiluted *sentence.* And the countless "tragedies" of *The Monk's Tale* lock onto automatic pilot rather than stopping once they have made their tragic point. Because each of these tales succeeds as an "unknowing" but instructive self-parody, it is essential that each be read "straight" as well as "awry." In other words, critical studies that discover literary depths in each tale are just as valid and necessary as those that interrogate the aesthetics of each work's literary shortcomings. But the only "self-knowing" parodic success in Fragment VII is its final tale, a beast fable that distills into the confines of 646 lines just about everything we might wish to find in a single literary artifact. Among the various reasons Chaucer chose to close out Fragment VII with this, his supreme parodic fiction, of paramount salience are the several ways it puts the reader's epistemological and critical agilities to the test.

We have already assessed Chauntecleer's critical reading of his troubling dream. And we have admired the mental acumen he displays in his instantaneous response to the fox-in-the-flesh. But it is obvious that Chauntecleer fails his next major test. Abandoning all caution, he succumbs to the fox's flattering invitation to fly down, close his eyes, and sing like his famous father, only then to find himself being transported to his carrier's den for dinner. Before this doomsday run to supper reaches its tragic consummation, however, Chauntecleer has the intellectual wherewithal to indulge in further creative thinking. His "gargat hente" in the fox's teeth, he manages to suggest to his captor that he might delight in cursing those in his pursuit: "A verray pestilence upon yow falle!" (VII.3410). The instant the fox opens his mouth to speak these words, the rooster escapes into a tree from which he refuses to descend, for all the fox's oily cajolings. And thus the fable's narrative ends with these two adversaries exchanging, from a safe distance, words of acquired wisdom: it is best to keep your eyes open; it is wise to keep your mouth shut.

In their interpretations of the overall meaning of *The Nun's Priest's Tale,* critics have made much of Chauntecleer's clever deployment of his linguistic skills as he escapes from the jaws of death. And they have also made much of the practical wisdom Chauntecleer acquires after his free and (un)fortunate fall. By concluding his narrative with these pithy apothegms, in other words, Chaucer fulfills the expectations generated by the beast fable genre itself: here the fable's pragmatically acquired wisdom places an emphasis on the eye and the tongue—on our ability to read phenomena in the world correctly, and our ability to speak judiciously, which sometimes means not to speak at all. There is, however, an earlier moment in the tale that also dramatizes matters epistemological and linguistic, although it scarcely translates these matters into any kind of pithy *moralitas.* As we have briefly noted, Chauntecleer reacts "natureelly" when he first confronts the fox by deploying his aestimative powers and fleeing to safety. But what might a reader do in an analogous situation? To what extent might the reader see himself mirrored in the rooster's aestimative ability to "read" the fox? What form of knowledge might the reader acquire if he were to transpose this literary fox into some phenomenal image lurking in the real world? Finally, what form of additional knowledge might the reader gain if he were to translate the rooster's "natural" utterance into human discourse? By asking these questions we are obviously addressing—perhaps belatedly—the foundational problematics concerning the utility and ethical truth of literature itself.

"COK! COK!"

Roger Bacon, Duns Scotus, Henry of Ghent, John of Reading, and several others in the late Middle Ages—all of them influenced by Averroes, Alhazen, and especially Avicenna—maintained that in animals and in human beings alike the middle chamber of the brain was occupied not only by the "aestimative" sense that we have already discussed, but also by a "discriminative" sense, the *virtus distinctiva*. This second power was also known as the "cognitive" sense or "phantasy," a name indicating, as Katherine H. Tachau explains, "its role as the faculty of the sensitive soul which 'imagines', or 'phantasizes', creating new images from those stored in the nearly adjacent imagination."[37] In several late medieval epistemological treatises, including Bacon's, these faculties were understood to "collectively complete the process of 'apprehension.'"[38] And even though the *virtus distinctiva* is located in the sensitive soul (and thus is not part of the intellectual soul), it actually manages to perform a "kind of syllogizing," a mode of intellection which "(a) does not involve words or propositions; and (b) is so rapid as to be imperceptible to our internal observation."[39] Understanding the "imaginative" or "phantastic" powers of the *virtus distinctiva*, in other words, should help us to appreciate in greater detail what actually occurred in Chauntecleer's brain the instant he saw the fox-in-the-flesh. Sensitively, accurately, and quasi-syllogistically, the rooster instantly apprehends the essence of the object before his gaze. And he succeeds in doing so by employing precisely the faculties belonging to the sensitive soul that human beings have equal access to, even though the mental motions of the *virtus distinctiva*, as the philosophers insisted, are imperceptible to our internal observation.

It is perhaps worth remarking at this point that in his recent best-seller *Blink: The Power of Thinking Without Thinking*, Malcom Gladwell makes a twenty-first-century claim for the mental agility of the human subject that philosophers of the mind were making about both human beings and animals in the thirteenth and fourteenth centuries:

> The part of our brain that leaps to [instantaneous] conclusions like this is called the adaptive unconscious, and the study of this kind of decision-making is one of the most important new fields in psychology. . . . This new notion of the adaptive unconscious is thought of . . . as a kind of giant computer that quickly and quietly processes a lot of the data we need in order to keep functioning as human beings. When you walk out into the street and suddenly realize that a truck is bearing down on you, do you have time to think through all your options? Of course not. The only way that human beings could ever have survived as a species as long as we have is that we've developed another kind of decision-making apparatus that's capable of making very quick judgments based on very little information.[40]

With the anecdotal support of Gladwell's *Blink* and with late medieval philosophers' much more formidable and technical analyses, I think we can now confidently assert that the mental powers of both reader and rooster in *The Nun's Priest's Tale* at a certain level of "intellection" are actually identical. This does not mean that rooster and reader are the same animal, but it does prove that they share a natural gift of instant knowing, of thinking without thinking, that on occasion is capable of saving them from extreme and sudden danger. What the reader is expected to make of this mirroring of his own uncanny ability to read life-endangering images is surely a critical question that requires further thought—concerning the nature of human nature, the capacities of our brain to instantly "know," as well as of our ability to gain some kind of future-oriented understanding of the world from lifelike figures provided by the imagination.

In his dramatization of these epistemological and literary-critical questions, Chaucer continues to complicate matters by incorporating additional issues concerning the signifying and denotative characteristics of language itself. Although the lightning-fast movement of the *virtus dis-tinctiva* "does not involve words or propositions," Chauntecleer never-theless utters a sound at precisely the same instant that his aestimative powers apprehend the fox:

> Nothyng ne liste hym thanne for to crowe,
> But cride anon, "Cok! Cok!" and up he sterte
> As man that was affrayed in his herte.

What might the spontaneous utterance "Cok! Cok!" at this moment possibly mean? Helen Cooper, as I noted earlier, argues that all six tales in Fragment VII are preeminently concerned with language. "If the Pri-oress's Prologue had declared the inadequacy of words to express spiri-tual meaning," she writes, "the Nun's Priest's Tale demonstrates how rhetoric can be manipulated to endow the most trivial of barnyard events with epic significance. At the other extreme, the analysis of the nature of words that Chaucer sets up in the group of tales gets its *coup de grace* from Chauntecleer's 'Cok! Cok!' Words can, after all, be pure sound, and mean nothing at all."[41] Now if Fragment VII, and especially *The Nun's Priest's Tale,* is preeminently concerned with "the nature of words," it would seem appropriate to ask whether "Cok! Cok!" is in fact something other than pure and meaningless sound. Is this locution possibly some kind of animal *crow* ("nothyng ne liste hym thanne for to crowe"), is it perhaps some kind of animal *cry* ("But cride anon"), is it some kind of quasi-human *sonus*, or is it some kind of fully human *vox?* As our hero's most passionate expression of his innermost feelings at a moment of intense danger and self-awareness, surely we are justified in wondering whether this iterated ululation might in some way be deeply meaningful.

These micro/macro questions may well appear linguistically trivial and critically *outré.* Yet throughout the Middle Ages philosophers of lan-guage actually expended a great deal of analytic energy classifying various animal as well as human sounds inside an all-encompassing taxonomy of linguistic, paralinguistic, and nonlinguistic signs. In "Animal Language in the Medieval Classification of Signs," a team of four scholars (includ-ing Umberto Eco) trace out the schematics of Aristotle, Boethius, Pri-scian, Avicenna, Abelard, Augustine, Peter of Spain, Lambert of Auxerre,

Roger Bacon, and many others concerning the semiotics of such locutions as a dog's bark and a rooster's crowing. A major discovery in their study is the "surprising fact" that the animal cry, like the wail of someone who is infirm, consistently appears in different positions in the same *de signis* taxonomies. That is, when a sound is emitted involuntarily by a sick man (*gemitus infirmorum*), it is seen as a "natural given," a pure "symptom" of that illness, and it is accordingly situated in one branch, the *signa naturalia* branch, in the *de signis* tree.[42] However, if the identical sound were "emitted in order to signify the same pain, but intentionally and according to a certain linguistic framework," it was understood to be a conventional "sign" similar in some respects to a word, and thus it is situated in a different branch, the *signa ordinata ab anima et ex intentione animae* branch.[43] In a similar fashion, the sound emitted by a rooster is a *signum naturalium* if it "merely" indicates the time of day or night. However, if it is impelled by some "intension" in the bird itself, that locution belongs to the conventional categories of *signa ordinata ab anima et ex intentione animae.*[44] Roger Bacon takes matters further by dividing the *signa ab anima* branch into two subgroups: first, there are signs *ad placitum et ex proposito cum deliberatione rationis et electione voluntatis,* that is, conventional words and iconic symbols generated via human free will; and second, there are *signa naturaliter, sine deliberatione rationis et sine electione voluntatis . . . , impetu naturae,* that is, involuntary expressions of the soul, or *anima,* such as sighs of the infirm and animal utterances, *voces brutorum animalium.*[45] Having constructed these two subdivisions, Bacon, rather surprisingly, then reunites them whenever they are *interiectiones ex deliberatione vel sine deliberatione*—interjections that are either intended or unintended. The unstableness of Bacon's categorizations of animal cries is striking: is a cock's crow (or cry) a *signum naturalia,* a *signum ordinatum ab anima (ad placidum),* a *signum ordinatum ab anima (naturaliter),* an *interiectio ex deliberatione,* an *interiectio sine deliberatione,* or something else?

Eco and his colleagues address these and related questions scientifically and at considerable length. But what happens to the unstable significance of a cock's cry when it appears inside the symbolic order of human language? Surely, whether or not this literary *sonus* is imitating, internalizing, or parodying a sound in nature, "Cok! Cok!" in *The Nun's*

Priest's Tale is now an integral element of poetry and is thus available to all the extrapolations that linguistic analysis and literary criticism might bring to bear. Yet because of its seeming semiotic vacuity, of all the verbal collocations in the tale "Cok! Cok!" may be, initially at least, the most resistant to any form of critical extrapolation. So a sensible way of beginning this critical test would be to allow that Chauntecleer's cry is a "pure sound" that "means nothing at all." But such a response to even a very small element in Chaucer's *ars poetica* should nevertheless prompt the careful reader to meditate, at least briefly, on the very idea of meaning itself. A possibly more enabling proposition could entertain the thesis that Chauntecleer is communicating the meaning of his intent, but only in a foreign language, namely the language of chickens. For Bacon as well as other medieval semioticians, as Eco and his colleagues explain, this would not have been a far-fetched conjecture:

> [In *Sumule Dialectices*,] Bacon is quite clear: *vox significativa* is that '*per quam omne animal interpretatur aliquid omni vel alicui sue speciei*', which is to say that there are *voces significativae naturaliter* which all the members of the species understand, as sounds of animals, and others (those *ad placitum*) which are understood only by subgroups of the same species: '*Gallicus Gallico, Graecus Graeco, Latinus Latino*'. Now, that animals understand each other '*possumus videre manifeste, quia gallina aliter garrit cum pullis suis quando invitat eos ad escam et quando docet eos cavere a milvo*'. Hence the chicken speaks with words which are different according to the circumstances, and is understood by its congeneres; and the ass is understood by the ass, the lion by the lion. For man, it is enough to have a little training and he will understand the language of the beasts. Or, as the pseudo-Marsilius of Inghen better clarifies: it is certain that the dog barks in order to signify something, and it is not important that everyone understands what he wants to say, it is enough that he is understood by those that know the properties and habits of dogs.[46]

In other words, after "a little training," we human readers might succeed in understanding what Chauntecleer means here *in his own animal lan-*

guage. A third mode of critical thinking moves away from zoosemiotics toward considering Chauntecleer's *interiectio* as a lexeme inside human language itself, namely, an onomatopoetic expression: thus the self-reflexive meaning of "Cok! Cok!" is its very own sound, or, more precisely, a referent in nature whose authenticity it attempts vainly to represent. A fourth and final interpretative stratagem, now much more literary than linguistic, would underscore the importance of Chauntecleer's essential artfulness: since he is much more a fictional than a factual fowl, perhaps this rooster's iterated *vox* has some semantic significance beyond the mimological. Aristotle was one of several philosophers who had "no difficulty in taking the sounds of animals as *voces significativae,* even if they were different from *nomina.*"[47] But could Chauntecleer's *vox significativa* actually be a *nomen*—that is, some kind of noun or name? Poets tend to be extremely mindful of the *nomina* they employ in their fictions, and this is especially true of those descriptive proper names which either overtly or obliquely express the essence of their protagonists' life and character. To provide critical support for this way of thinking, consider for a moment two extrapolations advanced by two major scholars concerning the deep-structure significance of a literary name. In a sequence of brilliant readings of the "logological reversibility" of Adam's name in the first three chapters of Genesis, Kenneth Burke offers a moment of seriocomic relief by considering other examples of essentialized names in narratives. The "simplest known instance of the temporizing of [a name's] essence," writes Burke, is as follows:

> Ooey Gooey was a worm. Ooey Gooey went for a stroll on a rail-road track. Along came a railroad train. Ooey gooey!

Burke then briskly unpacks the narratological, ontological, and teleological import of Ooey Gooey's name:

> Here Ooey Gooey's essence is defined in terms of his name, which implicitly contains his end. This perfect circularity is also translated into terms of the narratively rectilinear. Otherwise put: Both Ooey Gooey's name and Ooey Gooey's destiny proclaimed his nature. (Similarly, Adam's essence, as regards his name's punning

relation to the "earthy," was restated narratively in the story of his being formed from the earth and of all mankind's return to earth at death.)[48]

An equally ingenious exegesis of the narratological, ontological, and teleological significance of a literary name appears in Peter Brook's *Reading for the Plot*. In a chapter on Dickens's *Great Expectations,* Brooks finds that the qualities of the protagonist's self-given name, Pip, are qualities symptomatic not only of Pip and of the narrative shape of Pip's life, but of the reader's experience of reading and rereading the novel itself:

> In terms of the problematic of reading which the novel thematizes from its opening page, we could say that Pip, continuously returning toward origins in order to know the plot whose authority would lead him to the right end but never recovering origins and never finding the authoritative plot, never succeeds in going behind his self-naming to a reading of the missing patronymic. He is ever returned to a rereading of the unauthorized text of his self-given name, Pip. "Pip" sounded like a beginning, a seed. But, of course, when you reach the end of the name "Pip," you can return backward, and it is just the same: a repetitive text without variation or point of fixity, a return that leads to an unarrested shuttling back and forth. The name is in fact a palindrome. In the rereading of the palindrome the novel may offer its final comment on its expectative plot.[49]

Neither Burke's "logological" analysis of "Ooey Gooey" nor Brooks's "palindromic" analysis of "Pip" need be applied wholesale to Chauntecleer's existential cry: obviously "Cok! Cok!" is not the proper name of Chaucer's hero. Even so, inspired by Burke's and Brooks's nominal hermeneutics, an array of potential meanings of Chauntecleer's utterance may now begin to emerge. A *nomen* categorizing the hero's gender as well as his chicken nature, a phonic palindrome suggesting his origins and ends, and a "repetitive text without variety or point of fixity" that invites a rereading of the fable's own narrative design, "Cok! Cok!" might possibly carry a considerable amount of information that could enhance a reader's interpretation of the entire tale. And, of course, as a *nomen* declaiming and defining its speaker's animal essence at a moment of life-and-death urgency, it is actually possible that Chauntecleer's interjection could be translated, "syllogistically," to another level, into a corollary *nomen* defining the reader's own human nature.

Beginning with Rabelais' scornful satire of those logico-linguistic conundra enjoyed in the Middle Ages, interrogating the linguistic and meta-poetical implications of the *Tale*'s self-referential paradox, counterpointing Chauntecleer's reading of the image-without-a-name and the reader's rereading of that image from a different ontological plane, and concluding with a decryption of Chauntecleer's instinctive response and instantaneous locution when he first confronts his nemesis, this chapter has covered a good bit of ground. What holds it together is a consistent concentration on the dissemination of linguistic signs—the vexed relationship of different linguistic constructions to reality, to themselves, to the domain of meaning, and to the reader. While I have found it useful to invoke medieval philosophical studies and the relevant *subtilissimae quaestiones* they ask, I have been equally committed to tracking the motions of the reader's mind as it makes its way through the logico-linguistic-literary conundra foregrounded in the *Tale*. To provide a framework for tracing the reader's cognitive progress, I have invoked the inward wits, most notably *sensus communis, vis cogitativa, vis aestimativa, virtus distinctiva,* Memory, Intellect, Imagination, and the Agent Intellect. With the assistance of these terms, medieval philosophers engaged in a standard sequence of epistemological questions: how do we apprehend an object existing in the world, how do we internalize an image of that object into our minds, how do we correlate that image with a concept, and how do we align that idea with a name? The sequence our minds go through in order to "read" the world would initially appear to be quite different from the sequence involved in interpreting words on a page: in the first activity we transform apperceptions of reality into words, in the second activity we transform our comprehension of words into a re-cognition of the world. But, of course, in the act of reading, as our minds shuttle at lightening speed among images, ideas, and verbal signs, we are in fact processing in a complex fashion a vast array of signs and objects, interconnecting them epistemically and semiologically at precisely the same time. So one of the glories of *The Nun's Priest's Tale* is not only how it tests our agility as thinking readers, and not only how it invites us to reflect upon the motions of our mind as we read, but how it so affirmatively celebrates our critical ability to discover meanings in a text—even if the text itself is a congeries of resistant, logic-chopping, paradoxical, and dissseminal signs.

"Cok! Cok!" is a quintessential example of a disseminal verbal sign that deconstructs any semblance of semantic stability: as we have seen, it could mean nothing at all, it may belong inside the language of an animal other, it might link directly to the real, it may serve as a self-reflexive name, and it might even stand in for the significance of the entire *Tale*. Because the entire *Tale,* in turn, might be a self-enclosed semiocosm, as its own Liar paradox suggests, it may be questioning whether its signifiers actually have the power to escape the henhouse of language and reconnect with the real. It is via Chauntecleer's animal-with-no-name that Chaucer is able to raise, in turn, the inverse question about the relationship of *res* to *verba:* is it humanly possible to actually "know" a phenomenon if we lack the wherewithal to identify or invent its proper name? And emerging from this epistemological puzzle is a final question of considerable urgency to every reader. Like Chauntecleer's quasi-prophetic dream, is *The Nun's Priest's Tale* also a prescient figment of the "heigh ymaginacioun"? In other words, does the *Tale* anticipate the presence of a future Other whose nature cannot now be known? Because the only "real" answer to this question resides exclusively in the future experiences of the *Tale's* reader, this is one more puzzle that Chaucer's instructive parody leaves unsolved. As with the *Tale's* other *insolubilia*—be they logical, linguistic, epistemological, ontological, literary, or all of the above—that there is no available resolution here, even after the expenditure of much aggressive thinking, should no longer be cause for much alarm. Rather, it is the educative impact of all these *quaestiones subtilissimae* that illustrates the pedagogical ambitions of Chaucer's curricular parody while confirming the vitality of those three cognitive sciences that have been this chapter's major focus. In sum, *ars grammatica, ars noetica,* and *ars poetica* are all alive and well in the same, and rather crowded, literary chickenyard.

EIGHT

Moralitas

It is difficult
to get the news from poems
yet men die miserably every day
for lack
of what is found there.
—WILLIAM CARLOS WILLIAMS

Who, then, is Chaucer? In my introduction, I noted the common practice in Chaucer studies of characterizing Chaucer's authorial voice by prizing it cleanly apart from the voice of a tale's pilgrim-speaker. Typically, critics discussing individual Canterbury tales use "Chaucer" as a placeholder for the poem's genius—omnicompetent, wise, ethical, and all-knowing—while discerning in the poem another presence, that of its pilgrim-author, whose world vision is less perfect than Chaucer's and sometimes deeply flawed. And in certain tales, *The Nun's Priest's Tale* being a perfect case study, some critics actually discern a third voice, that of the "narrator": just as the Nun's Priest is Chaucer's fictional construct, this personage in turn is a literary confection of the Nun's Priest, a figure whose world views and aesthetic sensibilities both Chaucer and the

Nun's Priest are prepared to ironize. Even though most readers regard *The Nun's Priest's Tale* as the epitome of Chaucer's personal vision and poetic values, they nevertheless are often prepared to find authorial striations in the text, so that, at the very least, certain "untoward" passages (antifeminist asides, for example) can be attributed either directly to the Nun's Priest or obliquely to the ironized narrator, but only rarely to "Chaucer." While I suggested in my introduction that identifying the narrating "I" in *The Nun's Priest's Tale* may be yet another problematic issue foregrounded in Chaucer's *ars poetica,* up to the very end of this study I have used all three designations—Chaucer, the Nun's Priest, and the narrator—almost interchangeably. It is finally time to reflect on the theoretical issues this practice entails. In *Textual Subjectivity,* A. C. Spearing argues that identifying two or three subjectivities in any Chaucerian text is a wrong-headed critical practice absolutely antithetical to medieval ways of reading and of writing. The medieval aesthetics of reception, Spearing insists, differed radically from ours: rather than presuming, as we might, that consciousness precedes narrative, medievals assumed the opposite. Even though the pronoun "I" signals moments of subjectivity in a literary text, it need not add up to a unified speaking voice. In fact, in most medieval works, Spearing maintains, there simply is no voice whatever. Medieval narratives are therefore best read as "narratorless," and medieval poems, even first-person lyrics, are best read as instances of "subjectless subjectivity."[1]

With some careful qualifications, Spearing believes these generalizations apply equally well to Chaucer's *Canterbury Tales.* Spearing recognizes that Chaucer was "truly interested in the possibility of connections between stories and their tellers, and voiced narratives and unreliable narrators are the ultimate outcome of the process he set going."[2] However, "we must not suppose that Chaucer in the late fourteenth century could make an immediate transition into the world of the dramatic monologue (or would have wished to do so), and we cannot without gross distortion project the assumptions and expectations of our own time back into the early, exploratory stages of the development that he was only beginning."[3] In other words, even though the portraits of the *General Prologue* are attached to *The Canterbury Tales,* there is no need to associate any one of the tales very closely with the pilgrim to whom it is assigned: in fact, "we do not have to think of most tales as having a speaker or voice at all, in the sense of a fictional individual to whom the first-person pronouns of the narratorial discourse consistently refer."[4] Thus it would behoove all readers not only to put the portraits to the side, Spearing implies, but to set aside any prior assumption (until proved otherwise) that there is a speaking voice, let alone two or three, controlling the narrated events. If we were to make these against-the-grain moves, then our appreciation of the achievement of each of the Canterbury tales as an individual and "self-narrating" work of art would be enriched for the effort.

Towards the end of my generally very positive book review of *Textual Subjectivities,* I suggested its author might have taken into account recent work in performative studies: "Spearing is simply not prepared to interrogate the layers of signification, participation, contention, and contradiction that may be simultaneously at play in the performance of the first person pronoun—be it on the stage, in the appropriation of others' songs, in late medieval mystical identifications with the person of Christ, or in literary narratives where the author's presence and the presence of the fictive speaker may be discernible in the same words."[5] Nevertheless, I found Spearing's iconoclastic diagnostic of our deeply ingrained reading habits so "energizing, challenging, and instructive" that I suggested it "should be required reading in every graduate course on medieval literature."[6] Accordingly, even though Spearing never mentions Chaucer's beast fable, I want to suggest here that the central questions he raises concerning the labile ontologies of authorial voice and fictionalized voice are questions that *The Nun's Priest's Tale* also raises. In other words, when we claim to hear two or even three quite different voices in the same text, how do we know we are not deluding ourselves? What evidence do we have to illustrate the invisible seam where the poet's presence gives way to the consciousness of a ventriloquized speaker? Isn't our characterizing of the excellences of the arch-poet over against the failings of the unreliable narrator an all-too-obvious projection of our own self-esteem? Finally, how do we "know" what we profess to know about that absent/present identity within the text that we choose to name "Chaucer"?

Chaucer, I believe, actually anticipated all these questions. *Of course* he expected his readers would construct a personality out of *The Pardoner's Tale,* that they would create their versions of the Wife of Bath's character from her Prologue and tale, and that they would confect a list of attributes that the "voice" in *The Man of Law's Tale* reveals about its teller. And Chaucer of course knew his readers would fashion from *The Canterbury Tales* their own characterization of *him:* how could they (or we) not but do so? Famously, in response to our desire to know him better, Chaucer includes two of his own tales, the self-parodic tales of *Sir Thopas* and the *Melibee*. And in *The Nun's Priest's Tale* he ups the ante further, tweaking and teasing our desire to know him to no end. The effect of these peekaboo games is evidenced in the long history of the *Tale's* reception: Chaucer's authorial voice has been understood either as being *nearly* identical with the voice of the Nun's Priest (the majority position) or as being *totally* identical with it (the minority position). For example, in her 2008 study of the entirety of Chaucer's *ouevre*, Esther Quinn remarks that "the question of who is speaking, always a tricky issue in Chaucer's writings, is especially so in the *Nun's Priest's Tale*. Although the undescribed, unnamed priest who accompanies the Prioress is supposedly the speaker, the poet continues to speak in his own person."[7] But how, ultimately, does Quinn *know?* On the other side of the fence, in a study I will turn to in a moment concerning the *Tale's* compressed meditation on predestination vs. free will, Grover Furr determines that the Nun's Priest "basically comes down on the side of determinism," while Chaucer in all probability "evokes the opposite, nominalist position," even though the position assumed by the *Tale* itself is "indeterminate."[8] But how, again, does Furr ultimately *know?*

My intention is of course not to correct Quinn's and Furr's critical pronouncements, for their opinions are representative of all our "performative" and "characterological" readings of "Chaucer." Rather, I am suggesting that the intentional space that *may* be perceptible between authorial voice and narrating voice in *The Nun's Priest's Tale* is so nearly indiscernible that the self-critical reader is expected to ask how he or she is ultimately able to know of its very existence. In one way, then, my critical reading of Chaucer is diametrically opposed to Spearing's. Rather than being at a very early and exploratory stage, Chaucer has actually developed the art of free indirect discourse to such a sophisticated level that he has the confidence in *The Nun's Priest's Tale* to provide a subtle parody of the entire spectrum of issues relating to fictional subjectivity. But what this means in turn is that *The Nun's Priest's Tale* also supports Spearing's well-founded concern that by slicing a tale into a dyadic (or triadic) contest of disparate voices with foreordained personal characteristics, we coarsen a poem's subtleties and diminish our own experiences as readers of an extremely variegated text. So once again, I am professing that *The Nun's Priest's Tale* is an instructive self-parody reflecting Chaucer's own concerns about the successful or unsuccessful interpretation of his art. Yet in making this claim, I need to emphasize, especially in this theoretical context, that I too am obviously encoding into the *Tale* an authorial purpose that is very much to my liking. I am, in short, inventing my own "Chaucer." But ultimately I fear I have no choice but to do so. Since I find I cannot respond to *The Nun's Priest's Tale* as if it were a "narratorless narrative," and since, on the other hand, I cannot attribute any one line, sentiment, or thought to a single authorial voice over against another, I must insist to the very end on using these three powerful nominals—Chaucer, the Nun's Priest, and the narrator—almost, but not entirely, interchangeably.

One final way of appreciating Chaucer's *fort/da* game of authorial self-revelation, appearing and then disappearing as he invites his readers to capture his ever-vanishing presence, is in terms of the Cretan Liar paradoxes we considered in chapter 7. What if Chaucer were actually to decide to reveal himself in naked authorial splendor in order to uncover the real intent of his professed "intent"—in other words, to tell the pellucid "truth"? Would this then be the Chaucer whom we seek? Or, as with Chuck Close's self-portraits discussed in chapter 3, would Chaucer's self-revelation inside his own fiction succeed only in further problematizing the boundaries of his knowable poetic presence? As Rosalie L. Colie notes in her study of paradoxes in the Renaissance, the Cretan Liar paradox of self-referentiality is embedded in even the most "realistic" of Renaissance self-portraits:

> The Liar paradox is the classical paradox of self-reference, as well as the classical paradox of infinite regress. It cannot be verified internally, since there is no measuring rod for its accuracy; it cannot

be confirmed externally, since it refers only to itself. So is it also with self-portraits: the more faithful the likeness, the greater the falsity of the picture, the greater its isolation from any reference point outside the creating, re-creating self.[9]

By inviting us to consider *The Nun's Priest's Tale* as possibly his most self-referential work, Chaucer I believe is inviting us to meditate precisely on the indeterminate status of that "measuring rod" we employ as we contemplate art as a mirror of its author. We are free to believe that our measuring rod is accurate. But as with all the other *insolubilia* inside Chaucer's *ars poetica,* there is no resolution in sight: since the immanent figure of "Chaucer" exists only inside his own fiction, the authenticity of his authorial "self-portrait" is something that can never really be known.

So, having dedicated this entire book to *The Nun's Priest's Tale,* it is finally appropriate to ask, rather insistently: What *sentence,* what *moralitas,* might we now take away from all our critical labors? Throughout this study I have invoked a clutch of ideas concerning the disseminal play of the *Tale*'s literary language that can generally be called deconstructive. And while my theoretical influences and critical methods have varied from chapter to chapter, my high-intensity interrogations of many discrete passages have led rather consistently in the direction of interpretative irresolution. The "queered" metapoetics of the Nun's Priest's celibate sexuality; the semiotic "bouncing" inside the literary arts of imitation, translation, and irony; the generic instabilities burlesqued in the opening *exemplum;* the trivial "undecidabilities" interrogated in the *moralitas;* the logic-defying "category mistakes" of the *Tale*'s meta-metaphor; the mind-boggling *confusio* of historical noise; the persistence of *vis confundendi* in human attempts to measure time; and the self-canceling paradoxes embodying literature's relation to the real: all of these dominant effects, as well as many others, illustrate the tendency of Chaucer's Menippean parody to unravel and deconstruct the totalizing patterns of thinking that are distinctive to certain traditional discourses. To add further grist to the deconstructive mill, I have intermittently emphasized the resistance of *The Nun's Priest's Tale* to *any* kind of critical interpretation, a resistance at some times so adamantine that the *Tale* appears to border on being absolutely "unreadable."

In my introduction, I announced that I hoped to offer not only a new reading of *The Nun's Priest's Tale* but a new way, perhaps a radically new way, of thinking about everything that Chaucer has written. In retrospect this announcement may seem the height of "folye." Nevertheless, I have attempted throughout this book to suspend a number of traditional reading habits the better to grasp the inaugural power of Chaucer's literary masterpiece. Arguing that the *Tale* is designed to catalyze a series of independent responses, my emphasis has rested upon those intellectual breakthroughs, imaginative serendipities, and self-critical flashes experienced along the way as we search for "meaning." In order to celebrate the *Tale*'s multifaceted character, I have examined its parts in rather strict isolation one from another, thereby according overmuch credence to the theory that medieval poetics was more tolerant of "inorganic" artistic design than our modern reading practices are today—obviously *The Nun's Priest's Tale* is a perfectly unified, as well as unique, masterpiece. But the best way to appreciate the Tale's singularity, I have found, has been to read its parts with unusually close attention. Thus a major defining aspect of my own responses to the *Tale* is the degree of sustained attention I have given to extreme close-up critical readings.

In light of my definition of the *Tale* as Menippean didascalic parody, it follows that the poem is energized from beginning to end by some form of educative "intent." In its parodic redeployment of early classroom exercises, quadrivial problems studied in the universities, and major literary texts including Chaucer's earlier poems and tales, *The Nun's Priest's Tale* is engaged in fashioning a distinctively new curriculum with its readers. The "ideal reader" I have been constructing in this study has been especially well educated in the liberal arts—especially logic—as those *artes* were studied in the fourteenth century. But what I need to make emphatically clear at this point is that the new curriculum Chaucer is fashioning with his reader does not actually exist *inside* the *Tale*. It is not the *Tale*'s deepest substrate, its ultimate intellectual content. Rather, it exists only within every reader's individual responses. I have constructed one variant of those responses in my own step-by-step readings in the preceding chapters, and even though several of my critical readings arrive eventually at a *cul de sac*, I have made it clear that the sought-for effect has not been frustration or a sense of intellectual emptiness. Instead, it is the independent and creative progress each reader makes, bouncing back and forth from one never-quite-adequate site to the next, that constitutes the desired impact of Chaucer's pedagogical agenda. Thus if *The Nun's Priest's Tale* is a metapoetic hall of mirrors, the ultimate site of self-reflection is actually the reader's mind. Assisted by the mental faculties outlined in the preceding chapter, working with their own life skills, educational careers, and reading experiences (including, especially, the reading of Chaucer), each reader will invent a unique response to Chaucer's unique fable. This does not quite mean that each and every reader is Chaucer's "ideal reader," but it does mean that every reader is privileged to respond to *The Nun's Priest's Tale* in a uniquely inventive fashion.

The critical idea I am invoking here is Derek Attridge's definition of reading as an "inventive," "creative," and "literary" response. In *The Singularity of Literature,* Attridge characterizes the "event of reading" as a "singular" activity: it is neither an arbitrary "reaction" to the text nor is it a mere repetition of the text; rather, it is a creative "response" that emulates the literary inventiveness of the text as *other.* "Just as my response to another person as other is a response to the other in its relating to me," writes Attridge, "so my response to a work is not to the work 'itself' but to the work as other in *the event of its coming into being in my reading.*"[10] And because there is no one "correct" way of responding to any text, the singularity of each reader's reading will inspire other responses and thus provoke an unending succession of rereadings:

> [T]he reader attempts to answer to the work's shaping of language by a new shaping of his or her own (which will in turn invite further responses)—whether it be in the form of a literal act of writing, an inward composition, a speech or intervention in a discussion, a change of behavior. What this means, of course, is that it in turn will partake of the literary to some degree, and demand of its readers a response of the same inventive kind. This prospect of an endless chain of responses may sound alarming, but it only becomes so if we conceive of literature as possessing an extractable content which can finally be isolated—and hence possessing those qualities of self-presence, universality, historical transcendence, and absolute signification on which the Platonic tradition of aes-

thetics is based. But literature is characterized precisely by its lack of any such content—which, of course, is why we re-read, with no end in sight of our re-readings.[11]

Who, then, are Chaucer's readers? Because his readers' mental chemistries and life experiences differ radically one from another, Chaucer was surely aware that his works would be processed in ways over which he had little or no control. Chaucer's first inscribed reader, Harry Bailly, is a delightful illustration of that reader who, in Attridge's terms, "reacts" rather than "responds" to the text. Nevertheless, among all the fable's literary issues, there is surely one that Harry, like most readers, considers to be of paramount importance: how does a poem such as *The Nun's Priest's Tale* assist us in our daily lives? Chaucer's most straightforward answer to this question is one we are entirely familiar with: "al that written is, / To oure doctrine it is ywrite, ywis" (VII.3441–42). In other words, *everything* and *anything* in the *Tale* is capable of prompting an appropriately creative response, be it "a literal act of writing, an inward composition, a speech or intervention in a discussion, [or] a change of behavior." For Chauntecleer, as we have seen, it is the text of his own dream that prompts a creative response, although not until *after* the dream's partial reification does he belatedly undergoes a significant "change of behavior." Surely it is appropriate to ask how Chaucer's readers might experience a comparable change in response to catalysts that are discernible in the *Tale* itself. I therefore conclude by briefly imagining three reader-response scenarios.

Immediately before Russell's attack, the narrator suddenly finds himself embroiled in a confusing debate concerning divine foreknowledge, necessity, and human free will:

But what that God forwoot moot nedes bee,
After the opinioun of certein clerkis.
Witnesse on hym that any parfit clerk is,
That in scole is greet altercacioun
In this mateere, and greet disputisoun,
And hath been of an hundred thousand men.
But I ne kan nat bulte it to the bren
As kan the holy doctour Augustyn,

Or Boece, or the Bisshop Bradwardyn,
Wheither that Goddes worthy forwityng
Streyneth me nedely for to doon a thyng—
"Nedely" clepe I symple necessitee—
Or elles, if free choys be graunted me
To do that same thyng, or do it noght,
Though God forwoot it er that I was wroght;
Or if his wityng streyneth never a deel
But by necessitee condicioneel.
I wol nat han to do of swich mateere;
My tale is of a cok, as ye may heere . . .

                                   (VII.3234–52)

What are we to make of this odd intervention, so egregiously distinct in
its discursive register from all the rest of the *Tale*? It may well be another
one of those "small units of discourse" we have come to appreciate in
The Nun's Priest's Tale as a symptom, and perhaps a parody, of the "eine
kleine Einheit" aesthetics of medieval narrative construction. This quick
riff of abstract propositions also accords with the overarching definition
of the Menippea as a philosophical genre that enjoys parodying hubristic
philosophizings. And within the narrative arc of the *Tale*, the narrator's
meditation on determinism and free will is aptly positioned between the
fox's appearance in the chickenyard and Chauntecleer's confrontation
with his enemy. Nevertheless, in his critical essay focused on just these
nineteen lines, Grover Furr is justified in asking the quite straightforward
question: "[W]hat is this passage doing in this tale?"[12] After explaining
that reconciling human free will with divine foreknowledge was "the most
significant philosophical controversy of the fourteenth century,"[13] a controversy that "never resulted in an authoritative and final explanation,"[14]
Furr turns to the *Tale* itself: Pertelote, he finds, is a "fully-fledged nominalist"[15] who embraces free will; Chauntecleer and the Nun's Priest are both
antinominalists, which means they "basically [come] down on the side
of determinism";[16] Chaucer appears to align himself with "the opposite,
nominalist position";[17] while the position of the *Tale* is "indeterminate,"[18]
proving to be as "multivocal as any other work in Chaucer's canon."[19]

But rather than exploring (or challenging) the significance of this controversy as it relates directly to the characters in the *Tale,* I prefer instead to consider briefly how this free will vs. determinism agon might assist, at least obliquely, in guiding the responses of any "inventive" reader. That reader will surely feel a bond with the narrator when he confesses, "I ne kan nat bulte it to the bren" (VII.3240), for who, in this mare's nest of countervailing propositions, has ever fully succeeded in harmonizing divine foreknowledge and human free will? That reader, if a contemporary of Chaucer, might also recall the importance of future contingencies in fourteenth-century philosophical treatises. As I observed earlier, the Law of Contradiction was readily applicable to propositions if they obtain to situations in the past or the present: either proposition P is true and proposition not-P is false, or the reverse is the case. However, how does one determine the validity of a proposition whose verifying or unverifying referent will come into being only in the future? When this problem in formal logic is cast in a theological mode, as in the Nun's Priest's complaint, foreknowledge of future contingencies is seen as the privilege of divine providence. When cast in a less theological mode, forecertainty verges on a variant of "pagan" fatalism. In *Troilus and Criseyde,* an account of "pagan" historical events whose future outcome is already known, Chaucer brilliantly plays off individual free will, the reader's foreknowledge, "divine" foreknowledge, and a sense of unswerving doom.

Tragedy in the Middle Ages was almost universally defined as an ineluctable *de casibus* fall suffered by those who once "stoode in heigh degree, / And fillen so that ther nas no remedie / To brynge hem out of hir advertisee" (VII.1992–94)—as the Monk prescribes in his introduction to his eighteen tragedies. The Monk's fatalistic vision is iterated in Chauntecleer's nine *exempla,* each of which in its own way is a tragedy: despite the forewarning provided by a dream, the inevitable conclusion in each narrative is violent death. Although Chauntecleer's purpose is to prove that dreams are prophetic, none of his protagonists exercises free will, and none survives the outcome of the dream's dire prophecies. *The Nun's Priest's Tale* in this regard is utterly and absolutely different. In part because Chauntecleer belatedly exercises his own free will—extricating himself from the jaws of death to live another day—and in part because the prophetic meaning of his dream is open to interpretation, it would appear that the future is not entirely unknowable, nor is it entirely predetermined. After his first traumatic encounter with his own mortality, Chauntecleer is understandably ruffled and pensive. Yet at tale's end he appears ready to continue living his life with the "joye" and "plesaunce" that are the signatures of his rooster nature. Having been invited to reflect upon the postlapsarian prudence acquired by Chaucer's hero, the inventive reader might choose to emulate Chauntecleer's feisty resolve.

Secondly, the inventive reader might also respond "creatively" to the protagonist's fall itself, another moment where Chauntecleer exercises his free will. In *Blindness and Insight,* Paul de Man considers the fall to be the originary moment in the "plot of allegory" and of its twin trope, which is irony. Whether or not the fall is a literal fall or an allusion to the fall of Adam and Eve, it creates in the fallen protagonist a sudden awareness of his doubleness, turning him into an ironically "disinterested spectator" of his "phenomenal self." Even though I ultimately find this "disinterested spectator" tellingly different from Chaucer's "creative" reader, I quote de Man at some length:

> In the idea of the fall thus conceived, a progression in self-knowledge is certainly implicit: the man who has fallen is somewhat wiser than the fool who walks around oblivious of the crack in the pavement about to trip him up. And the fallen philosopher reflecting on the discrepancy between the two successive stages is wiser still, but this does not in the least prevent him from stumbling in his turn. It seems instead that his wisdom can be gained only at the cost of such a fall. The mere falling of others does not suffice; he has to go down himself. The ironic, twofold self that the writer or philosopher constitutes by his language seems able to come into being only at the expense of his empirical self, falling (or rising) from a stage of mystified adjustment into the knowledge of his mystification. The ironic language splits the subject into an empirical self that exists in a state of inauthenticity and a self that exists only in the form of a language that asserts the knowledge of this inauthenticity. This does not, however, make it into an au-

thentic language, for to know inauthenticity is not the same as to be authentic.[20]

Although de Man's somber exegesis scarcely accords with Chaucer's seriocomic representation of Chauntecleer's downward flight, Chaucer also insists on the absolute necessity of falling, for there is apparently no other way for his protagonist to gain even a modest degree of authentic wisdom or self-knowledge. And like de Man, Chaucer conceptualizes that fall linguistically as well as ontologically. De Man's postlapsarian protagonist is an "ironic, two-fold" subject divided by language into divergent identities: one is an "empirical self" and the other a self that "exists only in the form of a language that asserts the knowledge of this inauthenticity." Chaucer's interpretation of the fall is much less tragic, but no less instructive for being so. In fact, it is comically profound. Rather than dwelling upon the riven identity of its speaking subject, *The Nun's Priest's Tale* instead celebrates the capacious freedom and poetic creativity of postlapsarian language itself, as evidenced in its rivenness, its labile play, its parodic powers, and its disseminal undecideabilities. Even though the educational flight pattern of Chaucer's responding reader is a parody of the onwards and upwards ascent of the classic myth of the liberal arts, the fable's linguistic pleasure leads the reader, as Arthur Chapin has brilliantly explained, toward "a comic apotheosis, an un-solemn, sensuously alive elevation, in which earthly life is lifted, for a moment, back into innocence, enjoying a state of enlightenment indistinguishable from a *lightening up.*"[21]

The final "inventive" response I'll briefly address is oneiric. Published in 1991, Steven F. Kruger's *Dreaming in the Middle Ages* remains the most substantive examination of medieval dream theory to this day. Recently, at the 2008 New Chaucer Society Conference, Kruger returned to his book's subject, concluding a paper entitled "Dream Inheritance" with this "untested hypothesis":

[F]or the Middle Ages, as in many ways for Freud, the dream—with its push toward the future, whether in the form of wish fulfillment or in the promise of revelation, but, at the same time, with its necessary grounding in already experienced material—is a particularly rich site for the thinking through of questions about how what we inherit from the past might be reworded to fashion that future we most desire.[22]

A blend of medieval and modern dream theorizings, Kruger's hypothesis might actually serve as a respondant's guide to the entirety of *The Nun's Priest's Tale* in the twenty-first century. Reaching deep into the reader's personal past, plumbing the depths of that reader's experience and psyche, *The Nun's Priest's Tale* may also contain augurings of the future. We of course will never be certain. Yet in the context of these mysterious and preternatural literary powers, the troublesome expression that has given us pause, "by heigh ymaginacioun forncast," takes on further resonance. Perhaps metaphorical projections of the future are to be discovered somewhere between the text *as other* and the reader *as other,* in an imaginative space where a complex of agencies—God, the author, the reader, the rooster, the fox—give prophetic meaning to words. And even if the truths darkly "forncast" are at times forbidding, the beneficent effect of that "heigh ymaginacioun" is the opportunity to think through how we might translate our past experiences into a future we most desire.

A core ambition of *The Nun's Priest's Tale* is thus to keep the Memory alive, linked with the Imagination, and working with the estimative faculties and with Reason. Another ambition is to keep alive the freedom of the Will. Liberating its author from textual determinants of the past, an equally passionate aspiration of Chaucer's fable is to accord its readers a modicum of free choice in the future. Rereading a poetic *summa* that may be as useful as was Chauntecleer's dream, we might now wish to rewrite the future. That is, the name of the Name of the Fox is a Reality that our Agent Intellect, quite possibly, has already always known. Yet even if we are graced with such powers of Intellection, the abiding problem with our ways of envisioning the world is that abstractions, detached from particulars, are held poorly in the memory and are soon half-forgotten. This is where poetry does its best work. We know, as the *Tale* reminds us, that the fox will come: his color will be between yellow and red; black will be the tips of his ears, the tip of his tail. And when the fox appears with his small snout and his glowing eyes, his intent will surely be clear: he "wolde han had me deed." Yet between the fox's first and final incursions, we may have the choice of devising an interlude of mindfulness and creative pleasure. In composing an *ars poetica* that is resistant to all our critical incursions, Chaucer has thus in the end been most generous—insisting that we respond to *The Nun's Priest's Tale*, not as he might wish, but in our own quite singular fashions. So, as responsive readers, we are now at liberty to turn obliquely away from the *Tale*, in order to assess future contingencies, to invent narratives with grace notes of freedom, and to imagine an *argumentum* that might keep us "out of foul prisoun" (VII.2897), if only for the remainder of the day.

Notes

Introduction

1. Muscatine, *Chaucer and the French Tradition*, 237.

2. Strohm, *Social Chaucer*, 164.

3. Lerer, "The Canterbury Tales," 280.

4. Elliott, "Chaucer's Reading," 67.

5. D. Howard, *The Idea of the Canterbury Tales*, 370–71.

6. Bloomfield, "The Wisdom of *The Nun's Priest's Tale*," 70.

7. Lodge, *Small World*, 319.

8. Actually, as we shall see at greater length in chapter 2, beast fables in the Middle Ages were interpreted in wildly different ways. After reviewing a large number of fable manuscripts, Edward Wheatley concludes that "any fable could be interpreted according to any allegorical form, at the whim of the reader, or perhaps at the behest of a teacher"; Wheatley, *Mastering Aesop*, 91.

9. All citations of Chaucer's work are taken from Benson, *The Riverside Chaucer*. The line numbering indicates my acceptance of the Ellesmere sequence of tales, rather than the Hengwrt sequence.

10. Pearsall, *The Nun's Priest's Tale*, 257.

11. Beidler, "Desiderata," 74.

12. Donaldson, "Patristic Exegesis," 20.

13. Pearsall, *The Nun's Priest's Tale*, 50–81.

14. Ibid., 65.

15. Ibid., 12.

16. Elbow, *Oppositions*, 99–100.

17. Muscatine, *Chaucer and the French Tradition*, 242.

18. The paper was then published; see Boone, "Chauntecleer and Partlet Identified."

19. Wonderfully, there has been scholarly disagreement. Pearsall considers Boone's identification "unconvincing and ill-advised" because Golden Spangled Hamburgs cannot be traced back to the Middle Ages. Pearsall prefers the conservatism of Kenneth Sisam, who asserts that Chaucer's chickens are "old-fashioned varicolored barndoor-fowl, not one of the modern pure breeds"; Pearsall, *The Nun's Priest's Tale*, 150; Sisam, *The Nun's Priest's Tale*, 33.

20. This kind of Christianist reading, in its various allegorical and tropological forms, is well represented by Donovan, "The *Moralite* of the Nun's Priest's Sermon"; Dahlberg, "Chaucer's Cock and Fox"; and Levy and Adams, "Chauntecleer's Paradise Lost and Regained."

21. Donovan, "The *Moralite* of the Nun's Priest's Sermon"; Dahlberg, "Chaucer's Cock and Fox"; and Levy and Adams, "Chauntecleer's Paradise Lost and Regained."

22. Gallacher, "Food, Laxatives, and Catharsis," 51.

23. Ibid., 51–52.

24. Ibid., 50.

25. Ibid.

26. F. Anne Payne, *Chaucer and Menippean Satire*.

27. Ibid., 185.

28. Ibid., 202.

29. Ibid., 202–3.

30. Ibid., 204.

31. Ibid., 203.

32. Lowry, *Under the Volcano*, 175.

33. W. Wimsatt, "Northrop Frye," 103.

34. Bakhtin, *Problems of Dostoevsky's Poetics*.

35. Frye, *Anatomy of Criticism*, 308–12. I should note that Anne Payne also maintains that *The Nun's Priest's Tale* is a Menippean satire, a genre whose definition and applicability to *The Nun's Priest's Tale* I consider at some length in chapter 2.

36. Hussey, *The Nun's Priest's Prologue and Tale*, 4–5.

37. Ibid., 5.

38. Jordan, *Chaucer and the Shape of Creation*, xi.

39. Dagenais, *The Ethics of Reading*, 27 (cited by Wheatley, *Mastering Aesop*, 95).

40. See Rose, *Parody//Meta-fiction*, 98.

41. Orr, *Intertextuality*, 69.

42. Hutcheon, *A Theory of Parody*, 35.

43. Rose, *Parody//Meta-fiction*, 81.

44. See ibid., 63, 98.

45. See Norris, *Deconstruction*, 112–13.

46. Derrida, *Positions*, 46.

47. Derrida, *Dissemination*, 268.

48. Whittock, *A Reading of the Canterbury Tales*, 230.

49. See Suleiman, *Authoritarian Fictions*, esp. 199–238.

50. Reynolds, *Medieval Reading*, esp. 121–34.

51. Spearing, *Textual Subjectivity*, 118.

52. Ibid., 121.

53. Călinescu, *Rereading*, vi.

54. Ibid., 43.

55. Ibid., 14.

56. Balliett, *Ecstasy at the Onion*, 113.

One.   The Nun's Priest's Body, or Chaucer's Sexual Genius

1. Gaylord, "*Sentence* and *Solaas*."

2. Cooper, *The Structure of the Canterbury Tales*, 162.

3. See Astell, "Chaucer's 'Literature Group.'"

4. See VII.1907 and, more generally, 1893–1933, where Harry reveals that Goodelief considers him a "milksop" and a "coward ape."

5. While including the epilogue's lines, in brackets, in its mastertext, the *Riverside* edition explains: "These lines occur in a group of nine MSS generally taken to be of inferior authority and may have been canceled by Chaucer when he wrote lines 1941–62 of the Monk's Prologue, where the same ideas are repeated" (Benson, *Riverside Chaucer*, 941; see also 1133). For Harry's earlier and similar praise of the Monk as "a manly man" in the *General Prologue*, see I.167.

6. The thematics of masculinity in Fragment VII have been elucidated by Cohen in "Diminishing Masculinity," and also in Cohen, *Of Giants*, where he writes: "Male bodies of all kinds tumble along these dialogic bridges that connect the six tales [of Fragment VII]: celibate, hypersexual, overly physical,

otherworldly, diminutive, childlike, henpecked, hen serviced, ludic, and ludi-crous" (98). In addition see Patterson, "'What Man Artow?'" a study of the the-matics of children's literature and the rhetoric of authorial and masculine self-diminution in the central tales of Fragment VII.

7. Miskimin, *The Renaissance Chaucer*, 78.

8. Parker, "Virile Style."

9. *Epistle 899*, quoted ibid., 201.

10. Quoted ibid., 202.

11. See ibid., 201–22.

12. Ibid., 202.

13. Quoted ibid., 204.

14. Quoted ibid., 202.

15. Quoted ibid., 204.

16. Quoted ibid., 205.

17. Quoted ibid., 204.

18. For an application of these ideas to Boccaccio's linguistic predilections, see Barolini, "*Le Parole.*" As noted by Parker ("Virile Style," 214), the Old Italian proverb *Fatti maschii, parole femine* ("Deeds are male, words are female") still serves as the motto on the Great Seal of Maryland.

19. Quoted by Parker, "Virile Style," 203.

20. Matthew of Vendôme, *Ars Versificatoria*, 75.

21. *Ars Versificatoria*, 74 (translation modified slightly by Epp, "Learning to Write with Venus's Pen").

22. *Ars Versificatoria*, 75 (translation modified slightly by Epp).

23. Epp, "Learning to Write with Venus's Pen," 265–79.

24. Woods, "Rape," 73.

25. Wetherbee, *The Cosmographia of Bernardus Silvestris*, 96.

26. Ibid., 126.

27. Fanger, "The Formative Feminine," 81.

28. In their studies of Bernard's primary source, Plato's *Timaeus*, Luce Irigaray and Judith Butler both focus upon Plato's patriarchal valorizing of *hyle*, that is, the nature of feminine matter. Matter for Plato is "sterile," writes Iri-garay, "female in receptivity only, not in pregnancy . . . castrated of that impreg-nating power which belongs only to the unchangeably masculine" (Irigaray, *Speculum of the Other Woman*, 179). Butler expands upon Irigaray's analysis, arguing that the cosmogony of Forms in the *Timeaus* is "a phallic phantasy of a fully self-constituted patrilineality, and this fantasy of autogenesis or self-constitution is effected through a denial and cooptation of the female capacity for reproduction" (Butler, *Bodies That Matter*, 43).

29. The identification of the penis with the pen is a long-lasting trope in western letters. "Male sexuality," writes Sandra Gilbert in her landmark survey of this conceit, "is not just analogically but actually the essence of literary power. The poet's pen is in some sense (even more than figuratively) a penis" (Gilbert, "The Queen's Looking Glass," 4).

30. Alanus de Insulis, *The Plaint of Nature*, 216.

31. Ibid., 218.

32. Ibid., 71–72.

33. Ibid., 136.

34. Ibid., 137.

35. Ibid., 154–55.

36. See especially Ziolkowski, *Alan of Lille's Grammar of Sex*; Leupin, *Barbarolexis*, 59–78; Wetherbee, *Platonism and Poetry*, 188–211; Wetherbee, "The Function of Poetry"; Miskimin, *The Renaissance Chaucer*; H. White, *Nature, Sex, and Goodness*, 84–95; and Scanlon, "Unspeakable Pleasures."

37. Alanus de Insulis, *The Plaint of Nature*, 135.

38. Cowell, "The Dye of Desire," 116.

39. Minnis, *Magister Amoris*, 201.

40. Ibid., 169.

41. Ibid.

42. Shedding light on the semiotics of nakedness and of clothing in medieval poetry and aesthetics, Minnis connects Chaucer's opposition in the Prologue to the *Legend of Good Women* between "the naked text" and "glosyng" to "the crucial importance of the *sensus literalis*" in relation to the "fabulous garments of style which had adorned the *integumenta poetarum*" (Minnis, *Magister Amoris*, 137).

43. Guillaume de Lorris and Jean de Meun, *The Romance of the Rose*, 411, lines 19436–37.

44. Ibid., 415, lines 19610–11.

45. Minnis discusses the expectation in the Middle Ages that a priest should be sexually intact (Minnis, *Magister Amoris*, 195).

46. Jean never makes these vows explicit. In fact, Nature, as she sends her priest to Cupid, allows that "Of Forced Abstinence / I've much suspicion"; Guillaume de Lorris and Jean de Meun, *The Romance of the Rose*, 410, lines 19347–48.

47. For a revealing study of the polyvalent and conflicting symbolism of the cock—priapic, castrated, divinely intelligent, poetically inspired—as it relates to clerical potency and to medieval hermeneutics, see Minnis, *Magister Amoris*, 185–92.

48. The neologism "testeria" is, I believe, a coinage of Sandra Gilbert and Susan Gubar who accuse Frank Lentricchia of waxing testerical in his seemingly profeminist but ultimately phallocentric defense of the erotic (but not quite homosexual) world without women in Wallace Stevens's "Sunday Morning" (in Stevens, *Collected Poems*, 66–70). See Lentricchia, "Patriarchy Against Itself," 774. See next Gilbert and Gubar, "The Man on the Dump." In "Andiamo!" Lentricchia responds with an essay including a fictive exchange between him and his father (410):

> Dad, what's testeria?
> *Figlio!* What's happened to your Italian? It's TestaREEa. *Capisce?*
> Yes.
> Tell me.
> A store where they sell that stuff.
> In big jars!
> Let's go there!

The testerical debate did not end there. In a chapter entitled "Redeeming the Phallus," Lee Edelman reveals how "the 'stuff' of desire dispensed from the jars of this 'TestaREEa' constitutes the very essence of phallogocentric power insofar as it conflates associations of heads (the Italian 'testa') and texts (the Italian 'testo') with sperm (the 'stuff' of testicles) and testosterone (the 'stuff' of maleness)"; Edelman, *Homographesis*, 41. In short, all the terms in the medieval debate about the valence of sexual genius are still in play.

49. Freud, "The Uncanny," 160.

50. Derrida, *Dissemination*, 268, n. 67.

51. Brosnahan, "The Authenticity of *And Preestes Thre*," 306. "Rather than imagining that four characters were jammed into a bare two lines," Brosnahan reasons, "it is now possible to see that only one character [the second nun] and her description is cut off, a second character, the Nun's Priest, should obviously follow her portrait, but of it nothing survives, if it was ever written, and the last two characters [the two other priests] are not really part of the work. All tale tellers are now fully portrayed but the Second Nun and the Nun's Priest, and the admission of a hole in A 164 would explain both omissions" (307).

52. Birky, "The Word Was Made Flesh." See also Hass, "A Picture of Such Beauty."

53. Birky, "The Word Was Made Flesh," 171.

54. Ibid., 175.

55. Ibid., 177.

56. Ibid., 181.

57. Ibid., 182.

58. Ibid., 189.

59. Ibid., 109.

60. Matthew of Vendôme, *Ars Versificatoria*, 1.57; quoted by Hass, "A Picture of Such Beauty," 391.

61. Geoffrey of Vinsauf, *Poetria Nova*, 37.

62. Birky, "The Word Was Made Flesh," 191.

63. Matthew of Vendôme, *Ars Versificatoria*, 1.67, quoted by Hass, "A Picture of Such Beauty," 389.

64. Birky, "The Word Was Made Flesh," 190, 198.

65. See especially Lindley, "Inducing the Hole," and Scala, *Absent Narratives*, esp. 71–134.

66. Leicester, "The Art of Impersonation," 216.

67. Ibid., 217.

68. "Dramatic" and "biographical" readings of *The Nun's Priest's Tale* and of its teller have often been extraordinarily inventive. For an ample review (although such readings are presently less in fashion), see the sections titled "The 'Dramatic' Reading" and "Skepticism Concerning the 'Dramatic' Reading" in Pearsall, *The Nun's Priest's Tale*, 32–42.

69. Barthes, *The Pleasure of the Text*, 17.

70. Ibid., 10.

Two. *The Nun's Priest's Tale* as Grammar School Primer, Menippean Parody, and *Ars Poetica*

1. Clogan, "Literary Genres," 203.

2. For a review of Aesopic fables in the medieval classroom, see Wheatley, *Mastering Aesop*, esp. 32–51.

3. Ibid., 59.

4. Ibid., 77.

5. Ibid., 77.

6. Ibid., 78.

7. Ibid., 91.

8. Cato, *Disticha Catonis*.

9. Hazelton, "Chaucer and Cato," 358.

10. Ibid., 368.

11. Ibid., 360.

12. Ibid., 357, n. 2.

13. Ibid., 360.

14. Ibid., 373.

15. Ibid., 372.

16. Reed, *Middle English Debate Poetry.*

17. A late twelfth-century account by William of Fitzstephen describes ritual competitions acted out in a London churchyard between boys from different schools. Apparently twelve to fourteen years of age, these boys display an impressive mastery of the arts of scholastic disputation, all the while using the trivium to provide further artillery in their intellectual battles: "The scholars dispute, some in demonstrative rhetoric, others in dialectic. Some 'hurtle enthymemes,' others with greater skill employ perfect syllogisms. Boys of different schools strive against one another in verse, or contend concerning the principles of grammar, or the rules concerning past and future. There are others who employ the old art of the crossroads in epigrams, rhymes, and metre." Quoted by Murphy, "Rhetoric and Dialectic," 202.

18. A. Leach, *A History of Warwick School,* 79; also quoted in Miner, *The Grammar Schools,* 135.

19. John of Salisbury, *Metalogicon,* 66–71.

20. A. Leach, *A History of Winchester College,* 65; also partially quoted by Miner, *The Grammar Schools,* 125.

21. Zacharias, "Chaucer's *Nun's Priest's Tale,*" 60–61.

22. Pearsall, *The Nun's Priest's Tale,* 243.

23. See Thomson, *An Edition of the Middle English Grammatical Texts,* esp. 36–37, 82–83, 105.

24. As one example, consider simply the chapter titles of William Heytesbury's *On "Insoluble" Sentences,* chap. 1: "On Insoluble Sentences"; chap. 2: "Sophisms Involving the Words 'Know' and 'Doubt'"; chap. 3: "Logical Problems Arising from the Use of Relative Pronouns"; chap. 4: "Problems Concerning the Terms 'Begins' and 'Ends'"; chap. 5: "Maxima and Minima"; chap. 6: "Velocity and Acceleration."

25. For a discussion of the problems of "I" in *The Book of the Duchess,* see Travis, "White."

26. Besserman, "Chaucerian Wordplay," 68–73.

27. Pearsall, *The Nun's Priest's Tale,* 223.

28. Ibid.

29. Miner, *The Grammar Schools,* 181.

30. Ibid., 182.

31. John of Salisbury, *Metalogicon*, 68.

32. Lenaghan, "The Nun's Priest's Fable." For a study that touches on the influence of the *progymnasmata* on Shakespeare's plays, see Baldwin, *William Shakespere's Small Latine*, 464–753; for a more focused study of the influence of the *progymnasmata* on Milton, see D. Clark, *John Milton*, 230–49.

33. Priscian, "Fundamentals," 52–68.

34. Clark, *John Milton*, 231.

35. Priscian, "Fundamentals," 54.

36. Ibid., 54–55.

37. Ibid., 57.

38. Ibid., 58.

39. Ibid., 58–59.

40. Ibid., 59.

41. Ibid., 66.

42. Ibid., 66.

43. Kelly, *The Arts of Poetry and Prose*, passim. "Small units of discourse" is Kelly's translation of *Tendenz zur kleinen Einheit*, as used by Quadlbauer, "Zur Theorie der Komposition," 115–31.

44. Referenced in Costa, "Dialectic and Mercury," 44, citing Migne, *Patrologia Latina*, columns 853C–854A.

45. Honorius of Autun, "Concerning the Exile of the Soul," 198–206, at 199.

46. Ibid., 204.

47. Di Scipio and Scaglione, *The Divine Comedy*.

48. Ian Bishop, "*The Nun's Priest's Tale* and the Liberal Arts," 257–58.

49. Ibid., 258.

50. Weinbrot, *Menippean Satire Reconsidered*, 4, 19.

51. Relihan, *Ancient Menippean Satire*, 10.

52. Frye, *Anatomy of Criticism*, 308–12.

53. Ibid., 309.

54. Bakhtin, *Problems of Dostoevsky's Poetics*, 93–97, and passim.

55. F. Anne Payne, *Chaucer and Menippean Satire*, 7.

56. Relihan, *A History of Menippean Satire*, 13.

57. F. Anne Payne, *Chaucer and Menippean Satire*, 3.

58. My adaptation is constructed out of two other adaptations: Relihan, *Ancient Menippean Satire*, 6–7, and Weinbrot, *Menippean Satire Reconsidered*, 12.

59. F. Anne Payne, *Chaucer and Menippean Satire,* 7–11.

60. Fowler, *Kinds of Literature,* 119.

61. Weinbrot, *Menippean Satire Reconsidered,* 2.

62. Ibid., 4.

63. Ibid, xii.

64. Relihan, *Ancient Menippean Satire,* 194–97.

65. F. Anne Payne, *Chaucer and Menippean Satire,* 21.

66. Kirk, *Menippean Satire.*

67. Bronson, *In Search of Chaucer,* 32; quoted by F. Anne Payne, *Chaucer and Menippean Satire,* 31.

68. Kirk, *Menippean Satire,* 21–31.

69. Hutcheon, *A Theory of Parody,* 50.

70. Ibid. This is Hutcheon's characterization of Morson's thesis.

71. Cited by Hutcheon, *A Theory of Parody,* 51.

72. John of Salisbury, *Metalogicon,* 69.

73. Hutcheon, *A Theory of Parody,* 11.

74. See ibid., 62.

75. Ibid., 63.

76. Ibid., 60.

77. Ibid., 92.

78. Greene, *Light in Troy,* 28–53.

79. Ibid., 40.

80. Ibid., 45.

81. Geoffrey of Vinsauf, *Poetria Nova,* 26.

82. Ibid., 28.

83. Ibid., 29–31.

84. Cited in Pearsall, *The Nun's Priest's Tale,* 239.

85. Ibid.

86. Ibid.

87. Ibid.

88. Ibid., 240.

89. Ibid.

90. Ibid.

91. Ibid.

92. Culler, "Apostrophe," 59–69; cited by Hutcheon, *A Theory of Parody,* 63.

93. Hutcheon, *A Theory of Parody,* 4.

94. Ibid., 28.

95. Ibid.

96. In the judgment of Esther Quinn, *The Nun's Priest's Tale* serves as "a cover for writing about Richard": "Composed at a time when the young monarch was surrounded by men who were attempting to curtail his power, the tale conveys both a warning and a reassurance that disaster may be avoided"; Quinn, *Geoffrey Chaucer and the Poetics of Disguise*, 160–61.

97. Deschamps, *Oeuvres Complètes*, 103–4.

98. Brewer, "What is *The Nun's Priest's Tale* Really About?" 21.

99. Elbow, *Oppositions*, 107.

100. Pearsall's description of Owens's reading, from Pearsall, *The Nun's Priest's Tale*, 201.

101. Bishop, "*The Nun's Priest's Tale* and the Liberal Arts," 262.

102. Steiner, *After Babel*, 312–16.

103. Bloomfield, "The Magic of *In Principio*," 565.

104. Pearsall, *The Nun's Priest's Tale*, 199.

105. Augustine, *Confessions*, 256.

106. Stock, *Augustine the Reader*, 232; "an immense wood filled with snares and dangers" appears in *Confessions* 10.35.37.

107. For these two translations provided by editors (Pollard and Mac-Cracken) as well as others, see Law, "In Principio."

108. Pearsall, *The Nun's Priest's Tale*, 200.

109. William of Sherwood, *Introduction to Logic*, 115. It is appropriate in this light that William of Sherwood's examination of *Mulier que damnavit salvavit* appears in a chapter entitled "Simple Supposition and Singular, Indefinite, or Particular Propositions."

110. Cited by Kretzmann, William of Sherwood, *Introduction to Logic*, 115, n. 43.

111. Ibid.

112. Spade, "The Semantics of Terms," 196.

113. Dane, "*Mulier Est Hominis Confusio*," 276–78.

114. Ibid., 277–78.

115. Dinshaw, *Chaucer's Sexual Poetics*, 134.

116. Variants of this antifeminist latinate humor are to be found in many sites in late medieval English culture, as in this fifteenth-century poem (excerpted):

What Women Are Not

Of all creatures women be best,
Cuius contrarium verum est.

In every place ye may well see
That women be trewe as tirtill on tree,
Not liberal in langage but ever in secree,
And gret joye amonge them is for to be.

Of all creatures women be best,
Cuius contrarium verum est.

The stedfastnes of women will never be don,
So gentil, so curtes, they be everichon,
Meke as a lambe, still as a stone,
Croked nor crabbed find ye none.

Of all creatures women be best,
Cuius contrarium verum est. Etc.

Quoted in Davies, *Medieval English Lyrics,* 221–22.

117. See, especially, Birney, *Essays on Chaucerian Irony.*

118. "Risky" is employed in this context by Fish, "Short People," 176; see Hutcheon, *Irony's Edge,* 12.

119. M. Pratt, "Arts of the Contact Zone," 34; cited by Hutcheon, *Irony's Edge,* 93.

120. Culler, *Structuralist Poetics,* 158; cited by Hutcheon, *Irony's Edge,* 28.

121. Hutcheon, *Irony's Edge,* 28.

122. Ibid., 47.

123. See especially Bauschatz, "Chaucer's Pardoner's Beneficent Lie."

124. Baum, *Chaucer,* 221; cited in Pearsall, *The Nun's Priest's Tale,* 234.

125. E. Howard, *Geoffrey Chaucer,* 177–78; cited in Pearsall, *The Nun's Priest's Tale,* 234.

126. Baugh, *Chaucer's Major Poetry,* 379; cited in Pearsall, *The Nun's Priest's Tale,* 234.

127. Pearsall reviews the long tradition of "dramatic readings" of the *Tale,* wherein it is imagined that readers are able to descry a great deal about the Nun's Priest's life, his social relations, his personal appearance, and his private beliefs in *The Nun's Priest's Tale,* 32–39.

128. Ibid.; see as well the section titled "Skepticism Concerning the 'Dramatic' Reading," 39–42.

129. See Fish, "Short People."

130. Gordon, *The Double Sorrow of Troilus,* passim.

131. Pearsall, *The Nun's Priest's Tale,* 223.

132. Ibid., 223.

133. F. Anne Payne, *Chaucer and Menippean Satire*, 203 and 184.

134. Booth, *A Rhetoric of Irony*, 4.

135. Fish, "Short People," 176.

136. Ibid., 189. In the same issue, Booth provides a fully considered rebuttal to Fish: Booth, "A New Strategy."

137. Goldstein, "Chaucer, Freud, and the Political Economy of Wit," 148. See also Delany, "*Mulier est hominis confusio.*"

138. Most germane in this regard are Dane, "The Myth of Chaucerian Irony," and Pearsall, "Epidemic Irony."

139. Hartman, *Saving the Text*, 146; cited by Hutcheon in *Irony's Edge*, 9.

Three.   Close Reading: Beginnings and Endings

1. Kermode, *The Sense of an Ending*, 7.

2. See Davidoff, *Beginning Well*. In Davidoff's judgment, all medieval English narrative poems begin with one of six "basic opening modes": (1) a direct plunge into the material; (2) a statement of the content of the poem; (3) a prayer; (4) an explanation of how the poem came to be written; (5) an explanation of why the audience should listen to the poem; and, the most popular, (6) a framing fiction where an initial narrative event sets the stage for the interior, "core pattern," of the poem. For a sophisticated exploration of the theory and practice of beginnings in fourteenth-century literature and thought in England, see Smith, *The Book of the Incipit*.

3. Geoffrey of Vinsauf, *Poetria Nova*, 19–20.

4. Ibid., 20–21.

5. For the various uses of *argumentum* in classical literary theory, see Trimpi, *Muses of One Mind*, esp. 296–305.

6. Scanlon, *Narrative, Authority, and Power*, 3.

7. Ibid., 137. The eight tales Scanlon classifies as "clearly" *exempla* are *The Friar's Tale, The Summoner's Tale, The Physician's Tale, The Pardoner's Tale, The Monk's Tale* (an *exemplum* collection), *The Nun's Priest's Tale*, and *The Manciple's Tale*; see his note on 137.

8. See especially Robertson, "Some Disputed Chaucerian Terminology."

9. Robert Kilburn Root found the portrait enjoys "all the vividness and realism of a Dutch genre painting by Teniers or Gerard Dou" in *The Poetry of Chaucer*, 214; Percy Van Dyke Shelly felt it was "Homeric in its lifelike and homely details" in *The Living Chaucer*, 62; in *The Nun's Priest's Tale*, 140, Pearsall represents the view of Claus Uhlig, who saw it as "a pleasant picture, in the style of the Dutch Masters" in *Chaucer und die Armut*.

10. Donovan, "The *Moralite* of the Nun's Priest's Sermon"; Dahlberg, "Chaucer's Cock and Fox"; Engelhardt, "The Ecclesiastical Pilgrims"; Robertson, "Some Disputed Chaucerian Terminology."

11. Pearsall's representation of Uhlig's position, *The Nun's Priest's Tale*, 140.

12. Watkins, "Chaucer's *Sweete Preest.*"

13. Pearsall's representation of Friedman's thesis (Pearsall, *The Nun's Priest's Tale*, 37), as fully argued in J. Friedman, "The *Nun's Priest's Tale.*"

14. Pearsall's representation of Strange's thesis (Pearsall, *The Nun's Priest's Tale*, 46), as fully argued in Strange, "The *Monk's Tale.*"

15. Pearsall's representation of Robertson's thesis (Pearsall, *The Nun's Priest's Tale*, 145) as fully argued in Robertson, "Some Disputed Chaucerian Terminology."

16. Whittock, *A Reading of the Canterbury Tales*, 230.

17. John Lyons reviews the literature pertaining to this Greek model in *Exemplum*, esp. 6; 10; 246, n. 24. Scanlon reviews the Greek and Roman ways of understanding the *exemplum* genre in his *Narrative, Authority, and Power*, 32–34.

18. Lyons, *Exemplum*, 11.

19. Sheldon Sacks, for example, in *Fiction*, contrasts the apologue to the novel, or what he calls "represented action." "The informing principle" of apologues, Sacks writes, "is that each is organized as a fictional example of the truth of a formulable statement or closely related set of such statements" (8). In novels, by contrast, "characters, about whose fate we are made to care," are introduced "in unstable relationships which are then further complicated until the complications are finally resolved by the complete removal of the represented instability" (26).

20. Lyons, *Exemplum*, 5.

21. Ibid., 3.

22. Gelas, "*La Fiction manipulatrice*," 21; translation in Lyons, *Exemplum*, 21.

23. See Pearsall's notes, *The Nun's Priest's Tale*, 143.

24. See *Categoriae*, in Aristotle, *Basic Works*, 8.

25. Rowland, "A Sheep."

26. Hill, *Chaucerian Belief*, 139. Pearsall's extensive note on the economic status of the widow is extremely informative: *The Nun's Priest's Tale*, 139–40.

27. Pearsall, *The Nun's Priest's Tale*, 145.

28. Benson, *The Riverside Chaucer*, 531 (*Troilus and Criseyde*, III.1309).

29. Kuntz, *The Concept of Order*, xxiii.

30. Levy and Adams, "Chauntecleer's Paradise Lost and Regained."

31. Pearsall, *The Nun's Priest's Tale*, 146.

32. Suleiman, *Authoritarian Fictions*, 54.

33. Ibid., 199–238.

34. Parker, *Literary Fat Ladies*, 11.

35. One of the best studies of how authoritative discourse may contend with other discourses in the same literary text remains Mikhail Bakhtin's *The Dialogic Imagination*. Authoritative discourse, according to Bakhtin, is a monologic and "privileged language that approaches us from without; it is distanced, taboo, and permits no play with its framing context"; dialogism, on the other hand, is a consciousness of linguistic diversity that freely mixes "different semantic and axiological conceptual systems" by transgressing historical and social speech boundaries in order to celebrate "the living heteroglossia of language" (424, 306, 326). What is extraordinary about the Nun's Priest's *exemplum* is not only its heady admixture of axiological conceptual systems but the dialogical interplay of several semantic systems at once, such as the fetched-from-afar "halle and bour" and "hertes suffisaunce."

36. The coercion involved in the pursuit of an absolute Rule even in the reading of authoritarian fictions is evident earlier in this chapter, where I insisted that nothing could possibly divert one from the desired reading of Griselda's virtues: however, "No lecherous lust" and "Wel ofter of the welle than of the tonne" cannot but conjure up, if only momentarily, a subversive counterreading.

37. Said, *Beginnings*, 42.

38. Rather than finding Chaucer invariably undermining exemplarity at every turn, "what we actually get in the *Tales* is evidence of exemplary morality repeatedly going unheeded, and we need not on that account think exemplary rhetoric is faulty," writes J. Allan Mitchell in his useful study, *Ethics and Exemplary Narrative in Chaucer and Gower*, 82.

39. Scanlon, *Narrative, Authority, and Power*, 137.

40. Hardison and Golden, *Horace*, 11.

41. Sterne, *The Life and Opinions of Tristram Shandy*, 8.

42. Studies of narrative endings are legion. A few that are most germane to Chaucer are: Richter, *Fable's End*; Sklute, *Virtue of Necessity*; and McGerr, *Chaucer's Open Books*.

43. Edward Wheatley, in his comprehensive review of medieval fables, concludes that *moralitates* interpreted their fables in a wide variety of ways with no discernable overarching "system"; see his *Mastering Aesop*, 62–91.

44. Pearsall, *The Nun's Priest's Tale*, 12.

45. de Man, *The Resistance to Theory*, 3–20.

46. Ibid., 14.

47. Gasché, *The Wild Card of Reading*, 147.

48. Huntsman, "Grammar," 61.

49. Alanus de Insulis, *Anticlaudianus*, 97, n. 26.

50. Camargo, "Rhetoric," 108.

51. See Stump, "Dialectic."

52. See Bursill-Hall, *Speculative Grammars*.

53. An illustrative case in point is Henri d'Andely's thirteenth-century allegorical poem *The Battle of the Seven Liberal Arts*, where the figure of Logic, aided by Aristotle, Boethius, and others, issues forth from Paris to do battle with Grammar, supported by Donatus, Priscian, Virgil, Homer, and Ovid; but even when Logic wins the battle, we are told the war is not over, for, as Henri confidently predicts, in thirty years Grammar will again be in supremacy because without complete knowledge of the parts of speech no student will be able to advance in his academic career. See Paetow, *Two Medieval Satires*.

54. Suzanne Reynolds reviews these educational steps in her *Medieval Reading*, 7–44.

55. Ibid, 11.

56. Ibid., 21–22.

57. Ibid., 130–31.

58. For an authoritative analysis, see Kretzmann, "Syncategoremata, sophismata, exponibilia."

59. William of Sherwood, *Treatise on Syncategorematic Words*, 8.

60. Kretzmann, "Syncategoremata, sophismata, exponibilia," 217.

61. Ibid., 217, n. 24.

62. An academic skit from the 1960s Oxbridge review *Beyond the Fringe* (with Jonathan Miller, Alan Bates, Dudley Moore, and Peter Cook), where "Bertrand Russell" recounts a crucial moment in his philosophical career, brilliantly captures the survival of these syncategorematic concerns well into the twentieth century:

One of the advantages of living in Great Court, Trinity, I seem to recall, was the fact that one could pop across any time of the day or night and trap the then young G. E. Moore into a logical falsehood by the means of a cunning semantic subterfuge. I recall one occasion with particular vividness. I had popped across and had knocked upon his door. "Come in," he said. I decided to wait a while in order to test the validity of his proposition. "Come in," he said once again. "Very well," I replied, "if that is in fact truly what you wish." I opened the door accordingly and went in, and there was Moore seated by the fire with a basket upon his knee. "Moore," I said. "Do you have any apples in that basket?" "No," he replied, and smiled seraphically as was his wont. I decided to try a different logical tact. "Moore," I said, "do you then have some apples in that basket?" "No," he replied, leaving me in a logical cleft stick from which I had but one way out. "Moore," I said, "do you then have apples in that basket?" "Yes," he replied, and from that day forth we remained the very closest of friends. (Bennett, Moore, Cook, and Miller, *The Complete Beyond the Fringe*, 129–30)

63. Kretzmann suggests, at a miminum, that the reader would do well to acquire a general knowledge of the four properties of categorematic terms—signification, supposition, copulation, and appellation—before undertaking a study of Sherwood's syncategorematic treatise; William of Sherwood, *Treatise on Syncategorematic Words*, 5.

64. Kretzmann selects "totus" and "praeter" as the two premier examples to explore in detail because they are "two of the most frequently discussed syncategorematic words" in medieval logic; "Syncategoremata, sophismata, exponibilia," 216.

65. Ibid., 224.

66. In an introduction to his analysis of *praeter*, the fourteenth-century Mertonian logician Walter Burleigh defines the four things that are required for determining such an exception: "[1] the part that is excepted, [2] the whole from which the exception is made, [3] something in respect of which the exception is made, and [4] the act of excepting, which is conveyed by means of the exceptive word as by an instrument." Quoted in Kretzmann, "Syncategoremata, sophismata, exponibilia," 218.

67. Pearsall, *The Nun's Priest's Tale*, 255.

68. Kretzmann, "Syncategoremata, sophismata, exponibilia," 218.

69. For manuscript variants of NPT 3439, see Manly and Rickert, *The Text of the Canterbury Tales*, 8:613. Manly and Rickert's work on *The Nun's Priest's Tale* manuscript variants has been superceded by Thomas, *The Nun's Priest's Tale on CD-ROM*; see the collation of all witnesses for line 619.

70. Kretzmann, *William of Sherwood's "Treatise on Syncategorematic Words,"* 8.

71. Minnis, *Medieval Theory*, 206.

72. Caxton's translation, quoted in Minnis, *Medieval Theory*, 206.

73. I consider Chaucer's similar but scarcely identical use of Romans 15:4 in my "Deconstructing Chaucer's Retraction."

74. The most recent attempt to identify the referent of "my lord" as Christ is Field, "The Ending." Field also traces through all prior explications and non-explications of the identity of "my lord."

75. See de Man, *The Resistance to Theory*, 191.

76. Ibid., 17.

77. Ibid., 15.

78. Gasché, *The Wild Card of Reading*, 9.

79. Ibid., 20.

80. de Man, *The Resistance to Theory*, 17; Gasché, *The Wild Card of Reading*, 9.

81. Gasché, *The Wild Card of Reading*, 23.

82. In *Paul de Man*, Martin McQuillan explains the meaning of undecideability: "Reading is *never* a matter of resolving the meaning of a text, it is always a matter of the challenge of *undecideability* posed by meaning, where undecideability expresses itself. Undecideability is the experience of being unable to come to a decision when faced with two or more contradictory meanings or interpretations. It is not the same as 'indeterminacy,' a word that suggests a decision has been made and this decision is that a decision cannot be reached. In contrast undecideability stresses the active and interminable challenge of being unable to decide. In this sense, meaning is *radically* independent of the reader, if we conceive of 'the reader' in its traditional sense as a conscious individual exerting their will on a text" (55).

83. Lentricchia and duBois, *Close Reading*.

84. Ibid., ix.

85. Derrida, "Ulysses Gramaphone."

86. Storr, "Realism and Its Doubles," 18.

87. Quoted in Lyons and Storr, *Chuck Close*, 21.

88. Smith, "Medieval Fora," 79.

Four.   Chaucer's Heliotropes and the Poetics of Metaphor

1. Alanus de Insulis, *Anticlaudianus*, 46.

2. Ibid., 49.

3. As James J. Sheridan remarks in his notes to these passages, Alanus's extravagant admiration of Painting/Rhetoric was shared by his fellow Chartrians: for them, rhetoric not only embraced all forms of literature but was considered to be "the integrating factor of all education" (in Alanus de Insulis, *Anticlaudianus*, 97, n. 26).

4. Ibid., 97.

5. Ibid., 49.

6. That metaphor was absolutely central to medieval ways of thinking about poetry appears beyond dispute. "It would be safe to say," Lisa Kiser has written, "that the medieval theory of poetry was to a large extent dependent upon the understanding of how metaphors work"; Kiser, *Telling Classical Tales*, 50. In her review of medieval poetics, Margaret F. Nims concludes that "metaphor appears to be a basic unit of verbal meaning—of *poesis*, of *mimesis*. Metaphor, we might say, is a poeseme"; "*Translatio*," 221.

7. In *Time and the Crystal*, Robert M. Durling and Ronald L. Martinez provide an excellent review of the medieval lore of crystals generally and of heliotropes (both the gem and the plant); see 32–45, 114–16, and passim.

8. Text and translation provided by Durling and Martinez, *Time and the Crystal*, 120.

9. Valéry, *Oeuvres*, 1449–56.

10. For a study of this general poetic tradition (but with no special emphasis accorded the marguerite), see J. Wimsatt, *Chaucer and His French Contemporaries*.

11. The "Le dit de la Fleur de Lis et de la Marguerite" has been edited by J. Wimsatt, *The Marguerite Poetry*, 15–26. The description of the four parts of the marguerite's "person" appears in lines 203–42, pages 20–22.

12. Cited by J. Wimsatt, *The Marguerite Poetry*, 30. (My translation, with special thanks to Diane Marks.)

13. Machaut, "Le dit de la Fleur de Lis et de la Marguerite," lines 255–56, in J. Wimsatt, *The Marguerite Poetry*, 22.

14. Fourrier, editor of J. Froissart, *L'espinette amoureuse*, discovered these anagrams in lines 3386–89.

15. In "The Daisy and the Laurel," Sylvia Huot reveals how the marguerite proves to be a "multifaceted emblem," which, like poetry itself, is capable of taking on many associations: in one literary circumstance, Froissart's daisy is identifiable with the lady, in another with the poet's desire and loss, in another with unattainable and absolute perfection, and in still another with political figures. But as it moves through the entirety of Froissart's oeuvre, the

only apparent constant in the marguerite's significance is its self-identification as a "poetic flower," a "reified image, a work of art" (247).

16. The acrostic is formed by the first letter taken from each of the first sixteen lines of the opening stanzas of Machaut's "sixth complaint"; see J. Wimsatt, *The Marguerite Poetry*, 40–41.

17. J. Wimsatt, *The Marguerite Poetry*, 51. Wimsatt's source for this characterization of Marguerite of Flanders is Armitage-Smith, *John of Gaunt*, 29.

18. Although Wimsatt allows that "we can surely imagine that the [French] poets were celebrating an exemplar which had no existence outside their minds" (J. Wimsatt, *The Marguerite Poetry*, 9), a major part of his monograph is devoted to identifying Pierre de Lusignan as Machaut's Pierre.

19. Cicero, *De oratore*, 3.157.

20. Isidore of Seville, *Etymologiarum*, 50.27.

21. Bede, *Libri II De Arte Metrica*, 182.

22. Translations of Aristotle are taken from Aristotle, *Basic Works*.

23. Gordon, "The Enigma of Aristotelian Metaphor," 88.

24. In "Saint Augustine's Region of Unlikeness," Margaret W. Ferguson observes: "Augustine is haunted by the parallel between the nature of language and the nature of man 'lost in our present sad dispersal.' His analysis of language as a sequence of parts is in many ways a forerunner of Derrida's discussions of language as a 'play of differences' that necessarily ruptures any concept of truth as a totality. Unlike modern theorists, however, when faced with contradictions between a philosophy of essence and a linguistics of difference, Augustine chooses to relinquish language rather than God" (845).

25. Ricoeur, *The Rule of Metaphor*, 143–46.

26. Derrida, "The *Retrait*."

27. Parker, *Literary Fat Ladies*, 47.

28. The fantasy of a "green," antilogical, prelinguistic domain has been put into words in various ways by poets and philosophers. Two examples: Andrew Marvell in "The Garden" imagines a place that "Annihilat[es] all that's made / To a green thought in a green shade"; Noam Chomsky in his famous pseudoproposition discovers a similar metaphorical space: "Colorless green ideas sleep furiously."

29. Mansell, "Metaphor as Matter," 116.

30. Ibid., 115.

31. Mansell, "Written in Eden," 221.

32. Derrida, "White Mythology," 243.

33. Ibid., 250–51.

34. Gasché, "Quasi-Metaphoricity," 190.

35. For an interesting study that attempts to classify the paradigms that determine the hierarchical priorities of metaphor, see Lakoff and Johnson, *Metaphors We Live By.*

36. Levin, "Aristotle's Theory," 42.

37. Ibid., 43.

38. Postulated but not embraced by Ricoeur, *The Rule of Metaphor,* 270.

39. Ibid., 197.

40. The complexity of this name transference is enhanced by Chaucer's use of "daisy" as his own poetic name for the "flowers" of rhetoric. At first glance his equation appears to be an illustration of one of Aristotle's four metaphoric classes, wherein a name is transferred "from species to genus": the species "daisy" substitutes here for the genus "flower." But, in this context, "flower" is a metaphoric name designating the genus of all poetic tropes. Thus "flower" (botanical thing/proper name) = "flower" (rhetorical figure/metaphorical name) involves a transference that Aristotle does not include in his definition: not only is this a transfer of a name from genus to genus, it is a transfer of a proper name of a species that looks suspiciously metaphorical, the "eye of the day," to displace another name that is surely metaphorical, "the flower of rhetoric." Further evidence that Chaucer was well aware of the challenge of properly naming the sun is found in *Troilus and Criseyde* (II.904–5): "The dayes honour, and the hevens ye, / The nyghtes foo—all this clepe I the sonne." In a strikingly similar vein, Derrida writes, "If the sun is metaphorical always, already, it is no longer completely natural. It is always, already a luster, a chandelier, one might say an *artificial* construction . . . : father, seed, fire, eye, egg, etc."; Derrida, "White Mythology," 251.

41. Kiser, *Telling Classical Tales,* 56.

42. Ibid., 59.

43. In the fourteenth century as in the twentieth century, philosophers have agonized over the ways propositions such as "The morning star is the evening star" do or do not have logical meaning. It would appear in the foregoing proposition that two discrete things, A and B, are said to be identical, which is impossible, for how can two planets be one planet? Or else it would appear that two words, A' and B', are two names with the same meaning, a verbal equation that results in the meaningless tautology " 'Venus' is 'Venus.' " Apparently indifferent to the logical problems she has invoked, Kiser takes the equations of Chaucer's metaphor/proposition entirely literally (or entirely anagogically): the daisy as thing and word "equals" ("is," "means") the sun as thing

and word. For a study of these and related problems in medieval and modern philosophy, see Henry, *That Most Subtle Question,* especially chapter 1, "Propositional Syntax and Semantics," 1–45.

44. The appearance of the pearl in Alceste's habiliment ("o perle fyn, oriental") underscores a corollary tradition made possible by another fertile homonym: Old French *marguerite* was the name of both the daisy and the pearl. Like *heliotropia* and *heliotropium,* the two *marguerites* were understood to share analogous qualities and powers. Each was miraculously created without the intervention of natural or human agency: the flower from the effect of sunlight on tears, the pearl from the effect of moonlight on dew. And each was a symbol of absolute beauty and perfection subsisting in this world in whose refracted light, sublunar or subsolar, the spiritual light of the next world is visible. Thus Chaucer's English contemporary, the *Pearl* poet, was able to write an ornate Christian poem set in a garden with a precious pearl, ultimately the *margarita pretiosa* of Matt. 13:45–46, as its symbolic subject. Despite the narrator's acknowledgment that only God could have fashioned his *perle,* the poem's veneration of the precious stone at its center cannot but attract the reader's gaze toward admiring the beauty of the poet's own work of art. It is appropriate that the pearl should have become the proper name of the poem itself (untitled in the manuscript) as well as the descriptive name of its otherwise anonymous author.

45. See Black, "Metaphor," and Lakoff and Turner, *More than Cool Reason,* 131–35.

46. Kiser, *Telling Classical Tales,* 61–62. In "The Prologue," John Livingston Lowes argues, by contrast, that "the daisy is Alceste." Lowes then attempts to arrest any further forms of identification: "To argue further that Alceste is also somebody else is to introduce . . . an element of complexity which . . . is absolutely foreign to the poems [of the French tradition] whose simple formula is *marguerite* = Marguerite" (643). There is no doubt, however, that an implicit equation of Alceste with Richard's queen, Anne of Bohemia, is made possible by the God of Love's injunction in the F manuscript (but not in the G manuscript): "And whan this book ys maad, yive it the quene, / On my byhalf, at Eltham or at Sheene" (F.496–97). A cautious reassessment of this issue is offered by Paul Strohm in *Hochon's Arrow*: "The key to the relationship between Alceste within the poem and the historical Anne rests less in the denial or affirmation of particular congruencies than in a recognition of the environment of interpretive structures within which Alceste was invented and within which Anne seems at least partially to have invented herself" (116).

47. Black, "Metaphor," 78.

48. In *The Rule of Metaphor* Ricoeur writes, "The idea of category mistake brings us close to our goal. Can one not say that the strategy of language at work in metaphor consists in obliterating the logical and established frontiers of language, in order to bring to light new resemblances the previous classification kept us from seeing? In other words, the power of metaphor would be to break an old categorization, in order to establish new logical frontiers on the ruins of their forerunners" (197). The idea of the "calculated category mistake" in which "a term with an extension established by habit is applied elsewhere under the influence of that habit" derives from Goodman, *Languages,* 71. See also Ryle, *The Concept,* 10.

49. Mansell, in "Metaphor as Matter," writes, "It has been observed that metaphor seems *always* to mean something that could (albeit with difficulty) be translated into a statement. . . . But metaphor will never come into its own so long as it is thought of in this way. Interpretation actually leads away from metaphor's strength" (112).

50. In "Metaphor as Matter," Mansell calls metaphor "a garden run to seed" (116).

51. Pearsall, *The Nun's Priest's Tale,* 151.

52. Salter, "Medieval Poetry," 19.

53. Schaar, *The Golden Mirror,* 353.

54. Alanus de Insulis, *Anticlaudianus,* 97.

55. To my knowledge the first scholar to make this general observation in print is Frese, "*The Nun's Priest's Tale,*" 336. Hidden in acrostics, anagrams, icons, and rebuses, the extraordinary variety of "occulted signatures" found in medieval literature, art, and heraldry has generated several fascinating studies. See Friedman and Friedman, "Acrostics"; Kooper, "Art and Signature;" Hult, *Self-Fulfilling Prophecies*; and especially Middleton, "William Langland's 'Kynde Name.'" Graphic representations of Chaucer continue the tradition of the artist's self-identification with his work: Anne Middleton notes that in the famous Harvard portrait panel (frontispiece, *The Riverside Chaucer*), Chaucer points to himself "as an image of 'myn intent,' using the same gesture with which in the Ellesmere marginal portrait he points to his text, and thereby makes a functional equivalence between them" (Middleton, "William Langland's 'Kynde Name,'" 37). Yeager, in "British Library Additional MS. 5141," notes that to the upper left of the figure of Chaucer (who again is pointing to himself) there is a red-and-white shield bearing arms attributed to Chaucer and used by his son, Thomas, and to the upper right there is a carefully drawn flower "rendered both in bloom and in bud" (261). Yeager consulted Robert W. Kiger, director of the Hunt Institute for Botanical Documentation, Carnegie-Mellon

University, who wrote, "All the botanists on our staff have looked at it, and we agree that the only real plant species that it could be intended to represent is *Bellis perennis,* the common English daisy or marguerite" (261). Thus the marguerite, like the family arms, was understood to be an icon of Chaucer's identity. (I am grateful to Professor Yeager for calling my attention to his essay.)

Another interesting use of this self-inscribing authorial tradition is found in the editing history of Thomas Usk's poem to his "margarite-perle," the *Testament of Love.* The poem's garbled text was successfully rearranged once it was discovered that the head letters of its sections spelled out the acrostic "margaret of vertw haue mercy on thin usk." See Skeat, *Testament of Love,* 7:1–145.

56. The exploration of the female figure to elevate the male artistic ego has an extremely long history. Helen Solterer in "At the Bottom," writes, "The link between women and rhetorical invention is effective precisely because female experience is invented to a large degree by the prime movers of high medieval society. Such a link makes sense in a signifying world that has always perceived women as plastic entities to be molded like so many Galateas" (218). Solterer also notes that the allegorical transformation of the rose/woman into "a parable of *écriture*" is a repetition by modern critics of the medieval erasure of the feminine: "The rose, which functions first as a decorous figure of the female sexualized body, is transmuted yet again into a purely poetic sign" (214).

57. See Rowland, "The Wisdom of the Cock," and Steadman, "Chauntecleer."

58. See chapter 6 of this study, "Chaucerian Horologics and the Confounded Reader."

59. Duhem, *Medieval Cosmology,* 295–363.

60. Stevens, *Collected Poems,* 373.

61. How in fact does any analogy work? For an admirable attempt at explaining the analogical process, see Tversky, "Features of Similarity."

62. Cited by de Man, "The Epistemology of Metaphor," 16. The passage cited appears in Locke, *An Essay,* 3.9 (2:86).

63. George Lakoff, one of the most impassioned scholars of metaphor in this past century, found it necessary to write a lengthy book about the indeterminate nature of categories: *Women, Fire, and Dangerous Things.*

64. See, as an example, Sorabji, *Animal Minds*; Sorabji discusses the role of analogy in Aristotle's definitions of man and animal on page 14. See also Salisbury, *The Beast Within*; Salisbury argues that the "metaphorical" anxiety concerning the boundary lines between human and animal was a late-medieval

phenomenon: "Most people lived too closely to their animals to appreciate their value as metaphor. This changed in the twelfth century, which coincided with the beginnings of the increased ambiguity between people and animals" (114).

The most celebrated philosophical definition of humankind in Western philosophy is Aristotle's "Homo est animal rationalis grammaticus capax risus" ("Man is a rational, language-speaking animal capable of laughter"). But, alas, this definition suits Chauntecleer too well: an animal, he is verbal and rational, but, weak on irony, he is only *capax risus*. It is perhaps safer to retreat into a definition predicated exclusively upon humankind's unique zoomorphic differences from all other fauna. Thus, a second celebrated definition, attributed to Plato, "Homo est animal implume bipes" ("Man is a featherless bipedal animal") with a qualification provided by Diogenes the Cynic, "latis unguibus" ("Man is a featherless bipedal animal with flat toenails"). There is no doubt that Chauntecleer is fully fledged (*plume* rather than *implume*). However, he is like man in that he has two legs; he also has "toon" (do birds actually have toes?); he even has toenails whose whiteness (color, once again) should be the envy of any courtly lady. Therefore, taxonomically, Chauntecleer, when naked, is entirely human. In philosophical rebuttal, Diogenes is reputed to have thrown a plucked chicken into Plato's academy: see Laertius, *The Lives and Opinions of Eminent Philosophers*, 231. For an excellent modern study that explores the difficulties of philosophically defining that which is properly human, see Ryle, "A Rational Animal."

65. Ricoeur, *The Rule of Metaphor*, 279.

66. Durling and Martinez persuasively argue that all four of the important figures in Dante's *Rime* 1 need to be understood as heliotropes: the *petra*, or stone, from which his verses gain their name; the grassy or floral *erba* under which that stone is sometimes "magically" hidden; the *donna*, who if she were to obey her own heliotropic tendencies would depetrify her passions; and the *rime* itself, whose gemlike brilliance controls the movement of the sun. See their *Time and the Crystal*, chapter 3, "The Sun and the Heliotrope," 109–37, and chapter 4, "The Poem as Crystal," 138–64.

67. A matter yet to be studied is the *petra sott'erba* theme as part of an intertextual dialogue among medieval poets concerning the hidden powers of their craft (see n. 44 above). Dante's *erba/petra* configuration appears to be answered by Froissart's *marguerite/pierre*, by the Pearl poet's *erbere/perle*, and even by Chaucer's *daiseye/perle*. It is also worth noting that the narrator of the Prologue to *The Legend of Good Women* falls asleep in an "herbere," rather as the "perle" in *Pearl* disappears into an "erbere."

68. Ryan, *Possible Worlds*, 15. For studies that take into partial account the indebtedness of modern possible-world theory to medieval modal logic, see Ryan, *Possible Worlds*, and Pavel, *Fictional Worlds*.

Patricia Parker in *Literary Fat Ladies* has shown how sexual mystery, improper ownership, and intellectual conundrum are all embedded in the idea of metaphor. One example she provides that bears upon the medieval *heliotropia/heliotropium* puzzle of "ownership" is a quatrain from Shakespeare's "The Phoenix and the Turtle":

> Property was thus appalled
> That the self was not the same;
> Single nature's double name
> Neither two nor one was called.

69. This apocalyptic vision has been embraced by Jean Baudrillard, who maintains that every image in the postmodern world is not a representation of reality (even the absence of reality). Rather, it is a simulacrum: "It bears no relation to any reality whatsoever." Thus we find in contemporary culture a "panic-stricken" escalation of the figurative simply because "the object and substance have disappeared." See Baudrillard, "Simulacra and Simulations."

The place of the medieval heliotrope that I have been defining in this chapter is categorically different from Baudrillard's place of simulation. Rather, metaphor's hiding place, or "place apart," is analogous to the paradoxical "~~IS~~" of Derrida's *différance*: positioned between Being and Nonbeing, it both "is not" and also "is not not." Or to quote Derrida at his most pixilated, "Reserving itself not exposing itself, in regular fashion it exceeds the order of truth at a certain precise point, but without dissimulating itself as something, as a mysterious being, in the occult of nonknowledge. . . . In every exposition it would be exposed to disappearing as disappearance. It would risk appearing: disappearing"; Derrida, "Différance," 121.

Five.   The Noise of History

1. Cicero, *On the Commonwealth*, 193.
2. Augustine, *The City of God*, 456.
3. Spitzer, *Classical and Christian Ideas of World Harmony*, 40.
4. *Exemplaria* published a "special cluster" of essays (including parts of this chapter's central section) focused on "medieval noise": Cohen, "*Kyte oute*

yugilment"; Warren, "The Noise of Roland"; Allen, "Broken Air"; and Uebel, "Acoustical Alterity." Holsinger's *Music, Body, and Desire in Medieval Culture* is an extremely important contribution to the study of the cultural significance of music and its antitheses in the Middle Ages.

5. Leppert, *The Sight of Sound.*

6. Ibid, with slight modification, 2.

7. Ibid.

8. Boethius, *Fundamentals of Music,* 9–10.

9. Chamberlain, "The Music of the Spheres."

10. Ibid, 39–40 (emphasis added).

11. See, especially, Hawes, "More Stars, God Knows, than a Pair," and Aers, *Chaucer,* 16.

12. Aers, *Chaucer,* 2.

13. Strohm, *Social Chaucer,* xiii.

14. Patterson, *Chaucer and the Subject of History,* 49.

15. Wallace, *Chaucerian Polity,* xvii.

16. W. Wilson, "Scholastic Logic," 181–84. For a demonstration of the truth tables at work elsewhere in Chaucer, see Roney, *Chaucer's Knight's Tale and Theories of Scholastic Psychology,* 172–84.

17. Boitani, *Chaucer and the Imaginary World of Fame,* 209.

18. The preeminent Priscianic glosses were the early twelfth-century *Glosule super Priscianum maiorem,* William of Conches's *Glose super Priscianum,* Peter Helias's *Summa super Priscianum,* and the mid-thirteenth-century *Tractactus super Priscianum maiorem* normally attributed to Robert Kilwardby.

19. Priscian, *Institutiones grammaticae,* 5–6.

20. Quoted in Irvine, "Medieval Grammatical Theory," 863, n. 41.

21. Boethius, *Fundamentals of Music,* 11.

22. Ibid., 10.

23. The analogy enjoys a long history, originating apparently with Galen, given its full classical features by Vitruvius, rephrased by Adelard of Bath and then by Aquinas in his commentary on Aristotle's *De Anima;* see Bennett, *Chaucer's Book of Fame,* 79–80. Surprisingly, Bennett overlooked Dante's use of the image.

24. Boethius, *Fundamentals of Music,* 21.

25. Alighieri, *The Divine Comedy* (Singleton), 3:152–53. Further citations by canto and line number in the text.

26. Schnapp, *The Transfiguration of History,* 163.

27. Patterson, *Chaucer and the Subject of History,* 321.

28. Ibid.

29. Ibid.

30. Ibid., 246.

31. Justice, *Writing and Rebellion,* 207, emphases in the original.

32. Stahl, *Martianus,* 352.

33. Justice, *Writing and Rebellion,* 45.

34. Ibid., 125. There has been considerable mobility among recent scholarly studies in determining the proper name of this revolt/rebellion/uprising. See, especially, Justice's discussion here.

35. Hudson, *The Premature Reformation,* 374–75.

36. Quoted by Justice, *Writing and Rebellion,* 147.

37. Scase, *Piers Plowman,* 47–54. The erudition with which the friars supported their position is satirized, Scase notes, in *Piers Plowman B xx,* 273–76:

Enuye herde þis and heet freres go to scole
And lerne logyk and lawe and ek contemplacion,
And preche men of Plato, and preue it by Seneca
That alle þynges vnder heuene ouȝte to ben in comune.

38. See Benson, *Riverside Chaucer,* 878, note to 2126–28.

39. Georgianna, "Lords, Churls, and Friars," 158–59.

40. See Levitan, "The Parody of Pentecost"; Levy, "Biblical Parody"; and R. Clark, "Wit and Whitsunday."

41. Cited by Justice, *Writing and Rebellion,* 108.

42. Beckwith, *Signifying God,* 29–30.

43. Gurevich, *Medieval Popular Culture,* 11; cited by Justice, *Writing and Rebellion,* 135.

44. Quoted and translated by Green, "A Possible Source," 24–27.

45. Ibid.

46. Boethius, *Fundamentals of Music,* 89–91.

47. Chaucer, *Boece* 2, pr. 5, 26–33. The original passage is: "Et uox quidem tota pariter multorum replet auditum, uestrae uero diuitiae nisi comminutae in plures transire non possunt"; Boethius, *Philosophiae Consolatio,* 26.

48. For this insight I am indebted to Wright, "Jankyn's Boethian Learning."

49. Leppert, *The Sight of Sound,* 15.

50. Mel Brooks, "Mel Brooks," 64–65.

51. Bakhtin, *The Dialogic Imagination,* 291.

52. For these insights I am indebted to A. White, "Bakhtin, Sociolinguistics, and Deconstruction."

53. This reading of the fart has also been explored by Cox, in "Toward Vernacular Humor," 315.

54. The twelve-spoked critical cartwheel I have provided is of course not meant to represent *the* definitive interpretative circle—other interpretative circles are readily available; in this regard it is significant that the squire specifies that Thomas should give not only one, but "fartes thre" (III.2284).

55. Pearsall, "Interpretative Models."

56. Ibid., 68.

57. Morrison, *The Bluest Eye*, 1.

58. Ibid., 2.

59. Alighieri, *The Divine Comedy of Dante Alighieri* (Sinclair), 3:261. For "e io notai / le parti sì, come mi parver dette," I have opted for the translation provided in Alighieri, *The Divine Comedy* (Singleton), 3:205, canto 18, lines 89–90.

60. Reprinted from Alighieri, *The Comedy of Dante Alighieri* (Sayers), 3:221–22.

61. Alighieri, *The Divine Comedy of Dante Alighieri* (Sinclair), 266.

62. Ibid., 286–89.

63. The Eagle's explication of the workings of divine justice is offered in *Paradiso* 19; the physiological production of significant sound, I suggest, is a phonetic analogue to the preceding discursive justification. For further explorations of the semiotics of language in *Paradiso* 26, see Fyler, *Language and the Declining World*, 120–27.

64. See Irvine in "Medieval Grammatical Theory," 860. Irvine's study is an admirably thorough literary application of medieval grammatical theory to *The House of Fame*. My presentation of certain fundamental concerns of medieval grammar is very much indebted to Irvine's research.

65. Priscian, *Institutiones grammaticae*, 5–6.

66. Cited by Irvine, "Medieval Grammatical Theory," 860.

67. Ibid., 855.

68. Ibid., 856.

69. In "Old MacBerlitz Had a Farm," Noel Perrin marvels at the low fidelity of the human ear when it comes to transcribing animal sounds. Dogs, for instance: in French they say "ouâ-ouâ," in Dutch "waf-waf," in Polish "hau-hau," in Irish "amh-amh," in Japanese "wan-wan," in Chinese "wang-wang"; whereas in the Shangana-Tsonga language of the Bantu group, "pyee" is "the cry a dog makes after being kicked." Pig dialects in their variety are just as inscrutable: rather than "oink-oink," Polish pigs say "kwick-kwick," Portuguese pigs go "cué cué," Hungarian pigs say "röff-röff," Finnish pigs cry "snöf-snöf,"

whereas Italian swine insist upon "fron-fron-fron." Noel Perrin, *First Person Rural,* 106–11.

70. A very informative contribution to our understanding of medieval theories of sound, and especially concerning the differences between animal sounds and human sounds, is E. Leach, *Sung Birds.*

71. Genette, *Mimologics,* xxii–xiii.

72. Ibid., xxii.

73. For an extensive discussion of this descriptivist/antidescriptivist (and nominalist/realist) debate, see my study "White," esp. 21–35.

74. Genette, *Mimologics,* 123.

75. Ibid., 124–25.

76. Ibid., 125.

77. Ibid.

78. Ibid., 126.

79. Ibid., 129.

80. Ibid.

81. Ibid., 129–30.

82. Ibid., 129.

83. Ibid., 126.

84. Ibid.

85. Ibid.

86. Ibid., 131.

87. Ibid.

88. Attridge, *Peculiar Language,* 133.

89. Tyler, *The Unspeakable,* 20–21; for a more sober analysis of thought and motion, see Best, *Philosophy and Human Movement.*

90. Barney, "Chaucer's Lists," 219.

91. For an introduction to the semantics of terms in medieval logic, see in Kretzmann, Kenny, and Pinborg, *The Cambridge History of Later Medieval Philosophy*: D. P. Henry, "Predicables and Categories," 128–42; L. M. de Rijk, "The Origins of the Theory of the Property of Terms," 161–73; Paul Vincent Spade, "The Semantics of Terms," 188–96; and Gabriel Nuchelmans, "The Semantics of Propositions," 197–210. Also see Edwards, "History of Semantics," and Henry, *That Most Subtle Question,* 1–45.

92. Aristotle, *Basic Works,* 49–50.

93. Aristotle, *Aristoteles Latinus, II.1–2, De Interpretatione,* 20. William of Moerbeke's more accurate translation of Aristotle's *De interpretatione* deletes Boethius's additional *homo currit* propositions (see ibid., 51); however, unlike William of Moerbeke's other translations of Aristotle, which quickly established

themselves in the late thirteenth century as the most popular versions, the *logica vetus* (Boethius's translations of the *Categories* and *De interpretatione*, together with Porphyry's *Isagoge*) remained the authoritative logical texts throughout the later Middle Ages. See Dod, "Aristoteles Latinus," 45–79.

94. Reprinted from William of Sherwood, *Introduction to Logic*, 33. For the origin of the square of opposition in classical logic, see Bochenski, *A History of Formal Logic*, 140–41. The use of the square of opposition has been revitalized in modern logic by Fogelin, *Understanding Arguments*.

95. William of Sherwood, *Treatise on Syncategorematic Words*, 17–39.

96. Ibid., 22.

97. Ibid., 22, n. 23.

98. Ibid., 22.

99. Cited by Pearsall, *The Nun's Priest's Tale*, 246.

100. Ibid.

101. See Tuve, *Elizabethan and Metaphysical Imagery*, 97–99.

102. The effect is thus not so much antiquation (as in Spenser), but rather a mix of linguistic amelioration and pejoration, as the reader is drawn into a familiar relationship with lower-class diction. For a study of similar spatial strategies employed to quite different ends, see David Trotter's excellent analysis of T. S. Eliot's "here," "there," "this," and "that" in *The Making of the Reader*, 44–53. Also see Spearing's *Textual Subjectivity*, passim, for a close reading of Chaucer's "proximal diectics."

103. Curtius, *European Literature*, 162–65.

104. See Dobson, *The Peasants' Revolt*; in his "Introduction to the First Edition," 1–31, he offers a synopsis of the revolt, whose major events are then fully narrated in the subsequent chronicle accounts. For a collection of other studies of the Peasants' Revolt, see Hilton and Aston, *The English Rising of 1381*.

105. Cited by Dobson, *The Peasants' Revolt*, 5.

106. See, for example, Hutcheon, *A Theory of Parody*, passim, and Waugh, *Metafiction*.

107. Dobson, *The Peasants' Revolt*, 187.

108. Patterson, "'*No man his resoun herde*,'" esp. 473 and 492, n. 42.

109. Aers, "*Vox populi* and the Literature of 1381," 451, quoting Pearsall, *The Life of Geoffrey Chaucer* 146–47. See also John Ganim's Bakhtin-inspired analysis of medieval literary noise in his *Chaucerian Theatricality*, 113–20, and R. James Goldstein's insightful Freudian reading of Chaucer's classist humor: "Chaucer, Freud, and the Political Economy of Wit." Richard Fehrenbacher argues that, as in *The Canterbury Tales*, so in *The Nun's Priest's Tale*, Chaucer seeks

to remove himself from history into the realm of the literary; however, "the specter of Jack Straw and his meynee muscling their way into the text demonstrates how such attempts fail, and how history, attempt to contain it as one might, cannot be entirely banished from literature"; see his "'A Yeerd Enclosed Al Aboute,'" 135. For a persuasive critique of critical positions that focus on the Jack Straw passage as evidence of Chaucer's elitist tendency to trivialize and "literacize" contemporary political suffering, see Kane, "Language as Literature."

The critical reading of the fox chase I find most congenial to my own is Paul Strohm's careful assessment of the political dimensions of its different levels of literary discourse:

> A vivid instance of Chaucer's ability to deal with the most charged political materials in ways that forbid us to draw solid conclusions about his intentions is the apparent reference in the *Nun's Priest's Tale* to the rising of 1381. The *Nun's Priest's Tale* is itself the most consciously aesthetic of Chaucer's productions, constituting itself in an ultraliterary register that no longer even purports to reflect social reality but that revels in its dependence on established voices, themes, modes, and genres, many of which have been (or will be) encountered on the Canterbury pilgrimage. . . . The literary supersaturation of this tale in turn creates an environment of expectations within which even historically charged references like that to "Jakke Straw and his meynee" (VII. 3394) may be detached from their troubling social implications. . . . Rather than a historicization of the barnyard squabble, we actually have here a dehistoricization of the 1381 uprising with its presumably unsettling effects on most of the London populace and on Chaucer's stratum in particular. Its volatility substantially defused, Chaucer's reference is assimilated to the literary register of allusion and imagery in which the tale is arrayed.
>
> Yet to say that Chaucer excludes political references from the *Canterbury Tales,* and that he insulates his audience against the most startling aspects of those references he does include, is not to declare his work unhistorical. For history, suppressed at the level of allusion, is reintroduced at the level of form. The contribution of the *Nun's Priest's Tale* to history lies not so much in its allusions as in its socially charged assumption that diverse levels of argumentative style, socially conditioned genres and forms, and kinds of utterance can inhabit the same literary space, cooperating for the profit (here defined as literary *solaas*) of all. The *Nun's Priest's Tale,* together with

the *Canterbury Tales* as a whole, conveys the reassuring message that competing voices can colonize a literary space and can proliferate within it without provoking chaos or ultimate rupture.

Strohm, *Social Chaucer,* 164–66.

110. Dobson, *The Peasants' Revolt,* 162, 173, 183, 189.

111. Attali, *Noise,* 19.

112. Ibid., 6.

113. Ibid., 19.

114. Ibid., 33.

115. Gallant, *More Fun with Dick and Jane,* 48.

116. H. Rap Brown, *Die Nigger Die!* 21, 25.

117. For a brief study of several of these novels, see Cook, "Introduction: The Literature of Black America."

Six. Chaucerian Horologics and the Confounded Reader

1. See Landes, *Revolution in Time,* 86.

2. For a depiction of the cylinder dial, see North, *Chaucer's Universe,* 112.

3. Mooney, "The Cock and the Clock," 103.

4. The use of the term "cursive" I owe to Anne Higgins's useful study, "Medieval Notions of the Structure of Time." In "The Hours of the Day in Medieval French," W. Rothwell notes that "right up to the end of the fourteenth century indications of time in vernacular texts can only rarely be translated at all accurately into precise clock hours," and that "One of the most time-conscious writers of that age, Froissart, . . . changed from the old canonical hours to the new clock hours in the middle of his *Chroniques*" (249).

5. Professor Eisner informed me that his knowledge of astronomy was acquired entirely through self-instruction. With the exception of Mooney's "The Cock and the Clock," an essay concerned with modes of measuring time rather than the difficulties of Chaucer's *chronographiae,* and Marijane Osborn's *Time and the Astrolabe,* studies of Chaucer's temporal periphrases have tended to be allegorical, rather than scientific, in their allegiances. See, for example, Chauncey Wood, *Chaucer and the Country of the Stars,* 70–102, 161–72, and 272–97. See also the numerological readings of Frese, in *An Ars Legendi,* 141–63.

6. As late as 1532, Rabelais could still satirize the outrageous effects of the computists' calendar reckonings: "In that year the Kalends were fixed by the Greek date-books, the month of March was outside Lent, and mid-August

fell in May. In the month of October, I believe, or perhaps in September—if I am not mistaken, and I want to take particular care not to be—came the week so famous in our annals, that is called the Week of Three Thursdays"; Rabelais, *Histories of Gargantua and Pantagruel,* 171, cited by Higgins, "Medieval Notions," 234.

7. See Moyer, "The Gregorian Calendar," 146.

8. For detailed studies of the *computus* in the Middle Ages, see Cordoliani, "Contribution"; North, "The Western Calendar"; Wallis, "Images of Order"; Borst, *The Ordering of Time*; and Bede, *Bedae Opera de temporibus,* esp. the Introduction, 3–122.

9. Duhem, *Medieval Cosmology,* 299.

10. Ibid.; for a sustained analysis of the effects of these two condemnations as well as a still-enlightening discussion of fourteenth-century philosophical debates on the nature of time, see 295–363.

11. Ibid., 342–52.

12. Ibid., 352–62.

13. Needham, as quoted (but not cited) by Landes, *Revolution in Time,* 53.

14. For a survey of the mechanical clocks known to have existed in late-fourteenth-century England, see Mooney, "The Cock and the Clock," 104–8.

15. See Le Goff, "Merchant's Time" and "Labor Time."

16. Landes, *Revolution in Time,* 79.

17. North, *Chaucer's Universe,* 38.

18. Osborn, "The Squire's 'Steed of Brass.'" Although it appears as a life-size magical toy which "in the space of o day natureel" will "Beren youre body into every place," this "hors of bras," Osborn shows, is clearly an astrolabe, the horse's head holding the central pin in place: "whan yow list to ryden anywhere, / Ye mooten trille a pyn, stant in his ere," the Squire explains. Also see Osborn, *Time and the Astrolabe,* passim.

19. See Nicholas of Lynn, *The Kalendarium,* both for the text of this *kalendarium* and for a full description of its parts and uses.

20. Courtenay, *Schools and Scholars,* 3.

21. Ibid., 7.

22. Ibid., 9.

23. The ancient use of shadow-scales is discussed briefly in North, *Chaucer's Universe,* 243. The use of the shadow-scale in medieval computistic/world maps is noted briefly by Edson, "World Maps and Easter Tables," *Imago Mundi,* appendix 6.

24. Nicholas of Lynn, *The Kalendarium,* 31.

25. Ibid., 30.

26. As J. D. North dryly remarks, "It is not easy to imagine even scholarly pilgrims in real life exchanging pleasantries about the fraction of the arc of the artificial day traversed by the Sun"; North, *Chaucer's Universe*, 123.

27. Chaucer's shadow, to my knowledge, is the first human shadow to be recorded in English literature. Theoretically deduced from an almanac, it needs to be compared to the shadow cast by Dante's living body in Purgatorio: "Low at my back, the sun was a red blaze; its light fell on the ground before me broken in the form in which my body blacked its rays" (*Purgatorio* 3.16–18). Mark Peterson observes that Dante's shadow is "oddly precise and geometric," giving evidence that "Dante must have spent a little time examining shadows carefully." See Peterson, "Dante's Physics," 167. According to Philip R. Berk, Dante's is the first human shadow found in all of medieval literature; see Berk, "Shadows on the Mount of Purgatory," 47.

28. Peck, "Number Symbolism."

29. Nicholas of Lynn, *The Kalendarium*, 32–33.

30. The idea of time moving backwards is a phenomenon that Stephen Hawking says is scientifically feasible at certain phases of world history; see Hawking, *A Brief History of Time*, 143–53.

31. Nicholas of Lynn, *The Kalendarium*, 33.

32. For reasons that will shortly be clarified, lines 3188–89 are slightly different from the *Riverside* edition.

33. Admittedly, there is one small problem: the equation of the liturgical *hora* "pryme" with 9 a.m. is slightly willful, for as *The Riverside Chaucer* glossary reveals (1279), "prime" had at least three meanings for Chaucer: it could mean the canonical hour of 6 a.m.; or the first full hour of prime (6 to 7 a.m.); or the three hours from six to nine in the morning. But in Chaucer's corpus, only "fully pryme," or "pryme large," means 9 a.m. In light of the heavy emphasis I have placed on the many other "errors" of temporal measurement in Chaucer's *chronographiae*, this matter, at least for the moment, will be allowed to pass.

34. Luria and Hoffman, *Middle English Lyrics*, 109.

35. See Benson, *The Riverside Chaucer*, 939, nn. 3187–90. In *Time and the Astrolabe*, Osborn concurs with the long-standing critical conviction that "this bookishly accurate announcement" implies "a date of May 3" (205).

36. Manly and Rickert, *The Texts of the Canterbury Tales*, 7, 588–89. Manly and Rickert's variorum study of *The Nun's Priest's Tale* has been superceded, however, by Thomas, *The Nun's Priest's Tale on CD-ROM*; see the collation of all witnesses for line 370.

37. All cited by Pearsall in *The Nun's Priest's Tale*, 205–6.

38. Pratt, *The Tales of Canterbury*, 244.

39. Benson, *The Riverside Chaucer,* 939, n. 3190.

40. Ibid., 258.

41. Pearsall, *The Nun's Priest's Tale,* 206.

42. Quoted ibid.

43. The two major studies of this tradition are Murdoch, "The Analytic Character of Late Medieval Learning," with "Comment" by Kretzmann; and Kretzmann, "*Incipit/Desinit.*"

44. The fifteenth-century Middle English poem *The Court of Sapience,* ed. E. Ruth Harvey, includes a tour of the Castle of Knowledge where each of the seven liberal arts is housed in a discrete apartment. The apartment of Dame Dialectica gently satirizes the most important logical topics and strategies of her time (63):

> Her parlour fresshe, her clothyng proude and stout,
> Of *dyffert, scire,* and of *incipit*
> With sophysmes full depeynted was aboute,
> And other maters, as of *desinit.*
> The *Comune Treatys* taught she them therwyth:
> Whiche, whatkyns, what is proposicion
> What thyng he is, and his dyvysyon . . .
> She taught hem there with lust and all lykyng;
> Fast they dysputen in theyr comonyng,
> With sophyms strong straunge maters they discusse,
> And fast they crye oft, '*Tu es asinus!*'

Although *The Court of Sapience* hardly reveals a profound understanding of dialectics, it expects its readers to recognize the contemporary logical buzzwords, among the most prominent being the syncategorematic terms *incipit* and *desinit.* This passage from *The Court of Sapience* is cited by Murdoch, "The Development of a Critical Temper," 67.

45. Example provided by Kretzmann, "*Incipit/Desinit,*" 105.

46. Example provided by ibid., 107.

47. Murdoch, "The Analytic Character of Late Medieval Learning," 120.

48. Ibid., 121.

49. For an excellent introduction to these tracts, see C. Wilson, *William Heytesbury,* 32–37.

50. Ibid., 38–40. Peter of Spain's discussion of *incipit* and *desinit* has been translated by Norman Kretzmann as an appendix to his "*Incipit/Desinit,*" 122–28.

51. C. Wilson, *William Heytesbury,* 29–56.

52. Kretzmann, "*Incipit/Desinit,*" 133, n. 22.

53. Quoted by C. Wilson, *William Heytesbury,* 47; also cited by Murdoch, "The Analytic Character of Late Medieval Learning," 193.

54. Some of the functions of *vis confundendi* performed in *incipit/desinit sophismata* are explained by C. Wilson, *William Heytesbury,* 29–56.

55. See C. Wilson, *William Heytesbury,* 11–12.

56. Considering the enormous investment of the critical establishment in the numerological/allegorical significance of May 3, it is not likely that the emendation of this sacred date will happen very soon. For a review of many of the ingenious meanings critics have discovered in Chaucer's May 3, see Pearsall, *The Nun's Priest's Tale,* 206–8.

57. While I find no solution in sight, I do not claim that none is available. A sophistical proposition that shares a number of similarities with Chaucer's sophism can be found in Heytesbury's *Regule solvendi sophismata.* Here is Curtis Wilson's presentation of the proposition, as well as its solution—as supplied by Gaetano di Thiene (d. 1465): "Now there begins to be traversed some part which for the time ending at the present instant is as a whole still to be traversed. . . . The proof proceeds as follows: (a) Now no part is traversed which for the time ending at the present instant is as a whole still to be traversed; this statement is obvious. (b) But immediately after the present instant there will have been traversed some part which for the time ending at the present instant is as a whole still to be traversed; for there will be no instant after the present instant such that prior to that instant some (indeterminate) part will not have been traversed. From (a) and (b) the required conclusion follows"; C. Wilson, *William Heytesbury,* 53.

58. Mooney, "The Cock and the Clock," 96.

59. But this is not the convention used in John Somers's *Kalendarium.* The result is Somers's forenoons are all a day before Nicholas's: all the evidence in Chauntecleer's calculations (if one were to use Somers's *Kalendarium*) verify May 2 as the right date, whereas in Nicholas's *Kalendarium* May 3, as we have seen, is the "correct" day.

60. For example, J. D. North is certain that 1392 is the only year possible (the tale's events must fall somewhere between the Peasants' Revolt and Chaucer's death, he reasons); and the only concordant date within this year is Friday, May 3, 1392; see North, *Chaucer's Universe,* 457–58.

61. Chaucer's literary and cultural environment could also have provided a debate between April 1 and April 2. Although April 1 in the fourteenth

century had not yet acquired the burlesque features of April Fool's Day, it was nevertheless a holiday that enjoyed a touch of topsy-turvydom; it is perhaps appropriate that the Nun's Priest warns in his *moralitas* that his tale may be taken as a "folye." April 2, on the other hand, was admired in the Middle Ages for its symmetry as the second day of the second month: in Machaut's "Dit dou Lyon," for example, a poem that Chaucer may have translated as "the book of the Leoun," the crucial date is "Dou mois d'averil le jour secont" (see Benson, *The Riverside Chaucer*, 965, n. 1087). Thus, if Chaucer's readers wished to dispute this April 1/2 dialectic exclusively in regard to their cultural preferences (consider the equally "inconsequential" literary debate on the virtues of the flower and the leaf), there would be partisans on both sides.

62. Cornish, "Planets and Angels in Paradiso XXIX."

63. That Oresme was "one of the fourteenth century's greatest scientists" has been asserted by Kruger, *Dreaming in the Middle Ages*, 219, n. 87.

64. Oresme, *Tractatus*, 291–98.

65. Ibid., 313.

66. Ibid., 321–23.

67. Ibid., 311.

68. Kruger, *Dreaming in the Middle Ages*, 145.

69. Oresme, *Tractatus*, 287.

70. Ibid., 321.

71. Another text that may have direct bearing on Chaucer's appreciation of the inaccuracies of scientific calculations is *The Equatorie of the Planets* (see Price, *Equatorie*), an astrolabic study that has been conjectured to have been written by Chaucer. It includes in its margins (76 recto, 77 recto) the commentary "This canon is fals" ("This explanation is incorrect"). However, scholarly opinion at present tends to doubt Chaucer's authorship; see Arch, "A Case Against." My thanks to William Askins for providing, in private correspondence, expert analysis of this text's implications for Chaucer studies.

Seven.   The Parodistic Episteme: Learning to Behold the Fox

1. Rabelais, *The Works*, 1:325.

2. For further exploration of these matters, see Henry, *That Most Subtle Question*, 1–45, and passim.

3. Spade, *The Mediaeval Liar*.

4. This taxonomy is close to that provided by Hughes, *John Buridan*, 29. The bibliography of recent studies of the Liar paradox is vast. Book-length

analyses include: Cargile, *Paradoxes*; Mates, *Skeptical Essays*; Martin, *Recent Essays*; Barwise and Etchemendy, *The Liar*.

5. Buridan, *Sophisms on Meaning and Truth*, 73.

6. Ibid., 75.

7. In his *Ipomedon*, Hugh of Rutland wrote, "Ne mettez mie tout sur mei, / Seul ne sai pas de mentir l'art, / Walter Map reset bien sa part."

8. Nuchelmans, "The Semantics," 199.

9. Priscian, "Fundamentals," 58.

10. Sidney, "An Apology for Poetry," 1:185.

11. Ibid., 184.

12. Alighieri, *The Divine Comedy* (Singleton), 1:55.

13. Singleton, *Dante Studies I*, 62.

14. Boccaccio, *Il Commento Lez.* 20, 1:477–79, in Trimpi, *Muses of One Mind*, 350.

15. Ibid.

16. Ibid., 241–361.

17. Mansell, "Unsettling."

18. Iser, "Feigning in Fiction," 225.

19. Carroll, *The Complete Works*, 757.

20. Green, *A Crisis of Truth*, 1.

21. Hill, *Chaucerian Belief*, 138.

22. Rose, *Parody//Meta-Fiction*, 13.

23. Ibid., 108.

24. Ibid., 186.

25. Lecoy, *Le Roman de Renart*, 33; Terry, *Renard the Fox*, 31–33. For an excellent study of Chaucer's use of his sources, see R. Pratt, "Three Old French Sources."

26. See Bundy, "The Theory of Imagination," esp. 359–80; Harvey, *The Inward Wits*; Lindberg, *Studies*; and Akbari, *Seeing Through the Veil*.

27. Harvey, *The Inward Wits*, 45–55, and Bundy, "The Theory of Imagination," 371.

28. Numerous studies of medieval dream interpretation have been written. I recommend Hieatt, *The Realism of Dream Vision*, esp. 23–33; Spearing, *Medieval Dream-Poetry*, esp. 1–23; Lynch, *The High Medieval Dream Vision*; and Kruger, *Dreaming in the Middle Ages*.

29. For an extended study of this theme, see R. Payne, *The Key of Remembrance*.

30. Aquinas, *Summa Theologiae*, 1.83, 1; cited and translated in Harvey, *The Inward Wits*, 55.

31. Representatives of this homiletic critical position are Dahlberg, "Chaucer's Cock and Fox"; Donovan, "The *Moralite* of the Nun's Priest's Sermon"; and Levy and Adams, "Chauntecleer's Paradise Lost and Regained."

32. See Benson, *The Riverside Chaucer*, 939, n. 3217.

33. Burnley, *Chaucer's Language*, 110, and Wentersdorf, *"Heigh Ymaginacioun."*

34. Victor M. Hamm was the first to argue Chaucer's indebtedness to Dante, in his "Chaucer."

35. Hieatt, *The Realism of Dream Vision*, 42.

36. Regis, *Epistemology*, 225–52.

37. Tachau, "What Senses and Intellect Do," 658.

38. Ibid.

39. Ibid., 661.

40. Gladwell, *Blink*, 11–12.

41. Cooper, *The Structure of the Canterbury Tales*, 186.

42. Eco et al., "On Animal Language," 14.

43. Ibid., 14, 18.

44. Ibid., 18.

45. Ibid.

46. Ibid., 19–20.

47. Ibid., 7.

48. Burke, *The Rhetoric of Religion*, 257.

49. Brooks, *Reading*, 140.

Eight. *Moralitas*

1. Spearing, *Textual Subjectivity*, 30.

2. Ibid., 120.

3. Ibid., 120–21.

4. Ibid., 120.

5. Travis, "A. C. Spearing," 759.

6. Ibid., 760.

7. Quinn, *Geoffrey Chaucer and the Poetics of Disguise*, 157.

8. Furr, "Nominalism," 142, 140.

9. Colie, *Paradoxia Epidemica*, 360.

10. Attridge, *The Singularity of Literature*, 91 (emphasis in text).

11. Ibid., 93.

12. Furr, "Nominalism," 137.

13. Ibid., 135–36.

14. Ibid., 140.

15. Ibid., 142.

16. Ibid., 140.

17. Ibid., 142.

18. Ibid., 138.

19. Ibid., 139.

20. As quoted in Richard Neuse, *Chaucer's Dante*, 62, from de Man, *Blindness and Insight*, 214.

21. Chapin, "Morality Ovidized," 20.

22. Kruger, "Dream Inheritance," unpublished paper, courtesy of the author.

Works Cited

Aers, David. *Chaucer*. Atlantic Highlands: Humanities Press International, 1986.

———. "*Vox populi* and the Literature of 1381." In *The Cambridge History of Medieval English Literature*, edited by David Wallace, 432–53. Cambridge: Cambridge University Press, 1999.

Akbari, Suzanne Conklin. *Seeing Through the Veil: Optical Theory and Medieval Allegory*. Toronto: University of Toronto Press, 2004.

Alanus de Insulis. *Anticlaudianus or The Good and Perfect Men [by] Alan of Lille*. Translation and commentary by James J. Sheridan. Toronto: Pontifical Institute of Mediaeval Studies, 1973.

———. *The Plaint of Nature*. Translated by James J. Sheridan. Toronto: Pontifical Institute of Mediaeval Studies, 1980.

Alighieri, Dante. *The Comedy of Dante Alighieri*. Translated by Dorothy L. Sayers. New York: Basic Books, Inc., 1962.

———. *The Divine Comedy*. 3 vols. Translated and edited by Charles S. Singleton. Princeton: Princeton University Press, 1982.

———. *The Divine Comedy of Dante Alighieri*. Translated and edited by John D. Sinclair. Oxford: Oxford University Press, 1961.

Allen, Valerie J. "Broken Air." *Exemplaria* 16 (2004): 305–22.

Arch, Jennifer. "A Case Against Chaucer's Authorship of the *Equatorie of the Planets*." *The Chaucer Review* 40 (2005): 59–79.

Aristotle. *Aristotles Latinus, II.1–2, De Interpretatione vel Periermenias*. Edited by L. Minio-Paluello and G. Verbeke. Bruges: Desclée de Brouwer, 1965.

———. *The Basic Works of Aristotle.* Edited by Richard McKeon. New York: Random House, 1941.

Armitage-Smith, Sydney. *John of Gaunt.* New York: Barnes and Noble, 1964.

Astell, Ann. "Chaucer's 'Literature Group' and the Medieval Causes of Books." *Journal of English Literary History* 59 (1992): 269–87.

Atalli, Jacques. *Noise: The Political Economy of Music.* Translated by Brian Massumi. Minneapolis: University of Minnesota Press, 1985.

Attridge, Derek. *Peculiar Language: Literature as Difference from the Renaissance to James Joyce.* Ithaca: Cornell University Press, 1988.

———. *The Singularity of Literature.* New York: Routledge, 2004.

Augustine. *Confessions.* Translated by R. S. Pine-Coffin. London: Penguin Books, 1961.

———. *The City of God.* Translated and edited by Vernon J. Bourke and Gerald G. Walsh et al. Garden City: Image Books, 1958.

Bakhtin, M. M. *The Dialogic Imagination: Four Essays.* Edited by Michael Holquist and translated by Caryl Emerson and Michael Holquist. Austin: University of Texas Press, 1981.

———. *Problems of Dostoevsky's Poetics.* Translated by R. W. Rotsel. Ann Arbor: University of Michigan Press, 1973.

Baldwin, Thomas Whitfield. *William Shakespere's Small Latine and Lesse Greeke.* Volume 1. Urbana: University of Illinois Press, 1944.

Balliett, Whitney. *Ecstasy at the Onion: Thirty-one Pieces on Jazz.* New York: Oxford University Press, 1971.

Barney, Stephen A. "Chaucer's Lists." In *The Wisdom of Poetry: Essays in Early English Literature in Honor of Morton W. Bloomfield,* edited by Larry D. Benson and Siegfried Wenzel, 189–223. Kalamazoo: Medieval Institute Publications, 1982.

Barolini, Teodolinda. "'*Le parole son femmine e i fatti sono maschi*': Toward a Sexual Poetics of the *Decameron* (*Decameron* II, 10)." *Studi sul Boccaccio* 21 (1993): 175–97.

Barthes, Roland. *The Pleasure of the Text.* Translated by Richard Miller. New York: Hill and Wang, 1975.

Barwise, Jon, and John Etchemendy. *The Liar: An Essay on Truth and Circularity.* New York: Oxford University Press, 1987.

Baudrillard, Jean. "Simulacra and Simulations." In *Selected Writings,* edited and translated by Mark Poster, 166–84. Stanford: Stanford University Press, 1988.

Baugh, Albert C., ed. *Chaucer's Major Poetry.* New York: Appleton-Century-Crofts, 1963.

Baum, Paull F. *Chaucer: A Critical Appreciation.* Durham: Duke University Press, 1958.

Bauschatz, Paul C. "Chaucer's Pardoner's Beneficent Lie." In *Assays: Critical Approaches to Medieval and Renaissance Texts,* 2:19–43. Pittsburgh: University of Pittsburgh Press, 1983.

Beckwith, Sarah. *Signifying God: Social Relation and Symbolic Act in the York Corpus Christi Plays.* Chicago: University of Chicago Press, 2001.

Bede. *Bedae Opera de Temporibus.* Edited by Charles W. Jones. Cambridge: The Mediaeval Academy of America, 1943.

———. *Libri II De Arte Metrica et De schematibus et tropis: The Art of Poetry and Rhetoric.* Translated by Calvin B. Kendall. Saarbrücken: AQ-Verlag, 1991.

Beidler, Peter. "Desiderata." *The Chaucer Review* 15 (1980): 74.

Bennett, Alan, Peter Cook, Jonathan Miller, and Dudley Moore. *The Complete Beyond the Fringe.* London: Methuen, 2003.

Bennett, J. A. W. *Chaucer's Book of Fame: An Exposition of The House of Fame.* Oxford: The Clarendon Press, 1968.

Benson, Larry D. *The Riverside Chaucer.* 3rd ed. Boston: Houghton Mifflin, 1987.

Berk, Philip R. "Shadows on the Mount of Purgatory." *Dante Studies* 97 (1979): 47–63.

Besserman, Lawrence L. "Chaucerian Wordplay: The Nun's Priest and His *Woman Divyne.*" *Chaucer Review* 12 (1977–78): 68–73.

Best, David. *Philosophy and Human Movement.* London: George Allen & Unwin, 1978.

Birky, Robin Hass. "'The Word Was Made Flesh': Gendered Bodies and Anti-Bodies in Twelfth- and Thirteenth-Century Arts of Poetry." In *Medieval Rhetoric: A Casebook,* edited by Scott D. Troyan, 161–215. New York: Routledge, 2004.

Birney, Earle. *Essays on Chaucerian Irony (With an Essay on Irony by Beryl Rowland).* Edited by Beryl Rowland. Toronto: University of Toronto Press, 1985.

Bishop, Ian. "*The Nun's Priest's Tale* and the Liberal Arts." *Review of English Studies* 30 (1979): 257–67.

Black, Max. "Metaphor." Reprinted in *Philosophical Perspectives on Metaphor,* edited by Mark Johnson, 63–82. Minneapolis: University of Minnesota Press, 1981.

Bloomfield, Morton W. "The Magic of *In Principio.*" *Modern Language Notes* 70 (1955): 559–65.

———. "The Wisdom of *The Nun's Priest's Tale.*" In *Chaucerian Problems and Perspectives: Essays Presented to Paul E. Beichner,* edited by Edward Vasta and Zacharias P. Thundy, 70–82. Notre Dame: University of Notre Dame Press, 1979.

Bochenski, Joseph M. *A History of Formal Logic.* Translated and edited by Ivo Thomas. Notre Dame: University of Notre Dame Press, 1961.

Boethius, Manlius Anicius Severinus. *Consolation of Philosophy.* Translated by Richard H. Green. Indianapolis: Dover Publications, 2002.

———. *Fundamentals of Music.* Translated by Calvin M. Bower and edited by Claude V. Palisca. New Haven: Yale University Press, 1989.

———. *Philosophiae Consolatio.* Edited by Ludovicus Bieler. Turnhout: Brepols, 1982.

Boitani, Piero. *Chaucer and the Imaginary World of Fame.* Totowa: Barnes and Noble, 1984.

Boone, Lalia Phipps. "Chauntecleer and Partlet Identified." *Modern Language Notes* 64 (1949): 78–81.

Booth, Wayne C. "A New Strategy for Establishing a Truly Democratic Criticism." *Daedalus* 112 (1983): 193–214.

———. *A Rhetoric of Irony.* Chicago: University of Chicago Press, 1974.

Borst, Arno. *The Ordering of Time: From the Ancient Computus to the Modern Computer.* Translated by Andrew Winnard. Chicago: University of Chicago Press, 1993.

Brewer, Derek. "What is *The Nun's Priest's Tale* Really About?" *Trames (Travaux et Mémoires de l'U.E.R. des Lettres et Sciences Humaines de l'Université de Limoges)* 2 (1979): 19–25.

Bronson, B. H. *In Search of Chaucer.* Toronto: University of Toronto Press, 1960.

Brooks, Mel. "Mel Brooks: A Candid Conversation with the Emperor of Off-the-wall Comedy." *Playboy* 22 (February 1975): 47–67.

Brooks, Peter. *Reading for the Plot: Design and Intention in Narrative.* New York: Alfred A. Knopf, 1984.

Brosnahan, Leger. "The Authenticity of *And Preestes Thre.*" *Chaucer Review* 16 (1982): 293–310.

Brown, H. Rap. *Die Nigger Die!* New York: The Dial Press, 1969.

Bundy, Murray Wright. "The Theory of Imagination in Classical and Mediaeval Thought." *University of Illinois Studies in Language and Literature* 23 (1927): 183–472.

Buridan, John. *Sophisms on Meaning and Truth.* Translated by T. K. Scott. New York: Appleton-Century-Croft, 1966.

Burke, Kenneth. *The Rhetoric of Religion: Studies in Logology.* Boston: Beacon Press, 1961.

Burnley, J. D. *Chaucer's Language and the Philosopher's Tradition.* Cambridge: D. S. Brewer Ltd., 1979.

Bursill-Hall, G. L. *Speculative Grammars of the Middle Ages.* The Hague: Mouton, 1971.

Butler, Judith. *Bodies That Matter: On the Discursive Limits of "Sex."* New York: Routledge, 1993.

Călinescu, Matei. *Rereading.* New Haven: Yale University Press, 1993.

Camargo, Martin. "Rhetoric." In *The Seven Liberal Arts in the Middle Ages,* edited by David L. Wagner, 96–124. Bloomington: Indiana University Press, 1983.

Cargile, James. *Paradoxes: A Study in Form and Predication.* Cambridge: Cambridge University Press, 1979.

Carroll, Lewis. *The Complete Works of Lewis Carroll.* Introduction by Alexander Woollcott. Harmondsworth: Penguin, 1988.

Cato. *Disticha Catonis.* Edited by Marcus Boas Henricus Johannes Botschuyver. Amsterdam: North-Holland, 1952.

Chamberlain, David. "The Music of the Spheres and '*The Parlement of Foules.*'" *Chaucer Review* 5 (1970): 32–56.

Chapin, Arthur. "Morality Ovidized: Sententiousness and the Aphoristic Moment in the *Nun's Priest's Tale.*" *The Yale Journal of Criticism* 8 (1995): 7–34.

Cicero, Marcus Tullius. *De Oratore.* Cambridge: Harvard University Press, 1942.

———. *On the Commonwealth.* Translated by G. H. Sabine and S. B. Smith. Indianapolis: Bobbs-Merrill, 1976.

Clark, Donald Lemen. *John Milton at St. Paul's School.* New York: Columbia University Press, 1948.

Clark, Roy Peter. "Wit and Whitsunday in Chaucer's *Summoner's Tale.*" *Annuale Mediaevale* 17 (1976): 48–57.

Clogan, Paul M. "Literary Genres in a Medieval Textbook." *Medievalia et Humanistica* 11 (1982): 199–209.

Cohen, Jeffrey Jerome. "Diminishing Masculinity in Chaucer's Tale of *Sir Thopas.*" In *Masculinities in Chaucer: Approaches to Maleness in the Canterbury Tales and Troilus and Criseyde,* edited by Peter G. Beidler, 143–56. Cambridge: D. S. Brewer, 1998.

———. "*Kyte oute yugilment*: An Introduction to Medieval Noise." *Exemplaria* 16 (2004): 267–76.

———. *Of Giants: Sex, Monsters, and the Middle Ages.* Minneapolis: University of Minnesota Press, 1999.

Colebrook, Claire. *Irony.* New York: Routledge, 2004.

Colie, Rosalie L. *Paradoxia Epidemica: The Renaissance Tradition of Paradox.* Princeton: Princeton University Press, 1996.

Cook, William W. "Introduction: The Literature of Black America—The Noise of Reading." In *Tapping Potential: English and Language Arts for the Black Learner,* edited by Charlotte K. Brooks, 243–49. Urbana: National Council of Teachers of English, 1985.

Cooper, Helen. *The Structure of the Canterbury Tales.* Athens: University of Georgia Press, 1984.

Cordoliani, A. "Contribution a la litterature du comput au Moyen Age." *Studii Medievali* 1 (1960): 107–38; 2 (1961): 169–208.

Cornish, Alison. "Planets and Angels in *Paradiso* XXIX: The First Moment." *Dante Studies* 108 (1990): 1–28.

Costa, Gustavo. "Dialectic and Mercury (Education, Magic, and Religion in Dante)." In Di Scipio and Scaglione, *The Divine Comedy and the Encyclopedia of Arts and Sciences,* 43–64.

Courtenay, William J. *Schools and Scholars in Fourteenth-Century England.* Princeton: Princeton University Press, 1987.

Cowell, Andrew. "The Dye of Desire: The Colors of Rhetoric in the Middle Ages." *Exemplaria* 11 (1999): 115–39.

Cox, James M. "Toward Vernacular Humor." *Virginia Quarterly Review* 46 (1970): 311–30.

Culler, Jonathan. "Apostrophe." *Diacritics* 7 (1977): 59–69.

———. *Structuralist Poetics: Structuralism, Linguistics and the Study of Literature.* London: Routledge & Kegan Paul, 1975.

Curtius, Ernst Robert. *European Literature and the Latin Middle Ages.* Translated by Willard R. Trask. New York: Harper and Row, 1963.

Dagenais, John. *The Ethics of Reading in Manuscript Culture: Glossing the Libro de Buen Amor.* Princeton: Princeton University Press, 1994.

Dahlberg, Charles. "Chaucer's Cock and Fox." *Journal of English and Germanic Philology* 53 (1954): 277–90.

Dane, Joseph A. "*Mulier Est Hominis Confusio:* Note on Chaucer's Nun's Priest's Tale." *Notes and Queries* 39 (1992): 276–78.

———. "The Myth of Chaucerian Irony." *Papers on Language and Literature* 24 (1988): 115–33.

Davidoff, Judith. *Beginning Well: Framing Fictions in Late Middle English Poetry.* Rutherford: Farleigh Dickinson University Press, 1988.

Davies, R. T., ed. *Medieval English Lyrics: A Critical Anthology.* London: Faber & Faber, 1964.

Delaney, Shelia. "*Mulier est hominis confusio*: Chaucer's Anti-Popular *Nun's Priest's Tale*." *Mosaic* 17 (1984): 1–8.

de Man, Paul. *Blindness and Insight: Essays in the Rhetoric of Contemporary Criticism*. 2nd ed. Minneapolis: University of Minnesota Press, 1983.

———. "The Epistemology of Metaphor." In *On Metaphor*, edited by Sheldon Sacks, 11–28. Chicago: University of Chicago Press, 1979.

———. *The Resistance to Theory*. Minneapolis: University of Minnesota Press, 1986.

de Rijk, L.M. "The Origin of the Theory of the Property of Terms." In Kretzmann, Kenny, and Pinborg, *The Cambridge History of Later Medieval Philosophy*, 161–73.

Derrida, Jacques. "Différance." In *Critical Theory since 1965*, translated by Alan Bass and edited by Hazard Adams and Leroy Searle, 120–37. Tallahassee: University Presses of Florida, 1986.

———. *Dissemination*. Translated by Barbara Johnson. Chicago: University of Chicago Press, 1981.

———. *Positions*. Translated by Alan Bass. Chicago: University of Chicago Press, 1981.

———. "The *Retrait* of Metaphor." *Enclitic* 2 (1978): 5–33.

———. "Ulysses Gramophone: Hear Say Yes in Joyce." In *A Companion to James Joyce's Ulysses*, edited by Margo Norris, 69–90. Boston: Bedford, 1998.

———. "White Mythology: Metaphor in the Text of Philosophy." In *Margins of Philosophy*, translated by Alan Bass, 207–72. Chicago: University of Chicago Press, 1982.

Deschamps, Eustace. *Oeuvres Complètes de Eustache Deschamps*. 11 vols. Edited by le Marquis de Queux de Saint-Hilaire and Gaston Raynaud. Paris: Firmin Dodot, 1878–1903.

Dinshaw, Carolyn. *Chaucer's Sexual Poetics*. Madison: University of Wisconsin Press, 1989.

Di Scipio, Giuseppe, and Aldo Scaglione, eds. *The Divine Comedy and the Encyclopedia of Arts and Sciences*. Amsterdam: John Benjamins, 1988.

Dobson, R.B., ed. *The Peasants' Revolt of 1381*. 2nd ed. London: The MacMillan Press, 1983.

Dod, Bernard G. "Aristoteles Latinus." In Kretzmann, Kenny, and Pinborg, *The Cambridge History of Later Medieval Philosophy*, 45–79.

Donaldson, E. Talbot. "Patristic Exegesis in the Criticism of Medieval Literature: The Opposition." In *Critical Approaches to Medieval Literature, English Institute Essays*, edited by Dorothy Betherum, 134–53. New York: Columbia University Press, 1960.

Donovan, Mortimer J. "The *Moralite* of the Nun's Priest's Sermon." *Journal of English and Germanic Philology* 52 (1953): 493–508.

Duhem, Pierre. *Medieval Cosmology: Theories of Infinity, Place, Time, Void, and the Plurality of Worlds.* Edited by and translated by Roger Ariew. Chicago: University of Chicago Press, 1985.

Durling, Robert M., and Ronald L. Martinez. *Time and the Crystal: Studies in Dante's Rime Petrose.* Berkeley: University of California Press, 1990.

Eco, U., R. Lambertini, C. Marmo, and A. Tabarroni. "On Animal Language in the Medieval Classification of Signs." In *On the Medieval Theory of Signs,* edited by Umberto Eco and Costantino Marmo, 3–43. Philadelphia: John Benjamins, 1989.

Edelman, Lee. *Homographesis: Essays in Gay Literary and Cultural Theory.* New York: Routledge, 1994.

Edson, Evelyn. "World Maps and Easter Tables: Medieval Maps in Context." *Imago Mundi* 48 (1996): 25–42.

Edwards, Paul, ed. "History of Semantics." In *The Encyclopedia of Philosophy,* 7:365–75. New York: Macmillan Co., 1970.

Elbow, Peter. *Oppositions in Chaucer.* Middletown: Wesleyan University Press, 1975.

Elliott, Ralph W. V. "Chaucer's Reading." In *Chaucer's Mind and Art,* edited by A. C. Cawley, 46–68. London: Oliver and Boyd, 1969.

Emerson, Ralph Waldo. *Emerson in His Journals.* Edited by Joel Porte. Cambridge: Harvard University Press, 1982.

Engelhardt, George J. "The Ecclesiastical Pilgrims of the *Canterbury Tales*: A Study in Ethology." *Mediaeval Studies* 37 (1975): 287–315.

Epp, Garret P. J. "Learning to Write with Venus's Pen: Sexual Regulation in Matthew of Vendôme's *Ars versificatoria.*" In *Desire and Discipline: Sex and Sexuality in the Premodern West,* edited by Jaqueline Murray and Konrad Eisenbichler, 265–79. Toronto: University of Toronto Press, 1996.

Fanger, Claire. "The Formative Feminine and the Immobility of God: Gender and Cosmogony in Bernard Silvestris's *Cosmographia.*" In *The Tongue of the Fathers,* edited by David Townsend and Andrew Taylor, 80–102. Philadelphia: University of Pennsylvania Press, 1998.

Fehrenbacher, "'A Yeerd Enclosed Al Aboute': Literature and History in the Nun's Priest's Tale." *The Chaucer Review* 29 (1994): 134–48.

Ferguson, Margaret W. "Saint Augustine's Region of Unlikeness: The Crossing of Exile and Language." *Georgia Review* 29 (1975): 842–64.

Field, P. J. C. "The Ending of Chaucer's Nun's Priest's Tale." *Medium Ævum* 71 (2002): 302–7.

Fish, Stanley. "Short People Got No Reason to Live: Reading Irony." *Daedalus* 112 (1983): 175–92.

Fogelin, Robert J. *Understanding Arguments: An Introduction to Informal Logic.* New York: Harcourt Brace Jovanovich, 1978.

Fowler, Alastair. *Kinds of Literature: An Introduction to the Theory of Genres and Modes.* Cambridge: Harvard University Press, 1982.

Frese, Dolores Warwick. *An Ars Legendi for Chaucer's Canterbury Tales: A Re-Constructive Reading.* Gainesville: University of Florida Press, 1991.

———. "*The Nun's Priest's Tale*: Chaucer's Identified Masterpiece?" *Chaucer Review* 16 (1982): 330–43.

Freud, Sigmund. "The Uncanny." In *Literary Theory: An Anthology,* edited by Julie Rivkin and Michael Ryan, 418–30. Malden: Blackwell, 1998.

Friedman, John Block. "The *Nun's Priest's Tale*: The Preacher and the Mermaid's Song." *Chaucer Review* 7 (1973): 250–66.

Friedman, William F., and Elizabeth S. Friedman. "Acrostics, Anagrams, and Chaucer." *Philological Quarterly* 38 (1959): 1–20.

Froissart, Jean. *L'espinette amoureuse.* Edited by Anthime Fourrier. Paris: C. Klincksieck, 1972.

Frye, Northrop. *Anatomy of Criticism: Four Essays.* Princeton: Princeton University Press, 1957.

Furr, Grover. "Nominalism in the *Nun's Priest's Tale*: A Preliminary Study." In *Literary Nominalism and the Theory of Rereading Late Medieval Texts: A New Research Paradigm,* edited by Richard J. Utz, 136–46. Lewiston: Mellen, 1995.

Fyler, John M. *Language and the Declining World in Chaucer, Dante, and Jean de Meun.* Cambridge: Cambridge University Press, 2007.

Gallacher, Patrick. "Food, Laxatives, and Catharsis in Chaucer's 'Nun's Priest's Tale.'" *Speculum* 51 (1976): 49–68.

Gallant, Marc Gregory. *More Fun with Dick and Jane.* New York: Viking Penguin, 1986.

Ganim, John. *Chaucerian Theatricality.* Princeton: Princeton University Press, 1990.

Gasché, Rodolphe. "Quasi-Metaphoricity and the Question of Being." In *Hermeneutics and Deconstruction,* edited by Hugh J. Silverman and Don Ihde, 166–90. Albany: State University of New York Press, 1985.

———. *The Wild Card of Reading: On Paul de Man.* Cambridge: Harvard University Press, 1998.

Gaylord, Alan T. "*Sentence* and *Solaas* in Fragment VII of the *Canterbury Tales*: Harry Bailly as Horseback Editor." *PMLA* 82 (1967): 226–35.

Gelas, Bruno. "*La Fiction manipulatrice.*" In *L'Argumentation, linguistique et semiology,* 75–90. Lyon: Presses universitaires de Lyon, 1981.

Genette, Gérard. *Mimologics.* Edited and translated by Thaïs E. Morgan. Lincoln: University of Nebraska Press, 1995.

Geoffrey of Vinsauf. *Poetria Nova of Geoffrey of Vinsauf.* Translated by Margaret F. Nims. Toronto: Pontifical Institute of Mediaeval Studies, 1967.

Georgianna, Linda. "Lords, Churls, and Friars: The Return to Social Order in 'The Summoner's Tale.'" In *Rebels and Rivals: The Contestive Spirit in The Canterbury Tales,* edited by Susanna Greer Fein, David Raybin, and Peter C. Braeger, 149–72. Kalamazoo: Medieval Institute Publications, 1991.

Gilbert, Sandra M. "The Queen's Looking Glass: Female Creativity, Male Images of Women, and the Metaphor of Literary Paternity." In *The Madwoman in the Attic: The Woman Writer and the Nineteenth Century Literary Imagination,* by Sandra M. Gilbert and Susan Gubar, 3–44. New Haven: Yale University Press, 1979.

———, and Susan Gubar. "The Man on the Dump versus the United Dames of America; Or, What Does Frank Lentricchia Want?" *Critical Inquiry* 14 (1988): 386–406.

Gladwell, Malcolm. *Blink: The Power of Thinking Without Thinking.* New York: Little, Brown and Company, 2005.

Goldstein, R. James. "Chaucer, Freud, and the Political Economy of Wit: Tendentious Jokes in the *Nun's Priest's Tale.*" In *Chaucer's Humor: Critical Essays,* edited by Jean E. Jost, 145–63. New York: Garland, 1994.

Goodman, Nelson. *Languages of Art.* Indianapolis: Bobbs-Merrill, 1968.

Gordon, Ida L. *The Double Sorrow of Troilus: A Study of Ambiguities in Troilus and Criseyde.* Oxford: Clarendon, 1970.

Gordon, Paul. "The Enigma of Aristotelian Metaphor: A Deconstructive Analysis." *Metaphor and Symbolic Activity* 5 (1990): 83–90.

Green, Richard Firth. *A Crisis of Truth: Literature and Law in Ricardian England.* Philadelphia: University of Pennsylvania Press, 1999.

———. "A Possible Source for Chaucer's 'Summoner's Tale.'" *English Language Notes* 24 (1987): 24–27.

Greene, Thomas. *The Light in Troy: Imitation and Discovery in Renaissance Poetry.* New Haven: Yale University Press, 1982.

Guillaume de Lorris and Jean de Meun. *The Romance of the Rose.* Translated by Harry W. Robbins. New York: Dutton, 1962.

Gurevich, Aron. *Medieval Popular Culture: Problems of Belief and Perception.* Translated by Janos M. Bak and Paul A. Hollingsworth. Cambridge: Cambridge University Press, 1988.

Hamm, Victor M. "Chaucer: 'Heigh Ymaginacioun.'" *Modern Language Notes* 69 (1954): 394–5.

Hardison, O.B., Jr. and Leon Golden, eds. *Horace for Students of Literature: The Ars Poetica and Its Tradition*. Gainesville: University Press of Florida, 1995.

Hartman, Geoffrey H. *Saving the Text: Literature/Derrida/Philosophy*. Baltimore: Johns Hopkins University Press, 1981.

Harvey, E. Ruth. *The Inward Wits: Psychological Theory in the Middle Ages and the Renaissance*. Warburg Institute Surveys 6. London: The Warburg Institute, 1975.

———, ed. *The Court of Sapience*. Toronto: University of Toronto Press, 1984.

Hass, Robin R. "'A Picture of Such Beauty in Their Minds': The Medieval Rhetoricians, Chaucer, and Evocative *Effictio*." *Exemplaria* 14 (2002): 384–422.

Hawes, Clement. "'More Stars, God Knows, than a Pair': Social Class and the Common Good in Chaucer's *Parliament of Fowls*." *Publications of the Arkansas Philological Association* 15 (1989): 12–25.

Hawking, Stephen W. *A Brief History of Time: From the Big Bang to Black Holes*. New York: Bantam, 1988.

Hazelton, Richard. "Chaucer and Cato." *Speculum* 35 (1960): 357–80.

Henry, Desmond Paul. "Predicables and Categories." In Kretzmann, Kenny, and Pinborg. *The Cambridge History of Later Medieval Philosophy*, 128–42.

———. *That Most Subtle Question ('Quaestio Subtlissima'): The Metaphysical Bearing of Medieval and Contemporary Linguistic Disciplines*. Manchester: Manchester University Press, 1984.

Heytesbury, William. *On "Insoluble" Sentences: Chapter One of His Rules for Solving Sophisms*. Translated and edited by Paul Vincent Spade. Toronto: Pontifical Institute of Mediaeval Studies, 1979.

Hieatt, Constance B. *The Realism of Dream Vision: The Poetic Exploitation of the Dream-Experience in Chaucer and His Contemporaries*. The Hague: Mouton, 1967.

Higgins, Anne. "Medieval Notions of the Structure of Time." *The Journal of Medieval and Renaissance Studies* 19 (1989): 227–50.

Hill, John M. *Chaucerian Belief: The Poetics of Reverence and Delight*. New Haven: Yale University Press, 1991.

Hilton, R.H., and T.H. Aston, eds. *The English Rising of 1381*. Cambridge: Cambridge University Press, 1984.

Holsinger, Bruce W. *Music, Body, and Desire in Medieval Culture: Hildegard of Bingen to Chaucer*. Stanford: Stanford University Press, 2001.

Honorius of Autun. "Concerning the Exile of the Soul and its Fatherland; also called, About the Arts." Translated by Joseph M. Miller. In *Readings in Medieval Rhetoric,* edited by Joseph M. Miller, Michael Prosser, and Thomas Benson, 198–206. Bloomington: Indiana University Press, 1973.

Horace. *Satires, Epistles, and Ars Poetica.* Translated by H. Rushton Fairclough. Cambridge: Harvard University Press, 1961.

Howard, Donald R. *The Idea of the Canterbury Tales.* Berkeley: University of California Press, 1976.

Howard, Edwin J. *Geoffrey Chaucer.* Boston: Twayne, 1964.

Hudson, Anne. *The Premature Reformation: Wycliffite Texts and Lollard History.* Oxford: Clarendon Press, 1988.

Hughes, G. E. *John Buridan on Self-Reference.* Cambridge: Cambridge University Press, 1982.

Hugh of Rutland. *Ipomedon.* Breslau: Koblin and Hoschwitz, 1889.

Hult, David F. *Self-Fulfilling Prophecies: Readership and Authority in the First Roman de la Rose.* Cambridge: Cambridge University Press, 1986.

Huntsman, Jeffrey F. "Grammar." In *The Seven Liberal Arts in the Middle Ages,* edited by David L. Wagner, 58–95. Bloomington: Indiana University Press, 1983.

Huot, Sylvia. "The Daisy and the Laurel: Myths of Desire and Creativity in the Poetry of Jean Froissart." In *Contexts: Style and Values in Medieval Art and Literature,* edited by Daniel Poirion and Nancy Freeman Regalado. Special edition of *Yale French Studies* 80 (1991): 240–51.

Hussey, Maurice. *The Nun's Priest's Prologue and Tale.* Cambridge: Cambridge University Press, 1965.

Hutcheon, Linda. *Irony's Edge: The Theory and Politics of Irony.* New York: Routledge, 1994.

———. *A Theory of Parody: The Teachings of Twentieth-Century Art Forms.* New York: Methuen, 1985.

Irigaray, Luce. *Speculum of the Other Woman.* Translated by Gillian C. Gill. Ithaca: Cornell University Press, 1985.

Irvine, Martin. "Medieval Grammatical Theory and Chaucer's *House of Fame.*" *Speculum* 60 (1985): 850–76.

Iser, Wolfgang. "Feigning in Fiction." In *Identity of the Literary Text,* edited by Mario J. Valdés and Owen Miller, 204–30. Toronto: University of Toronto Press, 1985.

Isidore of Seville. *Isidori Hispalensis Episcopi Etymologiarum sive Originum Libri XX.* Edited by W. M. Lindsay. Oxford: Clarendon Press, 1911.

John of Salisbury. *The Metalogicon of John of Salisbury.* Translated by Daniel D. McGarry. Gloucester: Peter Smith, 1971.

Jordan, Robert M. *Chaucer and the Shape of Creation: The Aesthetic Possibilities of Inorganic Structure.* Cambridge: Harvard University Press, 1967.

Justice, Steven. *Writing and Rebellion: England in 1381.* Berkeley: University of California Press, 1994.

Kane, George. "Language as Literature." In *Lexis and Texts in Early English,* edited by Christian J. Kay and Louise M. Sylvester, 161–71. Amsterdam: Rodopi, 2001.

Kelly, Douglas. *The Arts of Poetry and Prose.* Turnhout: Brepols, 1991.

Kermode, Frank. *The Sense of an Ending: Studies in the Theory of Fiction.* New York: Oxford University Press, 1967.

Kirk, Eugene P. *Menippean Satire: An Annotated Catalogue of Texts and Criticism.* New York: Garland, 1980.

Kiser, Lisa. *Telling Classical Tales: Chaucer and the Legend of Good Women.* Ithaca: Cornell University Press, 1983.

Kooper, Erik S. "Art and Signature and the Art of the Signature." In *Court and Poet: Selected Proceedings of the Third Congress of the International Courtly Literature Society, Liverpool, 1980,* edited by Glyn S. Burgess et al., 223–32. Liverpool: Cairns, 1981.

Kretzmann, Norman. "Comment by Norman Kretzmann." In *Approaches to Nature in the Middle Ages,* edited by Lawrence D. Roberts, 214–20. Binghamton: Center for Medieval and Early Renaissance Studies, 1982.

———. "*Incipit/Desinit.*" In *Motion and Time, Space and Matter: Interrelations in the History of Philosophy and Science,* edited by Peter K. Machamer and Robert G. Turnbull, 101–36. Columbus: Ohio State University Press, 1976.

———. "Syncategoremata, sophismata, exponibilia." In Kretzmann, Kenny, and Pinborg, *The Cambridge History of Later Medieval Philosophy,* 211–45.

———, Anthony Kenny, and Jan Pinborg, eds. *The Cambridge History of Later Medieval Philosophy: From the Rediscovery of Aristotle to the Disintegration of Scholasticism, 1100–1600.* Cambridge: Cambridge University Press, 1982.

Kruger, Steven. *Dreaming in the Middle Ages.* Cambridge: Cambridge University Press, 1992.

Kuntz, Paul, editor. *The Concept of Order.* Seattle: University of Washington Press, 1968.

Laertius, Diogenes. *The Lives and Opinions of Eminent Philosophers.* Translated by C. D. Yonge. London: H. G. Bohn, 1853.

Lakoff, George. *Women, Fire, and Dangerous Things: What Categories Reveal about the Mind.* Chicago: University of Chicago Press, 1987.

———, and Mark Johnson. *Metaphors We Live By.* Chicago: University of Chicago Press, 1980.

———, and Mark Turner. *More than Cool Reason: A Field Guide to Poetic Metaphor.* Chicago: University of Chicago Press, 1984.

Landes, David S. *Revolution in Time: Clocks and the Making of the Modern World.* Cambridge: The Belknap Press of Harvard University Press, 1983.

Law, Robert Adger. "In Principio." *PMLA* 37 (1922): 208–15.

Leach, A. F. *A History of Warwick School.* London: Archibald Constable & Co., 1906.

———. *A History of Winchester College.* London: Duckworth & Co., 1906.

Leach, Elizabeth Eva. *Sung Birds: Music, Nature, and Poetry in the Later Middle Ages.* Ithaca: Cornell University Press, 2007.

Lecoy, Félix, ed. *Le Roman de Renart.* Paris: Champion, 1951.

Le Goff, Jacques. "Labor Time in the 'Crisis' of the Fourteenth Century: From Medieval Time to Modern Time." In *Time, Work, and Culture in the Middle Ages,* translated by Arthur Goldhammer, 43–52. Chicago: University of Chicago Press, 1980.

———. "Merchant's Time and Church's Time in the Middle Ages." In *Time, Work, and Culture in the Middle Ages,* translated by Arthur Goldhammer, 29–42. Chicago: University of Chicago Press, 1980.

Leicester, H. Marshall, Jr. "The Art of Impersonation: A General Prologue to the Canterbury Tales." *PMLA* 95 (1980): 213–224.

Lenaghan, R. T. "The Nun's Priest's Fable." *PMLA* 78 (1963): 300–307.

Lentricchia, Frank. "Andiamo!" *Critical Inquiry* 14 (1988): 407–13.

———. "Patriarchy Against Itself—The Young Manhood of Wallace Stevens," *Critical Inquiry* 13 (1987): 742–86.

———, and Andrew DuBois, eds. *Close Reading: The Reader.* Durham: Duke University Press, 2003.

Leppert, Richard. *The Sight of Sound: Music, Representation, and the History of the Body.* Berkeley: University of California Press, 1993.

Lerer, Seth. "The Canterbury Tales." In *The Yale Companion to Chaucer,* edited by Seth Lerer, 243–96. New Haven: Yale University Press, 2006.

Leupin, Alexandre. *Barbarolexis: Medieval Writing and Sexuality.* Translated by Kate M. Cooper. Cambridge: Harvard University Press, 1989.

Levin, Samuel R. "Aristotle's Theory of Metaphor." *Philosophy and Rhetoric* 15 (1982): 24–46.

Levitan, Alan. "The Parody of Pentecost in Chaucer's *Summoner's Tale.*" *University of Toronto Quarterly* 40 (1971): 236–46.

Levy, Bernard S. "Biblical Parody in the *Summoner's Tale.*" *Tennessee Studies in Literature* 11 (1966): 45–60.

———, and George R. Adams. "Chauntecleer's Paradise Lost and Regained." *Mediaeval Studies* 29 (1967): 178–92.

Lindberg, David C. *Studies in the History of Medieval Optics.* London: Variorum, 1983.

Lindley, Arthur. "Inducing the Hole: Paratactic Structure and the Unwritten 'Canterbury Tales.'" In *The Silent Word: Textual Meaning and the Unwritten,* edited by Robert J.C. Young, Ban Kah Choon, and Robbie B.H. Goh, 103–18. Singapore: Singapore University Press, 1998.

Locke, John. *An Essay Concerning Human Understanding; in Two Volumes.* Edited by John W. Yolton. London: J.M. Dent and Sons, 1967.

Lodge, David. *Small World: An Academic Romance.* New York: Macmillan, 1984.

Lowes, John Livingston. "The Prologue to the *Legend of Good Women* as Related to the French Marguerite Poems and the *Filostrato.*" *PMLA* 19 (1904): 593–683.

Lowry, Malcolm. *Under the Volcano.* New York: Reynal & Hitchcock, 1947.

Luria, Maxwell S., and Richard L. Hoffman, eds. *Middle English Lyrics: Authoritative Texts; Critical and Historical Backgrounds; Perspectives on Six Poems.* New York: Norton, 1974.

Lynch, Kathryn L. *The High Medieval Dream Vision: Poetry, Philosophy, and Literary Form.* Stanford: Stanford University Press, 1988.

Lyons, John. *Exemplum: The Rhetoric of Example in Early Modern France and Italy.* Princeton: Princeton University Press, 1989.

Lyons, Lisa, and Robert Storr. *Chuck Close.* New York: Rizzoli, 1987.

Manly, John M., and Edith Rickert, eds. *The Text of the Canterbury Tales, Studied on the Basis of All Known Manuscripts.* Chicago: University of Chicago Press, 1940.

Mansell, Darrel. "Metaphor as Matter." *Language and Literature* 17 (1992): 109–20.

———. "Unsettling the Colonel's Hash: 'Fact' in Autobiography." *Modern Language Quarterly* 37 (1976): 115–32.

———. "Written in Eden: Metaphor in Language." Unpublished book manuscript, courtesy of the author.

Martin, Robert L., ed. *Recent Essays on Truth and the Liar Paradox.* Oxford: Clarendon Press, 1984.

Mates, Benson. *Skeptical Essays.* Chicago: University of Chicago Press, 1981.

Matthew of Vendôme. *Ars Versificatoria.* Translated by Roger P. Parr. Milwaukee: Marquette University Press, 1981.

———. *The Art of Versification.* Edited and translated by Aubrey E. Galyon. Ames: Iowa State University Press, 1980.

McGerr, Rosemary Potz. *Chaucer's Open Books: Resistance to Closure in Medieval Discourse.* Gainesville: University Press of Florida, 1998.

McQuillan, Martin. *Paul de Man.* New York: Routledge, 2001.

Middleton, Anne. "William Langland's 'Kynde Name': Authorial Signature and Social Identity in Late Fourteenth-Century England." In *Literary Practice and Social Change in Britain, 1380–1530,* edited by Lee Patterson, 15–82. Berkeley: University of California Press, 1990.

Miner, John N. *The Grammar Schools of Medieval England: A.F. Leach in Historiographical Perspective.* Montreal: McGill-Queen's University Press, 1990.

Minnis, Alistair J. *Magister Amoris: The Roman de La Rose and Vernacular Hermeneutics.* Oxford: Oxford University Press, 2001.

———. *Medieval Theory of Authorship: Scholastic Literary Attitudes in the Later Middle Ages.* London: Scolar Press, 1984.

Miskimin, Alice S. *The Renaissance Chaucer.* New Haven: Yale University Press, 1975.

Mitchell, J. Allan. *Ethics and Exemplary Narrative in Chaucer and Gower.* Cambridge: D.S. Brewer, 2004.

Mooney, Linne R. "The Cock and the Clock: Telling Time in Chaucer's Day." *Studies in the Age of Chaucer* 15 (1993): 91–109.

Morrison, Toni. *The Bluest Eye.* New York: Rhinehart and Winston, 1970.

Moyer, Gordon. "The Gregorian Calendar." *Scientific American* 246 (May 1982): 144–52.

Murdoch, John E. "The Analytic Character of Late Medieval Learning: Natural Philosophy Without Nature." In *Approaches to Nature in the Middle Ages,* edited by Lawrence D. Roberts, 171–213. Binghamton: Center for Medieval and Early Renaissance Studies, 1982.

———. "The Development of a Critical Temper: New Approaches and Modes of Analysis in Fourteenth-Century Philosophy, Science, and Theology." *Medieval and Renaissance Studies* 7 (1978): 51–79.

Murphy, James J. "Rhetoric and Dialectic in *The Owl and the Nightingale.*" In *Medieval Eloquence: Studies in the Theory and Practice of Medieval Rhetoric,* edited by James J. Murphy, 198–230. Berkeley: University of California Press, 1978.

Muscatine, Charles. *Chaucer and the French Tradition*. Berkeley: University of California Press, 1966.

Neuse, Richard. *Chaucer's Dante: Allegory and Epic Theater in The Canterbury Tales*. Berkeley: University of California Press, 1991.

Nicholas of Lynn. *The Kalendarium of Nicholas of Lynn*. Edited by Sigmund Eisner and translated by Gary Mac Eoin and Sigmund Eisner. Athens: University of Georgia Press, 1980.

Nims, Margaret F. "*Translatio*: 'Difficult Statement' in Medieval Poetic Theory." *University of Toronto Quarterly* 43 (1974): 215–30.

Norris, Christopher. *Deconstruction: Theory and Practice*. London: Methuen & Co., 1982.

North, J. D. *Chaucer's Universe*. Oxford: Clarendon Press, 1988.

———. "The Western Calendar—'Intolerabilis, Horribilis, et Derisibilis': Four Centuries of Discontent." In *Gregorian Reform of the Calendar,* edited by G. V. Coyne, M. A. Hoskin, and O. Pederson, 75–113. Vatican: Pontifica Academia Scientiarum & Specolo Vaticana, 1983.

Nuchelmans, Gabriel. "The Semantics of Propositions." In Kretzmann, Kenny, and Pinborg, *The Cambridge History of Later Medieval Philosophy,* 197–210.

Oresme, Nicole. *Nicole Oreseme and the Kinematics of Circular Motion: Tractatus de commensurabilitate vel incommensurabilitate motuum celi*. Edited and translated by Edward Grant. Madison: University of Wisconsin Press, 1971.

Orr, Mary. *Intertextuality: Debates and Contexts*. Cambridge: Polity, 2003.

Osborn, Marijane. "The Squire's 'Steed of Brass' as Astrolabe: Some Implications for *The Canterbury Tales*." In *Hermeneutics and Medieval Culture,* edited by Patrick J. Gallacher and Helen Damico, 121–31. Albany: State University of New York Press, 1989.

———. *Time and the Astrolabe in The Canterbury Tales*. Norman: University of Oklahoma Press, 2002.

Paetow, Louis John, ed. and trans. *Two Medieval Satires on The University of Paris: La Bataille des Vii Ars of Henri D'Andeli, and The Moral Scolarium of John of Garland*. Berkeley: University of California Press, 1927.

Parker, Patricia. *Literary Fat Ladies: Rhetoric, Gender, Property*. New York: Methuen, 1987.

———. "Virile Style." In *Premodern Sexualities,* edited by Louis Fradenburg and Carla Freccero, 201–22. New York: Routledge, 1996.

Patterson, Lee. *Chaucer and the Subject of History*. Madison: University of Wisconsin Press, 1991.

———. "'*No man his resoun herde*': Peasant Consciousness, Chaucer's Miller, and the Structure of the *Canterbury Tales.*" *South Atlantic Quarterly* 86 (1987): 457–95.

———. "'What Man Artow?': Authorial Self-Definition in *The Tale of Sir Thopas* and *The Tale of Melibee.*" *Studies in the Age of Chaucer* 11 (1989): 117–75.

Pavel, Thomas G. *Fictional Worlds.* Cambridge: Harvard University Press, 1986.

Payne, F. Anne. *Chaucer and Menippean Satire.* Madison: University of Wisconsin Press, 1981.

Payne, Robert O. *The Key of Remembrance: A Study of Chaucer's Poetics.* New Haven: Yale University Press, 1963.

Pearsall, Derek. "Epidemic Irony in Modern Approaches to Chaucer's *Canterbury Tales.*" In *Medieval and Pseudo-Medieval Literature,* edited by Piero Boitani and Anna Torti, 79–85. Cambridge: Brewer, 1984.

———. "Interpretative Models for the Peasants' Revolt." In *Hermeneutics and Medieval Culture,* edited by Patrick J. Gallacher and Helen Damico, 63–70. Albany: State University of New York Press, 1989.

———. *The Life of Geoffrey Chaucer.* Oxford: Basil Blackwell, 1992.

———. *The Nun's Priest's Tale.* Part 9 of *A Variorum Edition of the Works of Geoffrey Chaucer,* vol. 2, *The Canterbury Tales.* Norman: University of Oklahoma Press, 1984.

Peck, Russell A. "Number Symbolism in the Prologue to Chaucer's *Parson's Tale.*" *English Studies: A Journal of English Language and Literature* 48 (1967): 205–15.

Perrin, Noel. *First Person Rural.* Boston: David R. Godine, 1978.

Peterson, Mark. "Dante's Physics." In Di Scipio and Scaglione, *The Divine Comedy and the Encyclopedia of Arts and Sciences,* 163–80.

Pratt, Mary Louise. "Arts of the Contact Zone." *Profession* 91 (1991): 33–40.

Pratt, Robert A. "Three Old French Sources of the Nonnes Preestes Tale." *Speculum* 47 (1972): 442–44, 646–68.

———, ed. *The Tales of Canterbury.* Boston: Houghton Mifflin, 1974.

Price, Derek J., ed. *The Equatorie of the Planets.* Cambridge: Cambridge University Press, 1955.

Priscian. "Fundamentals Adopted from Hermogenes." In *Readings in Medieval Rhetoric,* translated by Joseph Miller and edited by Joseph Miller, Michael H. Prosser, and Thomas W. Benson, 52–68. Bloomington: Indiana University Press, 1973.

———. *Institutiones grammaticae.* Vol. 2 of *Grammatici Latini.* Edited by Martin Hertz and Heinrich Keil. Leipzig: B. G. Teubner, 1855.

Quadlbauer, F. "*Zur Theorie der Komposition in der mittelalterlichen Rhetorik und Poetik.*" In *Rhetoric Revalued: Papers from the International Society for the History of Rhetoric,* edited by Brian Vickers, 115–32. Binghamton: Center for Medieval and Early Renaissance Studies, 1982.

Quinn, Esther Casier. *Geoffrey Chaucer and the Poetics of Disguise.* New York: University Press of America, 2008.

Rabelais, François. *Histories of Gargantua and Pantagruel.* Translated by J.M. Cohen. Harmondsworth: Penguin, 1955.

———. *The Works of Francis Rabelais.* 2 vols. Translated by Thomas Urquhart. London: H.G. Bohn, 1854–55.

Reed, Thomas L., Jr. *Middle English Debate Poetry and the Aesthetics of Irresolution.* Columbia: University of Missouri Press, 1990.

Regis, L.M. *Epistemology.* New York: Macmillan, 1959.

Relihan, Joel C. *Ancient Menippean Satire.* Baltimore: Johns Hopkins University Press, 1993.

———. *A History of Menippean Satire to A.D. 524.* Ann Arbor: University Microfilms International, 1985.

Reynolds, Suzanne. *Medieval Reading: Grammar, Rhetoric and the Classical Text.* Cambridge: Cambridge University Press, 1996.

Richter, David H. *Fable's End: Completeness and Closure in Rhetorical Fiction.* Chicago: University of Chicago Press, 1974.

Ricoeur, Paul. *The Rule of Metaphor: Multi-Disciplinary Studies of the Creation of Meaning in Language.* Toronto: University of Toronto Press, 1978.

Robertson, D.W., Jr. "Some Disputed Chaucerian Terminology." *Speculum* 52 (1977): 571–81.

Roney, Lois. *Chaucer's Knight's Tale and Theories of Scholastic Psychology.* Tampa: University of South Florida Press, 1990.

Root, Robert Kilburn. *The Poetry of Chaucer: A Guide to Its Study and Appreciation.* Boston: Houghton Mifflin, 1906.

Rose, Margaret A. *Parody//Meta-fiction: An Analysis of Parody as a Critical Mirror to the Writing and Reception of Fiction.* London: Croom Helm, 1979.

Rothwell, W. "The Hours of the Day in Medieval French." *French Studies: A Quarterly Review* 13 (1959): 240–51.

Rowland, Beryl. "A Sheep That Highte Malle (NPT, VII, 2831)." *English Language Notes* 6 (1968): 84–87.

———. "The Wisdom of the Cock." In *Third International Beast Epic, Fable, and Fabliau Colloquium, Münster 1979: Proceedings,* edited by Jan Goosens and Timothy Sodmann, 340–55. Köln: Böhlau Verlag, 1981.

Ryan, Marie-Laure. *Possible Worlds, Artificial Intelligence, and Narrative Theory.* Bloomington: Indiana University Press, 1991.

Ryle, Gilbert. *The Concept of Mind.* London: Hutchinson University Library, 1949.

———. "A Rational Animal." In *Collected Papers,* 2:415–34. New York: Barnes and Noble, 1971.

Sacks, Sheldon. *Fiction and the Shape of Belief: A Study of Henry Fielding, with Glances at Swift, Johnson, and Richardson.* Berkeley: University of California Press, 1964.

Said, Edward W. *Beginnings: Intention and Method.* New York: Basic Books, 1976.

Salisbury, Joyce E. *The Beast Within: Animals in the Middle Ages.* New York: Routledge, 1994.

Salter, Elizabeth. "Medieval Poetry and the Visual Arts." *Essays and Studies* 22 (1969): 16–32.

Scala, Elizabeth. *Absent Narratives, Manuscript Textuality, and Literary Structure in Late Medieval England.* New York: Palgrave, 2002.

Scanlon, Larry. *Narrative, Authority, and Power: The Medieval Exemplum and the Chaucerian Tradition.* Cambridge: Cambridge University Press, 1994.

———. "Unspeakable Pleasures: Alain de Lille, Sexual Regulation, and the Priesthood of Genius." *Romanic Review* 86 (1995): 213–42.

Scase, Wendy. *Piers Plowman and the New Anticlericalism.* Cambridge: Cambridge University Press, 1989.

Schaar, Claes. *The Golden Mirror: Studies in Chaucer's Descriptive Technique and Its Literary Background.* Lund: C.W.K. Gleerup, 1955.

Schnapp, Jeffrey. *The Transfiguration of History at the Center of Dante's Paradise.* Princeton: Princeton University Press, 1986.

Shelly, Percy Van Dyke. *The Living Chaucer.* Philadelphia: University of Pennsylvania Press, 1940.

Sidney, Philip. "An Apology for Poetry." In *Elizabethan Critical Essays,* edited by G. Gregory Smith, 1:148–207. Oxford: Clarendon Press, 1964.

Singleton, Charles S. *Dante Studies I.* Cambridge: Harvard University Press, 1954.

Sisam, Kenneth, ed. *The Nun's Priest's Tale.* Oxford: Clarendon Press, 1927.

Skeat, W.W., ed. *Testament of Love: The Complete Works of Chaucer.* Oxford: Clarendon Press, 1897.

Sklute, Larry. *Virtue of Necessity: Inconclusiveness and Narrative Form in Chaucer's Poetry.* Columbus: Ohio State University Press, 1984.

Smith, D. Vance. *The Book of the Incipit: Beginnings in the Fourteenth Century*
Minneapolis: University of Minnesota Press, 2001.

———. "Medieval Fora: The Logic of the Work." In *Reading for Form,* edited
by Susan J. Wolfson and Marshall Brown, 66–79. Seattle: University of
Washington Press, 2006.

Solterer, Helen. "At the Bottom of Mirage, a Woman's Body: 'Le roman de la
rose' of Jean Renart." In *Feminist Approaches to the Body in Medieval Literature,* edited by Linda Lomperis and Sarah Stanbury, 213–33. Philadelphia: University of Pennsylvania Press, 1993.

Sorabji, Richard. *Animal Minds and Human Morals: The Origins of the Western Debate.* Ithaca: Cornell University Press, 1993.

Spade, Paul Vincent. *The Mediaeval Liar: A Catalogue of the Insolubilia-
Literature.* Toronto: Pontifical Institute of Mediaeval Studies, 1975.

———. "The Semantics of Terms." In Kretzmann, Kenny, and Pinborg, *The
Cambridge History of Later Medieval Philosophy,* 188–96.

Spearing, A. C. *Medieval Dream-Poetry.* Cambridge: Cambridge University
Press, 1976.

———. *Textual Subjectivity: The Encoding of Subjectivity in Medieval Narratives and Lyrics.* Oxford: Oxford University Press, 2005.

Spitzer, Leo. *Classical and Christian Ideas of World Harmony: Prolegomena to an
Interpretation of the Word 'Stimmung.'* Edited by Anna Granville Hatcher.
Baltimore: Johns Hopkins University Press, 1963.

Stahl, William Harris, Richard Johnson, and E. L. Burge, trans. *Martianus Capella and the Seven Liberal Arts,* vol. 2, *The Marriage of Philology and Mercury.* New York: Columbia University Press, 1977.

Steadman, John. "Chauntecleer and Medieval Natural History." *Isis* 50 (1959):
236–44.

Steiner, George. *After Babel: Aspects of Language and Translation.* 3rd ed. Oxford: Oxford University Press, 1998.

Sterne, Lawrence. *The Life and Opinions of Tristram Shandy, Gentleman.* New
York: Oxford University Press, 1983.

Stevens, Wallace. *The Collected Poems of Wallace Stevens.* New York: Vintage,
1982.

Stock, Brian. *Augustine the Reader: Meditation, Self-Knowledge, and the Ethics
of Interpretation.* Cambridge: Harvard University Press, 1996.

Storr, Robert. "Realism and Its Doubles." In Lyons and Storr, *Chuck Close,* 9–23.

Strange, William C. "The *Monk's Tale*: A Generous View." *Chaucer Review* 1
(1967): 167–80.

Strohm, Paul. *Hochon's Arrow: The Social Imagination of Fourteenth-Century Texts*. Princeton: Princeton University Press, 1992.

———. *Social Chaucer*. Cambridge: Harvard University Press, 1989.

Stump, Eleonore. "Dialectic." In *The Seven Liberal Arts in the Middle Ages,* edited by David L. Wagner, 125–46. Bloomington: Indiana University Press, 1983.

Suleiman, Susan Rubin. *Authoritarian Fictions: The Ideological Novel as a Literary Genre*. New York: Columbia University Press, 1983.

Tachau, Katherine H. "What Senses and Intellect Do: Argument and Judgment in Late Medieval Theories and Knowledge." In *Argumentationstheories: Scholastische Forschungen su den logischen und semantischen Regelm korrekten Folgerns,* edited by Klaus Jacobi, 653–68. Leiden: E. J. Brill, 1993.

Terry, Patricia, trans. *Renard the Fox*. Berkeley: University of California Press, 1992.

Thomson, David, ed. *An Edition of the Middle English Grammatical Texts*. New York: Garland, 1984.

Thomas, Paul, ed. *The Nun's Priest's Tale on CD-ROM*. Birmingham: Scholarly Digital Editions, 2006.

Travis, Peter W. "A. C. Spearing, *Textual Subjectivity: The Encoding of Subjectivity in Medieval Narratives and Lyrics.*" *Speculum* 83 (2008): 756–60.

———. "Deconstructing Chaucer's Retraction." *Exemplaria* 3 (1991): 135–58.

———. "White." *Studies in the Age of Chaucer* 22 (2000): 1–66.

Trimpi, Wesley. *Muses of One Mind: The Literary Analysis of Experience and Its Continuity*. Princeton: Princeton University Press, 1983.

Trotter, David. *The Making of the Reader: Language and Subjectivity in Modern American, English, and Irish Poetry*. New York: St. Martin's Press, 1984.

Tuve, Rosemond. *Elizabethan and Metaphysical Imagery: Renaissance Poetic and Twentieth-Century Critics*. Chicago: University of Chicago Press, 1947.

Tversky, Amos. "Features of Similarity." *Psychological Review* 84 (1977): 327–52.

Tyler, Stephen A. *The Unspeakable: Discourse, Dialogue, and Rhetoric in the Postmodern World*. Madison: University of Wisconsin Press, 1987.

Uebel, Michael. "Acoustical Alterity." *Exemplaria* 16 (2004): 349–68.

Uhlig, Claus. *Chaucer und die Armut: Zum Prinzip der kontextuellen Wahrheit in den Canterbury Tales*. Mainz: Akademie der Wissenschaften und der Literatur, 1973.

Valéry, Paul. *Oeuvres*. Edited by J. Hytier. Paris: Gallimard, 1957.

Wallace, David. *Chaucerian Polity: Absolutist Lineages and Associational Forms in England and Italy*. Stanford: Stanford University Press, 1997.

Wallis, Faith. "Images of Order in the Medieval *Computus*." In *Ideas of Order in the Middle Ages,* edited by Warren Ginsberg, 45–67. Binghamton: Center for Medieval and Early Renaissance Studies, 1990.

Warren, Michelle R. "The Noise of Roland." *Exemplaria* 16 (2004): 277–304.

Watkins, Charles A. "Chaucer's *Sweete Preest.*" *Journal of English Literary History* 36 (1969): 455–69.

Waugh, Patricia. *Metafiction: The Theory and Practice of Self-Conscious Fiction.* London: Methuen, 1984.

Weinbrot, Howard D. *Menippean Satire Reconsidered: From Antiquity to the Eighteenth Century.* Baltimore: Johns Hopkins University Press, 2005.

Wentersdorf, Karl P. "*Heigh Ymaginacioun* in Chaucer's Nun's Priest's Tale." *Studia Neophilologica* 52 (1980): 3–34.

Wetherbee, Winthrop. "The Function of Poetry in the *De Planctu Naturae* of Alain de Lille." *Traditio* 25 (1969): 87–125.

———. *Platonism and Poetry in the Twelfth Century: The Literary Influence of the School of Chartres.* Princeton: Princeton University Press, 1972.

———, ed. and trans. *The Cosmographia of Bernardus Silvestris.* New York: Columbia University Press, 1973.

Wheatley, Edward. *Mastering Aesop: Medieval Education, Chaucer, and His Followers.* Gainesville: University Press of Florida, 2000.

White, Allon. "Bakhtin, Sociolinguistics, and Deconstruction." In *Carnival, Hysteria, and Writing: Collected Essays and Autobiography,* 135–59. Oxford: Clarendon Press, 1993.

White, Hugh. *Nature, Sex, and Goodness in a Medieval Literary Tradition.* Oxford: Oxford University Press, 2000.

Whittock, Trevor. *A Reading of the Canterbury Tales.* Cambridge: Cambridge University Press, 1968.

William of Sherwood. *William of Sherwood's Introduction to Logic.* Translated and edited by Norman Kretzmann. Minneapolis: University of Minnesota Press, 1966.

———. *William of Sherwood's Treatise on Syncategorematic Words.* Translated and edited by Norman Kretzmann. Minneapolis: University of Minnesota Press, 1968.

Wilson, Curtis. *William Heytesbury: Medieval Logic and the Rise of Mathematical Physics.* Madison: University of Wisconsin Press, 1956.

Wilson, William S. "Scholastic Logic in Chaucer's 'House of Fame.'" *Chaucer Review* 1 (1967): 181–84.

Wimsatt, James I. *Chaucer and His French Contemporaries: Natural Music in the Fourteenth Century.* Toronto: University of Toronto Press, 1991.

————, ed. *The Marguerite Poetry of Guillaume de Machaut.* University of North Carolina Studies in the Romance Languages and Literature 87. Chapel Hill: University of North Carolina Press, 1970.

Wimsatt, W. K. "Northrop Frye: Criticism as Myth." In *Northrop Frye in Modern Criticism,* edited by Murray Krieger, 75–107. New York: Columbia University Press, 1966.

Wood, Chauncey. *Chaucer and the Country of the Stars.* Princeton: Princeton University Press, 1970.

Woods, Marjorie Curry. "Rape and the Pedagogical Rhetoric of Sexual Violence." In *Criticism and Dissent in the Middle Ages,* edited by Rita Copeland, 56–86. Cambridge: Cambridge University Press, 1996.

Wright, Stephen K. "Jankyn's Boethian Learning in 'The Summoner's Tale.'" *English Language Notes* 26 (1988): 4–7.

Yeager, Robert F. "British Library Additional MS. 5141: An Unnoticed Chaucer *Vita.*" *Journal of Medieval and Renaissance Studies* 14 (1984): 261–81.

Zacharias, Richard. "Chaucer's *Nun's Priest's Tale.*" *Explicator* 32 (1974): 60–1.

Ziolkowski, Jan. *Alan of Lille's Grammar of Sex: The Meaning of Grammar to a Twelfth-Century Intellectual.* Cambridge: Medieval Academy of America, 1985.

Index

The Nun's Priest's Tale has been abbreviated as NPT.

"ABC, An," 92

Abelard, Peter, 328
  on *Mulier que damnavit salvavit,* 99

Adams, George R., 135, 352n.20
  "Chauntecleer's Paradise Lost and Regained," 390n.31

Adelard of Bath, 377n.23

Adorno, Theodor, 261

Aeneid, 67

Aers, David
  Chaucer, 208
  "*Vox populi* and the Literaure of 1381," 261

Alanus de Insulis
  Anticlaudianus, 73, 171, 191–92, 210
  Complaint of Nature, 28, 37–39, 43, 77
  on Genius, 18, 32, 36, 37–38, 41
  and Menippean satire, 77, 78
  on metaphor, 170–71, 176, 177, 178, 191–92
  on rhetoric as painting, 170–71, 176, 191–92, 369n.3

Albert of Saxony, 150, 271

Albertus Magnus: on *vis aestimativa,* 319

Alcuin: *Disputatio de Vera Philosophia,* 72

Alhazen, 326

allegory, 4–5, 185, 346

Allen, Valerie J.: "Broken Air," 376n.4

Allen, Woody: on comedy and tragedy, 89

ambiguity, 63–67, 100–101, 102, 112

"Amen," 160

analogy: relationship to metaphor, 182–83, 185, 187–88, 194–97, 374n.61

Andromache, 317

"Animal Language in the Medieval
  Classification of Signs," 328–31
Anne of Bohemia, 372n.46
Anonimalle Chronicle, 225, 259
antifeminism, 19–20, 64–65, 110,
  336, 356n.48, 361n.116
Aphthonius, 67
apologues vs. novels, 125, 364n.19
Apostrophe to Eleustria (England),
  86, 89, 90, 91–92
Apuleius, 74
  Golden Ass, 77–78
Aquinas, Thomas, 319
  on aestimative powers in animals
    and humans, 320
  on analogical participation, 195
  on categories of substance, 194
  commentary on *De Anima,*
    377n.23
  on logic, 145
Arch, Jennifer, 388n.71
Aristotle
  Categories, 380n.93
  on the categories, 130, 194
  on continuous vs. contradictory
    change, 288–91, 294–95
  on definitions of man, 374n.64
  De interpretatione, 252–54,
    380n.93
  De rhetorica, 145, 177
  on *exempla,* 124
  on limits, 288–92
  on logic, 134, 177, 252–54, 257,
    263–64
  on metaphor, 177, 179–80, 182,
    189, 371n.40
  On Sophistical Refutations, 304
  Physics, 288–91

Poetics, 177, 179–80
  on sounds of animals, 328, 331
  on time, 270, 271, 288–89
Armitage-Smith, Sydney: *John of
  Gaunt,* 370n.17
Askins, William, 388n.71
astrolabes, 272–73, 384n.18
  Treatise on the Astrolabe, 92,
    93–94, 272–73
Atkins, J. W. H., 87
Attali, Jacques
  on music and society, 201, 261–62
  Noise, 261–62
Attridge, Derek
  on onomatopoeia, 249–50
  on reading, 342–43
  The Singularity of Literature, 342
Auden, W. H.: on parody, 80
Augustine, St.
  Confessions, 97–98
  De Civitate Dei, 203–4
  on *in principio,* 97–98
  on language, 177–78, 370n.24
  on metaphor, 177–78, 191
  on political consonance and
    dissonance, 203–4
  on time, 267, 270, 297–98
  on truth, 98
Aureole, Peter: on time, 270
authorial intent, 14, 19, 231, 282
  and irony, 103–4, 113–14, 116
  and meaning of NPT, 2–8, 84,
    124, 142–43, 157, 340–49
  relationship to meaning of words,
    20, 148, 149, 157, 159
  See also Chaucer's voice
Averroes, 326
Avicenna, 319, 326, 328

Bacon, Roger, 62, 326, 329, 330–31
Baker, Houston A., Jr., 164
Bakhtin, Mikhail
  The Dialogic Imagination, 365n.35
  on encyclopedia parody, 9
  on heteroglossia, 232, 365n.35
  on Menippean satire, 75–76, 77, 79
  Problems of Dostoevsky's Poetics,
    75–76
Baldwin, Thomas Whitfield, 87,
  359n.32
Ball, John, 226
Balliett, Whitney: on Tatum, 26–27
Barney, Stephen A.: on the fox chase,
  251
Barolini, Teodolinda, 354n.18
Barthes, Roland, 164
  The Pleasure of the Text, 49
Baudrillard, Jean: "Simulacra and
  Simulations," 376n.69
Baugh, Albert C., 108
Baum, Paul, 108
beast fables
  of Aesop, 52, 54, 55, 56, 58, 59,
    68, 69, 71, 146, 309
  of Anianus, 54
  of Babrius, 54
  defined, 2
  vs. *exempla,* 125
  moralitates of, 2–3, 4, 55–56,
    141–42, 325, 365nn.42, 43
  vs. narrative truth, 196, 198–200
  and Priscian's *preexercitamina,* 12,
    67, 68, 309
  Romulus collection, 54–55
  satire in, 89
  types of allegory in, 55
  use in education, 54–56
  Wheatley on, 55, 351n.8

Beck, Philip R.: on Dante's shadow,
  385n.27
Beckwith, Sarah: on Christ's body,
  226–27
Bede: on metaphor, 177
beginnings
  logical analysis of *incipit/desinit,* 23,
    151, 269, 283, 287–97, 386n.44
  in narrative, 20, 84, 119–41,
    165–67, 363n.2
Bennett, J. A. W.: *Chaucer's Book of
  Fame,* 377n.23
Benson, Larry, 286–87, 353n.5,
  387n.62
Bernard of Chartres, 59–74, 73, 81
Bernardus Silvestris, 18
  De Cosmographia, 32, 36–37, 77,
    78, 354n.28
  and Menippean satire, 77, 78
Besserman, Lawrence: "Chaucerian
  Wordplay," 64–66, 112
Best, David, 380n.89
Beyond the Fringe, 366n.62
Bhaba, Homi, 164
Bible, the
  Adam, 4, 318, 331–32, 346
  allegory based on, 4–5
  Daniel, 317
  the Devil, 4
  Ecclesiastes, 108, 109
  Eve, 4
  Genesis, 4, 13, 97–98
  Gospel of John, 97
  Joseph, 317
  Last Judgment, 4
  Latin Bible as normative, 61–62
  Matt. 13:45–46, 372n.44
  Pharaoh, 317
  Romans 15:4, 158, 368n.73

Birky, Robin Hass, 49
  on rhetoric, 45–46
Bishop, Ian, 95
  "*The Nun's Priest's Tale* and the
    Liberal Arts," 73
Black, Max: on metaphor, 188
Blackmur, R. P., 164
Bloom, Harold: *A Map of
  Misreading*, 14–15
Bloomfield, Morton, 1
  "The Magic of *In Principio*," 97
Boccaccio, Giovanni, 354n.18
  on Francesca of Rimini, 310–11
  Il Filostrato, 92
Bochenski, Joseph M., 381n.94
Boece, 76, 92, 378n.47
Boethius, 74, 328
  Consolation of Philosophy, 78, 230,
    378n.47
  on consonance and dissonance, 201
  on *currit omnis homo*, 254,
    380n.93
  De differentiis topicis, 266
  De musica, 205, 206, 214–15, 217,
    223, 229
  on divisibility of musical tones, 229
  on efficient causality, 266
  on sound waves, 21, 214–15, 217,
    218, 223, 377n.23
Boitani, Piero: on Chaucer's *House
  of Fame*, 211
Bonaventure, St., 305
Book of the Duchess: Black Knight,
  317
Boone, Lalia: "Chauntecleer and
  Partlet Identified," 4, 190–91,
  352n.19
Booth, Wayne: *A Rhetoric of Irony*,
  113–14

Bradwardine, Thomas, 305
  Tractatus de incipit et desinit, 292
Brae, Andrew, 286
Brewer, Derek, 88, 95
Bronson, Bertrand: *In Search of
  Chaucer*, 78
Brook, Peter: *Reading for the Plot*, 332
Brooks, Cleanth, 164
Brooks, Mel: on farting scene in
  Blazing Saddles, 231
Brosnahan, Leger, 44, 356n.51
Brown, H. Rap: *Die, Nigger, Die!*, 265
Burckhardt, Sigurd: on poetry and
  words, 29
Buridan, John, 271, 305, 305–6, 306,
  312
Burke, Kenneth, 164
  on essentialized names, 331–32
Burleigh, Walter, 150, 271, 305
  De instanti, 292
  on *praeter*, 367n.66
Burton, Robert: *Anatomy of
  Melancholy*, 75
Butler, Judith, 354n.28

Cadmus, 202
Calinescu, Matei: *Rereading*, 25–26
Camargo, Martin: on rhetoric, 145
Canterbury Tales
  Fragment VII, 13–14, 24, 29–31,
    33, 40, 41, 324–25, 328, 353n.6
  General Prologue, 31, 33, 41, 43–44,
    47, 48, 79, 128, 138, 242, 336–37
  narrators in, 48–49
  relationship of NPT to, 1, 4,
    13–14, 24, 29–31, 33
Capella, Martianus: *The Marriage
  of Mercury and Philology*, 72,
  210, 223

cardinal virtues, 56
Carroll, Lewis: Bellman in "Hunting of the Snark," 311
Catholicon, 61
Cato
  Distichs/ethica Catonia, 56, 59, 146
  on dreams, 32, 52–53
Cervantes, Miguel de: *Don Quixote*, 9, 313
Chamberlain, David: on *Parliament of Fowls*, 206–7
Chapin, Arthur, 347
Chaucer Review, 3
Chaucer's voice, 1, 24–25, 49, 108, 335–40, 344
Chauntecleer
  and Aristotle's definition of man, 374n.64
  and the Bible, 4–5
  as category mistake, 193–94, 197–98
  vs. Chanteclere in *Roman de Renart, Branch II*, 315–16
  and Chaucer's name, 192, 373n.55
  colors of, 191–92, 196
  determination of time by, 51, 268
  downward flight of, 346–47
  dream of the fox, 23–24, 52–53, 314, 315–26, 321, 322–23, 334, 343, 348–49
  on dreams, 11, 57, 68, 94–95, 112, 314, 316–17, 319, 320, 321, 324, 343, 345
  erudition of, 3–4, 51–52, 73
  escape from fox, 325, 345
  flattered by fox, 69, 142, 325
  as Golden Spangled Hamburg, 4, 190–91, 352n.19

  as heliotrope/metaphor, 21, 172, 189–94, 195–200
  hens' lamentations regarding, 62–63
  imbalanced humors of, 6
  last words, 142, 325
  narrator's apostrophe on, 86–92, 96
  reaction to sight of fox, 320–21, 325–33, 333, 334, 344
  as reader, 314–15, 327
  and rhetoric, 52–53, 62
  translation of "in principio, mulier est hominis confusio," 19, 52, 58, 94–103
  vs. widow, 62
  See also fox chase
Chomsky, Noam, 370n.28
Cicero, Marcus Tullius
  De Inventione, 147
  De Re Publica, 202–3
  Erasmus on style of, 33–34
  on metaphor, 176–77
  on political harmony, 202–3
  Tacitus on style of, 34
Cicero, pseudo-: *Ad Herennium*, 147
Clark, D., 359n.32
Claudian, 211, 258
Clerk's Tale, 92
  Griselda as *exemplum* in, 126–28, 129–30, 132–33, 365n.36
Clogan, Paul, 54
Close, Chuck, 165, 339
close reading, 16–17, 112
  definitions of, 164–67
  of narrative beginnings/widow's portrait, 20, 119–41, 165–67
  of narrative endings/*moralitas* of NPT, 20, 122, 141–64, 165–67

Close Reading: The Reader, 164

Cohen, Jeffrey Jerome, 353n.6

"*Kyte oute yugilment,*" 376n.4

Colebrook, Claire: *Irony,* 104

Colie, Rosalie L.: on Cretan Liar paradox, 339–40

Colle, 256

Confessio Amantis, 122

Cooper, Helen: on Fragment VII, 30, 328

Cornish, Alison, 298

Courtenay, William J.: *Schools and Scholars in Fourteenth-Century England,* 275–76

Court of Sapience, 386n.44

Cowell, Andrew, 39

Cox, James M.: "Toward Vernacular Humor," 379n.53

Croesus, 317

Culler, Jonathan

  on apostrophe, 90

  on irony, 104

cultural materialism, 208

Curtius, 258

Dagenais, John, 11–12

Dahlberg, Charles, 124, 352n.20

  "Chaucer's Cock and Fox," 390n.31

dance, 14, 15, 26

Dane, Joseph: on *Mulier est hominis confusio,* 100–101

Dante Alighieri, 258, 323, 390n.34

  on *alta fantasia,* 322

  on center of his mind, 215–17, 223

  Commedia, 73, 210, 215–17, 236–39, 240, 282, 298, 310, 322, 379n.59, 385n.27

  Convivio, 73

  on the Eagle's voice, 237–38, 240, 243, 251, 379n.63

  on Francesca of Rimini, 310–11

  and *House of Fame,* 210, 215–17

  and liberal arts, 73

  Rime petrose, 199, 375nn.66, 67

  shadow of, 385n.27

  on sounds, 215–16, 237–38, 264

  on sphere of the just, 236–37, 240, 251

  on syzygy of sun, moon, and earth, 298

Davidoff, Judith: *Beginning Well,* 363n.2

deconstruction, 58, 143–44, 161–62, 163–64, 340

de Man, Paul, 164

  Blindness and Insight, 346–47

  The Epistemology of Metaphor, 196–97

  on the fall, 346–47

  The Resistance to Theory, 144–45, 149, 157, 159, 161–64

Derrida, Jacques

  on Aristotle, 179–80, 189

  on *différance,* 376n.69

  on dissemination, 17, 18, 33, 43, 45

  on the heliotrope, 169, 180–81

  on language as play of differences, 370n.24

  on linguistic signifiers, 33

  on metaphor, 169, 178, 179–81, 193

  "The *Retrait* of Metaphor," 178

  on the sun, 371n.40

  "Ulysses Gramophone," 165

  "White Mythology," 178, 179–80, 371n.40

Deschamps, Eustache: and the daisy, 174, 175, 184

Dick and Jane reader, 234–36, 238, 265

Dickens, Charles: Pip in *Great Expectations,* 332

Dinshaw, Carolyn: *Chaucer's Sexual Poetics,* 102–3

Diogenes the Cynic, 384n.64

disputation, 52–53, 57, 58, 59, 358n.17

dissemination, 323–24, 333–34, 340

  Derrida on, 17, 18, 33, 43, 45

  vs. polysemy, 17

Divine Comedy and the Encyclopedia of Arts and Sciences, 73

Dobson, R.B., 381n.104

Doctrinale, 61

Donaldson, Talbot: on moral of NPT, 3

Donatus, 205

  Ars Major/Barbarismus, 146–47

  Ars minor, 61, 146

Donovan, Mortimer J., 124, 352n.20

  "The *Moralite* of the Nun's Priest's Sermon," 390n.31

dreams

  Chauntecleer on, 11, 57, 68, 94–95, 112, 314, 316–17, 319, 320, 321, 324, 343, 345

  Chauntecleer's dream of the fox, 23–24, 52–53, 314, 315–26, 321, 322–23, 334, 343

  Emerson on, 303

  and imagination, 319

  Kruger on, 347–48

  Pertelote on, 11, 52, 57, 112, 316–17, 319

  as prophetic in literary texts, 320

  truth in, 23–24, 315–26

Du Bellay, Joachim, 176, 258

Durling, Robert M., 199

  Time and the Crystal, 369nn.7, 8, 375n.66

Eberhard of Béthune: *Grecismus,* 148

Eberhard the German, 85

Eco, Umberto, 328–31

Edelman, Lee, 356n.48

Eisner, Sigmund, 268–69, 278–79, 281, 282, 284–85, 383n.5

Elbow, Peter, 95

  on Chauntecleer, 3

Eliot, George, 119

Elizabeth I, 91

Elliot, T.S., 381n.102

Emerson, Ralph: on dreams and beasts, 303

endings

  logical analysis of *incipit/desinit,* 23, 151, 269, 283, 287–97, 386n.44

  in narrative, 20, 84, 122, 141–64, 165–67

Englehardt, George J., 124

Ennodius, 74

Epilogue to NPT, 17–18, 30–33, 41–42, 44, 46–49

Epp, Garret, 35

Equatorie of the Planets, 388n.71

Erasmus, Desiderius: on Ciceronian style, 33–34

"Erthe toc of erthe with wo," 166

Eucharist, the, 6

Everett, Dorothy, 88

exempla, 52–53, 365n.38
  vs. *argumentum/sentence*, 121,
    122, 128
  Aristotle on, 124
  Gélas on, 128
  Geoffrey of Vinsauf on, 121
  Lyons on, 125, 126
  Scanlon on, 122, 363n.7
  theory of manifestation regarding,
    128–29, 136

faculty psychology, 314–15, 320–23,
    342
  Agent Intellect, 323, 333, 348
  Common Senses (*sensus
    communis*), 319, 333
  Imagination, 318–19, 321–23,
    333, 334, 348
  Intellect, 321, 323, 326, 333, 348
  intellectus agens, 323
  Memory, 319, 320, 333, 348
  Reason, 319, 321, 323, 348
  virtus distinctiva, 326–27, 333
  vis aestimativa, 320–21, 325–26,
    328, 333, 348
  vis cogitativa, 319, 321, 333
Fall of Princes, 122
Fanger, Claire: on Bernardus
    Silvestris, 36–37
Fehrenbacher, Richard: "A Yeard
    Enclosed Al Aboute," 381n.109
Ferguson, Margaret W., 178
  *Saint Augustine's Region of
    Unlikeness*, 370n.24
Field, P.J.C.: *The Ending*, 368n.74
Fish, Stanley, 164
  on Booth, 114
  on irony, 19–20, 114, 116

Fland, Robert, 305
flattery, 69, 108–9, 142, 325
Fogelin, Robert J.: *Understanding
    Arguments*, 381n.94
food, 5–7
  and Nun's Priest, 6, 7
  widow's diet, 6, 131–33, 134, 137,
    138
Forster, E.M., 80
Foucault, Michel: on Liar paradox,
    313
Fowler, Alastair, 77
fox chase, 245–52, 255–64, 325
  and grammar, 241–42, 248–50
  and logic, 252, 255–57, 263–64,
    266
  and Peasants' Revolt, 21–22,
    71, 209, 258–64, 265–66,
    381n.109
  and rhetoric, 239, 257–59, 263
  sounds in, 21–22, 71, 209, 239,
    241–42, 243, 247–52, 257–58,
    260–61, 265–66
Francesca of Rimini, 310–11
Franklin's Tale
  Dorigen's task for Aurelius, 107
  the Franklin on "colours" of
    rhetoric, 169–70, 171, 176
free will vs. determinism, 71, 109,
    338, 343–47, 348
Frese, Dolores Warwick, 373n.55
  An Ars Legendi, 383n.5
Freud, Sigmund
  on dreams, 347
  on the eye and male organ, 42
  on jokes, 115
  on negation, 134
  on the uncanny, 177

Friar's Tale, 79, 363n.7

Friedman, John Block, 124

Friedman, William F. and
Elizabeth S., 373n.55

Froissart, Jean
Chroniques, 383n.4
and the daisy, 172, 175–76, 178,
184, 192, 369n.15, 375n.67
L'espinette amoureuse, 175–76
on Peasants' Revolt, 259

Frye, Northrop
Anatomy of Criticism, 8, 75
on Menippean anatomy, 9, 75,
77, 79

Fulgentius, 74

Furr, Grover, 338, 344

Fyler, John M.: *Language and the
Declining World,* 379n.63

Gaetano di Thiene, 387n.57

Galen, 377n.23

Gallacher, Patrick: "Food, Laxatives,
and Catharsis in Chaucer's
Nun's Priest's Tale," 5–6, 7–8

Gallagher, Catherine, 164

Ganim, John: *Chaucerian
Theatricality,* 381n.109

Gasché, Rodolphe
on Derrida, 181
The Wild Card of Reading, 145,
162

Gaylord, Alan: on Fragment VII,
29–30

Gélas, Bruno
on *exempla,* 128–29
on theory of manifestation,
128–29, 136

Genette, Gérard: *Mimologiques,* 242,
243–46

Genius
Alanus de Insulis on, 18, 37–38, 41
Jean de Meun on, 18, 39–40, 41
Nun's Priest as, 18, 32–33, 36, 44
genre of NPT, 2, 8–17, 18
as beast fable, 2–3, 4, 8, 52, 141–42
as Menippean satire/parody, 9–12,
13, 19, 53–54, 72, 74–84, 117,
340, 341–42, 344
and readers' expectations, 141–42
as self-parody, 13–17, 324–25
as simulacrum of Western
thought and letters, 12–13

Geoffrey of Vinsauf, 18, 85
on effeminized rhetoric, 45–46
on exempla and proverbs, 121
on female beauty, 46
on narrative beginnings, 120–21,
122
in narrator's apostrophe, 86, 87,
88–92, 96, 246
Poetria Nova, 19, 45, 86, 87, 88–92,
89–90, 96, 120–21, 140, 148, 246

Georgianna, Linda, 225–26

Gerland, 256, 260, 263

Gervais of Melkely, 85

Gilbert, Sandra, 164
on literary power and male
sexuality, 355n.29
on testeria, 356n.48

Gladwell, Malcom: *Blink,* 327

Glosule super Priscianum maiorem,
240, 377n.18

God, 6–7, 36–37, 185, 195
as Creator, 194, 296–97, 299
foreknowledge of, 71, 109, 322,
338, 343–46
justice of, 236–38, 251, 379n.63
and language, 178

Goldstein, R. James:
"Chaucer, Freud, and the Political
Economy of Wit," 381n.109
"Tendentious Jokes in the *Nun's
Priest's Tale*," 115–16
Goodelief, 32
Goodman, Nelson: *Languages of Art*,
373n.48
Gordon, Ida: on *Troilus and
Criseyde*, 111
Gordon, Paul: on Aristotle's views
regarding metaphor, 177
Gower, John, 261
grammar
ambiguity of pronouns, 63–64
art of *dictamen*, 62
etymology, 61, 62–67
as foundation of liberal arts, 62
and fox chase, 241–42, 248–50
vs. logic, 59, 150, 152, 366n.53
orthography, 61
prosody, 61
relationship to *enarratio*/literary
interpretation, 144–45, 146,
148–49, 155–57, 159–60,
161–62, 163, 241, 250–51
vs. rhetoric, 144–45, 147–49,
150, 155, 157, 159, 161, 162
syntax, 61, 62–67, 101
teaching of, 59–60, 61–64, 71
as trivial art, 20, 71, 144–45, 150,
161, 263
grammar school studies, 61–74
curriculum, 52–74, 146
disputation, 52–53, 57, 58, 59,
358n.17
distinctiones, 66–67
and hen's lamentations regarding
Chauntecleer, 62–63

Latin-English translation, 12, 58
Latin reading texts, 35, 61–62,
101, 146–49
Menippean parody of, 18–19, 78,
79, 117, 341–42
preexercitamina in, 12, 18–19, 60,
61, 67–72, 146, 257, 359n.32
and readers of NPT, 12–13,
18–19, 52–53, 71–72, 122,
146–49, 239, 245, 248
reading assignments, 12, 146–49
textual imitation in, 67–72, 80, 81,
83, 85–86, 148
Green, Richard Firth, 228
A Crisis of Truth, 312
Greenblatt, Stephen, 164
Greene, Thomas
The Light in Troy, 84–85
on textual imitation, 84–85, 89–90
Gregory of Rimini, 305
Grosseteste, Robert, 62, 305
Gubar, Susan, 164
on testeria, 356n.48
Guverich, Aron, 227

Hamm, Victor M.: "Chaucer,"
390n.34
Harmonia, 202
Harry Bailly
on the Monk, 30, 32, 353n.5
on the Nun's Priest, 17–18, 30–33,
41–42, 44, 46–49
quest for supremely masculine
male, 17, 30–33
as reader, 343
on studying "som sophyme," 306
time of day determined by, 22,
67–69, 276–80, 281, 282, 283,
284, 298, 300–301

Hartmann, Geoffrey: on irony, 116
Hawking, Stephen, 385n.30
Hazelton, Richard: on Cato's
   distichs, 56
"heigh ymaginacoun" passage,
   321–23, 334, 348
Helias, Peter: *Summa super
   Priscianum,* 240, 377n.18
heliotropes
   Chauntecleer as
      heliotrope/metaphor, 21, 172,
      189–94, 195–200
   daisy in the Prologue of *The
      Legend of Good Women,* 21,
      172, 183–89, 371nn.40, 43,
      372nn.44, 46, 373n.55,
      375n.67
   heliotrope (gem) and metaphor,
      171–72, 192, 199–200, 372n.44,
      376n.68
   heliotrope (plant) and metaphor,
      21, 169, 171–72, 174–75,
      179–82, 199–200, 372n.44,
      376n.68
   Machaut on, 172, 174–75, 176,
      178, 184, 370n.16, 18
Henry, Desmond Paul, 371n.43
Henry d'Andely: *The Battle of the
   Seven Liberal Arts,* 366n.53
Henry of Ghent, 150, 326
Heraclitus, 204
Hermogenes, 242, 250
   Progymnasmata, 67, 69
Heytesbury, William, 292
   On "Insoluble" Sentences, 358n.24
   Regule solvendi sophismata, 292,
      305–6, 387n.57
Hieatt, Constance B.: *The Realism of
   Dream Vision,* 389n.28

Higgins, Anne: "Medieval Notions
   of the Structure of Time,"
   383n.4
Hill, John M.: *Chaucerian Belief,* 312
Hinckley, Henry Barrett, 256
Holcot, Robert, 305
Holsinger, Bruce W.: *Music, Body,
   and Desire in Medieval Culture,*
   376n.4
Homer, 211
   Iliad, 80, 120
Honorius of Autun: *De animae exilio
   et patria,* 72–73
Horace, 146
   Ars Poetica, 120, 140
   on narrative beginnings, 120, 122,
      140–41
   on style, 17, 34
Householder, Fred: on parody, 80
House of Fame, 161, 379n.64
   Aeolus's trumpet of brass, 217–18,
      223
   the Eagle, 73, 210, 212–14, 317
   Fama, 210
   historiographical noise in, 21, 209,
      210–18, 221–22, 231, 239
   House of Rumour, 211, 222, 250
Howard, Donald, 1
Howard, Edwin, 108
Hudson, Anne: *The Premature
   Reformation,* 224
Hughes, G. E.: *John Buridan on
   Self-Reference,* 388n.4
Hugh of Rutland, 308
Hunstman, Jeffrey: on grammar, 145
Huot, Sylvia
   "The Daisy and the Laurel,"
   369n.15
   on Froissart, 176

Hussey, Maurice: *The Nun's Priest's Prologue and Tale,* 9–12
Hutcheon, Linda
  on irony, 82–83, 104, 105, 106, 108–9
  Irony's Edge, 104
  on parody, 15, 81, 82–83, 91, 108–9
  on satire, 82–83
  A Theory of Parody, 15, 82–83
Huxley, Aldous: *Brave New World,* 75

"I kan noon harme of no womman divyne," 19, 64–67, 70, 112
imitation, textual
  Chaucer's imitation of, 89–92
  as dialectic, 85, 89–91
  as eclectic/exploitative, 84–85, 89
  in grammar school studies, 67–72, 80, 81, 83, 85–86, 148
  Greene on, 84–85, 89
  as heuristic, 85, 89
  in narrator's apostrophe, 86–92
  as poetic skill, 19, 60, 67, 80, 81, 84–92
  as sacramental, 84, 85, 89
Innocent III: *De Contemptu Mundi,* 92
"In principio, mulier est hominis confusio": Chauntecleer's translation of, 19, 52, 58, 94–103
instinct vs. reason, 24
intertextuality: parodic text vs. target text, 8–9, 14–15, 80–81, 82, 83, 105, 107, 257
Irigaray, Luce, 354n.28

irony, 92–117, 320, 324, 346
  and authorial intent, 103–4, 113–14, 116
  Booth on, 113–14
  as Chaucer's signature trope, 103–4, 105, 107–9, 115, 116–17
  Colebrook on, 104
  Culler on, 104
  defined, 104
  as evaluative, 81–82
  Fish on, 19–20, 114, 116
  and homogeneous community of readers, 104–5, 115
  Hutcheon on, 82–83, 104, 105, 106, 108–9
  vs. parody, 19, 53, 79, 81–83, 105, 107, 112, 115
  as poetic skill, 19–20, 84, 92–117, 102
  Pratt on, 104
  readers of, 104–5, 107–8, 114–15, 117
  vs. satire, 79, 81–83, 107
Irvine, Martin: "Medieval Grammatical Theory and Chaucer's *House of Fame,*" 214, 379n.64
Iser, Wolfgang: "Feigning in Fiction," 311
Isidore of Seville
  Etymologiae, 214
  on metaphor, 177

Jacquerie of 1358, 260
Jameson, Fredric, 164
Jean de Meun
  on Genius, 18, 32, 36, 39–40, 41
  and Menippean satire, 77
  The Romance of the Rose, 39–40, 41, 77, 355n.46

Jesus Christ: as Incarnation, 45
John of Garland, 85
John of Holland: *Tractatus de primo
    et ultimo instanti,* 292
John of Reading, 326
John of Salisbury
    on dreams, 319
    on imitation, 81
    on liberal arts, 59–61, 67
    Metalogicon, 59–61
    on *Mulier que damnavit salvavit,*
        99
Johnson, Mark: *Metaphors We Live
    By,* 371n.35
Jonson, Ben: *Timber; or Discoveries,*
    34
Jordan, Robert: *Chaucer and the
    Shape of Creation,* 11
Joyce, James: *Ulysses,* 9
justice, 236–38, 239
Justice, Steven: *Writing and
    Rebellion,* 222, 224
Juvenal, 79

Kane, George: "Language as
    Literature," 381n.109
Keats, John: "The Fall of Hyperion,"
    145
Kelly, Douglas: on medieval
    composition, 72, 359n.43
Kermode, Frank, 120
Kiger, Robert W., 373n.55
Kilvington, Richard: *Sophismata,*
    292
Kilwardby, Robert, 62
    *Tractatus super Priscianum
    maiorem,* 240, 377n.18
Kirk, Eugene: *Menippean Satire,* 78

Kiser, Lisa
    on Chaucer's daisy, 185, 187,
        371n.43
    on poetry and metaphor, 369n.6
Knight, Stephen, 88, 261
Knighton, Henry, 259, 260
Knight's Tale
    as Menippean satire, 76
    and Statius's *Thebaid,* 202
Kooper, Erik S., 373n.55
Kretzmann, Norman, 254, 292,
        366n.58, 367nn.63, 64
    "Incipit/Desinit," 386nn.43, 50
Krieger, Murray, 164
Kruger, Steven
    Dreaming in the Middle Ages, 347,
        389n.28
    "Dream Inheritance," 347–48
    on Oresme, 300
Kuntz, Paul: *The Concept of Order,*
        134–35

Lakoff, George
    Metaphors We Live By, 371n.35
    *Women, Fire, and Dangerous
        Things,* 374n.63
Lambert of Auxerre, 328
Lancelot de Lake, 304–5, 307–14
Landes, David: on mechanical
        clocks, 272
language
    Augustine on, 177–78, 370n.24
    essentialized names, 331–32, 333
    masculine signified vs. effeminate
        signifier, 35
    in poetry, 17–18, 33–40, 42–43
    poet's mastery over, 42–43
    potency of, 17–18, 33, 43

as problematic sexual emission,
17–18
signified vs. signifier, 35, 41,
241–42, 243–46, 249–50, 256,
333–34
virile style, 17–18, 33–49
See also grammar; meaning of
words; poetry; rhetoric
Latin language
in grammar school studies, 12, 35,
57–58, 61–62, 101, 146–49
Latin Bible, 61–62
and levels of supposition, 99–100
Lavenham, Richard, 305
Leach, A. F.: on disputation, 57
Legend of Good Women
Alceste in, 21, 93, 185–88,
372nn.44, 46, 375n.67
daisy in, 21, 172, 183–89,
371nn.40, 43, 372nn.44, 46,
373n.55, 375n.67
God of Love, 21, 186–88, 317,
372n.46
pearl in, 186, 372nn.44, 46,
375n.67
Prologue, 21, 92, 138, 172,
183–89, 355n.42, 371nn.40, 43,
372n.46, 375n.67
LeGoff, Jacques: on mechanical
clocks, 271–72, 279
Leicester, H. Marshall, Jr., 48–49
Lenaghan, R. T.: on *progymnasmata*,
67
Lentricchia, Frank, 164, 356n.48
Leppert, Richard
The Sight of Sound, 205–6
on sounds produced by humans,
231

Leupin, Alexandre, 355n.36
Levy, Bernard J., 135, 352n.20
"Chauntecleer's Paradise Lost
and Regained," 390n.31
liberal arts, seven
and determination of time,
300–301
and genre of NPT, 12–13
grammar as foundation of, 62
John of Salisbury on, 59–61, 67
and medieval academic culture,
72–74, 83
quadrivium, 51, 59–60, 62,
73–74, 138–39, 144, 145, 206,
277, 341
trivium, 20, 52, 59–60, 62, 69,
71, 73–74, 101, 122, 144–64,
239, 259, 263, 265, 277
See also grammar; logic; rhetoric
Liddel, Mark, 286
literacy criticism, 3–4, 7–8,
323–24
and *exempla,* 125
grammar school studies in,
12, 55–56
and *moralitates* of beast fables,
4, 55–56, 122, 143–44
oral interpretation (*lectio*) and
enarratio/interpretation, 241,
250–51
parody as, 8–9, 94, 95–96
the trivium and *enarratio*/
interpretation, 144–64, 259,
263–64, 265
*Livre de Melibée et de Dame
Prudence,* 93
Locke, John: on properties vs.
essence of gold, 196–97

logic
  analysis of beginning and ending
    (*incipit/desinit*), 23, 151, 269,
    283, 287–97, 386n.44
  Aristotle on, 134, 177, 252–54,
    257, 263–64
  categoremata, 149–50, 252, 255,
    256, 287–88, 296–97, 367n.63
  and determinations of
    time/*chronographia* in NPT,
    23, 287–97, 298, 301
  and the fox chase, 252, 255–57,
    263–64, 266
  vs. grammar, 59, 150, 152,
    366n.53
  insolubilia/Cretan Liar paradoxes,
    305–14, 333, 334, 339–40
  law of contradiction, 345
  law of excluded middle, 23, 134,
    177, 211
  levels of supposition, 99–100, 101
  mental propositions, 309
  modal logic, 376n.68
  parody of, 257
  propositions, 252–56, 263–64
  relationship to *enarratio*/literary
    interpretation, 144, 146,
    149–60, 161, 163, 166
  vs. rhetoric, 59, 150
  sophismata, 23, 151, 152, 153, 154,
    156, 157, 166, 255, 284–97,
    305–15, 330–40, 333, 334
  square of opposition, 254–55,
    381n.94
  syncategoremata, 149–60, 161,
    252, 255, 287–91, 292, 293–94,
    296, 307, 366n.62, 367nn.63, 64,
    66, 386n.44
  as trivial art, 20, 59, 71, 144,
    145–46, 149, 150, 161, 239,
    252, 263–64
  vis confundendi in, 23, 293,
    296–97, 298, 300–301, 340,
    387n.54
Lowes, John Livingston: "The
  Prologue," 372n.46
Lowry, Malcolm: *Under the Volcano,*
  7
Lucan, 146, 211, 258
Lucian, 74
Lydgate, John: "Horse, Goose, and
  Sheep," 57
Lynch, Kathryn L.: *The High
  Medieval Dream Vision,*
  389n.28
Lyons, John: on *exempla,* 125, 126

Machaut, Guillaume
  "Dit dou Lyon," 387n.61
  on heliotropes/daisies, 172,
    174–75, 176, 178, 184,
    370n.16, 18
Macrobius
  *Commentary on the Dream
    of Scipio,* 204, 205, 206, 210,
    317, 319
  Saturnalia, 78
Malkyn, 256, 260, 263
Maniciple's Tale, 363n.7
Manly, John M., 87, 367n.69,
  385n.36
Man of Law's Tale
  determination of time of day in
    Introduction, 22, 277–80, 281,
    282, 283, 284, 298, 300–301
  readers' response to, 338

Mansell, Darrel
  on metaphor, 179, 191, 373nn.49,
    50
  "Metaphor as Matter," 179,
    373n.50
  "Unsettling the Colonel's Hash:
    'Fact' in Autobiography," 311
Map, Walter, 308
Marguerite of Flanders, 176,
  370n.17
Marsilius of Inghen, 271
Martianus Capella, 74
  Marriage of Mercury and
    Philology, 78
Martinez, Ronald L., 199
  Time and the Crystal, 369nn.7, 8,
    375n.66
Marvell, Andrew: "The Garden,"
  370n.28
Marxism, 208, 224
Matthew of Vendôme, 38, 85
  Ars Versificatoria, 35–36, 45, 148
  on Davus, 45
  on effeminate style, 18, 35, 45–46
  on Helen of Troy, 46, 47
  on praise of men, 47
McGarrigle, Persse, 2
McQuillan, Martin
  Paul de Man, 368n.82
  on undecideability and reading,
    368n.82
meaning of NPT, 2–8, 84, 124,
  142–43, 157, 325–26, 340–49
  See also moralitas of NPT
meaning of words
  as ambiguous, 63–67, 100–101,
    102, 112
  "Cok! Cok!," 328–33, 334

as figurative (rhetorical), 20,
  39, 40, 147, 149, 150, 155,
  157–58, 159–60, 161, 162,
  169–70
as literal (grammatical), 20, 39,
  40, 149, 150, 155, 157, 158,
  159–60, 162, 169–70
relationship to authorial intent,
  20, 148, 149, 157, 159
Melibee, Tale of, 30, 92, 93, 324, 338
Menippean satire
  as anatomy vs. satire, 9, 75
  Bahktin on, 75–76, 77, 79
  definitions of, 74–79
  as didascalic/educational, 78, 79,
    117, 341–42
  examples from Middle Ages,
    77–78
  Frye on, 9, 75, 77
  Kirk on, 78, 79
  Payne on, 76–77, 79, 352n.35
  Relihan on, 75, 77, 78, 79
  vs. Menippean parody, 53–54,
    75, 79
  Weinbrot on, 74, 77, 79
  See also genre of NPT, as
    Menippean satire/parody
Merchant's Tale
  encomium to marriage in, 107
  vs. NPT, 13
Merton College, 304
metaphor, 84, 158, 162
  Alanus de Insulis on, 170–71,
    176, 177, 178, 191–92
  and animals, 198, 374n.64
  Aristotle on, 177, 179–80, 182,
    189, 371n.40
  Augustine on, 177–78, 191

metaphor (*cont.*)
  as category mistake, 179–80,
    188–89, 193–94, 200, 340,
    373n.48
  "colours" of, 138, 169–70, 171, 176
  Derrida on, 169, 178, 179–81, 193
  as essence of poetry, 20–21,
    171–72, 369n.6
  vs. *exemplum*, 125
  and the heliotrope (gem), 171–72,
    192, 199–200, 372n.44, 376n.68
  and the heliotrope (plant), 21,
    169, 171–72, 174–75, 179–82,
    199–200, 372n.44, 376n.68
  interactionist theory of, 186
  Mansell on, 179, 191, 373nn.49, 50
  vs. narrative truth, 196, 198–200
  principal vs. subsidiary subjects
    in, 188–89
  relationship to analogy, 182–83,
    185, 187–88, 194–97, 374n.61
  relationship to hierarchical
    categories, 182–83, 190,
    193–95, 197–99
  signifier-signified relationship in,
    176–81, 198–200
metaphrasis, 58
Middle Ages
  attitudes toward poetic language
    during, 17–18
  definition of tragedy in, 345–46
  masculinity in, 17–18, 35–36
  poetry writing in, 11–12, 344
  reading practices in, 11–12, 20
Middleton, Anne, 373n.55
Mill, John M., 131
Miller's Tale
  Nicholas and quadrivial arts, 51, 52
  and politics, 221

Milton, John, 359n.32
  Paradise Lost, 120
mimologism, 244–45, 248
Miner, John N.: *The Grammar
    Schools of Medieval England*, 66
Minnis, Alistair
  Magister Amoris, 39–40,
    355nn.42, 45, 47
  on Romans 15:4, 158
Miskimin, Alice, 32, 355n.36
misogyny, 5, 19–20, 34, 41, 102,
    109–16
Mitchell, J. Allan: *Ethics and
    Exemplary Narrative in
    Chaucer and Gower*, 365n.38
mock epics, 88–89
Modistae, 146
Monk's Tale, 30, 324, 345, 363n.7
  Prologue to, 353n.5
Mooney, Linne, 296
  "The Cock and the Clock,"
    383n.5, 384n.14
moralitas of NPT, 55–56, 388n.61
  "Amen," 160
  apothegms in NPT, 2–3, 142
  close reading of, 141–64, 165–67
  and grammar, 20, 144–45, 146,
    148–49, 155–57, 159–60,
    161–62, 163
  and logic, 20, 149–60, 161, 340
  "my lord," 160–61
  as parody, 20, 122, 143–44, 163,
    166
  Pearsall on, 2, 143, 156
  and rhetoric, 20, 144–45, 146,
    148–49, 155–57, 159–60,
    161, 163
  as self-deconstruction, 143–44
Moretti, Franco, 164

Morgan, Thaïs E., 242
Morrison, Toni: *The Bluest Eye,*
    235–36, 238–39, 265
Morson, Gary Saul, 80
Murdoch, John, 290, 291
    "The Analytic Character of Late
    Medieval Learning," 386n.43
Muscatine, Charles, 4
music, 1, 26–27, 202–4, 206–7,
    261–62, 264

Nabokov, Vladimir, 25
necessity: simple vs. conditional,
    71, 109, 343–44
Neckham, Alexander: *Novus
    Avianus,* 54
New Chaucer Society Conference
    of 2006, 16, 164
New Chaucer Society Conference
    of 2008, 347–48
New Criticism, 16, 164
new historicism, 208
Newman, Randy: "Short People
    Got No Reason to Live," 111
Nicholas of Lynn's *Kalendarium,*
    22–23, 273–77, 296, 384n.19,
    387n.59
    and Chaucer's readers, 283
    and determination of time in
    the Prologue to *Parson's Tale,*
    281–82
    and Harry Bailly's determination
    of time, 278–79
    and Nun's Priest's determination
    of time, 284–85
Nietzsche, Friedrich: on grammar,
    161
Nims, Margaret F.: on poetry and
    metaphor, 369n.6

Nodier, Charles
    Dictionnaire des onomatopées,
    243–46, 248
    on mimologism, 244–45, 248
    *Notions élémentaires de
    linguistique,* 243–46
North, John D., 269, 272, 387n.60
    Chaucer's Universe, 385n.26
Norwish Cathedral: tower clock of,
    271
Nottingham, Roger, 305
Nuchelmans, Gabriel: on mental
    propositions, 309
Nun's Priest
    absence in the *General Prologue,*
    33, 43–44, 47
    apostrophe on Chauntecleer,
    86–92, 96
    celibacy of, 17, 43, 340
    defense of poetry, 198–200
    determination of time by,
    23, 268–69, 276–77, 283,
    284–301, 387n.61
    on determinism vs. free will,
    338
    and the Devil, 7, 113
    on flattery, 69, 108–9, 142
    and food, 6, 7
    as Genius, 18, 32–33, 36, 44
    Harry Bailly on, 17–18, 30–32,
    41–42, 44, 46–49
    on homicides, 70
    "I kan noon harme of no
    womman divyne," 19,
    64–67, 70, 112
    and linguistic dissemination, 33
    relationship to Chaucer, 25, 49,
    108, 335–39, 344
    relationship to narrator, 335–39

Nun's Priest (*cont.*)
  on truth of NPT and *Lancelot de
    Lake,* 69, 304–5, 307–14
  as unreliable narrator, 7, 112, 113
  on women, 19–20, 64–65, 70,
    109–17

onomatopoeia, 241–42, 258
  Attridge on, 249–50
  as mimologism, 244–45, 248
Oresme, Nicole: *Tractatus de
    Commensurabilitate vel
    Incommensurabilitate Motuum
    Celi,* 23, 299–300
Orr, Mary: *Intertextuality,* 15
Osborn, Marijane
  on Chaucer and the astrolabe, 273
  Time and the Astrolabe, 383n.5,
    384n.18, 385n.35
Ovid, 54, 146, 211
  on Clytie/heliotropes, 173–74
  heliotropic myth, 172
  Metamorphoses, 173
Ovide Moralisé, 158–59
Owen, Charles, 95
"Owl and the Nightingale," 57
Oxford University, 304, 305

Padua: de' Dondi clock of, 271
Papias: *Vocabulista,* 240
Pardoner's Tale, 107, 363n.7
Parker, Patricia, 139
  Literary Fat, 376n.69
  on metaphor, 178, 376n.68
  "Virile Style," 33–34, 354n.18
Parliament of Foules, 57
  Nature in, 317
  sounds in, 21–22, 206–7, 218,
    223, 239, 241, 248

parody, 18, 30, 47, 48, 232–33, 248,
    334
  and artistic freedom, 15–16
  definitions of, 53, 79–81
  encyclopedic parody, 9
  and Fragment VII, 24, 324–25
  of grammar school curriculum,
    53, 54–74
  Hutcheon on, 15, 81, 82–83, 91,
    108–9
  vs. irony, 19, 53, 79, 81–83, 105,
    107, 112, 115
  as literary criticism, 8–9, 94,
    95–96
  of logic, 257
  in narrator's apostrophe, 86–92
  NPT as Menippean satire/parody,
    9–12, 13, 19, 53–54, 72, 74–84,
    117, 340, 341–42, 344
  of Priscian's *preexercitamina,*
    18–19, 23
  readers of, 14–16, 83–84, 107–8
  Rose on, 16, 312–13, 314
  vs. satire, 5, 19, 44, 53, 74, 79–84,
    107
  self-parody, 13–17, 19–20, 53–54,
    83, 86, 105, 107–8, 112–17,
    324–25, 338, 339
  target text vs. parodic text, 5,
    8–9, 14–15, 80–81, 82, 83,
    105, 107, 257
  of translation, 58, 95–96
  and truth, 312–13
  widow's portrait as, 20, 62, 126,
    128–29, 136–37, 139–40, 141
Parson's Tale
  determination of time in, 22,
    268–69, 276–77, 280–83, 298,
    300–301

Prologue to, 22, 268–69, 276–77,
   280–83, 298, 300–301
readers' response to, 337
Patterson, Lee
   Chaucer and the Subject of
      History, 208, 220–21, 222,
      225, 233
   on peasants in Middle Ages, 260
   "What Man Artow?," 353n.6
Paul, St.
   Epistle to Titus, 305
   Romans 15:4, 158–59
Paul of Venice, 150, 305
   Logica magna, 292
Pavel, Thomas G.: *Fictional Worlds,*
   376n.68
Payne, F. Anne: *Chaucer and*
      Menippean Satire, 6–8,
      76–77, 79, 113, 352n.35
Payne, Robert, 88
Peacham, Henry, 258
Pearl poet, 372n.44, 375n.67
Pearsall, Derek, 261, 362n.127,
      364nn.11,13–16
   on Besserman, 65, 112
   on Chauntecleer's colors, 191
   on idealisation by negatives, 132,
      133–34
   on "In principio," 97, 98–99
   on *moralitas* of NPT, 2, 143, 156
   on moral of NPT, 3
   on narrator's apostrophe, 87, 88
   on Peasants' Revolt, 233
   on Pertelote's lamentation, 63
   on "Syn March bigan," 287
   on Talbot and Gerland, 256
   on widow's portrait, 132, 133–34,
      135, 363n.9, 364n.26
   on Zacharias, 65

Peasants' Revolt of 1381, 207–8,
      378n.34, 381n.104
   and fox chase in *Nun's Priest's*
      Tale, 21–22, 71, 209, 258–64,
      265–66, 381n.109
   Jakke Strawe, 258–61, 262, 264,
      381n.109
   and *Summoner's Tale,* 220–25,
      226, 233
Peck, Russell, 280–81
performative speech acts, 160, 161
Perrin, Noel: "Old MacBerlitz Had
      a Farm," 379n.69
Pertelote
   and the Bible, 4–5
   on dreams, 11, 52, 57, 112,
      316–17, 319
   as Golden Spangled Hamburg,
      190–91
   lamentation of, 63–64
   as nominalist, 344
   on purges, 6
Peter of Mantua: *De instanti,* 292
Peter of Spain, 150, 328
   Tractatus syncategorematum, 292,
      386n.50
Peterson, Mark: on Dante's shadow,
      385n.27
Petrarch, 176
Petronius, 74
   Satyricon, 77
philosophy
   analysis of time, 13, 23, 269,
      270–71, 274–75, 283, 287–97,
      298, 384n.10, 387n.57
   faculty psychology, 314–15,
      318–19, 320–23, 326, 333,
      342
   and the heliotrope, 172

philosophy (*cont.*)
  and metaphor, 172, 194–95, 198,
    199–200
  nature of change, 13, 288–91,
    294–95
  nature of motion, 13, 288–89
  See also faculty psychology; logic
Physician's Tale, 363n.7
Pierre of Lusignan, 176, 370n.18
Piers Plowman, 225, 378n.37
plagiarism, 58
Plato
  aesthetics of, 342–43
  Cratylus, 242, 245, 250
  on definition of man, 384n.64
  on Idea of the Good, 230
  on matter, 354n.28
  on philosopher–king, 227
  Timaeus, 6, 36, 37, 354n.28
Plowman in the *General Prologue*,
    128
poetic skills
  irony, 19–20, 84, 92–117, 102
  textual imitation, 19, 60, 67, 80,
    81, 84–92, 102
  translation, 19, 84, 92–103
poetry
  colors/flowers of, 169–70, 171
  construction in Middle Ages,
    11–12
  essence as metaphor, 20–21,
    171–72, 369n.6
  meaning in, 335
  relationship to real world, 6–8,
    160–61, 198–200, 239, 242,
    249–50, 304–5, 307–14,
    333–34, 340, 348–49
  sounds of, 239
  and truth, 309–12, 314, 318

politics, 91–92
  consonance and dissonance in,
    202–4, 205, 206–7, 216–17
  See also Peasants' Revolt of 1381
polysemy, 17, 64–65
Porphyry: *Isagoge*, 380n.93
postmodern theory
  and language, 313
  regarding reading, 144–45, 149,
    161–62, 163–64
  See also de Man, Paul; Derrida,
    Jacques
pragmatographia, 257–58
Pratt, Mary Louise: on irony, 104
Pratt, Robert, 286
preexercitamina
  comparison, 70
  deliberative rhetoric, 67–68
  demonstrative rhetoric, 67
  description, 70–71
  encomium, 70
  in grammar school studies,
    12, 18–19, 60, 61, 67–72,
    146, 205, 257, 359n.32
  impersonation, 70
  judicial rhetoric, 67, 69–70
  legislation, 71
  vs. NPT, 68–70
  vituperation, 70
  See also Priscian's *Preexercitamina*
Prioress's Tale, 30, 324, 328
Priscian, 328, 377n.18
  on "and," 153
  Duodecim, 67
  Partitiones, 147
Priscian's *Institutiones Grammaticae*,
    147, 214, 240–41, 245, 264
  four classes of *vox* in, 240, 241,
    242–43, 248–49, 250

Priscian's *Preexercitamina*
  and beast fables, 12, 67, 68, 309
  chria/anecdote, 67, 68
  in grammar school studies, 12,
    18–19, 60, 61, 67–72, 146, 205,
    257
  narration, 67, 68, 257, 259
  sententia/proverb, 67, 68
proverbs, 121
Puttenham, George, 257

Quadlbauer, F., 359n.43
Quinn, Esther, 338, 361n.96
Quintilian, 34, 61
  Institutes, 35
  on language, 35
  on parody, 79–80
  on teaching grammar, 59

Rabelais, François, 79
  on the book *Quaestio subtilissima*,
    303–4, 312, 333
  on calendar reckonings, 383n.6
Ransom, John Crowe, 164
readers
  and art of translation, 94–96, 102,
    116
  Chauntecleer as reader, 314–15,
    327
  and Chauntecleer's reaction to
    sight of fox, 327
  creative responses of, 24, 47–48,
    49, 83–84, 337–38, 341–49
  and determination of time,
    276–77, 279–80, 283,
    300–301
  as educated in logic, 304, 307,
    312, 314, 341
  expectations of, 141

gaps in Chaucer filled in by,
    47–48, 49
  and grammar school studies,
    12–13, 18–19, 52–53, 71–72,
    122, 146–49, 239, 245, 248
  and irony, 104–5, 107–8, 109–17
  logic studied by, 304, 307, 312,
    314, 341
  of parody, 14–16, 83–84, 107–8
  reading vs. cognition of reality,
    333–34
  rereading of NPT, 24, 25–26, 112,
    137–38, 163–64
  and undecideability, 163, 368n.82
  See also close reading
Reed, Thomas: on English debate
    poems, 57
Regement of Princes, 122
Relihan, Joel: *Ancient Menippean
    Satire*, 75, 77, 78, 79, 359n.58
Reynolds, Suzanne: *Medieval
    Reading*, 20, 147, 148–49,
    157, 159
rhetoric
  Alanus de Insulis on, 170–71, 176,
    191–92, 369n.3
  chaste rhetoric, 46
  and Chauntecleer, 52–53, 62
  Cicero on, 147
  colors of, 62, 169–71
  deliberative rhetoric, 67–68, 147
  demonstrative rhetoric, 67
  disembodied rhetoric, 45
  effeminized rhetoric, 45–46, 47
  epideictic rhetoric, 147
  and the fox chase, 239, 257–59,
    263
  vs. grammar, 144–45, 147–49,
    150, 155, 157, 159, 161, 162

rhetoric (*cont.*)
incarnational rhetoric, 45, 46
judicial/forensic rhetoric, 67,
69–70, 71, 147
vs. logic, 59, 150
Marian rhetoric, 46
masculine discursive paradigms
in, 45–46, 47
naked rhetoric, 45, 46
pedestalized rhetoric, 46, 47
and Priscian's *Preexercitamina*,
67–71
relationship to *enarratio*/literary
interpretation, 144–45, 146,
148–49, 155–57, 159–60,
161, 163
as trivial art, 20, 71, 144–45, 146,
147, 150, 161, 263
wanton rhetoric, 46
Richard I, the Lion-hearted, 19, 86,
87, 91
Richard II, 91, 108, 259, 361n.96
Richard of Campsall, 305
Rickert, Edith, 367n.69, 385n.36
Ricoeur, Paul: *The Rule of Metaphor*,
178, 194–95, 373n.48
Riffaterre, Michael, 25
Robertson, D.W., Jr., 5, 124
Roman de Renart, Branch II, 315
Romaunt of the Rose, 92, 109
Roney, Lois, 377n.16
Ronsard, Pierre de, 258
Root, Robert Kilburn: on widow's
portrait, 363n.9
Rose, Margaret
on parody, 16, 312–13, 314
Parody//Meta-Fiction, 312–13
Rothwell, W.: "The Hours of the Day
in Medieval French," 383n.4

Rowland, Beryl, 131
Russell the fox
and the Bible, 4–5
Chauntecleer's dream of, 23–24,
52–53, 314, 315–26, 321,
322–23, 334, 343, 348–49
on 'Daun Burnel the Asse,' 68
entry into chickenyard, 71,
348–49
as flatterer, 69, 142, 325
last words, 142, 325
as murderer, 70
as trickster, 7
See also fox chase
Russian formalists: on parody, 90
Ryan, Marie Laure: *Possible Worlds*,
376n.68
Ryle, Gilbert, 373n.48
"A Rational Animal," 375n.64

Sacks, Sheldon: on apologues vs.
novels, 364n.19
Said, Edward
on beginning, 139, 199
Beginnings, 139
Salisbury, Joyce E.: *The Beast Within*,
374n.64
Salter, Elizabeth: on Chauntecleer's
colors, 191
satire
vs. anatomy, 75
vs. irony, 79, 81–83, 107
mock epics, 88–89
vs. parody, 5, 19, 44, 53, 74,
79–84, 107
and social change, 75, 81, 107
See also Menippean satire
Satire of the Three Estates tradition,
79

Scanlon, Larry, 355n.36
　　on *exempla*, 122, 140, 363n.7
　　Narrative, Authority, and Power,
　　　140
Scase, Wendy: *Piers Plowman*
　　and the New Anti-Clericalism,
　　　225, 378n.37
Schaar, Claes: on Chauntecleer's
　　colors, 191
Schnapp, Jeffrey: *The Transfiguration*
　　of History in the Center of
　　Dante's Paradise, 216
Scotus, Duns, 305, 326
　　on time, 270
Second Nun, 44
Second Nun's Tale, 92
Sedgwick, Eve Kosofsky, 164
Seneca, 74
　　Apocolocyntosis, 77
　　on style, 17, 34
Shakespeare, William
　　"The Phoenix and the Turtle,"
　　　376n.68
　　Richard II, 91
Shelly, Percy Van Dyke: on widow's
　　portrait, 363n.9
Sheridan, James J.: on Alanus de
　　Insulis, 369n.3
Shipman's Tale, 30, 324
　　sundial of monk in, 267
Sidney, Sir Philip: *Apology for Poetry,*
　　176, 309
Singleton, Charles, 310
Sir Thopas, Tale of, 30, 324, 338
Sisam, Kenneth, 352n.19
Skeat, William, 287
Smith, D. Vance
　　The Book of the Incipit, 363n.2
　　"Medieval Fora," 166

Solterer, Helen
　　"At the Bottom," 374n.56
　　on women and rhetorical
　　　invention, 374n.56
Somers, John: *Kalendarium,* 273,
　　296, 387n.59
Sorabji, Richard: *Animal Minds,*
　　374n.64
sounds
　　of animals, 240, 241–42, 243,
　　　328–33, 379n.69
　　consonance and dissonance,
　　　201, 202–5, 206–7
　　as culturally coded, 205–6
　　Dante on, 215–16, 237–38, 264
　　fart in *Summoner's Tale,* 22, 209,
　　　218–34, 239, 379nn.53, 54
　　in fox chase, 21–22, 71, 209, 239,
　　　241–42, 243, 247–52, 260–61,
　　　265–66
　　insignificant (*sonus*) vs. significant
　　　(*vox*), 201–2, 205, 211–12, 214,
　　　220, 223–24, 231–32, 240–46,
　　　251, 328–33
　　music, 26–27, 202–4, 206–7,
　　　261–62, 264
　　as noise, 21–22, 201–2, 204–5,
　　　206, 207, 209, 210–18, 340,
　　　376n.4
　　in *Parliament of Foules,* 21–22,
　　　206–7, 218, 223, 239, 241, 248
　　and Peasant's Revolt, 260–61,
　　　264, 265
　　percussive sounds, 21–22, 84,
　　　204, 209, 210–18, 221–22,
　　　265
　　as waves, 21, 214–15, 217, 218,
　　　223, 377n.23
sources and analogues of NPT, 1

Spade, Paul Vincent, 305
    on levels of supposition, 99–100,
        101
Spearing, A. C.
    Medieval Dream-Poetry, 388n.28
    Textual Subjectivity, 25, 336–37,
        338–39, 381n.102
Spengler, Oswald, 261
Spenser, Edmund, 381n.102
Spitzer, Leo: on Augustine, 204
Squire's Tale: steed of brass in, 273
St. Albans clock, 271, 275
Statius, 146, 258
    Thebaid, 202
Steiner, George
    After Babel, 96–97, 101–2
    on translation, 96–97, 101–2
Sterne, Laurence: *Tristram Shandy,*
    9, 141, 313
Stevens, Wallace
    "Credences of Summer," 193
    "Sunday Morning," 356n.48
Stock, Brian: *Augustine the Reader,*
    98
Stoicism, 204
Storr, Robert, 165
Strange, William, 124
Strode, Ralph, 305
Strohm, Paul
    on fox chase, 381n.109
    Hochon's Arrow, 372n.46
    Social Chaucer, 208
style
    of Cicero, 33–34
    effeminized rhetoric, 45–46, 47
    Horace on, 17, 34
    Matthew of Vendôme on, 18, 35,
        45–46

Seneca on, 17, 34
Tacitus on, 17, 34–35
as virile, 17–18, 33–49
Suleiman, Susan
    Authoritarian Fictions, 136–37
    on authoritarian fictions, 20,
        136–37
Summoner's Tale, 79, 363n.7
    cartwheel, 22, 220, 223–32,
        379n.54
    and Christ's body, 226–27
    Friar John, 218–19, 222, 228
    and Holy Spirit at Pentecost, 226
    Patterson on, 208, 220–21, 222,
        225, 233
    and Peasants' Revolt, 22, 220–25,
        226, 233
    squire, 220, 227, 230
    Thomas's fart, 22, 209, 218–34,
        239, 379nn.53, 54
    Thomas's social status, 224
    village lord, 219–20, 222, 228,
        230
Swift, Jonathan, 79
Swineshead, Richard, 305

Tachau, Katherine, 326
Tacitus: on style, 17, 34–35
Talbot, 256, 260, 263
Tale of Melibee, 30, 92, 93, 324, 338
Tale of Sir Thopas, 30, 324, 338
Tatum, Art, 26–27
Tempier, Stephen, 270, 384n.10
Theon, 67
Thomas, Paul: *The Nun's Priest's
    Tale on CD-ROM,* 367n.69,
    385n.36
Thynne, Francis, 286

time, 340, 383n.4, 387n.56
  Aristotle on, 270, 271, 288–89
  astrolabic determination of, 272,
    274–75, 298
  Augustine on, 267, 270, 297–98
  Chauntecleer's determination of,
    51, 268
  computistical measurement of,
    269–70, 274–75, 298, 383n.6,
    384n.8
  determination by Harry Bailly,
    22, 67–69, 276–80, 281, 282,
    283, 284, 298, 300–301
  determination by Nun's Priest,
    23, 268–69, 276–77, 283,
    284–301, 387n.61
  determination in Prologue of
    Parson's Tale, 22, 268–69,
    276–77, 280–83, 298, 300–301
  errors in Chaucer's
    determinations of, 23, 269,
    279–80, 281, 282–83, 300–301,
    385n.33
  kalendric determination of,
    273–75, 298
  mechanical analysis of, 268,
    271–72, 274–76, 278, 298, 299,
    384n.14
  merchant's time, 272, 275, 279
  philosophical analysis of, 13, 23,
    269, 270–71, 274–75, 283,
    287–97, 298, 384n.10, 387n.57
  and scholarly community,
    275–76
  shadow-scale method of
    measurement, 267–68, 271,
    274, 278–79, 280–82, 284,
    384n.23, 385n.27
tithing, 225

translation
  and Chaucer's readers, 94–96,
    102, 116
  of "in principio, mulier est
    hominis confusio," 19, 52, 58,
    94–103
  masculinist bias in, 58
  parody of, 58, 95–96
  as poetic skill, 19, 84, 92–103
  postmodern theory regarding,
    102
  Steiner on, 96–97, 101–2
Treatise on the Astrolabe, 92, 93–94,
    272–73
Trimpi, Wesley: *Muses of One Mind*,
    311
Troilus and Criseyde, 76, 92, 111,
    133, 208, 345, 371n.40
Trotter, David: *The Making of the
    Reader*, 381n.102
truth, 303–15
  and ampliation, 310
  and *argumentum*, 311
  Augustine on, 98
  in dreams, 23–24, 315–26
  and fictional language, 309–14,
    318
  and *insolubilia*/Cretan Liar
    paradoxes, 305–14, 333, 334,
    339–40
  and *Lancelot de Lake*, 69, 304–5,
    307–14
  in literary texts, 69, 84, 250,
    304–5, 307–14, 318, 325–26,
    339–40
  and mental propositions, 309
  of NPT, 304–5, 307–14
  and parody, 312–13
  and poetry, 309–12, 314, 318

Tversky, Amos: "Features of
Similarity," 374n.61
Tyler, Stephen A.: on thinking,
250–51
Tyrwhitt, Thomas, 286

Uebel, Michael: "Acoustical Alterity,"
376n.4
Uhlig, Claus, 124
on widow's portrait, 363n.9
University of Paris, 304, 305
Usk, Thomas: *Testament of Love*,
373n.55

Valéry, Paul: on metaphor, 174
Varro, 74
Vendler, Helen, 164
Virgil, 54, 120, 146, 211
Vitruvius, 377n.23
Voltaire: *Candide*, 75

Wallace, David: *Chaucerian Polity*,
208
Walsingham, Thomas, 259
Walton, Sir Isaac: *Compleat Angler*,
75
Warren, Michelle R.: "The Noise of
Roland," 376n.4
Watkins, Charles, 124
Webern, Anton, 261
Weinbrot, Howard: *Menippean
Satire Reconsidered*, 74, 77, 79,
359n.58
Wetherbee, Winthrop, 355n.36
Wheatley, Edward: on beast fables,
55, 351n.8, 365n.43
White, A.: "Bakhtin, Sociolinguistics,
and Deconstruction," 378n.52
Whittock, Trevor, 124

widow's portrait
and the Bible, 5
and causation, 136, 137, 138, 139
close reading of, 20, 119–41,
165–67
and color, 134, 137, 138
diet, 6, 131–33, 134, 137, 138
as *exemplum*, 20, 62, 70, 121–22,
123–41, 143, 163, 165–66, 340,
363n.7, 365n.35
and gender, 135, 137, 138, 139
vs. Griselda's portrait in *Clerk's
Tale*, 126–28, 129–30, 132–33,
365n.36
and logic, 134, 137, 138
and marriage, 138
and number, 134–35, 137
as parody, 20, 62, 126, 128–29,
136–37, 139–40, 141
Pearsall on, 132, 133–34, 135,
363n.9, 364n.26
Wife of Bath, 337–38
William Heytesbury, 150
William of Conches: *Glose super
Priscianum*, 240, 377n.18
William of Fitzstephen, 358n.17
William of Moerbeke, 380n.93
William of Ockham, 150, 305
on time, 271
William of Sherwood, 305
hexagon of opposition of, 254–55
on *homo currit*, 254–55
Introduction to Logic, 254
on *Mulier que damnavit salvavit*,
99, 361n.109
on *omnis*, 255
*Treatise on Syncategorematic
Words*, 150–54, 156–57, 255,
292, 367n.63